MARXIST ETHICAL THEORY IN THE SOVIET UNION

SOVIETICA

PUBLICATIONS AND MONOGRAPHS

OF THE INSTITUTE OF EAST-EUROPEAN STUDIES AT THE

UNIVERSITY OF FRIBOURG/SWITZERLAND AND

THE CENTER FOR EAST EUROPE, RUSSIA AND ASIA

AT BOSTON COLLEGE AND THE SEMINAR

FOR POLITICAL THEORY AND PHILOSOPHY

AT THE UNIVERSITY OF MUNICH

Founded by J. M. BOCHEŃSKI (Fribourg)

Edited by T. J. BLAKELEY (Boston), GUIDO KÜNG (Fribourg), *and*
NIKOLAUS LOBKOWICZ (Munich)

VOLUME 40

PHILIP T. GRIER

Department of Philosophy, Northwestern University

MARXIST
ETHICAL THEORY
IN THE
SOVIET UNION

D. REIDEL PUBLISHING COMPANY

DORDRECHT : HOLLAND / BOSTON : U.S.A.

LONDON : ENGLAND

Library of Congress Cataloging in Publication Data

Grier, Philip T. 1942–
   Marxist ethical theory in the Soviet Union.

   (Sovietica ; v. 40)
   Based on the author's thesis, University of Michigan.
   Bibliography: p.
   Includes index.
   1. Ethics–Russia–History. 2. Communist ethics–History. 3. Philosophy,
Russian–History. 4. Values–History. I. Title. II Series.
BJ852.G73   171   78-12401
ISBN 90-277-0927-0

Published by D. Reidel Publishing Company,
P.O. Box 17, Dordrecht, Holland

Sold and distributed in the U.S.A., Canada, and Mexico
by D. Reidel Publishing Company, Inc.
Lincoln Building, 160 Old Derby Street, Hingham,
Mass. 02043, U.S.A.

To my Mother and Father

TABLE OF CONTENTS

PREFACE

A survey of the intellectual history of Marxism through its several phases and various national adaptations suggests, for any of at least three reasons, that the attempt to provide a widely acceptable summary of 'Marxist ethics' must be an enterprise with little prospect of success. First, a number of prominent Marxists have insisted that Marxism *can have no ethics* because its status as a science precludes bias toward, or the assumption of, any particular ethical standpoint. On this view it would be no more reasonable to expect an ethics of Marxism than of any other form of social science. Second, basing themselves on the opposite assumption, an equally prominent assortment of Marxist intellectuals have lamented the *absence* of a coherently developed Marxist ethics as a deficiency which must be remedied.[1] Third, less commonly, Marxism is sometimes alleged to possess no developed ethical theory because it is exclusively committed to advocacy of class egoism on behalf of the proletariat, and is thus rooted in a prudential, not a moral standpoint.[2] The advocacy of proletarian class egoism — or 'revolutionary morality' — may, strictly speaking, constitute an ethical standpoint, but it might be regarded as a peculiar waste of time for a convinced and consistent class egoist to develop precise formulations of his ethical views for the sake of convincing an abstract audience of classless and impartial rational observers which does not happen to exist at present. The phrase 'revolutionary morality' in the Russian revolutionary period usually implied just such a committed stance and a sharp impatience with verbal disputes over the morality of political actions.

The first consideration listed above, that as an empirical science Marxism cannot be understood to contain normative ethical commitments, was a view most widely espoused during the period of the Second International, particularly among intellectual leaders of the German Social Democratic party, such as Karl Kautsky. The emphasis placed upon this view, and the vehemence with which it was defended, can be properly understood only in the context of the larger debate which dominated much of German philosophy during this period between various doctrines of positivism, on the one side, and several versions of neo-Kantianism, on the other. There were protracted disputes over the proper characterization of empirical science, its presupposi-

ix

tions, and its modes of reasoning. Positivists generally insisted that empirical science offered the only valid source of knowledge, that no explanations in terms of transcendental or supernatural forces were admissible in science, that philosophy possessed no method and no knowledge distinct from the empirical sciences, and they broadly distrusted anything which might be labelled 'metaphysics'.

The neo-Kantians differed among themselves in many respects: some were primarily interested in the transcendental conditions of experience as well as the relation of the theoretical to the practical uses of reason; others tended to ignore the later parts of the *First Critique* as well as the *Second Critique* as excessively 'metaphysical', reading Kant primarily as an empiricist epistemologist. Even so it was often necessary to defend Kant against positivist critiques of his 'idealist' treatment of space and time.

Neither Engels nor Kautsky would have identified himself with the positivists, but both considered themselves enemies of idealism, and critics of certain sorts of metaphysical speculation. Their heavy emphasis on the *scientific*, anti-metaphysical nature of Marxian socialism dominated the movement at this time, and tended to keep Marxist orthodoxy out of the camp of the neo-Kantians, despite the influence of an articulate minority of neo-Kantian Marxists within the Party, and Marxist neo-Kantians without. The 'orthodox' in this context were inclined to incorporate discussions of ethics within Marxism only to the extent that ethics itself could be construed as an empirical science.

From this perspective, the genealogy of morals according to Darwin struck Kautsky in particular as providing just the right framework for a scientific inquiry into the subject, when supplemented by the tenets of historical materialism. For many adherents of evolutionary ethics, its greatest attraction lay in the apparent demystification of moral imperatives which resulted when their origins were traced to the animal kingdom. An important corollary of the thesis of the animal origins of morality was the suggestion that moral duties might be subject to evolutionary (even revolutionary) change. For adherents of a revolutionary political theory such as Engels and Kautsky, a science of ethics which authorized such a conclusion served very usefully to diminish the force of moral claims with which the old order might defend itself from destruction.

Controversies over evolutionist ethics were not restricted to Marxist circles during these years, but in whatever context they occurred, such debates tended to circle around the problem of defining 'nature' and 'society', so as to insist either on their mutual exclusivity, or on their continuity. On these conceptions depended one's views as to whether monkeys could be moral, duty a species of natural instinct, or principles of human conduct rooted in something transcending the realm of nature.

For positivistically inclined Marxists unattracted by Darwinian ethics, the science of ethics could be understood in effect as the sociology of morals, and as such incorporated along with the other special inquiries governed by historical materialism, without thereby admitting that Marxism itself contained any particular ethical norms. The admission that Marxism as a theory of the laws of social development incorporates a normative ethical standpoint would still threaten its scientific status in the eyes of some contemporary Marxists both inside and outside the USSR.

The second claim listed above, that Marxism requires but lacks an ethic has numerous sources in the history of the movement. The positivist and evolutionist attitudes toward a Marxist ethics were partly provoked by the claims of neo-Kantians who insisted that their own standpoint provided a superior account of the scientific enterprise, in particular one which explicated the true interrelations of the theoretical and the moral. Some neo-Kantians such as Conrad Schmidt saw the essential superiority of their position mainly in the neo-critical account of science, and were largely uninterested in Kantian ethics. Others, such as Hermann Cohen and Karl Vorländer, saw the greatest advantage of neo-critical philosophy in the account it provided of practical reason, and the relationship of the practical to the theoretical uses of reason. That account, when applied to Marxism, permitted the 'completion' or the 'grounding' of that science in ethical terms.

In France, Jean Jaurès, often cited as the founder of ethical socialism in that country, published a dissertation[3] in 1891 in which he argued that the true origin of socialism lay not in the materialism of the extreme Hegelian Left, but rather in the idealism of Luther, Kant, Fichte, and Hegel. In particular he emphasized the connection between the Kantian doctrine of the freedom of the will and the recognition of universally valid principles of duty in which freedom was considered 'identical with law and justice'. The freedom of each individual was bound up with that of every other individual in such a way that it could be realized only in a state governed by freely-accepted laws which was no mere sum of individual wills, but rather 'a kind of inner rational will of the people'.[4] In this respect Jaurès described Kant as a 'warm supporter' of what would come to be known as socialism.

A few years later in a less scholarly way, Bernstein also suggested that some greater element of moral idealism was required in the socialist movement. In the conclusion of his controversial work on evolutionary socialism[5] he declared that appeals to the material self-interest of the proletariat were inadequate justification for the socialist struggle, that contempt for the (moral) ideal was a self-deception, that the proletarian struggle must be inspired by a higher view of morals and of legal rights. In short, Marxism required an explicit ethical dimension.

The original source of the expectation that Marxism would supply an ethic, indeed a new ethic, for human conduct might be seen to lie in the Young Hegelian movement itself. That expectation arose from a particular attitude with which some of the Young Hegelians criticized the master's system. Hegel's system was thought to lack an ethic, not in the obviously false sense that Hegel had no account of the grounds of right, duty, or the good, but in the more subtle sense that Hegel's system failed to provide a set of prescriptions for action which would transform the historical present. Hegel bequeathed no program of political action. Within the Young Hegelian movement the conviction grew that a program for political action could somehow be generated from the critique of the Hegelian system, and since that system itself was peculiarly resistant to partial internal modifications, the critique was to be directed to the presuppositions of the system as a whole. Marx, following Feuerbach, concluded that the deficiencies of Hegel's system were to be explained by his insufficiently materialist starting-point; the system commenced with *abstract* being rather than real *sensuous* being. Hence the materialist critique of the Hegelian system was expected to issue in a concrete ethic – in the special sense of a program of revolutionary action transcending philosophy (realizing it, and simultaneously abolishing it).

The Young Hegelians were not alone in their judgement that Hegel's system lacked an ethic. Kierkegaard made the same complaint, but of course meant by it something rather different: that by offering an abstract system in which human existence is characterized *in general*, Hegel could offer us no understanding of what it is to be an existing individual.[6] In Kierkegaard's view, everything said in Hegel's philosophy about process and becoming was illusory. "This is why the System lacks an Ethic, and is the reason why it has no answer for the living when the question of becoming is raised in earnest, in the interest of action."[7]

The twentieth century French Marxist Maximilien Rubel cites Marx, Kierkegaard, and Nietzsche as three thinkers who undertook each in his own way to supply the deficiencies of the Hegelian system and provide the world with a new ethic. "In order to be fertile, the Hegelian philosophy of becoming had need of an ethic. Kierkegaard, Marx, and Nietzsche knew it: the first proposed to us the imitation of Christ, the last, that of Caesar. It was the vocation of Marx to bring us the ethic of the human individual (*l'homme humain*), made in the image of Prometheus."[8] Rubel argued that Marx's thought contains an ethical dimension, but one which is "characterized negatively by its amoralism [*sic*] and positively by its essentially pragmatic approach".[9] Rubel found in Marx's notions of the self-emancipation of the proletariat, and of the consonance of this end with the means provided by history for its realization, the fundamental postulates of Marx's ethics. In particular, Rubel found the ethical import of his thought in Marx's optimism that ordinary suffering and thinking human beings will prove adequate to the task of self-liberation. The optimistic call to action addressed to the proletariat is crucial in Rubel's view, because Marx's historical materialism offers no guarantee that the contradictions of capitalism will be resolved in a transition to socialism; chaos is a perfectly possible outcome of history and can be averted only by the acceptance of responsibility for the future.

Notwithstanding efforts of interpretation such as Rubel's, at least one contemporary Eastern European student of the problem has recently claimed that, "A Marxist ethics, at least one worthy of Marx's name, has yet to be constructed".[10] Throughout the history of Marxism, he notes, there have been two interpretations of Marx, ethical and "a-ethical".[11] In Stojanović's opinion the explanation of this fact lies in an ambiguity in Marx's own thought; numerous passages can be cited on behalf of *either* view. Stojanović himself sees Marx as an heir of the 'great European humanistic-ethical tradition'[12] which Stojanović interprets broadly to include "the concepts of de-alienation, freedom, social equality and justice, the abolition of exploitation, the disappearance of social classes, the withering away of the state, the creation of self-managing associations of producers, and so on".[13] Marx's ethical contribution must be seen in his "radicalization and concretization of these values"[14] rather than in the formulation of a new or alternative ethical criterion. From the extensive list of humanistic values just cited, Stojanović follows the Polish writer Marek Fritzhand[15] in proposing two principles, the socialization and the self-realization of man, which he sees as components of de-alienation, as the fundamental value commitments of Marx's work. From this point of view, "Marx was a sort of ethical perfectionist: he stood for the realization of every human potential which does not threaten man's social nature".[16] Marxism then in Stojanović's interpretation constitutes in part an injunction to the maximum of self-cultivation or development of talents consonant with social harmony.

This last assertion is challenged by a third view sometimes encountered in discussions of Marxism and ethics. This third source of doubt about Marxist ethical theory can be characterized as 'revolutionary morality' – the view that Marxism presupposes a moral commitment to furthering the interests of the proletariat through socialist revolution, but not an ethical theory. The absence of an ethical theory on this view may be interpreted in either of two ways: first, there is no explicit Marxist theory of the right or the good for all humanity; the class interest of the proletariat exhausts the whole of its concern; revolutionary morality is a species of ethical egoism and excludes the moral point of view. Hence the construction of an ethical justification for the conduct of the proletariat is simply beside the point. Second, questions of strategy and tactics of the revolution preempt attention; the formulation of ethical theories lies outside the range of tasks of the revolutionary. Thus in a recent work Donald Hodges has argued, "Marxism does not offer an ethic for revolutionaries, only a revolutionary method".[17]

Hodges specifically objects to the universalism, as opposed to class egoism, which he sees in the doctrine of 'socialist humanism' in the forms in which that view has developed, especially among Eastern European Marxists, in the last two decades. The value of self-cultivation at the heart of it, Hodges argues, represents a concession by Marxists to the classical European humanist tradition deriving from the Greek and Roman ethic of self-cultivation which should be rejected by revolutionary Marxism. The acquisition of culture in this sense cannot be divorced from the acquisition of material goods and the leisure which wealth makes possible; "the two lead in practice to that preeminence of some individuals over others which follows from human oppression . . .".[18] Hence the elaboration of an ethic of socialist humanism in the name of Marxism can only serve to distract the individual toward self-cultivation, away from the problem of providing the material pre-requisites of culture for the entire population; and finally, it functions as a justification for policies of economic development in the Eastern European socialist countries which presuppose the continued exploitation of the workers for an ever-lengthening 'interim' period during which the educated elites of the ruling bureaucracies enjoy the perquisites of culture in the name of some future when the uneducated and the less educated strata will have been 'levelled-up' to the conditions of life prevailing now for the elite.

Hodges advocates instead a 'revolutionary Communism' unabashedly egoist, committed to the elimination of exploitation of the oppressed, which contains no view of the good of humanity in general, and does not purport to adopt the moral point of view, rather exercises a sustained class hatred against wealth, power, and privilege of the few. Hodges has in effect positively 're-evaluated' the slave morality depicted by Nietzsche and adopted it as the appropriate posture of Marxism. The hatred of the inhabitants of the under-world for their overlords, whom they define as *evil*, is sufficient to justify and to orient action; no more elaborate ethical theory is required of, or should be sought in, Marxism.

These controversies over the nature of Marxist ethics are deeply rooted in conflicting interpretations of Marxism. To choose between them is to commit oneself on some of the most disputed issues in the history of the movement, and also on a number of larger philosophical issues such as the nature of science, of values, and of moral judgment. A sample of the more obvious exegetical problems in Marxism would include the following.

In what sense is Marxism a science? If Marxism provides knowledge of 'the laws of social development', does this not imply that society develops accord-ing to laws, that history is determined? And if history is determined, what is the scientific relevance of inspirational appeals to the proletariat to take responsibility for their self-liberation? And if socialism will only come about as a result of self-conscious revolutionary praxis on the part of an aroused and determined proletariat, in what sense can Marxism, as the doctrine of that movement, be 'merely' a science?

Does Marx presuppose a concept of authentic human nature, as opposed to a succession of historically produced class natures? If there is no governing concept of authentic human nature in Marx, by what criterion is one to gauge historical progress? And if 'progress' and 'progressive' are not normative terms, why is socialism a desirable direction of historical development?

Does the mature Marx have a view about the good of humanity as a whole, as he appears to in the early writings for example, where he criticizes 'politi-cal' emancipation as falling short of 'human' emancipation? Is the humanism of the early writings to be regarded as a youthful aberration, not carried over into the scientific system of the mature Marx, or do the humanist views devel-oped so strikingly in the early writings underlie the whole of Marx's work?

To develop, or to summarize, a Marxist ethics is to adopt a certain set of answers to such questions as these, namely a set of answers in terms of which the elaboration of a Marxist ethics appears to be an appropriate and legiti-mate enterprise of Marxist philosophy. Despite the controversial nature of this very assumption, we have the testimony of a substantial number of Marx-ist theoreticians, since the end of the nineteenth century, that the enterprise is indeed legitimate, that Marx's work is properly interpreted as implying a definite ethical standpoint.

In recent years some Soviet Marxist philosophers have attempted to arti-culate such a standpoint, thereby commiting themselves to a reading of Marx

which makes room for such a theory. There is of course nothing like unanimity among Soviet Marxists as to the nature of a Marxist ethic nor of
the relationship between such an ethic and the central concerns of Marx's
work.

The present work offers a survey of the history of twentieth century (Russian and) Soviet Marxist discussions of ethical theory, examines the principal
claims of recent writings where a consensus can be discovered, and explores
the major areas of controversy where there is none. In certain respects Russian
and Soviet Marxist discussions of ethics represent a continuation of the debate
begun in the late nineteenth century, within the German Social Democratic
movement. As has been suggested, that discussion centered on two concerns,
the preservation of Marxism as a strict science, and the relationship of Kantian
ethics to Marxism. Both of these concerns are evident in recent Soviet writings. The survey of the original disputes among the German Social Democrats,
in which the Russian Marxist Plekhanov was an influential participant, supplied in Section 3 of the first Chapter, provides an important element of the
background to subsequent Soviet discussions which will be explored in the
remainder of the present work.[19]

ACKNOWLEDGEMENTS

The author would like to express his appreciation to several persons and organizations whose help and encouragement were a great assistance at various stages of this project. Professors Donald J. Munro, Thomas J. Blakeley, George L. Kline, and Richard T. DeGeorge have all given substantial assistance at various times with their encouragement, their criticisms of an earlier manuscript on the same subject, and by the models they provided in their own works on the same and related subjects.

The present work is based in part on a dissertation submitted to the University of Michigan, and that work was materially assisted by a grant from the Inter-University Committee on Travel Grants which enabled me to spend a year in the Soviet Union as a scholar on the cultural exchange program, and by a Ford Foundation Foreign Area Fellowship which facilitated the writing of that earlier work. I would also like to thank the Friends Service Council of Great Britain which provided further opportunities for Western and Soviet philosophers to discuss problems of ethical theory together in congenial circumstances, and of course all those philosophers in the Soviet Union whose hospitality made the present work possible. In particular I would like to mention Oleg Grigor'evič Drobnickij, whose untimely death was a substantial loss to that community of scholars seeking to further the mutual understanding of Soviet and Western philosophers and philosophies.

Northwestern University PHILIP GRIER

CHAPTER ONE

MARXISM AND ETHICAL THEORY: A BRIEF HISTORY

1. INTRODUCTION

The process of discovery and dissemination of Marx's more explicitly humanist writings extended throughout the first half of the twentieth century. The major documents involved were his doctoral thesis (written in 1840–41, first published in 1902),[1] the *Contribution to the Critique of Hegel's Philosophy of Law* (written in 1843, first published in 1927),[2] the *Economic and Philosophic Manuscripts* (written in 1844, first published in full in 1932),[3] the *German Ideology* (written in 1845–46, first published in full in 1932),[4] and the *Grundrisse*, (written in 1857–58, published in 1939, when it was obscured by the outbreak of war, and republished in 1953, after which it became widely available for the first time).[5] The translations of these works into other languages sometimes required many more years; for example, a relatively complete English translation of the *Grundrisse* appeared only in 1973.

Since Marx's writings were being interpreted and explained to ever widening audiences of the uninitiated by self-appointed intellectual executors before their author had himself passed from the scene, the nearly century-long interval required for the discovery and dissemination of a number of his major works could not have failed to have serious consequences for the development of Marxism as a movement. For example, despite Engels' effort to restore some awareness of Feuerbach's place in the evolution of Marx's thought by the publication of *Ludwig Feuerbach and the Outcome of Classical German Philosophy* in 1888, the development of the first great 'system' of Marxist orthodoxy in the German Social Democratic movement around the turn of the century took place during the period of maximum ignorance of those works of Marx which most clearly displayed his Hegelian origins and his humanist inclinations. After Marx died in 1883, and Engels in 1895, there were no major voices in the movement for a number of years capable of supplying the missing elements or correcting the exaggerations of Marx's followers in these respects. The process of recovering the true context of Marx's intellectual origins by a new generation of scholars did not get underway until the 1920's, especially in the work of Lukács and Korsch. By that time however, an 'orthodoxy' of German Marxism was largely established and had been bequeathed in part to Russian and Soviet Marxism.

A second major contributing influence to the 'orthodoxy' of its first established national party originated in certain fairly dramatic changes of intellectual fashion in Germany, as well as elsewhere in Europe, in the period following 1848. Continental interest in Hegel and German Idealism dropped precipitously after the failed revolutions of 1848, and was not to be seriously revived in some respects until the 1930's. As Charles Taylor remarks, in the 1850's and 1860's Hegel's philosophy fell into virtual oblivion;[6] materialism, mechanism, positivism, and evolutionism tended to dominate intellectual developments after 1850. Slightly later, a revival of interest in Kantian philosophy as a corrective to some of the above-mentioned trends of thought took place, and it was the rivalry between various doctrines of positivism and evolutionism on the one hand, and neo-Kantianisms on the other, which formed the intellectual background against which the first major Marxist orthodoxy developed. At the turn of the century substantial controversies over the 'orthodox' interpretation of Marxism took place which bore influences of these two perspectives of evolutionary positivism and of neo-Kantianism. It was in the course of these controversies, especially that over Bernstein's writings, that certain interpretations of Marxism began to receive the label 'revisionism', and others, by implication, 'orthodoxy'. Throughout this period the dominant influences of the philosophical world in which both Marx and Engels came to maturity were remembered as a rather remote development of German intellectual history affecting only a previous generation. Hegel was remembered, if at all, mainly as the 'state philosopher' of William Frederick III's Prussia. Engels' somewhat nostalgic backward glance at all that in 1888 had the flavor of an obituary, a summing up; 'classical German philosophy' itself had decomposed, and the proletariat of 1888 were the only legitimate inheritors of its spirit. Even the tributes to Feuerbach, whom he credits with having 'exploded and cast aside' the Hegelian system, pulverizing the contradiction of Young Hegelianism and liberating Marx from its spell, turn out to be exceedingly ambivalent.[7] Engels is "struck by Feuerback's astonishing poverty when compared with Hegel".[8] "He was incapable of disposing of Hegel through criticism; he simply threw him aside as useless, while he himself, compared with the encyclopedic wealth of the Hegelian system, achieved nothing positive beyond a turgid religion of love and a meager, impotent morality."[9] What begins as praise of Feuerbach for having liberated Marx from the toils of Young Hegelianism, ends with muted praised of Hegel.

In fact, Marx was so strongly influenced by Feuerbach in one short but crucial phase of his development that it would seem appropriate to call Marx a Feuerbachian during the years 1843–44.[10] It is the writings from this period of strongest Feuerbachian influence, and those from the immediately succeeding period which offer the most detailed and explicit statement of Marx's humanism. The exposition of Marxian humanism must begin therefore with the consideration of Feuerbach and Marx.

2. FEUERBACHIAN AND MARXIAN HUMANISM

The humanism of both writers was marked first of all by a strong perfectibilist element. This emerges in Marx's well-known school-leaving essay, written some years earlier.

> Nature herself has determined the sphere of activity in which the animal should move, and it peacefully moves within that sphere, without attempting to go beyond it, without even an inkling of any other. To man, too, the Deity gave a general aim, that of ennobling mankind and himself, but he left it to man to seek the means by which this aim can be achieved; he left it to him to choose the position in society most suited to him, from which he can best uplift himself and society.
>
> . . . .
>
> But the chief guide which must direct us in the choice of a profession is the welfare of mankind and our own perfection. It should not be thought that these two interests could be in conflict, that one would have to destroy the other; on the contrary man's nature is so constituted that he can attain his own perfection only by working for the perfection, for the good, of his fellow men.[11]

In this passage Marx echoes one of the most striking themes of Renaissance humanism as represented in the writings of Pico della Mirandola. Pico wrote that God created man, only after having completed the entire universe, because he desired to produce a being capable of contemplating the beauty of the creation. However, since all possible 'natures' had already been employed in the creation, no archetype for an additional creature remained, so God created man as 'a creature of indeterminate nature', unique in the universe. Man alone had the power to choose his own place in the scheme of creation. God announced that,

> ... Thou, constrained by no limits, in accordance with thine own free will, in whose hand We have placed thee, shalt ordain for thyself the limits of thy nature ...[12]

One contemporary commentator has described Pico's *Oration* as an example of Renaissance Pelagianism, the strongest resurgence of that doctrine since the condemnation of Pelagius himself. Perhaps by extension Marx's humanism should be viewed in part as a modernization of that same doctrine. Marx 'modernizes' Pelagianism above all by rejecting the notion of divine creation. Since the whole of world history is only the creation of man through human labor and the development of nature through man, "he has evident and incontrovertible proof of his *self-creation*, his own *formation process*".[13] Mankind stands in relation of creator to itself. (The elaboration of this doctrine leads directly into Marx's historical materialism).

This perfectibilism, for Feuerbach as well as for Marx, led to a critique of prevailing conditions of human existence which was intended to expose the sources of limitation, suffering, and finitude, to remove the socially-imposed obstacles to human self-development. An important element in this perfection of human nature was reflected in the notion of the *integrity* or *wholeness* of the human personality which was conceived as the appropriate outcome of the self-expressive development of the human subject.[14] According to this notion of the wholeness appropriate to the developed human personality, almost any form of division in the human psyche, or even conflict between individuals, could be understood as a tragic evidence of the failure of humanity to achieve an existence appropriate to its true (though as yet unrealized) nature. All this of course could be found in any number of German authors in the late eighteenth and early nineteenth centuries. German philosophy had supplied a ready term to embrace the profundities as well as the ambiguities of this theme – *alienation* (*Entfremdung*). What distinguished Feuerbach and Marx in particular was their resolute insistence that the *causes* of this alienation could be traced to specifically identifiable structures of belief and social institutions, and were subject to radical transformation by the efforts of humanity itself.

In Feuerbach's thought, the notion of alienation soon came to be centered on the phenomena associated with the Christian doctrine of original sin, broadly construed; in the contrast between the perfection (infinitude) of the Divinity and the fallenness (finitude) of the human condition. He argued that the attributes of divinity such as goodness, justice, and wisdom are not such because God possesses them, but rather, God possesses them because these attributes are in themselves divine. "Justice, wisdom, and, in fact, every determination which constitutes the divinity of God, is determined and known through itself; but God is known and determined by the predicates."[15] But, Feuerbach argues, "nothing is to be found in the essence and consciousness of religion that is not there in the being of man, that is not there in his consciousness of himself and the world."[16] In truth there is an identity of the divine and the human predicates, or in other words, "the anti-thesis of divine and human is illusory".[17] The true content of the distinction between the divine and the human is simply that between the essence of humanity at large and the being of the individual.

In replacing traditional theology by this anthropologism, Feuerbach did not understand himself to be denying what he took to be a vitally significant truth disguised by the older forms of religion and theology, but rather rescuing it from its alienated form. The true atheist, says Feuerbach, is he to whom the predicates of the divine Being — for example, love, wisdom, and justice — are nothing, not he to whom only the subject of these predicates is nothing.[18] Indeed, within the circle of Young Hegelians, Feuerbach was attacked for *not* having liberated himself from the toils of theology, for having only reasserted it in a particularly convoluted guise.

Mankind, having hypostasized each of the so-called 'divine' predicates, attributes them to an abstract God and in that act denies them to its own nature. It is in this act of self-abnegation by humanity that Feuerbach locates the alienation which characterizes the human condition religiously conceived. In phrases which Marx was to echo two years later in the Paris manuscripts, Feuerbach claims,

... the more human the being of God is, the greater is the apparent difference between God and man; that is, the more is the identity of the human and the Divine Being denied by theology ... and the more is the human ... depreciated.[19]
In order to enrich God, man must become poor; that God may be all, man must be nothing.[20]

Another group of Feuerbach's most characteristic notions are indicated by the term 'species-being' (*Gattungswesen*). In order to make plausible his claim that the Divine Being is nothing other than the being of man himself, Feuerbach had to supply some account of how such a mistake or illusion could occur. Attempting to distinguish between animal and human, Feuerbach claims that consciousness, understood in a special sense, is the definitive human trait:

Strictly speaking, consciousness is given only in the case of a being to whom his *species*, his *mode of being* is an object of thought.[21]

The consciousness of the animal provides only an experience of itself as an individual; there is no distinction between the inner and the outer life. The human individual however is capable of taking 'the essential mode of being' of his species — the 'Thou' as opposed to the 'I' — as an object of thought. Feuerbach makes frequent use of a special epistemological 'principle', namely that no being can cognize an object which is not an intrinsic part of its own mode of being. For example, "A really finite being has not even the slightest inkling, let alone consciousness, of what an infinite being is, for the mode of consciousness is limited by the mode of being."[22] But in religion, humanity is conscious of the infinite. But there could be no such state of consciousness unless infinity characterized the mode of being of consciousness itself. Hence, "in its consciousness of infinity, the conscious being is conscious of the infinity of its own being."[23]

The distinction in traditional theology between the infinity of divine predicates and the finitude of human predicates by virtue of which God is held to be a totally different being from humanity merely misplaces the distinction between the finite limitations of any individual human being and the 'infinite plenitude'[24] of predicates which characterizes humanity as a whole. In its idea of God humanity has only grasped its own nature in an estranged form.

The consciousness of God is the self-consciousness of man; the knowledge of God is the self-knowledge of man. Man's notion of himself is his notion of God, just as his notion of God is his notion of himself — the two are identical.[25]

In a further application of the notion of 'species-being' in the *Principles of the Philosophy of the Future*, Feuerbach interprets human being as communal being.

The single man *in isolation* possesses in himself the essence of man neither as a *moral* nor as a *thinking* being. The *essence* of man is contained only in the community, in the *unity of man with man* — a unity, however, that rests on the reality of the distinction between the 'I' and the 'You'.[26]
Solitude means being *finite* and *limited, community* means being *free* and *infinite*. For *himself* alone, man is just man (in the ordinary sense); but man *with* man — the unity of 'I' and 'You' — that is God.[27]

Like Feuerbach, Marx was convinced that the causes of humanity's present alienated form of existence could be identified and eliminated through human effort. He shared Feuerbach's attitude toward established religion as an important component of contemporary alienation. What Feuerbach tended to see as a cause, however, Marx regarded as merely a symptom of a deeper disease, one rooted in the mode of production, in the prevailing social relations under which the material conditions of life were produced and reproduced. The I–Thou relationship of love in which Feuerbach saw the resolution of alienated existence and the free realization of infinite human spirit, would be realizeable for Marx only through a transformation of the economic relations which constitute the prevailing forms of social existence. The prevailing social relations inevitably *dehumanize* the participants.

The details of Marx's analysis of alienated labor are by now very familiar, as should also be the larger motives of his analysis. The trilogy of concerns which preoccupied much of the preceding period of German literature and philosophy — the threat of loss of unity between man and man, man and nature, man and God — appear in Marx only somewhat modified. The consequence of alienated labor is an "external relation of the worker to nature and to himself".[28] And the other alienation, of man to himself "is realized and expressed in the relation between man and other men".[29] Only alienation of humanity from God drops from view in Marx's analysis, or more strictly speaking, is transmuted into alienation from species-being, the unity of I and Thou that is God in Feuerbach's analysis.

In Marx's use of Feuerbach's notion of species-being is revealed once again his commitment to a strong thesis of perfectibilism. Human consciousness exhibits the unique capability, according to Feuerbach, of taking the essential mode of being of its species, the Thou as opposed to the I, as an object of thought. Marx reiterates that man is a conscious being, i.e., his own life is an object for him, since he is a species-being.[30] Humanity's capacity to take its own essence as an object of thought gives it the capacity to do what no other creature is capable of, to produce *universally*, to *reproduce the whole of nature.*

The animal only produces itself, while man reproduces the whole of nature. . . . The animal builds only according to the standard and need of the species to which it belongs while man knows how to produce according to the standard of any species and at all times knows how to apply an intrinsic standard to the object. Thus man creates also according to the laws of beauty.[31]

Most discussions of Marx's humanism lead sooner or later to the fundamental question of its intended scope. Did Marx always intend to offer a general view of the ultimate good of all mankind, as his distinction between political emancipation and *human* emancipation in the early writings suggests, or are these early writings to be viewed as a stage in the development of his thought which was transcended by a narrower focus upon the problem of economic liberation of the proletariat and no view at all about the ultimate good of the remainder of mankind? Is the humanism of the early Marx eclipsed by the subsequent shift of focus and method in his work? A complete answer to this question can be supplied only by a review of the whole of his work, if then. However, an indication of the present writer's interpretation of this problem can be supplied by way of a discussion of a passage drawn from a 'mature' work of Marx, the *Grundrisse*, his notes and sketches for the *Preface to the Critique of Political Economy* and *Capital*.

In Notebook V of these sketches, Marx raises the question of whether the production of wealth is to be considered an end in itself, or merely a means to the realization of some other good, such as creation of the best citizens. He concludes that in Greek and Roman antiquity, the production of wealth was never an end in itself. Rather a particular mode of production was regarded as most conducive to the development of civic character and a healthy polis. Accordingly, Marx suggests that the attitude of antiquity, in which the human being appears as the aim of production seems lofty when contrasted to the modern world where production appears to be the aim of mankind, and wealth the aim of production.

In fact, however, when the limited bourgeois form is stripped away, what is wealth other than the universality of individual needs, capacities, pleasures, productive forces, etc., created through universal exchange? The full development of human mastery over the forces of nature, those of so-called nature as well as of humanity's own nature? The absolute working out of his creative potentialities, with no presupposition other than the previous historic development, which makes this totality of development, i.e., the development of all human powers as such the end in itself, not as measured on a *predetermined* yardstick? Where he does not reproduce himself in one specificity, but produces his totality? Strives not to remain something he has become, but is in the absolute movement of becoming? In bourgeois economics – and in the epoch of production to which it corresponds – this complete working-out of the human content appears as a complete emptying-out, this universal objectification as total alienation, and the tearing-down of all limited one-sided aims as sacrifice of the human end-in-itself to an entirely external end. This is why the childish world of antiquity appears on one side as loftier. On the other side, it really is loftier in all matters where closed shapes, forms and given limits are sought for. It is satisfaction from a limited standpoint; while the modern gives no satisfaction; or, where it appears satisfied with itself, it is vulgar.[32]

It would be difficult to find in the mature works a passage richer in content relevant to the discussion of Marx's humanism than this one. First of all it is a passage from the mature Marx; yet it could easily be imagined as an excerpt from the manuscripts of 1844. The concept of alienation is central and explicit; the motive of mastery over nature and self (created nature) is clear; the commitment to perfectibilism again manifest.

In this passage Marx's humanist ethic occurs as a constituent element of an implicit philosophy of history; the two inquiries are inseparable. This is just as true for Marx as it was for Hegel.[33]

In the passage above Marx articulates a conception of intrinsic good for humanity as a whole: the development of all human powers as such. This conception is simultaneously a criterion for the evaluation of historical development and itself a product of history. Marx sees this criterion as a generalized schema, and not a commitment to any particular conception of human nature, not a 'pre-determined yardstick'. The absolute working out of humanity's creative potentialities is to take place under 'no presupposition other than the previous historic development'. In the task of self-development humanity is always compelled to take the realities of the present moment and its present nature as its starting-point, but in all other respects humanity is a free creator of its own future, meaning, presumably, that there are no laws determining the human future independently of human consciousness. Again Marx seems to appeal implicitly to a doctrine of the unlimited potential for development of the human spirit, with echoes of Pico della Mirandola as well as of Hegel and Feuerbach.

If the general intent of this passage is clear, the view as expressed is not without ambiguities. Surely no Marxist would wish to deny any dialectical logic connecting the present with the past. Such a logic is invoked in this very passage: what is in reality the complete working-out of the human content appears under the present form of production as a complete emptying out; what is in reality a universal objectification of the human spirit now takes the form of total alienation; what is in reality the tearing-down of all limited, one-sided aims appears in the historical present as the sacrifice of the human end-in-itself to an entirely external end.

Humanity will have attained mastery over its own nature (and its own future) when it becomes capable of grasping its own existence as a manifestation of this dialectic, as 'the absolute movement of becoming', and ceases striving to remain something it has become, ceases reproducing itself in one specificity, (i.e., as worker, capitalist, etc.) and devotes itself to the realization of the 'universality' of individual needs, capacities, pleasures, productive forces, etc.

Above all Marx is determined not to *specify* an ultimate human essence, not to provide 'closed shapes, forms and given limits' for it. The concerns of Marx and of Pico della Mirandola's God are in this respect identical.

Taken out of context, this concern to specify no human essence, to apply no pre-determined yardstick to it or history, might spell the defeat of any attempt to specify a structure or logic of history. In fact Marx does commit himself to one defining feature of humanity sufficiently specific to ensure the possibility of a philosophy of history. It is a defining characteristic of *authentic* human nature to possess complete mastery over itself and the rest

of nature, to be free in the self-conscious 'absolute' working-out of its creative
potentialities. A dialectical logic of history can be inferred from this perspective: its constitutive event, though not its culmination, must be the coming to
self-consciousness of humanity. Humanity at some historical juncture must
recognize and begin to realize its potential for mastery over itself and nature.
Communism, even in the early Marx, represents this most significant event in
history, but not its culmination. "*Communism* is the necessary form and
dynamic principle of the immediate future but not as such the goal of human
development — the form of human society."[34] That process of self-development itself, free and potentially infinite, cannot be specified in advance.

In Marx's conviction that the only destiny appropriate to humanity lay in
the indefinitely great extension of powers, needs, and capabilities must be
seen his often-cited Prometheanism. In this passage he reveals a very characteristic attitude: only the bourgeoisie could contemplate with satisfaction the
limits within which the development of human nature up to the present has
been confined. The very possibility of that satisfaction was sufficient to con-
vict the bourgeoisie of irredeemable vulgarity in Marx's eyes.

The argument over whether Marx's works contain an ethical theory may
now be regarded in the following light. Normative ethical theory has been
defined by one contemporary authority, William Frankena, as containing (1)
judgments of moral obligation, (2) judgments of moral value, and secondarily,
(3) judgments of non-moral value.[35] A study of the last is not as such a part
of ethics or moral philosophy according to Frankena, but since it turns out
that a consideration of what is intrinsically good in a non-moral sense is
logically involved in determining what is morally right or wrong, we must
include a discussion of such value judgments in an account of ethics. It seems
to this writer that Marx's works do not contain an ethical theory, strictly
speaking, according to this usage (which seems to me proper), because Marx
nowhere offers a general account of judgments of moral obligation or moral
value. On the other hand his notion of the development of all human powers
as an end in itself seems to me precisely a judgment of intrinsic good, or non-
moral value, and one which is asserted universally by Marx. The further problem of the defensibility of such a criterion will not be pursued here. 'Creative
self-expression', 'self-development', 'power and achievement' are all items
that have occurred on moral philosophers' lists of intrinsic goods, but Marx's
references to such a criterion are too sparse and imprecise to admit of much
detailed discussion. However it does seem possible from this perspective to
argue that Marx did not simply take the view that whatever the dialectic of
history produced was right.[36]

In light of the above, I would claim that attempts to construct an ethical theory proper, incorporating a Marxist notion of intrinsic good, cannot be dismissed as un-Marxist or inappropriate in any fundamental sense. It is clear that Marx considered such a project a waste of time in the circumstances of his own life, that he viewed existing moral codes as elements of prevailing class ideology, and appeals to traditional notions of justice, for example, as irrelevant, even when expressed as demands by the proletariat. On the other hand, if Marx as a theorist could be in a position to stipulate a universal criterion of intrinsic good, there would appear to be no reason why similarly universal judgments of moral obligation and value could not be provided, in the context of an appropriate philosophy of history, in a manner similar to Hegel. I shall argue in the conclusion of this chapter that the general structure of Hegelian ethics is the appropriate context for interpreting many of Marx's views, and that, considering Marx's own intellectual origins, this should hardly be surprising.

3. ENGELS, KAUTSKY, AND NEO-KANTIAN ETHICAL THEORY

Perhaps the most protracted and detailed discussion of Marxism and ethical theory in the history of that movement, with the possible exception of the discussions of socialist humanism in the 1960's, occurred during the interval from approximately 1895 to the beginning of World War I. The principal forum for that debate was the German Social Democratic movement, although significant contributions also came from French, Russian, Austrian, and Italian participants. The discussion eventually involved much of the intellectual leadership of the Social Democratic party, with Mehring and Kautsky periodically taking up the subject in the pages of *Neue Zeit*. It involved a number of Marxists who considered themselves neo-Kantians, and some neo-Kantian philosophers who considered themselves Marxists.

In order to appreciate how a dialogue between neo-Kantianism and Marxism could become a dominant intellectual occupation in those years of German Social Democracy, it is necessary to recall some features of the history of philosophy in nineteenth century Germany.

The decade of the 1850's, perhaps philosophically the least memorable of that century in Germany, produced the materialism of Büchner, Moleschott, and Vogt (toward which Feuerbach gravitated in his later years), accompanied by a tendency toward positivism, scientism, and consequent neglect of the philosophical tradition. After approximately a decade and a half during which these developments occupied the center of the philosophical stage, a revival of interest in Kant made its first appearance in the 1860's, and began to take hold in some German universities in the 1870's. One of the major events signalling this return to Kant was the publication in 1866 of Lange's famous *History of Materialism*[37] in which he evaluated this tradition from a perspective which made Kant's philosophy the major event in recent philosophical history. Under the circumstances this renewed attention to Kant constituted a dramatic revival of the fortunes of philosophy in Germany.

For a younger German philosopher beginning his intellectual career in the last two decades of the nineteenth century, there would have appeared to be two major alternatives for one's philosophical allegiance: either some form of evolutionary postivism, or neo-Kantianism. The issue of which philosophy provided the proper account of empirical science tended to be the most common battleground between them. The memory of Hegel was a dim one, and distorted at that through the Young Hegelians' critiques of his system after his death.

Of much greater immediate relevance for Marxist disputes over ethical theory was the context provided by Engels' discussion of morality in his *Anti-Dühring*, published in 1878. In this work Engels was chiefly concerned to dispute Herr Dühring's assertion of the existence of eternal truths in the sphere of human morality. Engels, on the contrary, insisted that the three classes of contemporary society – the feudal aristocracy, the bourgeoisie, and the proletariat – each possessed its own special morality derived in the last resort from the practical relations on which their class position was based.[38] Admitting that these three moralities shared much in common, Engels considered the view that this common element shared by all three might constitute a universal moral code, and dismissed that possibility on the grounds that the common component could be taken as reflecting nothing more than the fact of a common historical background shared by the three classes in question. He emphatically rejected any suggestion of an immutable moral law which could be construed as trans-historical.

We maintain on the contrary that all former moral theories are the product, in the last analysis, of the economic stage which society had reached at that particular epoch. And as society has hitherto moved in class antagonisms, morality was always a class morality; ....[39]

These class moralities have always functioned either as a justification for oppression by the ruling class, or for revolt by the oppressed class, according to Engels.

These assertions are immediately qualified in an interesting though somewhat puzzling way when Engels proceeds to acknowledge in the next sentence that "there has on the whole been progress in morality, as in all other branches of human knowledge . . .", without suggesting what the criterion of such progress might be. He then introduces the possibility of "a really human morality which transcends class antagonisms" in some future society which has overcome and forgotten class contradictions. The characteristics of such a single universal moral code which would justify terming it 'really human' are not explored by Engels at this point. The position bequeathed by Engels can be summarized in the following points:

1.   All morality is class morality.
2.   There are no eternal, immutable, or transhistorical moral truths (although the succession of moral codes through history is to be viewed as a *progress*).
3.   Moral principles and values shared in common by various class moralities are not to be construed as manifesting a universal code of human conduct (although the morality of a future classless society might be 'truly human').
4.   The morality of each class is a product of the practical, economic relations of which that class is constituted.

This series of points made by Engels on the subject of morality, with all its ambiguities, came to be regarded by many as the heart of Marxist orthodoxy on that subject, to be defended by such champions as Kautsky and Mehring against the revisionist tendencies of neo-Kantians in later years.

In the same year in which Marx died, 1883, the journal *Neue Zeit* was founded, with Kautsky as its chief editor. For many years he and Mehring in particular presided over the intellectual fate of Marxism in the pages of that journal, contributing several pieces every month in response to political and literary events of significance for the socialist movement. While he lived, Engels also contributed occasionally, in the role of elder statesman of the movement. This circle of primary editors of *Neue Zeit*, together with Kautsky and other figures such as Plekhanov, came to be seen as the principal defenders of genuine Marxism or 'scientific socialism', engaging in criticism of various centrifugal tendencies within the larger socialist movement, and defending it against attacks from without.

Early in the history of *Neue Zeit* Kautsky displayed an interest in subjects related to ethical theory. About the same time that Engels was preparing the *Origins of Private Property, the Family, and the State*, Kautsky contributed two articles to *Neue Zeit* with a somewhat Darwinian flavor on the social instinct in the animal and the human worlds.[40] More directly on the subject of morality, Kautsky became involved in the dispute between Mehring and Tönnies over the German Society for Ethical Culture which Mehring had criticized at its founding late in 1892.[41] The German Society for Ethical Culture announced the aim of assisting the German proletariat by introducing an ethical dimension into the economic and political class struggle. Mehring responded by denying any possibility of a 'neutral' position in the class struggle, calling the struggle itself the only 'ethic' required by the proletariat. Tönnies, as a defender of the Society wished to criticize Marx for ignoring the ethical component of the proletarian struggle, but admitted a certain ambiguity in the political commitment of the Society. Mehring and Kautsky firmly insisted that whatever the intentions of the Society, its presumption of an 'ethically neutral position' in the existing class struggle rendered it effectively an ally of the bourgeoisie.

When Bernstein presented a series of articles in *Neue Zeit* beginning in 1897 on the present position of the socialist movement and recommending certain directions of policy for the future, he provoked a controversy which also touched on the problem of Marxist ethics. Bernstein was invited to summarize and elaborate his views in a single book, which he produced in 1899,[42] and that book occasioned the famous debate at the 1899 Hannover congress of the Social Democratic Party over the orthodoxy or 'revisionism' of Bernstein's views. In the conclusion of that book, Bernstein, making a slight bow in the direction of the neo-Kantian concern with ethical theory, charged that the Marxist movement had failed to articulate its moral ideals in a manner adequate to inspire the working class in the struggle with the bourgeoisie. While the problem of Marxist ethical theory remained only an incidental issue in the immediate controversy, Kautsky was repeatedly forced to defend Marxism against Bernstein's charge in subsequent years.

As editor of *Neue Zeit* Kautsky continued to be drawn into debate from time to time over ethical theory. For instance in 1901 he found himself in a minor polemic with a Dr. F. W. Foerster who was arguing that the English experience had proven that worker's movement founded merely upon Marxist conceptions of a class struggle was incapable of supplying the moral guidelines necessary for the development of genuine self-government within the working class.[43] Kautsky of course replied that Dr. Foerster had misunderstood the ethical dimension of the proletarian struggle, which brought about the highest feelings of solidarity, of self-sacrifice, and of loyalty to one's co-workers.

Kautsky's concern with Marxism and ethical theory culminated in the years 1905–1907, in a struggle with the editorial board of the Party daily, *Vorwärts*, in August of 1905, in the publication of his book *Ethics and the Materialist Conception of History* in 1906, and in numerous articles written in defense of his views in the months following the appearance of the book.[44] While the revolution of 1905, the 'hurricane on the Russian ocean' raged, Kautsky was caught up in the 'storm in a teacup' in Berlin, accusing Karl Eisner and several other members of the editorial board of *Vorwärts* of a revisionist inclination toward neo-Kantianism, and particularly toward Kantian ethics. Kautsky resolved this dispute by forcing out Eisner and five other members of the board.[45] In the immediate aftermath of this organizational struggle, Kautsky determined to set down his own view of the Marxist analysis of ethics, one suspects, largely in order to dispense once and for all with a subject that had proved to be exceedingly fractious within German Marxism.

In the Preface to this work Kautsky explains that he did not wish to delay setting out his views on Marxism and ethics "in face of the influence which has been won in our ranks by the ethics of Kant."[46] The appearance of Kautsky's book naturally brought forth numerous reviews and further discussions to which Kautsky contined to contribute in the next two years, and it is from all of these materials that one is able to assess Kautsky's contribution to Marxist 'orthodoxy' on the subject of ethics. The details of Kautsky's views will be considered below, after an examination of some of the neo-Kantian views which provoked his response.

The first 'generation' of neo-Kantians included Hermann Cohen, who demonstrated an interest in 'the social question' as well as an interest in the philosophical doctrines espoused by contemporary socialists. Karl Vorländer, one of the second 'generation' neo-Kantians, who was, among the more sophisticated members of that group, the most dedicated to the dialogue with Marxism and its chief historian, treats Cohen as its main initiator.[47] According to Vorländer, as early as 1877, in his *Kants Bergründung der Ethik*,[48] Cohen had stressed the fundamentally political nature of Kant's conception of the highest good as a kingdom of ends.[49] In a similar vein, Vorländer himself argued in 1900 that "Kant's ethic is, despite its apparently individualistic garb, in the last analysis, chiefly an ethic of community. And socialism is nothing else, ethically understood."[50]

It was the Kantian conception of a kingdom of ends interpreted as a description of the socialist ideal, and a definition of humanity, which proved to be one of the most enduring attractions of that philosophy for socialists inclined toward Kant. Kant himself had described the kingdom of ends as a practical idea used to bring into existence what does not exist but can be made actual by our conduct.[51] Vorländer pointed out that Kant also spoke of "this principle of humanity" as "an end in itself" and as "a principle which is the supreme limiting condition of every man's freedom of action".[52] Of this conception Vorländer inquires, "Can the basic idea of socialism, the idea of community, simply expressed, be more significantly proclaimed?"[53]

Common to a majority of the neo-Kantian socialists was the conviction that Marxism as a social theory required 'completion' or 'grounding' by an ethical system. The materialism, or naturalism, of writers such as Engels, Kautsky, or Plekhanov was held to be inadequate to support any such ethical system, especially by neo-Kantians like Hermann Cohen. Where materialism perforce limited its understanding of scientific socialism to 'causal-genetic' terms, the critical philosophy could reconcile science and ethics. In 1896 Cohen voiced the opinion, which was often quoted by later participants in the discussion, that "Socialism is in the right so far as it is grounded in ethical idealism. And ethical idealism has grounded it."[54] In one of his subsequent works, *Ethik des reinen Willens,*[55] much quoted by contemporary Marxists, Cohen attempted just such an ethical grounding for social theory. Speaking of this work, Vorländer claimed that "for the first time ethics as the logic of the social sciences, especially as the logical foundations of the theory of justice (*Rechtswissenschaft*) was established."[56] "Thus emerged the purely idealistic foundation of socialism, if possible, still more significantly and sharply."[57]

Cohen argued that the materialist conception of history embraced a contradiction when it attempted to speak of improving the human condition merely by means of improving the economic conditions of life.[58] To regard good conduct in human beings as nothing more than a reflex of good (social) health would not only reduce morality to a chimera, but deprive justice (*Recht*) not only of its ethical, but also of its logical foundation.[59] In this consequence lay the mistake of the so-called materialist conception of history, according to Cohen.[60]

'Society' in its modern usage involved a double meaning, one moral and one legal-economic.[61]

Precisely speaking, it is not correct to say that the concept of society issues in two meanings, one as an economic, and the other as an ethical correction of the positive idea of the state. These two meanings constitute, in the same concept, the contradiction of the materialist and the idealistic view of history. According to the first meaning of 'society' the individual is judged and evaluated not so much as a social being, but rather as an economic one. According to the other meaning man as a social being in the ethical sense is taken as the problem. From one meaning arises social physics, from the other, social ethics.[62]

Cohen rejected that interpretation of Marx which limited his concern exclusively to the economic conditions of human life. "Ethical inspiration spurred on his entire great work, the theoretical as well as the practical."[63] He felt that any adequate social theory must concern itself as much with the ethical as with the economic dimension, and Marxism could be no exception. "A logical contradiction pricks at the materialist view of history; however the ethical spirit which pulses through the entire theory must bring it to self-correction."[64] Cohen goes on to develop a doctrine of 'ethical freedom' in Kantian terms of autonomy and moral law which he places at the foundation of any adequate social theory.

In the same work, Cohen referred to Kant's categorical imperative as the chief contribution of Kantian philosophy to socialism. In a passage which Kautsky singled out for special criticism the following year in his *Ethics and the Materialist Conception of History*, Cohen described the categorical imperative as "the ethical program of the new epoch, and the entire future of world history."[65] (Kautsky was to complain that this 'program of the entire future of world history' was too narrowly conceived. This 'timeless moral law', the categorical imperative, would itself come to an end under socialism, when in actual practice men will no longer be tempted to treat each other as means.[66] In this Kautsky appears to echo a bad argument of Engels to the effect that 'Thou shalt not steal' will no longer be a moral commandment under Communism because there will be no theft.)

Vorländer, in his 1900 work, *Kant und der Sozialismus* followed Cohen's lead in identifying the categorical imperative as a description of the political ideal of socialism.

The true and actual connection of socialism with critical philosophy is founded rather in the 'purely moral', in the consequences – never drawn in practice by Kant – of that simple yet exalted formula of the categorical imperative, which teaches us to respect humanity in the person of every other fellow human being at all times as an end in himself, never merely as a means. On this foundation socialism must build, if it would have any ethical foundation at all.[67]

Among the consequences of the categorical imperative which Kant did not spell out of course would be the necessity for the abolition of capitalism, whereby the proletariat is treated as mere means for the capitalists' end of multiplying capital.

In a rather respectful but nevertheless dissenting review of Vorländer's book on Kant and socialism, Mehring took particular exception to Cohen's and Vorländer's references to the categorical imperative as containing the ethical ideal of socialism.

The maxim is first of all at present not such a forgotten little thing, only re-discovered by the neo-Kantians, as Vorländer appears to believe. It belongs to those remarks of Kant which are universally known, and has played a large role in the political literature of the nineteenth century, only most certainly in quite another sense than Vorländer and Cohen believe. To the founding of German socialism it has not contributed a grain of sand, though it has rolled up several stones to the foundation of liberalism, and quite particularly, of anti-socialist liberalism.[68]

Mehring's review tended to confirm the view of the 'Marxist center' that Kantian ethics could only lead to revisionism, or even 'anti-socialist liberalism'. Vorländer's book and Mehring's review appeared only a few months after the Hannover party congress at which Bernstein's views, including his modest signs of approval toward the neo-Kantian Marxists, were condemned as revisionist. After 1900 the centrists appeared to harden their opposition to Kantianism in general, but this by no means eliminated neo-Kantian influences within the active intellectual leadership of the party.

Another perspective on the relationship between Kant and Marx was supplied by Conrad Schmidt. Reacting to the discussion which followed the publication of Vorländer's book in 1900, he argued that modern socialism, with its 'thoroughly naturalistic' mode of comprehension, 'disregarding every religion and metaphysics' must in the end also be thoroughly opposed to the practical philosophy of Kant, which is itself based upon a particular metaphysical system.[69] Vorländer eventually replied that Schmidt had misunderstood Kant: "Kant's most characteristic service consists much more precisely in the pure delimitation of the sphere (of ethics); and thus his ethics is distinguished in principle from religion and metaphysics."[70] Here it would appear that Vorländer allows his enthusiasm for Kantian ethics to carry him away; it is difficult to see how an account of Kant's ethics could be given without reference to the metaphysical concept of *noumena*. Nevertheless, Vorländer insists that the "naturalistic mode of thought which dominates the new theoreticians of socialism is not rendered impossible by Kantian epistemology, but rather that epistemology forms the necessary completion, the philosophical foundation, of the 'naturalistic mode of thought'."[71] Schmidt wished to argue that the "socialist ideal of humanity", "the free, unhindered development of all human talents in a society regulated in a planned manner through the social will" was only a "product of the natural-social development proceeding forward through the class struggle."[72] To this Vorländer retorts, "Toward which goal does this development proceed 'forward'?" "What ought to be the measure of this 'social will'; which should be the highest guiding principle of these socially-regulated plans? Does our 'naturalist' not notice that he is no longer dealing here with developmental-historical, but with ethical, concepts?"[73]

Schmidt did indeed acknowledge that his own 'socialist' account of morality did not differ substantially in practical consequences from that of Kant.[74] However he remained convinced that Kant's ethic was inseparably tied to a particular metaphysics which had no place in socialist theory. Attempting to support this view, Schmidt argued that no norm such as the Kantian categorical imperative which applied to this world, as opposed to some metaphysical otherworld could remain 'exceptionless'. No norm of this kind could possess any more than 'relative universal validity' (sic).[75] Kant's claim to universal validity or objective lawfulness of the categorical imperative thus proves, according to Schmidt, that Kant's moral philosophy is rooted in metaphysics. He goes on to admit that such 'exceptions' would themselves have to be 'justified', so that Vorländer is correct in replying that this implies only a reformulation of the original maxim, not an abrogation of it, and thus Schmidt undermines his own contention.

Whatever the difficulties in his interpretation, Schmidt remained convinced that the formal adoption of Kantian ethics as a 'completion' of socialist theory would smuggle unwanted metaphysical notions into that theory. He was much more favorably disposed to Kant's sociological notions in The Idea of a Universal History, and considered Marx's historical materialism to be the fulfillment of that universal scheme of history defended as a possibility in Kant's work.

Regarding Kantian ethics, Schmidt finally attempted to make a distinction between the 'ethico-social idealism' implicit in the system, and the 'specifically rationalist moral philosophy' contained therein. Schmidt then claimed that the first was 'completely independent' of the second.[76] He then suggested that the recognition of the necessity for the development of a planned socialist society by means of the proletarian class struggle conditioned by the economic structure, "has therewith at the same time attained the foundation for that idealism on which it can depend."[77] In effect Marx represents the completion of Kant, rather than the other way around.

Parallel to the development of neo-Kantianism, another influence began to make itself felt among theoreticians of social democracy during the same period — evolutionary thought. The decade of the 1870's produced several of the major works in which the theory of evolution was specifically applied to the species Homo sapiens, and in particular to its institutions of morality. Darwin published the Descent of Man in 1871; Haeckel, his Anthropogenie in 1874; and the first volume of Spencer's Principles of Ethics appeared in 1879.

These developments constituted an important element of the background against which Kautsky and other socialist theorists would read Engels' comments on morality in the *Anti-Dühring* of 1878.

Kautsky was by no means the only socialist thinker attracted to evolutionist ethics. Ludwig Woltmann, an avowed socialist, attempted to develop his own unique synthesis of Kant, Marx, and Darwin in three books published in successive years from 1898 to 1900.[78] Woltmann sought to develop an ethics which would be 'evolutionist and socialist' in content and at the same time 'unconditionally subordinated' to Kantian ethics. For that reason Kant's moral philosophy would be for Woltmann an 'ethic of socialism', and socialism would be the 'socio-economic fulfillment of the moral law'.[79]

Woltmann's view of the relationships of Marx to Hegel and Marx to Kant was typical of many neo-Kantian socialists.

That my book stands under the sign of the return to Kant is taken by some Marxists as a regress. However, anyone who knows precisely the critical position of Marx towards Hegel, and his own scientific method, must comprehend that Marx's conception of scientific reasoning corresponds throughout to Kant's critical philosophy, and that Marx's rejection of Hegel, and his turn toward natural science and history was basically a return to the genuine source of classical German philosophy, whether or not Marx was clearly conscious of this connection of principle.[80]

In *Die Darwinsche Theorie und der Sozialismus* Woltmann described the views of eighteen writers whom he counted as 'Darwinist supporters of socialism', including Lafargue, Bebel, Liebknecht, Kautsky, Cunow, Bernstein, among others, confirming the impression that evolutionary thought played a major role in the background of late nineteenth century Marxism. For all of the enthusiasm over Darwinism however, Woltmann was quite definite about the necessity of a Kantian correction to evolutionary socialist ethical theory. In his view the subordination of socialist, evolutionist ethics to Kantian ethics was required because the universal validity of moral concepts depended not upon their origins, but upon the possibility of providing a ground or justification for them.[81] He protested against the "eternally trivial objections of the historians of morality from the Darwinist and Marxist school" who "have so little methodological self-consciousness that they would undertake the investigation of a subject whose concepts they have never clarified."[82] The details of Woltmann's ethical theory may be passed over in favor of an examination of Kautsky's views, which had a much greater impact upon subsequent Marxist ethical theory.

Kautsky had been a Darwinian even before he discovered Marxism,[83] and the motives which impelled him to endorse evolutionary theory were in large part the same which attracted him to the materialist conception of history, namely "the strong desire to bring the entire world, including our intellectual functions, under a unitary conception, and to exclude all factors besides the natural from it."[84] In this Kautsky merely shared the common aspiration of that naturalism which had developed swiftly after the middle of the 19th century in Europe, inspired by the simultaneous developments of evolutionary theory and the theories of conservation of matter and energy which were just then gaining widespread acceptance in the scientific community.[85] Man was to be brought entirely within the sphere of nature through the demonstration of his ties with the animal kingdom, and nature as a whole was to be conceived as a vast but unitary, closed system of matter and energy incorporating both life and mind. A new, more restricted contrast was to be drawn between nature and society, or nature and culture. The distinctiveness of the latter was no longer to be conceived in terms of its relations to the supernatural, to a transcendent divinity. Instead, the distinction between nature and society was to be drawn in terms of those characteristics which distinguish the species *Homo sapiens* from the others, remembering that all belong equally to the same natural order.

In the sphere of ethical theory an analogous ambition led to the attempt to provide a complete account of the phenomena of human morality in strictly naturalistic terms. For Kautsky this was, at bottom, the major question of ethical theory. Could the phenomena of morality be explained in 'materialistic' terms, or was it necessary in the end to incorporate reference to some supernatural or metaphysical element in the account? For Kautsky it seemed sufficient 'explanation' of moral phenomena to provide an account of their genesis. If their origins could be described in naturalistic ('materialistic') terms, the motive of the inquiry would have been satisfied. Such an approach deflected attention from the prior problem of analyzing the possibly unique properties of moral concepts, judgments, and principles, as Woltmann had emphasized. Kautsky apparently did not take seriously Woltmann's objections to Darwinist and Marxist historians of morality who would investigate a thing the concept of which has not been previously clarified.

The phenomenon to be explained, in Kautsky's view, was the discovery 'soon after the Persian wars' of an internal 'regulator', of a 'highly mysterious power' which 'dwelt in the breast of every man', as well as of judgments of right and wrong 'which appeared so natural and self-evident'.[86]

The mysterious internal regulator of conduct, or sense of the moral law could initially be explained in only two ways, Kautsky believed. Materialists such as Epicurus could refer to experiences of happiness or pleasure as the motive force of human action, explaining ethical disagreements as rooted in different types of pleasure as well as in ignorance of the true durations of various pleasures.[87] Such an explanation of the moral law encounters two great difficulties, according to Kautsky: it fails to explain action in accordance with moral duty, as opposed to prudence, and it fails to explain the rapidity and certainty of moral judgments (on the assumption that the calculus of pleasures must require some time to operate).[88]

The alternative explanation of the moral law rests upon the apparent inability of the naturalistic one to explain action in accordance with duty, where more pain than pleasure is likely to result. This puzzle led some thinkers, above all Plato, to conclude that man lives not only a natural life but also a life outside of nature; that supernatural or nonnatural forces operate in the human spirit. From this source arose the ethics of philosophical idealism and monotheism.[89]

The subsequent careers of these two positions, the materialist and the spiritualist, Kautsky traces as follows: materialism is represented in the eighteenth century egoistic utilitarians (Lamettrie, Holbach, Helvetius), the English moral sense theorists, Darwinian ethics, and Marxist ethics; the spiritualist position is dominated in the modern period by the ethics of a single thinker – Kant.

French utilitarianism was a progressive development in that "it stood in close logical connection with a materialist view of the universe. The world as experience presents it to us appeared as the only one which could be taken into account by us."[90] Moral passions and views are determined by the conditions of human life, especially those supplied by education and by the state. According to Kautsky there can be an inherent conflict between the interests of the individual and those of the society at large only where the state, society, and education are defectively constructed, affected by ignorance. In the consequent demand for the reformation of the state and society lies the revolutionary value of French utilitarianism. Its greatest defect lay in the absence of any naturalistic account of the *source* of revolutionary zeal to accomplish these transformations: "Whence . . . is a moral ideal to be derived in a world of vice?"[91]

The moral sense theory of the English constituted a partial retreat from materialist ethics. They still sought to supply a purely naturalistic account of morality, but did not believe that considerations of utility could account for the complexity of moral life or for the sense of obligation. Accordingly, they distinguished between an egoistic and a sympathetic sense to account for moral conduct. The moral and the egoistic senses were opposed, but equally natural, and in this Kautsky saw the greatest virtue of the moral sense theorists. Their greatest defect lay in an inability, in his view, to account for the *origin* of such a moral sense in strictly natural terms. Only Darwinian ethical theory would prove equal to this task.

The occurrence of Kantian ethics *after* the development of utilitarianism and the moral sense theories of the eighteenth century illustrates the contradictory path of development to which humanity is subject in Kautsky's view. Contemplating this paradox of dialectical development, Kautsky was moved to observe, "Certain people like to cry now, 'Back to Kant!'. But those who mean by that the Kantian ethic, might just as well cry 'Back to Plato!'."[92]

Not all of Kantian philosophy fell under Kautsky's scorn. He was prepared to countenance certain empiricist elements of the first *Critique*, in which Kant stands on the same ground as the materialists: that the world outside us is real, and that all knowledge is derived from the senses. He would also agree with Kant that our knowledge of the world is conditioned by our cognitive faculties, and that accordingly an investigation of our own cognitive powers is a necessary prelude to the investigation of the external world. The first investigation is the task of philosophy – the science of science.[93]

Kautsky would also be content to accept Kant's distinction between the unknowable noumenal world and the phenomenal world of sense experience – if Kant had merely used this distinction to support a conclusion that there are no absolute truths, no final and complete knowledge.[94] According to Kautsky, all the errors of the Kantian philosophy originated in Kant's attempts to characterize the noumenal. First of all, by asserting the ideality of space and time, Kant in effect makes an assertion about the noumenal – that it is not characterized by space and time. In Kautsky's view, Kant was constitutionally unable to resist the temptation of 'break-neck leaps over the bounaries of knowledge' which he had himself established.[95] In his ethics this tendency takes over. "It seemed to him quite impossible to bring the moral law into a necessary connection with nature; that is with the world of phenomena. Its explanation required another world, a timeless and spaceless world of pure spirit, a world of freedom in contrast to the world of appearance (phenomena) which is ruled by the necessary chain of cause and effect."[96] The fundamental law of the pure practical reason then proves to be the crucial *entrée* into the noumenal world. In Kant's view the law is purely formal in that it represents merely the form of universal law necessarily inherent in any adequate maxim of conduct. Kautsky notes that the law must be 'independent of all conditions appertaining to the world of the senses' in order that its purely formal character not be compromised, and the heart of Kautsky's criticism lies in the claim that Kant fails to achieve this 'independence' of the world of the senses necessary for the moral law.

Kautsky first attempts to identify the moral law with an empirical thought, and observes that "we cannot possibly grasp a thought which is independent of all conditions appertaining to the world of the senses."[97] The moral law fails the test of independence in several senses according to him: first it is not a law of the 'pure will' in itself, but a law of the control of my will when brought in contact with my fellow men; secondly it assumes a world of men outside of me, and still more, the wish that these other men should conduct themselves in a particular fashion; it assumes a harmonious society as desirable and as possible; and "it assumes that the moral law is the means to create such a society, that this result can be achieved through a rule which the individual sets to himself."[98] Thus Kant was thoroughly deceived when he thought that this moral law was independent from all conditions appertaining to the world of sense.[99] Kautsky's main thrust against Kantian ethics is so briefly made that it would appear not to support the weight of much consideration. Kautsky's requirement of 'independence' appears so strong that any moral law which proved capable of application in the phenomenal world would be ruled out, and if this is so, perhaps all that can be said is that Kautsky failed to grasp Kant's position.

Curiously enough for a theorist whose primary interest centers on demonstrating that mankind's moral feelings must be understood as the creations of a natural order in which strict causal necessity reigns, Kautsky explicitly and unambiguously acknowledges that moral reasoning is quite distinct from causal reasoning. "If in the world of the past, the sequence of cause and effect (causality) rules, so in the world of action, of the future, the thought of aim (teleology)."[100] Having rejected Kant's two worlds of the phenomenal and the noumenal, Kautsky introduces two worlds of his own: the Past and the Future. Although the concept of moral choice is absurd with respect to the past, where 'iron necessity' rules, such choice is unavoidable with respect to the future.[101] The freedom which characterizes the world of the future is described as a "feeling' which is an 'indispensable psychological necessary which is not to be got rid of by any degree of knowledge."[102] As such it is a precondition of rational action. Two further worlds must be introduced in order to expound Kautsky's own doctrine of freedom: nature and society. My actions even with respect to the future are subject to causal determination in the sphere of nature, and are not free. Only my actions with respect to the future in the social sphere are free.

The obvious conclusion to Kautsky's argument would be that moral reasoning and causal psychological reasoning presuppose two distinct viewpoints, as he himself just explained. We may exercise one viewpoint or the other, but shifting from one to the other does not dissolve the first in the second; it is merely to suggest that we have changed the point of our inquiry. In this discussion Kautsky came much closer than many 'materialists' to acknowledging the distinctive nature of moral reasoning which was the principal concern of their neo-Kantian opponents.

Darwin greatly improved the eighteenth century English moral sense theory of ethics in Kautsky's opinion by proving that "the altruistic feelings formed no peculiarity of man, that they are also to be found in the animal world".[103] The altruistic feelings are among the impulses which develop spontaneously among those species of animals in which the social bond becomes a weapon in the struggle for life.[104] Among those impulses which form the necessary conditions for social forms of existence Kautsky lists altruism (self-sacrifice for the whole), bravery in defence of common interests, fidelity to the community, submission to the will of society, obedience and discipline, truthfulness to society, and ambition (sensibility to the praise and blame of society).[105]

According to Kautsky these social impulses are none other than the highest virtues; they constitute the entire moral code, with the possible exception of justice. All of these moral virtues are 'a product of the animal world'.[106] "An animal impulse and nothing else is the moral law."[107]

In this conclusion Kautsky adopted an extreme view of the origins of human morality in the social behavior of animals. The general issue of the suitability of animal behavior as a model for the explanation of human social conduct was much disputed in these years. Darwin's original evolutionary theory depended in part upon the supposition that the behavior of primitive animals could be modelled on that of humans caught in the Malthusian struggle for economic survival in late eighteenth century England. Despite this analogy at the heart of evolutionary theory, men such as Thomas Huxley argued that the analogy was misplaced, that "cosmic nature is no school of virtue, but the headquarters of the enemy of ethical nature."[108] The attempt to discover the origins of human morality in nature was too far-fetched in Huxley's view. Kropotkin argued on the contrary that Darwin had been unfair to the animal kingdom in attributing the Malthusian mechanism to them as the dominant principle of evolution, and stressed the role of cooperative social behavior in animal and human conduct alike, thereby tending to rescue somewhat the usefulness of the analogy.

This entire controversy has recently been started up again by the publication of E. O. Wilson's *Sociobiology: A New Synthesis*,[109] and the fundamental questions at issue seem not to have changed much since the nineteenth century. The shock value of tracing human social behavior to origins in animal behavior in nature depends entirely upon how rigidly we restrict our concept of animal nature at the outset. At one extreme the analogy between nature and society threatens to collapse; at the other the contrast between nature and society tends to disappear.[110]

At any rate, the answers to the puzzles which Kautsky originally noted with respect to moral feeling — that they occur with great rapidity, and convey a sense of compulsoriness which cannot be easily analyzed — are all supposedly found in the fact that the moral law is a universal instinct, with a force equal to the instinct for self-preservation and reproduction.[111] (In a curiously nihilistic extension of this argument Kautsky adds that when reason begins to analyze the grounds for our moral convictions "then one finally finds that to comprehend all means to pardon all, that everything is necessary, that nothing is good and bad."[112] But this seems to ignore his own discussion of moral freedom with respect to choices of conduct in society.)

Darwin satisfactorily accounts for all these basic moral virtues or traits of character according to Kautsky and thus was the first to make an end to the division of human nature into an animal and a supernatural part. But the Darwinian hypothesis cannot account for one crucial feature of human morality: the moral ideal. "Of that there is not the least sign in the animal world."[113] The materialist conception of history alone is capable of explaining the human capacity for setting ideals and following them in a naturalistic manner. Tenets of morality, or moral precepts, are a component of morality which did not exist in the animal world, dependent as they are on the prior development of language. These moral tenets are themselves brought into existence as a product of social needs.[114] Even though it is not always possible to fix the exact connection between particular moral conceptions and the social relations from which they arose, sufficient numbers of such connections have been demonstrated to take it as a general rule.[115] Although moral precepts are originally a product of social needs, social conditions may change without bringing about an immediate, corresponding alteration of moral precepts. In such a situation, these moral precepts, as elements of the social superstructure, may have an influence upon the economic base. Just as the prevailing ideology of a ruling social class may gradually be outmoded by development of the mode of production, a moral code may become so inappropriate to existing circumstances that hypocrisy becomes the rule in human conduct. This, Kautsky insists, is not *im*morality. As all moral codes are merely conventional fashions "that which is called immorality is simply a deviating kind of morality."[116] (The nihilism which appeared in connection with his Darwinism here becomes generalized). Finally, Kautsky characterizes the moral precepts which arise in an oppressed class as an *ideal* morality. It is 'ideal' in the sense that it constitutes a protest against the actual prevailing hypocrisy of the ruling class. It does not emerge from any scientific knowledge of the social organism, but from a deep social need, a burning desire for something other than the existing conditions. Kautsky insists that such an ideal morality is only something "purely negative, nothing more than opposition to the existing hypocrisy".[117]

In these passages, which are surely aimed at Bernstein's demand for moral ideals which would inspire the proletariat to take up the struggle for a better world, Kautsky grants that an 'ideal morality' does have importance as a motivational force; but given its 'purely negative' character and the absence of a scientific understanding of social conditions in its foundations, "the moral ideal will be deprived of its power to direct our policy".[118] The policy of the social democratic movement must be based upon science, not upon a morality of ideals. The moral ideal becomes a source of error in science. Having painstakingly worked up to this point, where he can drive a sharp wedge between the scientific and the ethical analysis of social conditions from a Marxist perspective, Kautsky then unwittingly appears to throw it all away by announcing that science can after all be viewed as a source of prescriptions: it can certainly prescribe an 'ought', but dares to issue this 'ought' only as a result of the insight into the necessary.[119]

The confusion apparent in the conclusion of Kautsky's work is perhaps indicative of the convoluted debates on Marxist ethics which took place in the German social democratic movement. If Kautsky desired an account of science which linked it so closely with ethical prescriptions perhaps he should have simply endorsed the views of the neo-Kantians instead of leading the battle against them; for it was precisely the goal of providing a detailed account of the relationship between the aims of Marxist social inquiry and rationally defensible moral ideals which motivated the majority of them.

The discussion of the place of Kantian ethics within scientific socialism reached its highest plane of sophistication in the exchanges between Karl Vorländer and Max Adler, the Austrian Marxist. For Adler, the problem of Marxist ethics led to the question of the relationship of the practical to the theoretical philosophy of Kant. That problem in turn was to be approached mainly through the question of the possible role of teleological reasoning in social science. Adler was one of the participants in the argument also involving Dilthey, Münsterberg, Rickert, Simmel, Stammler, and Windelband among others, over the appropriateness of some form of 'teleological' reasoning in the social sciences analogous to causal reasoning in the natural sciences. The outcome of this discussion in Adler's view was negative: there could not be a distinction between the natural and the social sciences in terms of their fundamental mode of reasoning.[120] This in turn meant that the foundation of social science was not to be sought in the sphere of Kantian practical philosophy, but in the sciences of nature.[121] Adler denied explicitly that he belonged to the ranks of the neo-Kantians, but Vorländer insisted that Adler's views made him, if not a member, at least a follower of the neo-Kantian camp.[122]

In one of his major works, *Kausalität und Teleologie im Streite um die Wissenschaft*, Adler distinguished two spheres of thought: 1. that of the necessary relations of thought, i.e., the consistent elaboration of the thought forms through which the entire world around us is constructed, and 2. that of value relations, which are themselves always referred to norm-recognizing wills.[123] To refuse to recognize an obligation may separate a person from the ethical community, and perhaps from all human community, but not from nature in general.[124] The law-like character of the moral principle depends upon the existence of its cognizer; the law-like character of the theoretical or natural judgment does not.[125] (Vorländer retorts that were there no men, there would also be no 'natural law').[126]

Adler distinguishes the lawfulness of wills from the lawfulness of events. The lawfulness of wills, or of ends willed, or of ethics, constitutes no science, and cannot provide 'absolute and objectively valid knowledge'. Such knowledge comes only from the sphere of the cognition of nature, where by 'nature' is meant "the existence of the thing, insofar as it is determined in accordance with universal laws".[127] What goes beyond the cognition of nature, such as ethics, aesthetics, or philosophy itself, is not science strictly speaking. It does not augment the system of objectively valid judgments; rather, it supplies only viewpoints of judgment, or sketches of the form of a *Weltanschauung*.[128]

After rejecting teleological reasoning from the social as well as the natural sciences, Adler then admits that science always presents only one side of existence, and so also of social life, namely that side which can be fixed in the form of an object, abstracted in universal concepts, and brought under laws.[129] Man is in the first instance a practical, goal-setting creature, and therein consists the true 'primacy of practical reason'. To grasp this is no longer to allow the sphere of science to be disrupted by value concepts, but to regard science as a means for the realization of moral goals, as a value to be realized itself.[130] In this respect Kant thinks like Marx, according to Adler.[131] The leap from the realm of necessity into that of freedom is accomplished for

Marx and Engels as well as for Kant, only in the practical deed.[132] The rejection of teleological conceptions from science thus in no way puts into question Kant's great teaching of the primacy of practical reason, but on the contrary, for the first time puts it in its true light. Kant's philosophy of practical reason finds its direct continuation in the saying with which Marx began the great work of his life: "Philosophers have only tried in various ways to interpret the world; but the point is to change it."[133]

In spite of his refusal to endorse the views of neo-Kantians such as Vorländer, Adler himself sounded very like a neo-Kantian in his criticisms of Kautsky's *Ethics and the Materialist Conception of History.* In a review published in the Vienna *Arbeiterzeitung* he remarked that the materialist conception signifies for Marxists only that standpoint which endeavors to conceive the sum of all appearances without remainder according to causal laws. It seeks a "radical and methodical exclusion of all religious and speculative miracles from the 'honest nutritive soil of experience'."[134] That however is a principle to which the critical philosophy would annex itself with its whole heart. What is new in historical materialism, as opposed to vulgar scientism, is the attempt to get away from any metaphysic, including materialism as a metaphysic, into a pure science.

Adler asserts somewhat charitably that Kautsky's book repudiates any 'shallow scepticism and empirical relativism' in the matter of ethics:[135] he denies in no way the significance or even the existence of ethical problems. Indeed Kautsky recognizes the obligatory force of ethical judgments as their essential character. However he is not able to grasp this character methodically, since he fails to distinguish between the 'is' and the 'ought', between the description of, and the demand for, an event. To fail to consider the nature of this obligation would be to set aside the whole problem of ethics, to leave unsolved the twin problems of the nature of ethical obligation and of the ethical ideal, on which problems the previous materialism ran aground.[136] The founding of a new moral order requires a double accomplishment: the framing of a new moral ideal, and the arousal of sufficient moral passion to carry out the struggle. Unfortunately, Kautsky's inquiry comes to a halt with the distinction. He does not ask what differences these moral ideals, or moral senses, make. Instead he adopts the posture of a merely theoretical, as opposed to an ethical, inquiry and in a kind of mental confusion, asks only what are the *causes* of these moral ideals and passions. But of course the causal explanation of ethical phenomena can only touch upon their historically determined manner of occurrence, their appearance and disappearance, but can never illuminate for us "the

existence of the ethical itself, that by which I know it as an ethical evaluation."[137]

As a consequence of his purely naturalistic-scientific standpoint, Kautsky
resists the methodological solution which a proper interpretation of the relationship between the theoretical and the practical reason in Kant provides.
Ethics construed as a natural science must be contrasted to ethics as practical
philosophy, a thesis which leads us back to the characteristic problem of
ethics: the 'ought'. The materialist conception of history is an excellent
maxim (as Kant would have said) of causal explanation, an instrument of
scientific reasoning similar to Newton's principle of gravity or Darwin's
hypothesis of natural selection, but it is not a practical philosophy. Within
the limits of the materialist conception of history, ethics can only be a social
science, an investigation of determinate existences and events, fundamentally
only a branch of sociology. The limits of the materialist conception of history
coincide with the limits of natural science generally. It follows, according to
Adler, that if Marxism does not wish to remain in an uncompleted state, it
must proceed to the critique of reason in both its theoretical and its practical
respects, as performed by the critical philosophy. It must proceed to the
analysis of 'the formal action-conditions of the self as a thinking and acting
being'. It speaks for the 'scientific character' of Marxism that its fundamental
concept of its own limits leads, just as in modern science, immediately to the
critical philosophy, which is undeniably required for the proper understanding of both.[138]

Vorländer pointed to passages such as these in order to claim Adler as
essentially an adherent of his own neo-Kantian views of the necessity for
'completing' Marxism with the Kantian practical philosophy, especially in his
major work *Kant und Marx* published in 1911. Two years later, in his own
book, *Marxistische Probleme,*[139] Adler continued to insist that a substantial
difference divided them, and rejected Vorländer's accusation of inconsistency.[140] In Adler's view, as expressed in 1913, in light of the strict logical
and epistemological distinction of science from ethics, any project for the
'grounding' or 'completion' of socialism by ethical theory was out of the
question. He complained that the neo-Kantians were too ready to speak of
any systematization of insights as a 'science'. From this perspective Kant's
practical philosophy was also a science. Vorländer had in fact complained
that it was a mistake "to limit the name and concept of science one-sidedly
to causal explanation."[141] Adler agreed that every science was a systematization of insights; "however is every such system therefore a science?"[142] Adler
refers the reader to his work on causality and teleology for arguments against

such a view. It is only systematization from the viewpoint of causal regularity that deserves the name of science, strictly speaking, a conclusion to which Kantian philosophy itself leads directly.[143] The refusal to label ethics a science is no merely verbal matter, as Vorländer would imply, because not to do so leads to fundamental confusions over the methodology of the social sciences.

Adler 'fully accepts' the practical philosophy of Kant, for its 'magnificent contribution' and 'continuing effectiveness', but still refuses to see in it a foundation or even a completion of Marxism, understood as a theory of the causal lawfulness of social development.

Adler sees in Kantian ethics an irrefutable demonstration of the "classic formal properties . . . which belong to the nature of human consciousness insofar as it is considered from the practical side" and of "the formal elements of theoretical experience, insofar as it is considered from the epistemological side."[144] This formal ethical judgment, equally operant in every human consciousness, comes into consideration in causal investigation as the universal direction-determinant of social events, so that ethical evaluation is imminent in historical causation. In this apparent psychologization of the Kantian categorical imperative, along with the categories, Adler was perhaps misled by a prevailing tendency among some of the neo-Kantians towards the same misreading of Kant. Having psychologized the categorical imperative, it is then easy for Adler to view the main service of the Kantian practical philosophy for Marxism as the identification of an important causal factor in historical development — namely the formal properties common to every human faculty of ethical judgment. And this seems to be Adler's central contention with respect to the relationship between Kantian ethics and Marxism.

On the whole no intellectual resolution of this dispute over the role of Kantian ethics in Marxism emerged during this period, apart from the organizational 'resolution' which Kautsky brought about in 1905, when he pushed those inclined toward neo-Kantianism off the editorial board of *Vorwärts*.

The intellectual problem of the relationship of Kantian ethical theory to Marxism was left hanging, and it was to prove a constant temptation to Russian as well as Soviet writers to incorporate the categorical imperative somehow into the doctrines of Marx. The further adventures of the categorical imperative in Russian and Soviet Marxism will be described below.[145]

4. MARX AND HEGELIAN ETHICAL THEORY

Many of the participants in the discussion of Marxism and ethical theory during the height of the German social democratic movement agreed on one point: that Marx's relationship to Hegel did not require prolonged examination. Kant appeared to be "a much more modern spirit than Hegel", standing "much closer to the age of natural science and the socialist *Weltanschauung*".[146] Vorländer concluded his 1900 work on Kant and socialism with the declaration that, instead of 'Back to Kant!', the slogan 'Forward with Kant!', toward a unified conception of social events and social goals, offered the most promising future for Marxist theory.

In view of the prevailing attitudes toward Hegel, it is not surprising that in the discussion of Marxism and ethical theory in these years the relationship between Hegel's ethics, philosophy of history, and Marx's treatment of both, received comparatively little attention. It can be argued however, that Marx's views on ethical theory cannot be satisfactorily examined outside the context of Hegel's ethical theory and philosophy of history.

For Hegel, morality was a subject which could not be rationally comprehended in abstraction from history. The dialectic of spirit, culminating in the realization of freedom, negated and transcended the prevailing moral codes of a succession of cultures; and the 'world-historical individuals' who defied prevailing standards of conduct were sometimes justified by the consequences of their crimes. Noble individuals who resisted on moral grounds what the advance of spirit made necessary, may stand higher in moral worth than those whose crimes proved justified in the dialectic of history.[147] It was no part of Hegel's ultimate intention to establish a thesis of ethical relativism. He remarked in the *Science of Logic* that "insofar as dialectic abrogates moral determinations, we must have confidence in reason that it will know how to restore them again, but restore them in their truth and in the consciousness of their right, though also of their limitations."[148] The relationship between moral evaluation and what might be termed 'historical' evaluation constitutes a central problem of Hegel's ethical theory.

Hegel's most thorough consideration of the problems of ethical theory occurs in the *Philosophy of Right*. There we discover not simply a theory of moral judgments, but four topics – civil law, morality (*Moralität*), ethical life (*Sittlichkeit*), and world history – joined in a single inquiry.[149] To this must be added the *Philosophy of History*, for a fuller account of Hegel's views on the relationship of morality and history.

The treatment of morality in Hegel depends upon his distinction between *Moralität* and *Sittlichkeit*. 'Morality' (*Moralität*) as a technical term for Hegel refers to *abstract* morality, or *conscientiousness*, which is to say the *form* of all genuinely moral action; however it is used by Hegel to refer to the situation in which we think of actions performed by the individual in abstraction from concrete social institutions, historically situated, which would provide the actual circumstances and content of universally rational conduct. 'Morality' refers to principles of conduct regarded in their purely subjective aspect, as founded on what the individual agent himself holds to be right and wrong, good and evil, and not, as Hegel says, on a principle which is considered to be in and for itself right and good.[150] So long as one confines one's thinking about the subject to the level of abstract thought, adopting the formal concept of morality (mere conscientiousness) as one's criterion of right and wrong, any maxim of conduct whatever could turn out to be justified.[151] Moreover, when one undertakes the justification of moral judgments at the level of understanding (as opposed to reason), the suggestive evidence of history − that there is no universal, objective standard of right or good − turns out to be correct. But this conclusion is no more adequate than is the understanding generally as a means of representing the truth. It is precisely this consequence of ethical relativism which Hegel points to as proof of the inadequacy of the concept of *Moralität* as opposed to *Sittlichkeit*. This last concept reflects the right and the good as grasped by speculative reason, and can only be discussed within the context of Hegel's philosophy of history.

By 'ethical life' (*Sittlichkeit*), or as some translators would have it, 'concrete ethics', Hegel means the concrete morality of an actual historically-situated social order, where rational institutions and laws provide the content of conscientious conviction and conduct.[152] The validity of moral judgment for Hegel is thus qualified by the dialectic of reason in history, and moral philosophy cannot proceed independently of the philosophy of history. Ethical life is "a subjective disposition, but one imbued with what is inherently right."[153] It is "the concept of freedom developed into the existing world" in the form of "absolutely valid laws and institutions" which are "above subjective opinion and caprice."[154] Now these 'absolutely valid laws and institutions' can only be realized in a rational state, and that in turn can only be realized through history.

History, according to Hegel, is the development of the consciousness of freedom on the part of spirit, and the consequent actualization of that freedom in social institutions. This development is first of all a *self-development* of the idea, a self-development which proceeds dialectically. The course of this dialectical self-development of the idea is displayed in the *Logic*. It is one of the conclusions of the *Logic* "that every step in the process, as differing from any other, has its determinate peculiar principle."[155] The 'determinate principle' of each historical stage constitutes the unifying principle of a particular national spirit which characterizes and dominates that period of history. "Now that such or such a specific quality constitutes the peculiar genius of a people, is the element of our inquiry which must be derived from experience, and historically proved," Hegel says.[156] But to accomplish this, not just in the case of a single culture, but in the succession of national cultures which comprises world history, presupposes that the historian be "familiar *a priori* with the whole circle of conceptions to which the principles in question belong".[157] The philosophical examination of the materials of history proceeds according to the categories of reason, not merely of the understanding, and the chief category of that examination, its criterion of historical progress, is the idea of freedom. The philosophical study of history presupposes a knowledge of the idea of freedom. Just as Keppler had to be familiar *a priori* with the logic of ellipses, squares, cubes, and their various possible relations before he could discover from empirical data his famous laws, so the historian must have a disciplined appreciation of all the *a priori* elements or moments which contribute to the idea of freedom, an appreciation one could obtain by reading the *Logic*.[158]

The exegesis of Hegel's views on morality and history also requires reference to his famous notion of the 'cunning of reason'. The actualization of the idea of freedom which is the historical process, involves two elements, the idea itself, and the complex of individual human passions, the warp and the woof of history. The goals at which individual human passions are directed are always limited and special. The individual human agents themselves are intelligent, thinking beings, and their passions are "interwoven with general, essential considerations of justice, good, duty, etc.".[159] However these general considerations do not as such constitute the objects of individual human passion. The object of their passion must always be some particular thing, which they identify as good or obligatory. In these particular commitments, individuals, guided by their finite comprehension of their duties, subject themselves to 'momentous collision' with historical contingencies "which are adverse to this fixed system; which assail and even destroy its foundations and existence; whose tenor may nevertheless seem good — on the large scale advantageous — yes, even indispensable and necessary."[160] These contingencies realizing themselves in history involve a general principle of a different order from these fixed systems of judgment, a principle which is an essential phase in the development of the idea. Such a general principle, in bringing ruin to fixed systems of moral judgment, lies in the aims of world-historical individuals, whose actions may contribute far more substantially to the realization of the idea, than those of the most noble, indeed moral, individuals.

In this 'combat of history' which tends to the frustration and destruction of individual aims and passions, the idea of freedom makes no sacrifice of itself; it remains in the background, untouched and uninjured.[161] Instead, it makes use of the subjective passions, private aims, and selfish desires of individual actors in history, sacrificing them on the altar of the self-development of spirit. The individual actor whose hopes, interests, and passions are mangled by it, remains largely ignorant and unsuspecting of the process in which he is caught up. This view of matters leads of course to Hegel's famous description of history as "the slaughter-bench at which the happiness of peoples, the wisdom of states, and the virtue of individuals have been victimized."[162] In similar fashion Marx was to speak of human progress as resembling "that hideous pagan idol, who would not drink the nectar but from the skulls of the slain."[163]

It is a further apparent implication of Hegel's notion of the cunning of reason that a double perspective must be introduced in the evaluation of human action. The first of these can be termed 'moral evaluation'; the second, perhaps, 'historical evaluation'. Hegel discusses the potential conflict between these two perspectives of evaluation in the context of the great deeds of history. The perspective of morality is that of the evaluation of the individual actor's character in terms of "what the agent holds to be right and wrong, good and evil."[164] It is the issue of concientiousness, of the evaluation of personal character. The perspective of historical assessment is a different matter, as Hegel says, "for the history of the world occupies a higher ground than that on which morality has properly its position."[165] These world-historical individuals whose crimes spirit employs are not to be condemned by comparison with the virtuous nobility of those who on moral grounds oppose what the advance of spirit makes necessary.

In this respect Hegel's philosophy of history provides ample support for relativists who wish to speak of moralities being transcended, outmoded through the dialectic of history, and to conclude from this that nothing is objectively right or wrong. But that this was not Hegel's intention is clear: ". . . in so far as dialectic abrogates moral determinations, we must have confidence in reason that it will know how to restore them again . . . ."[166]

Historical evaluation cannot be treated as logically independent of the making of moral judgments. The problem of the apparent divergence of moral evaluation (good and evil, right and wrong) and historical assessment (progressive and reactionary) is in part an illusion. It is created by the fact of our retrospective posture. Our grounds for making such judgments of the divergence of abstract right or of morality from the requirements for the development of spirit are available only with respect to the past. The owl of Minerva takes flight only at dusk. With respect to our own day and circumstances, no such perspective for a critique of ethical obligation is available. No such distinction between the demands of morality and the 'higher' historical interests of spirit can be made with respect to the present for the citizen of a rational state. One's objective duty is that publicly attached to one's station in the social and political order. There is no critical standpoint available to the would-be autonomous individual who aspires to transcend the morality of the present. The critique of moralities from the standpoint of the requirements of historical progress can never be more than a retrospective commentary on the past. The present and future are beyond its reach.

The writings of Marx contain substantial evidence that his own view of history, historical progress, and the relation between the historically progressive and the moral are quite parallel to Hegel's. The most substantial body of materials for examining Marx's treatment of the problem of history and morality consists of his writings on British rule in India, done mostly in the form of his articles for the *New York Daily Tribune* in the 1850's.

In these Marx can be seen to be a sharply ironic chronicler of history as the slaughter-bench of the happiness of peoples and a highly consistent student of the cunning of reason. Marx's scathing commentary on the brutality, rapacity, and stupidity of British imperialism in India, particularly in the aftermath of the Indian mutiny of 1857, could scarcely be exceeded without transcending the limits of journalistic good taste. In fact Marx's concern over the horrors of British rule in India is interrupted only briefly by a still more basic concern — that the British armies might lose. When there appeared to be a serious prospect of a complete British defeat in India, all of Marx's invective is directed against the stupidity of the British army. As soon as the military basis of the British presence seemed secure again, Marx returned to the task of communicating to his American readers the details of the rapacity and stupidity of British colonial rule. But Marx, as any good Hegelian in these questions, does not become fixated on the business of making moral evaluations.

England, it is true, in causing a social revolution in Hindustan, was actuated only by the vilest interests, and was stupid in her manner of enforcing them. But that is not the question. The question is, can mankind fulfill its destiny without a fundamental revolution in the social state of Asia? If not, whatever may have been the crimes of England she was the unconscious tool of history in bringing about the revolution.[167]

In all of Marx's writings on European colonialism, he is perfectly consistent, so far as one can see, with the ironies implicit in the cunning of reason.

Historical progress is a bloody business. But nowhere does Marx betray the slightest doubt about the historical mission of European civilization.

England has to fulfill a double mission in India: one destructive, the other regenerating – the annihilation of old Asiatic society, and the laying of the material foundations of Western society in Asia.[168]

The process will condemn an entire generation of Indians, and perhaps the next as well, to degradation, poverty, and to the destruction of their entire way of life. The benefits will be realized only by generations yet unborn.

In case there is any remaining moral squeamishness in his readers, Marx deliberately adopts the moral perspective and pronounces upon the rights and wrongs of the British intervention in India:

Now, sickening as it must be to human feeling to witness these myriads of industrious, patriarchal, and inoffensive social organizations disorganized and dissolved into their units, thrown into a sea of woes, and their individual members losing at the same time their ancient form of civilization and their hereditary means of subsistence, we must not forget that these idyllic village communities, inoffensive though they may appear, had always been the solid foundation of Oriental despotism, that they restrained the mind within the smallest possible compass, making it the unresisting tool of superstition, enslaving it beneath traditional rules, depriving it of all grandeur and historical energies.[169]

For Marx the objective inferiority of Hindu morality is proved in the fact that man, the sovereign of nature, falls down on his knees in adoration of Hanuman, the monkey, and Sabbala, the cow.[170]

In short, one is objectively justified in exercising the moral judgments of one's own society, retrospectively, against the morality of a national culture which has been transcended in the development of history. To the extent that one is right in arguing that Marx subscribes to the above-mentioned features of Hegel's philosophy of history, then there is an objective criterion of historical progress, and one which is *not* independent of our ethical judgments. That criterion of intrinsic good must be understood as 'the unlimited development of humanity's creative powers with no presupposition other than the previous historical development.'

One significant difference between Marx's view of the relationship between morality and history, and Hegel's, lies in the fact that Marx was willing, as Hegel was not, to forsee the outlines, in a limited sense, of the near future, taking the developed contradictions of the present as a guide. To this extent, and only to this extent, some basis for a distinction between the demands of morality and the requirements of historical progress in the present is provided, a basis which did not exist in Hegel's system.

But this cannot justify the conclusion that Marx's theory is ultimately independent of any particular value commitments, because for Marx, the full realization of human potential is an historical project for which we assume full, conscious responsibility as a consequence of the revolution. In a sense the whole point of Marx's notion of the socialist revolution was that it would mark the inception of humanity's self-conscious and knowing assumption of responsibility for the realization of human potential. If this is true, it is diffi-cult to see how humanity could dispense with a system of judgments for obligating and forbidding, for praising and blaming individuals for their contributions or hindrances to the realization of the intrinsic good. In other words, from the moment of the revolution on, the apparent divergence be-tween moral evaluation and historical evaluation must tend to disappear. (In this sense as well, Prof. Kamenka is correct in asserting that for Marx, "Only with the full fruition of the human spirit or essence could morality arise."[171])

The above-mentioned un-Hegelian peculiarity of Marx's views — that he maintains a distinction between historical evaluation and moral evaluation in the present — in conjunction with his insistence on using the vocabulary of historical evaluation ('progressive' or 'reactionary') rather than that of moral evaluation, leads to a serious ambiguity in Marx's humanism. First of all, until the revolution has been accomplished, historical evaluation of individual con-duct appears to supercede moral evaluation entirely. Actions immoral from the perspective of prevailing moral standards may be justified as conducive to historical progress — the revolution. The moral appears to be subordinated to the political. After the revolution, when humanity has assumed full, conscious responsibility for its own self-development, it would appear that the institu-tion of moral praise and blame for individual contributions, or lack thereof, to the realization of the intrinsic good, would be unavoidable. If Marx had little or nothing to say about the specific criteria of moral judgment under Communism, he had equally little to say about the organization of the eco-nomy, for example, under Communism. From the absence of details concern-ing socialist ethical theory in Marx, one should not conclude that there is no such thing, any more than one should conclude that there is no such thing as socialist economic theory from its absence in *Capital*.

But there is a second ambiguity in Marx which has still more serious poten-tial consequences. When he refers to 'the development of all human powers as such' as an end in itself, it is not clear that Marx would apply this criterion to individuals as such, rather than to humanity as a whole. Indeed, as Prof. Kline has argued,[172] it would appear that most of Marx's references to this problem can be interpreted as referring to the development of humanity as a whole —

a process which might entail treating individuals as instruments for collective development, rather than regarding the development of the potential of each individual as an intrinsic good. In Prof. Kline's phrase, it may be that Marx had only "a humanist *ideal* for the future, but no humanist *principles* for the present."[173] The dependence of the possibility of morality on the occurrence of the revolution for Marx has just been disucssed; Marx will permit 'historical' evaluation to be replaced by moral evaluation only in the future. The other problem indicated by Prof. Kline, the absence of unequivocal concern with the moral conditions of individual existence as opposed to that of collective 'humanity' in Marx, can be illuminated in an interesting way by a suggestion of Prof. Kamenka: that Marx employs a "metaphysical notion of the human essence as truly universal in a qualitative, intensional sense and not in a merely distributive sense."[174] The use of this notion would signal the disappearance of the very distinction between one individual and another. As Prof. Kamenka argued in another passage, since the human essence for Marx is universal, "its first and primary condition is the rational society, in which the traditional problems of morality and law are entirely resolved. The true basis of morality is not individual conduct, but social organization."[175] There is a definite basis in Marx's writings for this conclusion, and if true, it tends to deepen the first as well as the second ambiguity discussed above.

In summary, there are at least two serious ambiguities about the nature of Marx's humanism, both related to the conflation of historical evaluation with moral evaluation. Both these ambiguities result in part from Marx's departure from Hegel's view that no (historical or political) perspective could be available with respect to the present from which to criticize or supercede the prevailing morality of a nation state which has achieved rational laws, by which of course Hegel meant primarily the freedom and equality before the law which were seen by him as goals of the French revolution. Post-revoluttionary Soviet discussions of these problems will be explored below.

CHAPTER TWO

SOVIET PHILOSOPHY: THE AMBIGUOUS INHERITANCE
OF MATERIALISM

1. INTRODUCTION

By its own account the fundamental identifying trait of Soviet Marxist-Leninist philosophy has been and is its dialectical-materialist standpoint. Engels', and more particularly Plekhanov's insistence that all philosophies belong to one or the other of two great camps, materialism or idealism, which together exhaust the most important tendencies of philosophical thought has been adopted as the first premise of all philosophical commentary.[1] Within the camp of the materialists, two major groups are distinguished, the 'vulgar' or 'mechanistic' materialists and the 'dialectical' materialists. The differences between these two varieties of materialism were thought to be so great that 'dialectical' or 'intelligent' idealism was to be preferred in Lenin's eyes to 'metaphysical' or 'stupid' materialism.[2] Thus, in the view of most Soviet philosophers, the identity of Marxist-Leninist philosophy depends entirely upon success in maintaining the distinction between 'dialectical materialism' and all other species of materialism, as well as all varieties of idealism. This commitment, and the assertion that dialectical materialism constitutes the only true interpretation of Marx's and Engels' philosophical writings, are perhaps the two most fundamental dogmas of Soviet philosophy.

As was argued in the *Preface* the problem of articulating a Marxist ethical theory also involves the task of interpreting, or re-interpreting, Marx's writings in such a way as to indicate the appropriateness of such an undertaking, and its logical relation to the rest of his system. Since materialism represents the central philosophical theme of Soviet Marxism, that issue will be explored here in summary fashion as an introduction to the general framework of thought which governs the development of Soviet ethical theory. The development of dialectical materialism rests ultimately on the critique of the Hegelian dialectic supplied by Feuerbach and Marx, and constitutes a particular interpretation of that critique; dialectical materialism will be surveyed here in terms of the history of that critique.

Since the 1920's the complex issue of the relation of Marx to Hegel has provided one of the most sensitive means of discrimination among the numerous interpretations of the former to be found in Eastern as well as Western

Europe. That issue was effectively raised by the publication of Korsch's *Marxism and Philosophy* and Lukàcs' *History and Class Consciousness*, both in 1923. During that decade in the Soviet Union, the issue of Marx's relation to Hegel was sharply contested in the dispute between the 'mechanists' and the 'Deborinites' or 'dialecticians'. The mechanists among other things were opposed to the suggestion that dialectical reasoning had any serious role to play in scientific Marxism, preferring a straightforwardly empiricist conception of that science, and denigrated Hegel's role in the development of Marxism. This dispute was resolved in favor of the dialecticians, and since the end of the 1920's no serious challenge to the claim that Marxian materialism incorporates the 'dialectical method' developed by Hegel has been countenanced in the Soviet Union. Marx's claim that he extracted the 'rational kernel' of the Hegelian system is reiterated constantly. But where Hegel employed the dialectic idealistically, Marx and Engels applied it materialistically, it is claimed. But the problem of explaining precisely what dialectical materialism owed to Hegel was not fully resolved. In an important sense, the basic justificatory task of Soviet Marxist-Leninist philosophy has been and is to explain in what the 'materialist' transformation of the Hegelian dialectic consists, and hence also to explain precisely the intended meaning of 'materialism'.

As many commentators have recognized, this last problem is infected with a radical ambiguity in the meaning of 'materialism', afflicting the Marxist tradition from its very origins in the critique of Hegel's system supplied by Feuerbach which Marx endorsed and repeated in the 1844 *Manuscripts*. That ambiguity, it can be argued, set the stage for an apparent oscillation within the Marxist tradition from an implicitly pre-Kantian empiricism (in many respects comparable to Locke) on one hand, to a near endorsement of the Hegelian dialectic on the other, all in the name of Marxist orthodoxy. Obviously, any account given of the relation of Marxism to Hegel's philosophy will be largely determined by the choice of empiricist or dialectical terms to describe Marx's own position. However, the choice between these two very different emphases in the interpretation of Marx's work remains subject to controversy. For the source of this ambiguity one must return to its origin in Marx's own temporary mentor, Feuerbach.

2. FEUERBACHIAN MATERIALISM AS A CRITIQUE OF HEGEL

In the intellectual circles to which Marx belonged as a university student and for a few years thereafter, the philosophy of Hegel excited deeply ambivalent feelings. It was generally viewed as "the culmination of modern philosophy" and "the most perfect system that has ever appeared".[3] But at the same time it was experienced as a potentially "oppressive burden" and "a prison of the intellect".[4] Hegel's system stood as an indomitable peak, largely blocking out their view of the sun. How to live in the shadow of the mountain was a problem which preoccupied most of them in one way or another. The ambivalence of their attitudes toward the master is exemplified particularly well by Feuerbach who had sat in Hegel's lectures, and was known both for his able defense of Hegel in 1835 against Bachman's *Anti-Hegel*, as well as for his work of 1839, 'Toward the Critique of Hegelian Philosophy', which repeats practically the whole of Bachman's criticism as his own.[5] In this initial critique we discover Feuerbach earnestly attempting to *prove* "that the Hegelian philosophy is really a definite and special kind of philosophy" on the ground that despite its being "distinguished from all previous philosophies by its rigorous scientific character, universality, and incontestable richness of thought", it nevertheless came into being at a definite point in human history and *therefore must* be based upon certain accidental presuppositions in addition to those which are necessary and rational![6]

The Hegelian philosophy is "the most perfect *system* that has ever appeared",[7] but it cannot be "*the absolute reality of the idea* of philosophy" because it is impossible that an entire species realize itself in a single individual — "art as such in *one* artist, and philosophy as such in one philosopher".[8]

In his 1839 critique of Hegelian philosophy, Feuerbach develops an elaborate doctrine of the *ownership* of ideas, in which he distinguishes between *ideas themselves*, and the *forms of communication* of ideas. Demonstration and inference are necessary forms of communication, but the demonstration of one philosopher's ideas does not actually communicate the original philosopher's ideas themselves to the second philosopher. "Demonstration is therefore only the means through which I strip my thought of the form of 'mineness' so that the other person may recognize it as his own . . . ."[9] In this sense "every system is only an expression of or image of reason" and not reason itself.[10] But Hegel's system was supposed to be "reason itself; all immediate activity was to dissolve itself completely in mediated activity, and the presentation of philosophy was not to presuppose anything, that is, *nothing was to be left over in us and nothing within us — a complete emptying of ourselves*".[11] (underlining mine) One of Feuerbach's deepest anxieties thus seems to have been that if Hegel's system were truly without presuppositions, if the 'being' with which the *Logic* began were *real* being, then nothing would remain thinkable which was one's own, as opposed to Hegel's; Feuerbach himself would have been 'emptied' by Hegel.

In retrospect one can only be struck, not by Feuerbach's denials and objections, but by the awe which made them necessary. To be confronted with such a colossus in the shape of one's own professor would be enough to traumatize any ambitious student aspiring to make a contribution in the same field, and evidence of this trauma in the history of the Young Hegelian movement abounds.

The 'solution' generally seized upon was to present their own work as a *realization* of the Hegelian philosophy, "but a realization which is simultaneously a *negation*, and indeed the negation *without contradiction*, of this philosophy".[12] Hegel was accused of having remained merely *contemplative* in his solution of the various riddles and alienations which afflicted mankind, especially established religion, and later in the writings of the Young Hegelians, the state. This accusation appeared in a great variety of forms; on occasion it amounted to an accusation of having failed to overcome Cartesian dualism, having failed to achieve the identity of thought and being (or having achieved this identity only in the realm of thought),[13] having failed to account for the *active* as opposed to the *passive* subject in the cognition of the objective world, having failed to account for the reality of the material world (or having accounted for it only in thought), or, in a somewhat different perspective, having presented philosophy as capable of comprehending the world only *post festum*, as the owl of Minerva, and not achieving a philosophical anticipation of the future; or still more strongly, not *bringing about* that future through a critique of the present. The alleged 'conservatism' of the Hegelian system was presented in the form of various accusations: that he failed to transcend theology, that he failed to repudiate Christianity as an historical institution, that he hypostasized the constitutional monarchy in the form of the Prussian state as the realization of reason, and so forth.

Typical of the difficulties into which these attempts to criticize the master led is the following passage from Feuerbach:

Hegel is a *realist*, but a *purely idealistic* realist, or rather an abstract realist; namely, a realist abstracting from all reality. He *negates* thought – that is abstract thought – but he does so *while remaining within abstractive thought* with the result that his negation of abstraction still remains abstraction. Only 'that which is' is the object of philosophy according to Hegel; however, this 'is' is again only something abstract, only something *conceived*. Hegel is a thinker who *surpasses* himself in thought. His aim is to capture the thing itself, but only in the *thought* of the thing; he wants to be *outside* of thought, but still remaining *within thought* – hence the difficulty in grasping the *concrete* concept.[14]

This paradoxical desire 'to be outside of thought, but still remain within thought' attributed to Hegel might better serve as an epigram for much of the Young Hegelian movement, especially Feuerbach and the Feuerbachian Marx. 'To be outside of thought' meant to engage in action, to transform the human situation in accordance with the needs of true humanity, to determine the future; it also meant to get outside the Hegelian system. But the primary instrument of this struggle remained 'within thought'; it was philosophy; and, (the possibility remains significant) perhaps even *Hegel's* philosophy. Marx, commenting on the impracticality of the 'practical' political party in Germany which demanded the 'negation of philosophy' insisted that "you cannot transcend [*aufheben*] philosophy without actualizing it," (although to be sure the actualization of philosophy was also to be its abolition).[15]

Of all the accusations against Hegel, perhaps the soundest, or most easily defended, was also one of the simplest: Hegel's philosophy was fundamentally contemplative. In the famous image of the owl of Minerva spreading its wings only at dusk, Hegel confirmed that philosophy could not serve as a futurology. It could comprehend the necessity of what had taken place in human history only at the end of the development in question; it could not command the future. Against this particular 'failing' of the Hegelian system, one senses that the deepest frustration of the Young Hegelians accumulated, and that these frustrations motivated their most persistent criticisms of that system.

Given the commitment of the Young Hegelians (including Marx) to the belief that philosophy was the essential instrument of that critique of the present which would determine the future, Hegel's claim that philosophy was a purely *retrospective* science could obviously not be credited. There had to be some reason, a flaw within the system, which *prevented* the Hegelian philosophy from achieving its appointed task of unambiguously revolutionary critique leading to political or social action. Feuerbach and Marx were both convinced that Hegel's 'problem' lay somehow in a failure to overcome 'idealism', in an insufficiently 'materialist' or 'realist' starting-point of the system.

The most usual definitions of 'materialism' and 'idealism' however are utterly inadequate to capture the sense of the criticism which Feuerbach, and soon Marx, wished to make of the Hegelian system. In the pre-Kantian sense, in the context of the Cartesian tradition, to call Hegel an 'idealist' would make of him a Berkelyian, as Lenin implicitly attempted to do in *Materialism and Empirio-Criticism*, denying the reality of material substance.[16] And to call Marx a 'materialist' would place him in the same school as Lamettrie and the other French materialists of the eighteenth century. The explicit criticisms offered by Feuerbach and Marx of these erstwhile ancestors should indicate that neither category, understood in its Cartesian sense, is adequate to represent their views.

What must be kept in mind to assess the meaning of 'materialism' for either Feuerbach or Marx is the desire of both to preserve what they generally held to be one of the greatest achievements, or at least aspirations, of Hegel's philosophy: its monism, overcoming the metaphysical distinction between thought and being.[17] A relapse into dualism would have been considered a failure by either thinker; only some form of monism which presupposed the underlying identity of thought and being, would have been taken as a worthy successor to Hegel's philosophy.

Both Feuerbach and Marx suspected that Hegel's monism had somehow slighted the reality of the objects comprising nature and society in their existence independent of individual consciousness. Feuerbach had tentatively advanced his own alternative criterion of the real as early as his doctoral dissertation in 1828, ostensibly an orthodox Hegelian work. That criterion was intended to remedy the 'defect' of the mind-dependence of objects in Hegelian metaphysics, and at the same time preserve the greatest aspiration of the Hegelian system, the elimination of the metaphysical gap between thought and being, permitting one to conceive man as an integral whole, mind and body. This new criterion of the real Feuerbach termed 'sensuousness' (*Sinnlichkeit*), and it remained a fundamentally important notion in many of his later works, especially those which most influenced Marx.[18]

Taken in its reality or regarded as real, the real is the object of the senses – the *sensuous*. Truth, reality, and sensuousness are one and the same thing. Only a sensuous being is a *true* and *real* being.[19]

In his doctrine of *sensuousness* Feuerbach mixed a variety of elements, including suggestions of an empiricist, sensationist epistemology, and a metaphysics of love.

Feuerbach believed his own philosophy superior to Hegel's in part because his own cognizing subject had 'real eyes', and Hegel's lacked human eyes: "it is forever unable to cross over to the object, to being; it is like a head separated from the body, which must remain unable to seize hold of an object because it lacks the means, the organs to do so."[20] In several senses the instrument of liberation from the Hegelian absolute for Feuerbach was to be the human eye. Whereas the 'cruel hand' of Hegel's dialectical system robbed nature's creatures of their independence, the passive organ of perception, the 'sympathetic' eye cognized them without imposing itself upon them.[21] Cognizing the world of things through thought, the Hegelian system "imposes

on them *laws* that are only too often despotic." Sensuous perception on the
other hand "leaves things in their *unlimited freedom*."[22]

Feuerbach's sensationist epistemology must be regarded as more of an
inclination than an accomplished fact however, for despite its occasionally
almost naive realist tone, the account of perception in Feuerbach remains
closer to Hegel's than to any empiricist's. Had Feuerbach's doctrine of
perception gone so far as a classical empiricism (or its twentieth century
sense-datum variants), claiming the existence of some discriminable nucleus
of content in the percept uncontaminated by judgment, he would have at
least succeeded in opposing Hegel's epistemology in an umambiguous way.
But instead he endorsed the thoroughly Hegelian notion that "true perception is perception determined by thought."[23] Feuerbach criticizes Hegel for
letting that thought which purports to present the world as perceived exist in
"uninterrupted continuity with itself" and thereby constitute a world which
circles around itself as its center, in contradiction to reality.[24] In Feuerbach's
conception, the real world of objects, unconstrained by the 'cruel laws' of
the Hegelian dialectic, is meant to speak directly for itself to the cognizing
subject, suggesting perhaps the metaphor of a straight line, in contrast to
Hegel's alleged circle. But Feuerbach opposes to the Hegelian 'circle' no
straight and open-ended line of a genuine empiricist philosophy of perception;
he only wishes to modify Hegel's circle to an *ellipse*! ". . . The *ellipse* is the
symbol, the coat of arms of sensuous philosophy, of thought that is based on
perception."[25]

In this period Feuerbach's empiricist aspirations are left surrounded by
ambiguities. To take the numerous empiricist passages seriously would make
of him more of a Lockean representative realist than a post-Hegelian thinker.
But he nowhere admits that firm distinction between the pure sensory content, and judgments concerning it, which any classical empiricist epistemology
requires. Instead he rests with Hegel in claiming that "true perception is perception determined by thought." His 'critique' of Hegel in this respect constitutes
a genuine critique only on the assumption that Hegel's account of perception
somehow failed utterly, so that Hegel's cognizing subject remained 'blind'.

In a further dimension of Feuerbach's notion of 'sensuousness' he presents
it as a metaphysics of love. "Thus, for example, love is the true *ontological*
demonstration of the existence of objects apart from our head: there is no
other proof of being except love or feeling in general."[26]

The *old* philosophy maintained that that which *could not be thought of also did not
exist*; the *new* philosophy maintains that that which is not loved or *cannot be loved does
not exist*.[27]

The reality of the individual human being cannot be given in isolation from the human community. "The *essence* of man is contained only in the community, in the unity of man with man — a unity however, that rests on the reality of the distinction between 'I' and 'You'."[28] This last extension of the notion of 'sensuousness' from 'capable of being sensed' to 'capable of being loved' seems more of a pun than a philosophical argument, but it cannot be said that Feuerbach was not in earnest; he saw in it a new criticism of Hegel, who "derives these ideas from man understood as an isolated being, as mere soul existing for himself."[29] Since Feuerbach's own view suggests a very simplified re-telling of Hegel's argument for the necessity of mutual recognition in the development of self-consciousness toward objective spirit, the justice of Feuerbach's criticism cannot be easily demonstrated.

3. MARXIAN NATURALISM AND MATERIALISM

Marx like Feuerbach sought a monism which transcended the Cartesian separation of thought and being, and at the same time, like Feuerbach, claimed to repudiate Hegelian idealism, the position which led to many of the ambiguities of Feuerbach's views. In the chapter on Hegelian philosophy in the 1844 *Manuscripts* Marx began by applauding Feuerbach as "the only one who has a *serious, critical* relation to Hegel's dialectic," and as the one who established "*true materialism* and *real science* by making the social relationship of 'man to man' the fundamental principle of his theory."[30] Marx then proceeded to restate many of Feuerbach's arguments against Hegelian idealism, on the basis of a very Feuerbachian criterion of reality: "To be *sensuous* or actual is to be an object of sense or *sensuous* object and thus to have sensuous objects outside oneself, objects of sensibility. To be sentient is to suffer."[31] Like Feuerbach, Marx was convinced that Hegel's system failed to include 'actual man' and 'objective nature', that Hegel's categories *man* and *nature* were only abstractions, products of alienated mind comprehending itself abstractly.[32] For Hegel human nature is equivalent to self-consciousness, Marx says, and thus all alienation of human nature for Hegel is nothing but the alienation of self-consciousness.[33] For this Hegelian man, who is not *actual* man but only the abstraction of man, thinghood can only be externalized self-consciousness.[34] But real man, "actual corporeal man with his feet firmly planted on the solid ground inhaling and exhaling all of nature's energies"[35] should have real natural objects confronting him, and his self-externalization should establish an actual objective world (if an alienated one).[36] "An objective being acts objectively and would not act objectively if objectivity did not lie in its essential nature" says Marx, again echoing Feuerbach. This view Marx terms a "consistent naturalism or humanism" and claims that it is distinguished from both idealism and materialism, but is "the unifying truth of both."[37]

Marx's critique of Hegelian idealism finally focuses on the transition from the *Logic* to the *Philosophy of Nature* in the *Encyclopedia*. The motives which Marx attributed to Hegel for this transition refer to the absolute idea, the culmination of the *Logic*. The absolute idea, says Marx, is an abstraction which comprehends itself to be an abstraction, and a self-comprehending abstraction knows itself to be nothing.[38] It must therefore abandon itself as abstraction and arrive at its exact opposite, nature, which is something.[39] It decides to let nature speak freely for itself. The entire transition from the *Logic* to the *Philosophy of Nature* is thus only the transition from abstracting to intuiting. In this process the abstract thinker discovers that the nature which he "thought he was creating out of nothing from pure abstraction" was merely an abstraction from nature's characteristics, now discovered by intuiting. But this intuiting itself remains abstract. Nature, taken abstractly, for itself and fixedly isolated from man, is nothing for man.[40] "Nature as nature, that is so far as it is sensuously distinguished from that secret meaning hidden within it, . . . is nothing, a nothing proving itself to be nothing."[41]

The nature which interests Marx is that 'actual objective world' which real men established by their self-externalization, the world of society, or culture, the 'second nature' of which Enlightenment writers spoke. Within a few months of writing the 1844 *Manuscripts* Marx criticized Feuerbach in the *German Ideology* for *failing* to grasp the truth that nature apart from man is of no consequence for man:

And after all, the kind of nature that preceded human history is by no means the nature in which Feuerbach lives, the nature which no longer exists anywhere, except perhaps on a few Australian coral islands of recent origin, and which does not exist for Feuerbach either.[43]

Marx's general lack of interest in untransformed, or virgin nature, abstracted from the process of human appropriation, has quite properly been interpreted as meaning that Marx has no fundamental interest in the traditional metaphysical problem of mind and body, at least as it occurs within the Cartesian tradition. To signal this shift of interest away from the traditional 'idealist-materialist' controversy in metaphysics, it would have been fortunate if Marx's expressed preference for the term 'naturalism' rather than 'materialism' had prevailed.[44]

In order to assess Marx's relation to any of the standard forms of materialism, it is important to remember that unlike Hegel, he declines to elaborate
anywhere a pure philosophy of nature. For Marx, pre-historical nature, untransformed by human action, does not constitute an object of theoretical
interest. This concept of pre-historical or untransformed nature plays a significant role, according to Marx, only in the 'pure' natural sciences. These same
natural sciences are, however, an activity rooted in human society:

Even this 'pure' natural science receives its aim, like its material only through commerce
and industry, through the sensuous activity of men. So much is this activity, this continuous sensuous working and creating, this production, the basis of the whole sensuous
world as it now exists, that, were it interrupted for only a year, Feuerbach would find
not only a tremendous change in the natural world but also would soon find missing the
entire world of men and his own perceptual faculty, even his own existence.[44]

The world confronting humanity is the world constituted by social activity;
the world man cognizes is the world *for* man, the world transformed by
human activity. A Communist society, says Marx in the 1844 *Manuscripts*,
will be man-naturalized-and-nature-humanized, and as such will form the
object of a single science incorporating both the history of nature and the
history of man.

The process of the transformation of nature which is also the history of
humanity's creation of itself, constitutes the subject matter of historical
materialism, and hence Marxian 'materialism' signifies an inquiry quite distinct from that indicated by 'materialism' in the Cartesian tradition.

Feuerbach probably intended, and Marx suggested more clearly, a transformation of the problems of Cartesian metaphysics. Neither rejected the
dichotomy between consciousness and material objects in one sense, but both
presupposed a more fundamental cosmological category, a monistic one,
embracing both consciousness and the Cartesian external (material) world, –
'material' or 'sensuous' nature. 'Nature' in this peculiarly Marxian sense refers
to 'all there is (in the world) *for man*.'[45] Marx supposes that the world of
things exists for humanity only as a totality of possible satisfactions of its
needs. Humanity develops its conceptual apparatus for differentiating and
cognizing elements of the world as an integral part of its practical activity
aimed at compelling the world to supply its needs. Because the structure of
human concepts is determined by specific needs, the world as known by
humanity is the world as related to those needs. As humanity's needs develop,
so does the conceptual structure for knowing the world. In this sense humanity *produces* its world as a continuous by-product of the struggle to satisfy
those needs, produces it conceptually as well as 'materially'. Not only does

Marx constantly insist on the fact that humanity *produces* nature, but also that nature in this sense is capable of being *humanized*, made into the "inorganic body of man."

Nature developing in human history – the creation of human society – is the actual nature of man; hence nature as it develops through industry, though in an *alienated* form, is truly *anthropological* nature.[46]

Just as nature is destined to be humanized, man is destined to become naturalized; the conflict between man and nature is to be resolved in a new entity, society.

Thus *society* is the completed, essential unity of man with nature, the true resurrection of nature, the fulfilled naturalism of man and humanism of nature.[47]

If 'nature' in the usual philosophical sense refers to the world of extended bodies in contrast to mind, Marx expands the notion to include, in effect, all there is; specifically all that humanity is, including its conscious activities. As a contemporary German commentator, Schmidt, has remarked, "Nature in this broad sense is the sole object of knowledge. On the one hand it includes the forms of human society; on the other, it only appears in thought and in reality in virtue of these forms."[48] In this respect Marx fails to exorcize the ghost of Hegel in convincing fashion. Nature (as Marx would say, 'real', 'objective' nature) is the sole object of knowledge; but Schmidt is correct in saying that it appears in thought *and in reality* only in virtue of its social forms. Just as for Hegel objective spirit (society) ranked higher in reality than nature, 'social' or 'transformed' nature constitutes the truth ("the secret meaning hidden within") of 'abstract' or 'virgin' nature for Marx. Thus, 'society' can be treated as a synonym for 'reality' or 'cosmos' for Marx, in that it will eventually designate all there is for humanity, including within its reference untransformed nature insofar as the latter constitutes anything for humanity.[49]

In these respects one can agree with Schmidt's conclusion that Marxian materialism should not be interpreted as an answer to any of the central problems involved in the traditional metaphysical inquiry signified by the terms 'materialism' and 'idealism'. However, it is not true, as Schmidt tends to imply, that Marx offers no doctrine of matter in the traditional metaphysical sense. In one of his earliest works, *The Holy Family*, he does venture to present an extraordinarily vitalistic conception of matter:

Among the qualities inherent in *matter, motion* is the first and foremost, not only as *mechanical* and *mathematical* but even more as *impulse, vital spirit, tension,* or – to use

Jakob Böhme's expression – "Qual" of matter. The primitive forms of matter are living, individualizing, *essential capacities* inherent in it, producing specific differences.

In *Bacon*, its first creator, materialism conceals within itself, still in a naive way, the germs of an all-sided development. On the one hand, matter smiles upon the whole of man in poetic-sensuous splendor. On the other, this aphoristic doctrine itself is still full of theological inconsistencies. [50]

In this essay, one of his earliest attempts to characterize 'materialism', Marx did not hesitate to hint at a philosophy of nature which would appear to have far more in common with the metaphysics of German idealism than with any accepted sense of 'materialism'.

Feuerbach's intention to combine a thorough-going rejection of Hegelian idealism with preservation of some version of an identity thesis, without reducing consciousness to a property of matter in any usual sense of the term, should probably be seen as the immediate progenitor of this rather special doctrine of matter hinted at by Marx. Given all of these philosophical commitments, the precise motives for the rejection of Hegel's metaphysics must necessarily have been rather convoluted. If Hegel's system was the most nearly successful of all nineteenth century attempts to defend the thesis of the identity of thought and being (we have Feuerbach's authority for this in part), and if Feuerbach and Marx remained firmly wedded to some version of that monism, then a Hegelian 'naturalism' may well have been the most coherent alternative open to them. As J. N. Findlay remarked, "There is, for Hegel, nothing ideal or spiritual which does not have its roots in Nature, and which is not nourished and brought to full fruition by Nature." [51]

On the other hand, to the extent that any genuinely materialist critique of the Hegelian system succeeded, Hegel's thesis of the identity of thought and being would have to be radically modified or abandoned. This peculiar combination of theses advocated by both Marx and Feuerbach placed a great tension on the term 'material' which is quite evident in the passage quoted from the *Holy Family*, as well as in subsequent Marxist philosophy.

In order to understand how Marx could, even as a young man in Germany in the 1840's, advocate such a doctrine of matter with no apparent doubt about its plausibility, one must recall a now obscure intellectual development of nineteenth century Germany which seemed to offer precisely what was required: an alternative account of the identity of thought and being which could claim to be 'materialist' in a certain sense, yet distinct from and superior to the reductionist materialism of the eighteenth century French variety, and still better, could claim the authority of 'science'. That tradition resided in Schelling's philosophy of nature and in the scientific works inspired by it in the field of biology, most notably those of Lorenz Oken and Henrich Steffens. A substantial controversy over the proper aims and procedure of scientific biology took place in the first half of the nineteenth century. The controversy centered on the issue of whether that science consisted in the ever more detailed accumulation and study of individual specimens in order to develop the most refined possible classificatory schemes registering their *differences*, or whether the future of biological science lay primarily in exploring the morphological *similarities* among them, relating these in tentative developmental sequences. The latter tendency was manifest in Goethe's *Morphology of Plants*, and of course received cosmic justification in Schelling's *Naturphilosophie*. Followers of Schelling such as Oken and Steffens also took it as their aim to develop a general evolutionary scheme which applied to the cosmos as a whole, and the earth in particular, illustrating their theses with vastly more detailed empirical observations of nature.[52]

Oken's work in particular enjoyed wide esteem through much of the first half of the nineteenth century, as a major representative of one of the extremes contending over the proper conception of biological science.[53] One must remember that this controversy had by no means been resolved by the 1840's; conceptions of empirical science in these areas were still very much in dispute, and a German intellectual who became disenchanted with the details of Hegel's unification of nature and spirit, but not with the entire tradition which produced it, need only have retreated the relatively short distance to 'scientific' versions of a *Naturphilosophie* such as that of Oken to have felt comfortable in the general supposition of identity of nature and spirit – from a 'scientific' perspective which presupposed the 'primacy' of nature. Given the unsettled state of conceptions of empirical science, especially of biological science, in the early and middle parts of the nineteenth century, one should be quite wary of assuming that Marx understood by 'empirical science' the same positivist conception that came to dominate the later part of the century.

Marx's published works from this period and later contain so few detailed discussions bearing directly upon the problems of a philosophy of nature in the usual sense that one can only speculate about Marx's attitude to 'scientific' versions of a *Naturphilosophie* such as Oken's.[54] At a minimum one can say that Marx did not consider the elaboration of a philosophy of nature relevant to his enterprise; whether he also considered such a project incoherent, as some have alleged, is less certain. The complex relation between 'scientific' doctrines such as Oken's, and the Hegelian *Naturphilosophie*, might serve as an illuminating analogue of the relation between Marxian 'materialism' and the Hegelian system. Such an analogue might further illustrate the truth of Nicholas Lobkowicz's remark that "all such inconsistencies and dilemmas are, in the last resort, due to the basic paradox of Marxism-Leninism, namely that it wants to be a materialism without leaving the heights of Occidental metaphysics which, to Soviet philosophers, is exemplified in Hegel."[55]

4. ENGELS, PLEKHANOV, AND LENIN ON DIALECTICAL MATERIALISM

Whereas Marx displayed no serious interest in systematic speculation on a concept of nature independent of human activity directed to the transformation and appropriation of it, Engels displayed an unmistakeable ambition to supply Marxism with a *Naturphilosophie*, a doctrine of the laws of dialectical development exhibited by nature itself, independently of human history or thought. This ambition is first articulated in detail in Engels' preface to the second edition of the *Anti-Dühring* in 1885, in the second year after Marx's death. In the Preface to the first edition, Engels was primarily concerned to register his distaste at having been prevailed upon to rebut the views of Dühring, disclaiming professional competence in the subject matter of the natural sciences. In the second Preface however, he invoked the authority of Marx for the doctrines contained in the book ("I read the whole manuscript to him before it was printed,")[56] and explicitly presents it as an attempt to complement Marx's work on the dialectics of history with "a conception of nature which is dialectical and at the same time materialist".[57] Engels claims that

the same dialectical laws of motion as those which in history govern the apparent fortuitousness of events; the same laws as those which similarly form the thread running through the history of the development of human thought and gradually rise to consciousness in the mind of man

are to be discovered in nature.[58]

On the relationship of mind to matter, Engels holds that

thought and consciousness . . . are products of the human brain and that man himself is a product of Nature, which has been developed in and along with its environment; whence it is self-evident that the products of the human brain, being in the last analysis also products of Nature, do not contradict the rest of Nature but are in correspondence with it.[59]

Neglecting the interrelation of praxis and cognition suggested by Marx, Engels also re-invoked the copy theory of knowledge in a manner reminiscent of Lockean representative realism. In the introductory part of *Anti-Dühring*,

Engels asserts that "an exact representation of the universe, of its evolution and that of mankind, as well as of the reflection of this evolution in the human mind, can therefore only be built up in a dialectical way . . ."[60] The commitment to a copy theory of knowledge is still more explicit in his later work, *Ludwig Feuerbach and the Outcome of Classical German Philosophy*, in the second part on 'Idealism and Materialism.' There he explains that "the influences of the external world upon man express themselves in his brain, are reflected therein as feelings, thoughts, instincts, volitions − . . .".[61]

His general view seems to have been that thought must be dialectical because we are so taught by nature; the processes of nature take place in accordance with dialectical laws, and hence only dialectical thought can accurately reflect these processes. It was a deficiency of contemporary science that "the scientists who have learned to think dialectically are still few and far between . . .".[62] His view that the laws of the dialectic as he formulated them were exhibited by nature itself could hardly be put more succinctly than in his discussion of the 'law of the negation of the negation':

What therefore is the negation of the negation? An extremely general − and for this reason extremely comprehensive and important − law of development of Nature, history and thought; a law which, as we have seen, holds good in the animal and plant kingdoms, in geology, in mathematics, in history and in philosophy . . . .[63]

Engels' determination to produce a full-blown philosophy of nature unquestionably transgressed the bounds Marx set for his own intellectual endeavors, as many commentators have pointed out.[64] Whether Engels' project must be considered an incoherent or mistaken extension of Marx's work cannot be so easily decided. In addition to Engels' claim that Marx approved the *Anti-Dühring*, there is the evidence discussed above that Marx himself in his early years saw nothing offensive in a doctrine of matter which would have fit fairly comfortably within either Hegel's or Oken's *Naturphilosophie*. Marx himself had no interest in developing such an inquiry, but the question of its legitimacy or illegitimacy can only be settled in the context of the larger issue of the coherence of Marx's critique of Hegel's system as a whole; whether Marx succeeded in developing a distinct alternative, or whether in the absence of such an alternative Marx's deeper presuppositions must be seen as locked into orbit about those of Hegel.

Plekhanov confidently endorsed Engels' general program of providing a 'dialectical materialist' philosophy of nature to complement the 'dialectical materialist' philosophy of history: "Like every modern philosophical system, materialist philosophy must give an explanation of two kinds of phenomena, on the one hand of nature and on the other of the historical development of mankind."[65] Since Plekhanov served as teacher to a whole generation of Russian Marxists, in Lenin's famous words, the consonance between Plekhanov's and Engels' views on this question appears to have established beyond serious question for many subsequent Russian and Soviet Marxists, that Marxist philosophy incorporates a specific philosophy of nature as well as of history: dialectical materialism.

For Plekhanov all modern materialism, metaphysical as well as dialectical, rests on the supposition that matter possesses the capacity of sensation.[66] This doctrine is attributed alike to Locke, to Holbach, and to Marx.[67]

The chief respects in which dialectical materialism differs from the metaphysical variety are summarized by Plekhanov in two points:

1. The essence of everything finite lies in the fact that it cancels itself and passes into its opposite. This change is realized with the assistance of each phenomenon's own nature: every phenomenon itself contains the forces which give birth to its opposite.

2. Gradual quantitative changes in the given content are finally transformed into qualitative differences. The moments of its transformation are the moments of leap, of interruption in graduality. It is a great error to think that nature or history makes no leaps.[68]

Plekhanov's own predilection was for the study of leaps in human history — revolutions — and he did not share Engels' fascination with the progress of the natural sciences in his own day as demonstrating the truth of dialectical materialism. This preference for the social over the natural did not diminish the importance which Plekhanov attached to dialectical materialism as a *monistic* view of reality applying equally to nature and history, however. Repeatedly in the *Development of the Monist View of History* and in the *Essays in the History of Materialism* he stressed the superiority of *monism*, idealistic or materialistic, over dualism.[69] Plekhanov's vigorous and literate defense of materialism in its eighteenth century French as well as dialectical varieties served to confirm the 'orthodoxy' of Engels' views in the *Anti-Dühring*, especially in the eyes of Lenin.

Against the background of Engels' and Plekhanov's conceptions — some would call it *invention* — of dialectical materialism as a philosophy of nature as well as of history, Lenin's 1908 work, *Materialism and Empirio-Criticism* served to establish this doctrine once and for all as a component of orthodox Soviet Marxist philosophy. Lenin unhesitatingly attributed the doctrine in question to Marx: "Marx frequently called his world outlook dialectical materialism, and Engels' *Anti-Dühring, the whole of which Marx read through in manuscript*, expounds precisely this world outlook."[70] Far from imitating Marx's lack of interest in any discussion of a concept of nature independent of the process of human appropriation of it, Lenin takes the two central problems of philosophy to be, one, establishing the reality of external nature existing independently of the cognizing subject (essentially the Cartesian problem), and two, establishing that our perceptions are reliable 'copies' of this independently existing reality.

His general position would be more appropriately termed 'realism' than 'materialism', as has been pointed out by numerous commentators: ". . . the concept 'matter', as we already stated, epistemologically implies *nothing but* objective reality existing independently of the human mind and reflected by it."[71] In general Lenin tended to conflate the epistemological doctrine of realism with the metaphysical doctrine of materialism.[72] Materialism as a metaphysical doctrine would normally consist of a specific definition of 'matter' plus the claim that nothing but matter is ultimately real. However by 'materialism' Lenin often meant only the denial of the mind-dependence of external objects, plus the claim that they really possess the properties they appear to have, i.e. the epistemological doctrine of realism.

As further confirmation of the essentially epistemological focus of Lenin's inquiry, he omits any account of the metaphysical problem of the relation of mind to matter, but is quite specific as to the epistemological relation of ideas to their objects – they are accurate 'copies' of these objects. Nevertheless the metaphysical problem of the relation of mind to matter must be viewed as an unavoidable one for Lenin, because he insists that mind is not the same as matter, only a property.

That the concept of 'matter' must also include 'thoughts', is a muddle, for if such an inclusion is made, the epistemological contrast between mind and matter, idealism and materialism . . . loses all meaning. That this contrast must not be made 'excessive', exaggerated, metaphysical, is beyond dispute . . . .[73]

By insisting in this manner upon the distinction between mind and matter, and yet failing to give any positive characterization of matter beyond "being an objective reality", Lenin leaves open a variety of possible metaphysical positions as compatible with his interpretation of dialectical materialism. It could be argued that he succeeds in eliminating only Berkeleyian subjective idealism as incompatible with dialectical materialism, leaving a consistent metaphysical materialism, or even dualism of the Cartesian or Lockean varieties as possibilities. In this respect the position Lenin defends in *Materialism and Empirio-Criticism* is arguably pre-Kantian in substance, if not in vocabulary, and certainly pre-Hegelian, in that no significant role is provided for dialectical reason.

Such was the opinion of at least one well-known German Marxist philosopher who was a younger contemporary of Lenin. In his 1923 publication *Marxism and Philosophy* Karl Korsch argued that the true purport of Marx's materialist dialectics had been lost in the scientistic 'vulgar Marxism' of the Second International.[74] In Korsch's view, the primary defect of the vulgar interpretation of Marxian socialism was its refusal to countenance anything but naive realism "in which both so-called common sense, which is the 'worst metaphysician', and the normal positivist science of bourgeois society, draw a sharp line of division between consciousness and its object."[75] Korsch asserted that this distinction had ceased to be completely valid even for Kant, and has been 'completely superseded' in dialectical philosophy, because every dialectic is characterized by the coincidence of consciousness and reality.[76]

In a subsequent defense of his views published in 1930, Korsch elaborated his criticism of Lenin's materialism, accusing him of having dragged the entire debate between materialism and idealism back to a pre-Kantian stage, prior to the emergence of German idealism. In Korsch's view, after the Hegelian system, the 'Absolute' was definitively excluded from the *being* of both spirit and matter, and was transferred into the dialectical movement of the idea. Lenin, however went "back to the absolute polarities of 'thought' and 'being', 'spirit' and 'matter', which had formed the basis of philosophical dispute in the seventeenth and eighteenth centuries."[77] Such a materialism, Korsch alleged, was derived from a metaphysical idea of being that is absolute and given, thus no longer fully dialectical, much less dialectically materialist, and rather collapses into "a *dualism* comparable to that of the most typical bourgeois idealists."[78]

Unknown to Korsch, Lenin had pursued his philosophical education significantly beyond the ambiguously pre-Kantian metaphysics of *Materialism and Empirio-Criticism* and the copy theory of knowledge. In the years 1914 and 1915 Lenin undertook a serious study of Hegel's philosophical system, especially the *Science of Logic* and the *History of Philosophy*, as evidenced in extensive notes and comments which he made for his own use. A small portion of these was published in 1925 and the majority of them in 1929–30 as volumes IX and XII of the *Lenin Miscellanies*.[79] In Hegel's *Logic*, Lenin discovered, apparently for the first time, the significance of dialectical reason in the Hegelian system, and therefore also in Marx:

Movement and '*self*-movement' . . . 'change', 'movement and vitality', 'the principle of
all self-movement', 'impulse' (*Trieb*) to 'movement' and to 'activity' – the opposite of
'dead Being' – who would believe that this is the core of 'Hegelianism', of abstract and
abstruse (ponderous, absurd?) Hegelianism. This core had to be discovered, understood,
hinüberretten, laid bare, refined, which is precisely what Marx and Engels did.[80]

Lenin's interest in Hegel revolved about one central 'idea of genius', the idea
of the dialectic; he was uninterested in the 'nonsense about the absolute' and
tried to read Hegel 'materialistically' by which he meant, "I cast aside for the
most part God, the Absolute, the Pure Idea, etc."[81] Lenin offered many
abbreviated formulations of this 'idea of genius', among the first of which was
"the universal, all-sided *vital* connection of everything with everything and
the reflection of this connection . . . – in human concepts, which must likewise be hewn, treated, flexible, mobile, relative, mutually connected, united
in opposites, in order to embrace the world."[82] Having discovered the notion
of dialectics, Lenin insisted that any continuation of the work of Hegel and
Marx "must consist in the *dialectical* elaboration of the history of human
thought, science, and technique."[83]

In the briefest definition Lenin offered of his newly discovered dialectics
he described it as "the doctrine of the unity of opposites."[84]

Dialectics is the teaching which shows how *Opposites* can be and how they happen to be
(how they become) *identical* – under what conditions they are identical, becoming transformed into one another, – why the human mind should grasp these opposites not as
dead, rigid, but as living, conditional, mobile, becoming transformed into one another.[85]

In a development closely related to his discovery of the dialectic, Lenin also
made a substantial advance upon the copy theory of knowledge as the central
doctrine of his epistemology. In place of discussions of the copy theory Lenin
explored the notion of truth in its connection with practical reason.

Theoretical cognition ought to give the object in its necessity, in its all-sided relations, in
its contradictory movement, *an-und für-sich*. But the human notion 'definitively' catches
this objective truth of cognition, seizes it and masters it, only when the notion becomes
'being-for-itself' in the sense of practice. That is, the practice of man and of mankind is
the test, the criterion of the objectivity of cognition.[86]

Notwithstanding Lenin's fascination with Hegel's dialectic, and the concept
of practice as crucial for a dialectical theory of knowledge, it would be wrong
to suggest that Lenin has entirely abandoned the standpoint of *Materialism
and Empirio-Criticism* in his subsequent study of Hegel. Occasional remarks
in his notes on the *Logic* suggest that Lenin has correctly grasped the nature
of Hegel's realism, e.g., "The dialectic is not in man's understanding, but in

the 'idea', i.e., in objective reality."[87] But such insights as these do not prevent Lenin from re-asserting his own version of realism on numerous occasions: "But he leaves aside the question of Being *outside* man!!! A sophistical dodge *from* materialism."[88] "The crux here — *aussen ist* — outside man, independent of him. That is materialism. And this foundation, basis, kernel of materialism, Hegel begins *wegschwätzen*."[89] "In particular there is suppressed the question of existence *outside* man and humanity!!! = the question of materialism!"[90]

This uneliminable, metaphysically fundamental contrast between individual consciousness and external reality persists as an underlying theme throughout much of Lenin's discussion of Hegel's *Logic*, not excluding echoes of a copy theory of knowledge in the midst of his exposition of Hegelian epistemology. Lenin characterizes 'truth' in one note as "the *totality of all* sides of the phenomenon, of reality and their (reciprocal) *relations*."[91] The main content of the logic is described as the relations "by which these concepts (and their relations, transitions, contradictions) are shown as *reflections of the objective world*."[92] (underlining mine) Hegel is described as having "brilliantly divined the dialectics of *things* (phenomena, the world, *nature*) in the dialectics of concepts."[93] But, insists Lenin, the dialectics of *things* produces the dialectics of *ideas*, and not vice versa.[94] He is tempted to describe Hegel's assertion of the dialectical relations inherent in reality as a 'brilliant guess' because in Lenin's view Hegel actually grasped these dialectical relations in 'mere' concepts. "Hegel actually *proved* that logical forms and laws are not an empty shell, but the *reflection* of the objective world. More correctly, he did not prove, but made a brilliant guess."[95]

In one of his summative judgments on the contribution of Hegel's *Logic* to Marxist philosophy, Lenin claims that it cannot be applied in its given form, it cannot be taken as given. "One must separate out from it the logical (epistemological) nuances, after purifying them from *Ideenmystik*: that is still a big job."[96]

From the collection of Lenin's various commentaries and marginal notes on Hegel a single interpretive thesis emerged as Lenin's central claim: that in the Hegelian system, dialectics is identical with the content of logic, and with the theory of knowledge (essentially a correct statement). This claim first appeared publicly in 1925 in *Bolshevik* (Nos. 5, 6), in a short essay entitled 'On the Question of Dialectics' which had been written in 1915. In this essay he asserted that "dialectics *is* the theory of knowledge of (Hegel and) Marxism. This is the 'aspect' of the matter (it is not 'an aspect' but the *essence* of the matter) to which Plekhanov not to speak of other Marxists, paid no attention."[97] The same claim, identification of the dialectic and theory of knowledge with the logic, appears or is alluded to at least six times in his notes on the *Greater* and the *Lesser Logics.*[98] Subsequent Soviet works on the interpretation of Hegel have tended to take Lenin's thesis as defining the fundamental task in the explication of Hegel.

The tensions inherent in Feuerbach's and Marx's uses of the term 'material' were in effect magnified by Lenin's philosophical legacy. The problem of the relation between 'dialectical materialism' and 'dialectical idealism', or the relation between Marx and Hegel, was if anything, intensified and still further complicated by Lenin's *Philosophical Notebooks*: "The sum total, the last word and essence of Hegel's logic is the *dialectical method* – this is extremely noteworthy. And one thing more: in this most *idealistic* of Hegel's works there is the *least* idealism and the *most materialism*. 'Contradictory', but a fact!"[99]

The entire range of Lenin's philosophical writings would seem to embrace at one extreme a largely pre-Kantian response to what was essentially the epistemological problem inherent in Cartesian dualism, and at the other an endorsement of the Hegelian dialectic (modified in some appropriately 'materialist' fashion which has yet to be satisfactorily clarified) as the heart of Marxist philosophy. Between these two poles Soviet Marxist philosophy has been free to oscillate, and from this perspective it is clear at least that the problem of interpreting the philosophy of Hegel, and supplying the details of a 'materialist' critique of it, can be regarded as the most sensitive measure of the general position of Soviet philosophy, and of individual philosophers as well.

5. DIALECTICAL MATERIALISM AND THE CRITIQUE OF DIALECTICAL IDEALISM IN SOVIET THOUGHT

As noted in a recent Soviet collective work on Hegel, "the question of the evaluation of the philosophy of Hegel, particularly his dialectics, is one of the sharpest of the problems which have been vigorously discussed throughout the existence of Soviet philosophical science."[100] The problem of the role of dialectics in Marxist philosophy, and hence the relation of Marx to Hegel, constituted a central issue of the philosophical disputes of the 1920's. In the early twenties there were brief echoes of 'vulgar materialism'; there were advocates of an eliminative reduction of psychic phenomena to neurophysiological processes, and demands that philosophy be entirely replaced by empirical investigations.[101] While such demands were not central in the thinking of the majority of those writing on philosophical subjects at the time, a certain suspiciousness concerning the possible contributions of philosophy to science appears to have been widely shared in the scientific community, which was itself heavily influenced by mechanist views.[102] The prevalence of mechanist views in parts of the scientific community led to particular scepticism about any role for dialectical thought in connection with the study of nature, and that in turn tended to reflect on the claims of dialectical thought generally.

In the years 1924–25 a major dispute erupted over I. I. Stepanov's book *Historical Materialism and Contemporary Natural Science: Marxism and Leninism*, in which he articulated the mechanist position, simply identifying Marxist philosophy with the general conclusions of the natural sciences.[103] Such challenges as these eventually led to sharp public polemics between critics and defenders of dialectical reasoning, as well as to scholarly works on the subject.

Continuing public scepticism over the usefulness of the study of Hegelian dialectics eventually provoked such philosophers as Deborin and his students to a spirited defense of both the importance of the Hegelian dialectic for the proper interpretation of Marxism, and of the necessity of dialectical reasoning in the study of nature. The repudiation of dialectical reasoning in science was of course a corollary of the central conviction of the mechanists that neither contradictions nor 'dialectical leaps' were to be encountered in nature. Nature and society as well were to be investigated with the methods of empiricism, proceeding on the assumption of universal determinism and the possibility of ultimately physical, or even mechanical explanations of all natural processes.

Two publication events in 1925 affected the course of the dispute. Engels' unfinished manuscript, *The Dialectics of Nature*, appeared for the first time, during the midst of the mechanist-Deborinite controversy, and Lenin's essay 'On the Question of Dialectics' also appeared in print then for the first time.[104] Both these events tended to intensify the debate. This posthumous intervention by Engels created several difficulties for the mechanist position, because a major motive for Engels in writing the book had been rooted in opposition to Newtonian mechanism as he understood it.

Lenin's essay on dialectics stressed the "contradictory, *mutually exclusive*, opposite tendencies in all phenomena and processes of nature (including mind and society),"[105] suggesting that Marx's *Capital* should be understood as a study of the dialectical contradictions of modern bourgeois society, showing the development of these contradictions. He claimed that the method of investigation used by Marx "must also be the method of exposition (or study) of dialectics in general (for with Marx the dialectics of bourgeois society is only a particular case of dialectics)."[106] This essay also contained Lenin's subsequently much-quoted thesis that the dialectic constitutes the theory of knowledge of (Hegel and) Marxism, to which Plekhanov 'not to speak of other Marxists paid no attention.'[107] These two publications were used by Deborin and his supporters to attain something like a victory over the mechanist faction. Deborin insisted that the doctrine of dialectical materialism was "historically and logically an immediate adjunct of Hegelian dialectics, constituting its continuation and further development."[108] Referring to Hegel's *Science of Logic*, Deborin claimed that "If one abstracts from the fundamental inadequacies of Hegelian logic which we have indicated, then we must recognize that in general the Hegelian system must be considered correct from the materialist point of view."[109] Deborin took it to be the primary task of Marxist philosophy to elaborate Hegel's dialectical structure of thought systematically from the materialist point of view.

The triumph of the dialecticians should have been complete after the publication in 1929 and 1930 of the bulk of Lenin's philosophical notebooks, revealing his painstaking study of Hegel's *Science of Logic*, including such aphorisms as "It is impossible completely to understand Marx's *Capital*, and especially its first chapter, without having thoroughly studied and understood the *whole* of Hegel's *Logic*."[110]

However, just at the point when it appeared that Hegel studies had secured a firm basis and a serious intellectual leader in the Soviet Union, Deborin's views on the relation of dialectical materialism to dialectical idealism were condemned.[111] A recent Soviet account of the philosophical motive for that condemnation reads as follows:

Finally, also condemned was that idea (although never formulated succinctly by Deborin or any of his students), that the Hegelian analysis of the categories of the dialectic as a whole are fully sufficient for Marxism and are in need only of a cleansing from idealist forms.[112]

This author however thought Deborin was responsible for "a significant strengthening of scientific research in the sphere of materialist dialectics."[113] Another author writing on the same subject praises Deborin for defending the idea of a "materialist re-working of Hegel's dialectics arid the development on that basis of Marxist dialectics," and explains that Deborin maintained an "insufficiently critical attitude toward the Hegelian idealistic dialectic, and an incorrect merging of it with the dialectic of Marx."[114]

Following this turn of events, an attempt was made to provide an acceptable commentary on the relationship of Hegelian philosophy and dialectical materialism under the new conditions established as a result of the resolution of the Deborin affair. This resulted in the publication in 1932 of an anthology entitled *Hegel and Dialectical Materialism.* [115] Quite recently this work was still being described as 'the most thorough analysis' of 'scientific approaches' to the study of Hegel produced in the 1930's. It also provided the first substantial commentaries on Lenin's recently published *Philosophical Notebooks*; however the commentaries contained in it are not now regarded as especially valuable.

One Soviet writer, B. V. Bogdanov, has offered the following periodization of Hegel studies in the Soviet Union. The period from 1917 through the criticism of Deborin's work was characterized by significant amounts of 'propadeutic and in part propagandistic' work on Hegel under the difficult conditions immediately following the revolution and civil war. The work of Deborin and others in criticizing the mechanist faction is praised, but the claim is made that materialist dialectics during this period was developed almost entirely in the form of Hegelian dialectics rather than on the basis of "a theoretical generalization of the experience of the revolutionary movement." [116]

A second period, from 1931 to the mid-1930's began with a scrutiny of Deborin's work and a criticism of his errors, stressing the opposition of Hegelian and materialist dialectics. It continued with the study of Lenin's writings on Hegel, and substantial publications of Hegel's works (eleven volumes of Hegel's writings published in the 1930's). [117] During the period from the mid-1930's until 1953 the task of developing a materialist re-working of Hegel is described as suffering from 'serious hindrance' caused by the dogmatism "connected with the cult of personality of Stalin." [118] In this period of little investigation into the development of Marxism, 'underestimation' of Lenin's *Philosophical Notebooks* occurred from time to time. Following sharp criticism in the press in 1943 of the third volume of the *History of Philosophy* for the absence of criticism of the conservative side of German idealist philosophy, the erroneous evaluation of Hegelian philosophy as the aristocratic reaction to the French bourgeois revolution and French materialism predominated until 1953. [119] The literature of that period was restricted mainly to journal articles and brochures.

In a third period, beginning after the death of Stalin, Soviet studies of Hegel have been characterized, according to Bogdanov, by an illumination of the positive achievements of Hegelian philosophy, with the rational content of his dialectic predominating by comparison with criticism of its negative tendencies.[120] He reports no unanimity on this score, however.

The re-evaluation of Hegel has taken a number of avenues in the last two decades of Soviet philosophy. The largest single category of Soviet interpretive efforts focuses on Lenin's thesis of the identity of the logic, the dialectic, and the theory of knowledge in Hegel's system. One recent Soviet study lists more than twice as many bibliographical items devoted to this problem than to any other aspect of Hegel studies since the mid-1950's.[121] It is in this form that Soviet philosophers commonly address the fundamental problem of attempting to reconcile insofar as possible, the Marxist use of the Hegelian dialectic with the materialism from which Marxist philosophy is held to be inseparable. The difficulty presents itself in the following way: Soviet Marxists wish to employ Hegel's dialectic as a logic (or method) governing all forms of scientific inquiry, on a materialist basis. It is clear however that within Hegel's system, the dialectic is not merely a logic of inquiry. As presented, especially in the *Phenomenology*, the dialectic of the successive 'shapes of consciousness' also constitutes Hegel's theory of knowledge, for the objects of knowledge are themselves moments of the dialectical succession of relations of subject to object which constitute the history of natural consciousness. But this dialectic constitutes a theory of knowledge only on the 'idealist version' of the identity of thought and being, which is inadmissible for Soviet materialism. The problem in part thus becomes, how to characterize the relation between the logic, the dialectic, and the theory of knowledge so that the dialectic can be employed without involving oneself in all the assumptions behind Hegel's theory of knowledge. There is after all a well-known alternative 'solution' for this problem – Lenin's copy theory of knowledge.

One distinctive attempt to deal with this dilemma, or rather to dissolve it, was offered by K. S. Bakradze, but is apparently not widely shared among other Soviet philosophers.[122] Bakradze asserted that one can speak of the identity of the dialectic, logic, and theory of knowledge in Hegel only in a certain limited sense: the laws of logic as a logic of development, and the general laws of the dialectic coincide, but as a whole, dialectic as science does not coincide with the theory of knowledge. The dialectic is significantly wider; it is not only a doctrine of the development of knowledge, but a doctrine of the most general laws of development of nature and society. Further, Bakradze considered logic proper to consist of formal logic. He did not consider Hegel's dialectical logic to be in essence a logic, rather only a theory of knowledge worked out on the logical plane.[123]

By qualifying Lenin's thesis of the identity of the logic, dialectic, and theory of knowledge, Bakradze created an opportunity to deal boldly with another difficult problem for Soviet Marxist interpretations of Hegel. In the usual formula, Marx took over the revolutionary *method* of Hegel's philosophy, the dialectic, while discarding the reactionary idealistic content of the system itself. In his book, Bakradze provided an exposition of a central thesis of Hegel's *Logic* — the impossibility of making an ultimate distinction between form and content of the logical categories — and insisted that Hegel's *method* must be understood analogously, as ultimately identical with his *system*, the content of the dialectic. Hence the thesis of the independence of Hegel's method from the content of his system cannot be defended, and Marxism cannot be understood to develop from Hegel's method exclusive of his system. Having reached these essentially sound conclusions, Bakradze appeared to retreat somewhat, restoring the distinction in an altered form:

It is not the dialectical method, in that form in which Hegel constructed it, which contradicts his system; rather the rational moment, the 'rational kernel' in the dialectical method of Hegel. What requires endless development is not the Hegelian dialectical method in its mystified form, but that moment in his dialectic which needed to be threshed out, saved, and further developed on a new materialistic basis.[124]

An evidently more widely shared view of Hegel is presented by V. I. Šinkaruk in *The Logic, Dialectic, and Theory of Knowledge of Hegel.*[125] Šinkaruk sees no difficulty in agreeing with the thesis of identity of dialectical logic with the dialectic as a theory of knowledge (a theory of the dialectical method of cognition). They are one and the same science: dialectical logic as the theory of dialectical method is the dialectic as a theory of knowledge, for Hegel as well as for Marx.[126]

However he argues that a qualification must be introduced to deal with the problem adequately. He speaks of the *coincidence* (but not identity) of the logic and the dialectic, which he defines as 'identity of content and difference of object and form'.[127] According to Šinkaruk the problem of the *coincidence* of the logic and the dialectic is one of the relation between dialectical logic and the dialectic as a *theory of development* (i.e., the dialectic as a science of the universal laws of development of nature, society and thought). He asserts that Hegel 'solved' this problem by interpreting the laws of thought, studied by dialectical logic, as laws of being, and the latter as laws of thought. As a result, the logical principles of cognition were "dialectically ontologized (the laws of development of the system of knowledge were converted into [the laws of] the development of material systems), and the laws of development of material systems were logicized, brought under the categories of the process of thought, of logic."[128]

The object of dialectical logic in Hegel is confused, and idealistically identified, with the object of dialectics as the science of the laws of development of nature, society, and thought. Reiterating Lenin's phrase, Šinkaruk insists that Hegel only *guessed* (a brilliant guess) that in the laws of the development of concepts one could discern the laws of development of *things*, a guess which could be correct only to the extent that the laws of development of thought happen to coincide with the universal laws of being. But in order to know *to what extent* this coincidence obtains, it is necessary to *discover* [presumably empirically?] the universal laws of development of nature and society. "In Hegel, *all* dialectical regularities of thought are interpreted as regularities of being itself (being = thought)."[129]

Therefore the Marxist dialectic as the science of the laws of development of nature, society, and thought proceeded not from the bosom of the Hegelian dialectic, but resulted from the application of the dialectical means of thought to the study of social life and the generalization of the achievements of natural science.

In order to create the dialectic as a science, it was necessary to scientifically discover the dialectic of things only guessed at by Hegel, and then only on that basis (on the basis of knowledge of the objective dialectical laws of development of nature, society and human thought) produce a materialist reworking of the idealistic dialectic of Hegel into the *system* of the materialist dialectic as a theory of development and as a theory of knowledge.[130]

Lenin's phrase describing Hegel's dialectic of concepts as containing a 'brilliant guess' wherein was revealed the dialectic of things finds its fruition in views such as Šinkaruk's. Since the materialist dialectic is conceived as a dialectic of things, not of concepts, the latter may be conceived as a simple *reflection* of the former. One could thus introduce a copy theory of knowledge into the midst of the dialectic.

Moreover, since the materialist dialectic is to be developed by the study of social life and generalization from natural science, it appears that the essential method of that investigation is to be conceived simply in empiricist terms. The transformed Hegelian dialectic is to be discovered and demonstrated through the process of empirical inquiry — a triumph of Engels' conception.

In a curious irony, since the most general laws of thought and being are to be discovered through 'scientific' investigation, one could even argue that the mechanists triumphed after all. Depending upon one's interpretation of that ambiguous word 'scientific' it could turn out that the 'method' of much philosophical inquiry is implicitly construed as a form of armchair sociology. Such a conception of philosophical method is in fact encountered in many Soviet writings on ethical theory. Hence the fundamental ambiguity of Marx's and Feuerbach's 'materialist critique of Hegel' is preserved where it began — in the interpretation of the Hegelian dialectic.

CHAPTER THREE

THE ORIGINS OF SOVIET ETHICAL THEORY

The disputes over ethical theory conducted within the German Marxist movement were monitored in great detail by Russian Marxists. In the period from 1900 up to the revolution, most of the major German contributions to the debate over ethical theory and socialism were translated promptly into Russian, and discussed at length in Russian publications. Multiple translations of some of these German works appeared almost simultaneously in various parts of Russia, and certain contributions were published repeatedly in anthologies over a period of years. Books by Vorländer, Woltmann, and Hildebrand, not to mention Kautsky and Engels, were translated; numerous articles by Kautsky, Bauer, Mehring, and other leaders of the German social democratic movement were also translated and published in anthologies, including nearly all the major articles on ethical theory appearing in the pages of *Neue Zeit* both prior to and during the period.

Russian Marxists were not merely observers of the German Marxists' debates, of course; Plekhanov, Berdjaev, Peter Struve, and Tugan-Baranovskij, among others, all either wrote contributions in German for publication abroad, or had works translated into German which played a part in the evolution of the debates within the Marxist movements of Western Europe. Russian Marxists took a prominent role in the discussions of Bernstein's 'revisionism' and in the debates over the neo-Kantian tendency within the Marxist movement which emerged in part from the controversy over Bernstein's writings.

During the period from 1898 to 1900 a number of contributions from Russian Marxist authors appeared in German journals reacting to Bernstein's theses. In 1897 Bernstein had begun publishing a series of articles in *Neue Zeit* under the general title 'Problems of Socialism', containing most of the views which were shortly to be collected in his celebrated 'revisionist' book.[1] Plekhanov leapt into the ensuing polemic with great energy, attacking Bernstein, Conrad Schmidt, and Peter Struve in particular for their 'revisionist' views on a variety of subjects.[2] In defense of a 'materialist' critique of Kantian metaphysics and epistemology against Conrad Schmidt, Plekhanov argued that Kant's notion of the 'thing-in-itself' involved a radical inconsistency: on the one hand, the 'thing in itself' is a cause of our perceptions, and on the other, the category of cause is inapplicable to it.[3] This unknowable 'thing in itself' constituted the chief source of metaphysics in the Kantian system, its 'meta-phenomenalism', which left in question the reality of objects independent of our perceptions of them, a defect from which 'materialism' did not suffer. The chief *motive* for this renaissance of interest in Kantian philosophy on the part of the bourgeoisie, Plekhanov insisted, was their desire to 'moralize' the proletariat and combat atheism, combined with the supposition that Kant's philosophy, theoretical and practical, would be the most appropriate weapon in this class struggle.[4]

Some of Plekhanov's most pointed criticisms of the neo-Kantian movement within Marxism were published a few years later in the form of greatly expanded notes for his second Russian edition (1905) of Engels' *Ludwig Feuerbach*.[5] There Plekhanov specifically took up the question of the categorical imperative and endorsed some of Hegel's criticism of it — namely that Kant's three examples of conduct forbidden by the categorical imperative are inadequate: that Kant's conclusion in each of them follows only if one adds a further moral premise to each of them. "Kant's teaching, as Hegel says, does not contain a single law of morality clear in itself, without any further arguments and without contradictions, independently of other qualifications."[6] Most seriously in Plekhanov's view, Kant's ethical doctrine was fundamentally misguided in its objection to any form of utilitarianism. Kant's objection to utilitarianism was motivated by his understanding of the utilitarian principle as that of " 'personal happiness' which he correctly calls the principle of self-love".[7] Such an understanding of utilitarianism prevents Kant from coping "with the basic questions of morality", because "morality is founded on the striving not for personal happiness, but for the happiness of the whole: the clan, the people, the class, humanity. This striving has nothing in common with egoism. On the contrary, it always presupposes a greater or lesser degree of self-sacrifice."[8] Plekhanov then goes on to suggest that this 'social feeling' is selected and strengthened in its transmission from generation to generation by the Darwinian mechanism of evolution.

Nikolaj Berdjaev, in a lengthy three-part article on Albert Lange, published in *Neue Zeit* in 1900, similarly criticized Kantian epistemology, but also criticized 'dialectical materialism' as an invention of Engels' *Anti-Dühring* which had little to do with Marx's sociological doctrines, and which was bound to be superceded in the development of Marxist social theory.[9] Berdjaev, while much more respectful of Kant's philosophy than Plekhanov at this point, nevertheless considered it an inadequate basis for Marxist social theory.

The philosophy of Kant, perhaps the most profound in the history of thought, and in the highest degree suited to stimulate new human thought, is from the socio-historical stand-point a philosophy of compromise. It suffers from half-measures and contradictions.[10]

As did Plekhanov, Berdjaev objected most strongly to Kant's doctrine of the unknowable thing-in-itself, which he considered ultimately self-contradictory. This supposed contradiction in Kant's epistemology according to Berdjaev resulted from a contradiction in his psychology which in turn was produced by disharmonious social conditions.[11]

Kant and critical philosophy as a whole superceded both naive realism and the common forms of idealism as well.

For Kant knowledge is a product both of the subject and of the object: the first gives the form, the second, the content; all cognizable things (with secondary and primary qualities) are only appearances for us, i.e., not for the individual consciousness, but for the universal transcendental consciousness which makes knowledge also objective and universally valid.[12]

This according to Berdjaev was the "most profound thought in the history of epistemological ideas"; however Kant's 'bifurcated' psychology led him to the concept of the thing in itself, an unknowable something which acts upon me and can be cognized only as appearance. Hence Kant's philosophy culminates in an unacceptable dualism. Berdjaev himself predicted (and aspired to) a 'harmonization' of life which would lead to the 'harmonization' of thought, and to a "unified, monistic *Weltanschauung*" which would be tightly bound up with life.[13]

Berdjaev's own 'rectified' Kantianism (he termed it 'critical realism') was allegedly distinct from naive realism in that it recognized no object which was not cognized by a subject, and distinct from idealism because it conceded 'no privilege whatever' to the subject. Finally, it was distinct from Kantianism because it permitted no epistemological dualism: the concept of the thing-in-itself was for Berdjaev "meaningless".[14]

He was equally critical at this point of Kant's practical philosophy. "What Kant takes as an eternal postulate of practical reason, we hold to be a temporary postulate of the humanly determined socio-psychological formation."[15] Other times will arrive, and other interests will assert themselves; what Kant took as sacred we will tear down. "We do not need the 'intelligible world' without which Kant could not live, and we have, on our side, our own realm of sacred things in the name of which we condemn the social foundation of the 'intelligible world'."[16]

At the time of writing this article, Berdjaev described himself as an enthusiastic supporter of Marxism, however embracing the 'critical direction' within it. His disaffection with Marxism became still more marked in his first book, *Subjectivism and Individualism in Social Philosophy*, which appeared soon after the publication of the article just discussed.[17] Directed in the first instance against the 'subjective sociology' of Mixajlovskij, the book also constituted a reaction to the first of Ludwig Woltmann's three Kantian-socialist, Darwinian treatises on ethics, which Berdjaev undoubtedly had in mind when he spoke of being "sick to death" of hearing about the usual view of social phenomena from "German 'academic socialists' ".[18] Although he did not repudiate his previous criticisms of Kant, he appeared on the whole to be more favorably disposed toward Kant, and less so toward Marx in this work. He rejected the view that moral obligation and moral ideals could be considered only as subjectively justifiable, and argued that "there must be some objective standard which would enable us to set one subjective ideal above the others".[19] The subjective sociologists, in which group he apparently included Marx as well as Mixajlovskij where ethics was concerned, believed that social ideals could be grounded in two ways: first, that a given social ideal is objectively necessary, i.e., historically inevitable; and second, it is subjectively desirable for some social class. Berdjaev considered such a 'justification' of a social ideal 'absolutely inadequate'. He claimed instead that

it is necessary to show that our social ideal is not only objectively necessary (the logical category), not only subjectively desirable (the psychological category), but also that it is objectively moral and objectively just, ... that it is binding on all, has unconditional value, is something *obligatory* (the ethical category).[20]

He stressed the distinct character of the ethical as a subject of inquiry ultimately fitted only for philosophical as opposed to scientific inquiry. He emphatically disputed the tendency current in some Marxist as well as other circles to suppose that philosophy was destined to be replaced by scientific social theory. Only philosophy would be capable of demonstrating the basis for an objective moral ideal. He then turned to Kant for the starting point of this philosophical inquiry, arguing that the source of the objectively moral, as well as of the objectively true, is rooted in transcendental consciousness.[21] "Objective morality is possible only if one accepts the *a priori* character of a moral law which distinguishes unconditionally between good and evil."[22] "The formal difference between good and evil or between the moral and the immoral precedes every sense experience; the category of justice is given *a priori* to our transcendental consciousness, and this ethical *a priori* is what makes moral experience and moral life possible."[23]

In this new work, Berdjaev acknowledged "one postulate of practical reason, the postulate of moral order," in contrast to his criticism of the "eternal postulate" in the *Neue Zeit* article. He still maintained however that this moral order was not located "in the intelligible world, nor in unknown things in themselves", but rather in "the one real world of phenomena, in that progress which is being accomplished within the worldly and historical process and is actualizing the 'realm of ends' ".[24] Thus in place of the Kantian 'intelligible world' Berdjaev rested the reality of his moral order on one fundamental empirical assumption, "the presupposition of universal progress", and admitted that "if the latter falls, our argument too will inevitably collapse".[25] Vorländer viewed Berdjaev's ethical theory on the whole as threatening to collapse into a purely natural-scientific, merely causally explanatory one, and as Professor Kline has argued, Berdjaev's single empirical assumption constitutes a very frail reed upon which to hang one's entire theory of moral order.[26]

In the same period when Berdjaev was commenting upon the Kantian direction in contemporary Marxism and developing his own distinctive attitudes toward the problem of Marxism and ethical theory, the emerging debate over these problems within German Marxism was being presented to a Russian audience. In December, 1900, the journal *Žizn'* in St. Petersburg published a lengthy article entitled 'The Neo-Kantian Tendency in Marxism' which contained a sympathetic summary, indeed almost a paraphrase, of Vorländer's just-published *Kant und der Sozialismus*.[27] The author, Evgenij Lozinskij, referred approvingly in a postscript to Berdjaev's article on Lange, which appeared after Lozinskij's had been prepared for publication, as the most distinctly neo-Kantian article yet to appear in the pages of *Neue Zeit*. Lozinskij's article thus had the effect of drawing his Russian reader's attention to the development of neo-Kantianism in German Marxism within months of Vorländer's original declaration of its status as a coherent movement.

A negative reaction to all of this appeared from the hand of Ljubov' Aksel'rod, an associate of Plekhanov and like him a defender of 'orthodox' Marxism, under the title 'Why Don't We Want to Go Back?' (a rejoinder to the 'Back to Kant!' slogan).[28] In regard to Kantian ethics, Aksel'rod first of all echoed Plekhanov in attributing the fashionableness of the categorical imperative to the desire of the threatened bourgeoisie to ward off the impending revolution.[29] The categorical imperative itself she described as an "abstract formula, suitable for all times, for all social orders, and all classes, which in actuality condemns not a single form of human communal life".[30]

The capitalist sincerely convinced of the rectitude of the institution of private property is as moral as the socialist striving to destroy it.

Aksel'rod further argued that Berdjaev could not consistently discard the three postulates of pure practical reason and retain the categorical imperative, quoting Windelband's *History of Modern Philosophy* in support of her view.

If you believe in the necessity and universal obligatoriness of the moral law, then you must believe also in those conditions under which alone the necessity and universal obligatoriness are possible. These conditions are freedom and the suprasensuous world; consequently you must, if the whole of your conviction is not unfounded, believe also in the reality of freedom and the suprasensuous world. Accordingly Kant terms the ideas to which the activity of practical faith must apply, the postulates of pure practical reason.[31]

She then suggests that Berdjaev thought he could ignore this aspect of the Kantian doctrine because in fact he accepted approximately the same postulates himself on other, partly religious, grounds.[32] Aksel'rod showed a certain prescience in these remarks, written in 1901, for within approximately a year Berdjaev had renounced Marxism and begun to develop his own explicitly religious existentialism. As one of the contributors to the famous *Vexi* anthology in 1909 criticizing the Russian intelligentsia tradition, including Marxism, Berdjaev's hostility to the latter was to become still more pronounced.

Another of the temporary neo-Kantian Marxists of Russia, Peter von Struve, also entered the debates over Bernstein's 'revisionism' and the Kantian tendency within Marxism from the beginning. In 1899 he published a substantial article in the *Archiv für Soziale Gesetzgebung und Statistik* criticizing the Marxist conception of social revolution.[33] In particular he criticized the notion of a 'contradiction' between the forces of production and the prevailing social relations, arguing that the distinction between them was an artificial one, that in reality no such regular contrast could be discovered; hence this could not be the main mechanism of revolution. He argued further that the single theoretical model of contradiction employed by Marx, which pictured the resolution of such contradictions as invariably a violent qualitative change in phenomena, was incorrect. There was in fact more than one theoretical model of contradiction, and other models did not lead to resolutions involving sudden qualitative changes or 'dialectical leaps'. In support of his views Struve drew upon Kant's discussion of the 'law of continuity of all alteration' in the Second Analogy from the *Critique of Pure Reason*.[34] Concluding that the theoretical and evidentiary basis on which Marx claimed to predict scientifically the inevitable revolutionary transition from capitalism to socialism

was quite inadequate, Struve then attributed the certainty of Marx's conviction to a distinctly utopian component of his theory, rooted in passionately
held social ideals: "Scientific socialism is no pure culture of science: as a
social ideal it is necessarily a combination of science and utopia."[35]

Plekhanov devoted a great many pages of the journal *Zarja* in 1901 and
1902 to a defense of Marxism against Struve's criticisms; however as these
articles by Plekhanov touched only indirectly on the problems of ethical
theory, they will not be discussed here.[36]

Another Russian neo-Kantian socialist, Prof. Tugan-Baranovskij, went even
farther than Struve in this question of the relationship of Marxism to socialism as a social ideal. He claimed that the essence of modern socialism as a
doctrine lay in its proclamation of a new social ideal, and that ideal was one
developed not by Marx but by the utopian socialists. Still more, he claimed
that Marxism had not added anything to the ideal as it was created by the
early socialists.

Thus the tactics of Marxism, crowned by so brilliant a success in practical life, have in
theory resulted in weakening the interest in the final issue of socialism. Nothing can,
therefore, be more erroneous than the opinion generally entertained, that the theory of
socialism is entirely to be found in the writings of Marx and his school.[37]

At the heart of this new social ideal, according to Tugan-Baranovskij, lay the
idea of the human personality as the greatest aim in itself. "The best founder
and interpreter of this system" was "the greatest philosopher of modern time
– Kant".[38] The slogan promulgated in the French revolution, 'liberty, equality, and fraternity', above all *equality*, was supplied a foundation 'solid as
granite' by Kant's practical philosophy. As was true for most of the German
neo-Kantian Marxists, Kant's 'kingdom of ends' represented the ideal of
human society at the heart of socialism for Tugan-Baranovskij.[39]

This critical attitude toward Marxism grew sharper in the following years.
When four of Vorländer's essays on Kant and Marx were translated and
published as a book in St. Petersburg in 1909, Tugan-Baranovskij wrote a
foreword in which he declared that the attempt to base Marxism upon Kant's
practical philosophy was impossible. "The ethical grounding of socialism is
marked not by the supplementation of Marxism, but by the fundamental
transformation – more precisely, dissolution – of it."[40] Tugan-Baranovskij
argued that socialism was in clear need of a reformation which would incorporate the theoretical foundations for its moral ideals. This 'new theory of
socialism' would be constructed on the ruins of Marxism which could itself
not survive the attempt to provide an ethical foundation; hence while agreeing

with Vorländer's concern to supply such a foundation, he rejected the entire supposition of a possible reconciliation between Marx and Kant (to Vorländer's evident surprise).[41]

The dialogue between German and Russian Marxists over the place of Kantian ethical theory in Marxism was not restricted to bilingual contributors. (Indeed Vorländer himself did not read Russian, but was able to summarize the views of three Russian philosophers at length in his 1911 work). The rate of translation from German into Russian on this subject remained quite high for several years. For example, in 1907 an anthology, *The Ethical Problem in Historical Materialism*, was published in Moscow containing essays from *Neue Zeit* on the subject by Kautsky, Joffe, and Bauer. Vorländer's works received special attention from the 'Pulse of Life' (*Pul's žizni*) publishing house in Moscow, which published three of his works in the years 1906 and 1907.[42] These were followed in 1909 by the anthology of Vorländer's essays from St. Petersburg just mentioned.[43] All three of Ludwig Woltmann's works mentioned above had been translated and published in 1900 and 1901.[44]

Opponents of the Kantian tendency received aid from the complete translation of Engels' *Anti-Dühring* which appeared in 1904, and from a minor industry engaged in the translation and publication of the works of Kautsky. His two early articles from *Neue Zeit* on the social instinct in animals and humans were published three times in translation (1890, 1907, and 1922).[45] His polemic with Quessel in *Neue Zeit* after the appearance of *Ethics and the Materialist Conception of History* appeared as a separate pamphlet in 1907.[46] An anthology of Kautsky's essays published in 1918 also contained a number of his writings on ethical theory.[47] Above all, his book *Ethics and the Materialist Conception of History* appears to have descended upon Russian readers in a blizzard of at least eight separate editions in 1906, another in 1918, two more in 1922, with substantial excerpts reprinted in 1923 and 1925.[48] A major anthology entitled *Marxism and Ethics* appeared in 1923, containing many of the *Neue Zeit* articles plus substantial parts of Kautsky's book; and it was followed by a second, much enlarged edition in 1925 which contained practically all the exchanges on ethical theory which had appeared in *Neue Zeit* involving Kautsky, excerpts from his book, and the entire dispute among Plekhanov, Martov, and Aksel'rod concerning 'simple moral norms' and the categorical imperative. While not publishing a representative sample of the works of neo-Kantian Marxists, the anthology nevertheless included a detailed bibliographical guide to most of their works available in Russian.[49]

The Russian extension of the debate originating in Germany between 'neo-Kantian' and 'orthodox' Marxists was clearly a major episode in the early history of twentieth century Marxism in Russia. At the same time, as Professor Kline has pointed out, there was a quite distinctive Russian development in the discussion of Marxism and ethical theory which had almost no counterpart in Germany: a school of 'Nietzschean' Marxists whose views coincided with neither of the two camps discussed above.[50] Professor Kline describes four persons as the principal writers in this group: A. A. Bogdanov (Malinovskij), V. A. Bazarov (Rudnev), A. V. Lunačarskij and S. Vol'skij (Sokolev). Lunačarskij and Vol'skij both objected to the constraints placed upon the individual by abstract concepts of moral duty, by universal moral ideals, and by the various forms of moral pressure on the individual to conform to socially dictated standards of conduct. The goal of both these persons was a release of the individual personality for the fullest possible expansion of his powers. Whereas Lunačarskij tended to oppose any attempt to "transform the individual into a cell of the social organism," and expected that only in some "splendid future" could the interests of the individual and those of society achieve harmony, Vol'skij argued that tactical considerations dictated the temporary renunciation of individualism for the immediate future, and that only following the defeat of capitalism would an ethics liberated from the concept of duty be possible.[51] In his book *The Philosophy of Struggle: an Essay in Marxist Ethics*, Vol'skij claimed that the idea of duty was "the inevitable companion of bourgeois society".[52] In a Nietzschean extreme of individualism, Vol'skij argued that "the class sees in itself something to be eliminated, the individual something to be asserted".[53] Prof. Kline states that Vol'skij's work in 1909 was one of the last defenses of naturalistic ethical individualism to appear in Russia.[54]

The other two prominent Nietzschean Marxists, Bogdanov and Bazarov, were 'collectivists', intent on liberating the individual from an ethics of duty, yet conceiving the future primarily in terms of an organically fused, vital social organism in which the individual perceived no disparity between his own and the collective's interests.[55] Bazarov even employed the Slavophile term *sobornost'* to describe the "fusion of all human souls" which he envisioned as the outcome of the repudiation of the ethics of individual duty, of the rejection of abstract ethical norms in general.[56] In their collectivism, Bogdanov and Bazarov were less consistent with their Nietzschean inspiration than either Lunačarskij or Vol'skij, but much more consistent with the collectivism of the future Soviet order.

By the end of the first decade of the twentieth century, the focus of debates over ethical subjects within the Russian Marxist movement had begun to shift, and the year 1909 may be usefully regarded as a pivotal one for several reason. First, it was the year in which the last of the translations of Vorländer's works appeared, and in reviewing it Deborin felt confident enough to claim, with perhaps only a certain amount of polemical exaggeration, that "at the present time the theme of 'Kant and Marx' has lost its topicality and already has to a significant degree only historical interest".[57] Deborin may well have had in mind the fact that the original representatives of neo-Kantian ethics within the socialist movement, Berdjaev, Struve, and Tugan-Baranovskij, had all for various reasons declared their opposition to the doctrine of Marxism in particular, if not to socialism in general, and their views on ethics no longer had to be taken seriously within the Russian Marxist movement.

Second, the famous *Vexi* (Signposts) anthology also appeared in 1909, openly hostile to the socialist-intelligentsia tradition within Russian culture, with essays by Berdjaev, Struve, and four other theorists. Thereafter the confrontation between Marxists and '*Vexovcy*' was to be an established feature of Russian intellectual life (until about 1922 when most of the *Vexovcy* were driven into emigration); but it no longer had the character of an intellectual exchange in which the opponents could take each other and their respective arguments as worthy of serious consideration. The assumptions under which each group operated had diverged too widely for mutually profitable interchanges. The *Vexovcy* group published another anthology in 1918 reacting with extreme pessimism to the events surrounding the revolution, and a number of them contributed to a third in 1922.[58]

Third, Vol'skij's major work, *The Philosophy of Struggle*, also appeared in 1909; however as Professor Kline observed, it was not only the most significant and consistently argued of the Nietzschean individualist works to appear, it was also the last. In the preceding year, the 'Nietzschean' group as a whole had suffered a strenuous attack by Lenin in the form of his *Materialism and Empirio-Criticism*, directed against their epistemological views, which had the political consequence of identifying them as a deviationist group and isolating them from the 'orthodoxy' defended by other leaders of the Bolsheviks.

In summary, after 1909 the more original and adventurous views on ethical theory within the Marxist movement, from both Kantian and Nietzschean sources tended to be driven into opposition (in the case of the main neo-Kantians of course the path of opposition was freely chosen and taken somewhat earlier). Disputes over ethical theory within the Russian Marxist movement did not cease, but they tended to revolve more closely about the formulations of Engels' *Anti-Dühring*, Kautsky's *Ethics*, and various alleged 'deviations' from these.

The most philosophically talented opposition group was that informal one known as the *'Vexovcy'* or simply the *'idealisty'* who criticized the Bolshevik revolution, especially on moral grounds, as it unfolded. The most visible philosophical opponents of the Bolsheviks were people such as Berdjaev, Frank, Shestov, S. Bulgakov, Radlov, and N. Losskij, who at various times represented almost everything from neo-Kantianism to Christian mysticism. Between the February and October revolutions of 1917 Frank published *The Moral Watershed in the Russian Revolution*, dividing all its participants into two groups, those who sought "justice, liberty and individual dignity, culture, broad political development based on mutual respect" and those on the side of "violence, arbitrariness, unbridled class egoism, contempt for culture, indifference to the common national good", i.e., the Bolsheviks.[59] In the summer of 1917 Berdjaev published two works, *Is Social Revolution Possible?* and *People and Class in the Russian Revolution*, interpreting Marxism as an eschatological utopia of heaven on earth in the name of which the masses were being whipped into a frenzy of evil, hate-filled passion.[60] The doctrine of class revolution threatened to erect a social order founded upon hate rather than love, a catastrophe for Russian history.

The confrontation between the Bolsheviks and this philosophical opposition was less marked during the Civil War, but immediately upon the close of the war in 1921, until the forced emigration of its main participants in 1922, the opposition group generated one last burst of public criticism of the revolution within Russia. The main instruments of this final outpouring were the journal *Mysl'* in Petrograd, which succeeded in publishing three issues in the first half of 1922, the philosophical annual *Mysl' i slovo* in Moscow, the 'Philosophical Society' at the University of Petrogard which was resurrected in 1921, chaired by Radlov, and the 'Free Ecclesiastical Academy' in Moscow.[61] The most sweeping moral criticism of the revolution was rooted in the Christian historiosophy of such writers as Berdjaev, Frank, and Stepun. In their view capitalism and the socialist revolution alike were products of the same spiritual collapse stemming from loss of faith during the Enlightenment. They reached back to Solovëv's and Dostoevsky's criticisms of the spiritual poverty of capitalism and its child, socialism, and recalled the Slavophile notion of a special destiny of the Russian people to establish an ideal of moral harmony on earth. Needless to say, that moral ideal, and therefore the destiny of the Russian people, they saw utterly betrayed by the Bolshevik revolution. Such views were presented by Berdjaev in *The Fate of Russia* (Moscow, 1918), by L. Karsavin in *The East, the West, and the Russian Idea* (Petrograd, 1922), and in the anthology *Oswald Spengler and the Decline of Europe*, containing articles by Berdjaev, Frank, Stepun, and Bukspan (Petrograd, 1922). Radlov, in a work entitled *Ethics* (Petrograd, 1921) criticized the revolution from the perspective of 'moral principles' which were "as unchanging as the fundamental laws of thought".[62] The development of this wide-ranging discussion of Russian history, ethics, Christianity, and the socialist revolution was abruptly transferred to Western Europe when its main leaders were forced out of the Soviet Union in 1922. In particular Berdjaev continued to develop this interpretation of Russian history and the revolution in a series of well-known books published in Western Europe.[63] As mentioned above, however, this particular dispute over the ethics of the revolutionary movement had long since ceased to be one between opponents who recognized the legitimacy of each other's fundamental position and hence bore the character of a hostile polemic, rather than a reasoned argument.[64]

Focusing once again on the Marxist movement in these years, an example of the type of dispute over ethical theory still occurring within the ranks broke out in 1915 when Plekhanov accused the Germans of violating "simple norms of morality and right" in their invasion of neutral Belgium, and castigated German social democrats for not resisting these developments more energetically.[65] He borrowed the phrase from the first *Manifesto of the International Brotherhood of Workers*, to which Marx had been a contributing author. When criticized for this reference to 'simple norms of morality and right', Plekhanov in a second essay called on Kant's *Critique of Practical Reason* for support.

> You know that I am not a Kantian, and do not like to lean on Kant. But when one begins speaking about simple norms of morality and right, it is impossible not to recall the author of the *Critique of Practical Reason*.[66]

Plekhanov's 'reliance' on Kant amounted to little more than a favorable mention of the categorical imperative, but it sufficed to bring forth a severe attack from Martov, accusing him of "capitulation before idealism and metaphysics".[67] Martov confined his attack largely to quoting a letter from Marx to Engels in which Marx complained about the circumstances in which the references to 'morality' and 'right' found their way into the *Manifesto*, explaining that he had been forced to permit a few such harmless phrases to remain in the document in deference to the sensibilities of other members of the drafting committee.[68] Aksel'rod then entered the fray in defense of her associate Plekhanov and his assertions concerning "simple laws of morality and right".

Class ethics and the relative character of right and morality notwithstanding, humanity has worked out in its long socio-historical life general norms of mutual existence. These general norms, penetrating the whole of our life, have become functions of the social organism as unnoticeable to the simple eye as the physiological functions of the individual organism.[69]

Despite her own previous attacks upon the Kantian categorical imperative, in defense of Plekhanov she argued that,

The categorical imperative in all of its ramifications and with all of its rules and norms is a fully clear and fully evident product of socio-historical development. And as such, it is an actually existing fact, possessing real significance.[70]

Martov chose not to let the matter rest there, and composed a very lengthy rebuttal of Aksel'rod's view, which appeared only somewhat later.[71]

This same dispute erupted a second time when about 1926 the philosopher Deborin found himself engaged in a very wide-ranging public dispute with Aksel'rod. He chose among other things to attack her views on moral philosophy, especially the Kantian sympathies expressed in the 1916 article, as decidedly anti-Marxist. In the course of this second dispute Aksel'rod restated her views in the following passage, equivocating somewhat on the question of the ultimate obligations of the proletariat:

... There do exist general simple laws and norms of morality, and ... these laws are obligatory likewise for the proletariat, but only insofar as they do not contradict the class revolutionary tasks of the latter, since the victory of socialism over capitalism is not only a historical necessity, but also the highest moral ideal for the proletariat and all who are oppressed, ...[72]

Deborin insisted that no genuinely Marxist account of ethics could contain any universally obligatory norms of conduct:

The concept of the universally obligatory signifies for them that which is obligatory for all times and peoples, something supra-experiential, not dependent upon real life, standing above history, above reality .... The origin of these laws and norms is purely metaphysical, supra-experiential; they are rooted in a suprasensuous world.[73]

In support of this criticism he quite properly cited Engels' *Anti-Dühring*, in which very similar assertions are to be found.

Deborin's positive views on the subject of ethics very clearly pose the problem so frequently encountered in Marxist discussions of ethical theory which was pointed out repeatedly by the neo-Kantians: the dissolution of ethics into sociology.

Ethics, generally speaking, is nothing other than the study of the behavior or life of people corresponding to ideals in which are formulated definite requirements arising from the social position of these people. [74]

On the subject of moral obligation, Deborin asserted that moral duty is nothing other than 'social instinct' or 'social feeling' become conscious.

Duty or conscience is the voice of the collective in the individual, the reflection of the interests and strivings of the collective in the individual consciousness, the 'pressure' of the collective on the individual . . . [75]

The doctrine of 'social instinct' or 'feeling' was not developed at length by Deborin; he referred to Darwin and Spencer as the sources of his analysis. The evolutionary reference was evidently thought sufficient to deflect inquiry from the possibly vexatious problem of the ground of moral obligation.

Social feelings, present to some degree in animals which live in herds are transformed over the course of human history into social stimuli and social obligations laid upon the individual by the corresponding collective.
. . . .
All social instincts or feelings and the moral laws resting upon them, that is, man's social obligations toward the collective, developed gradually in the historical process of social life. [76]

To inquiry about the possible *grounds* of moral obligations, such a view supplies an irrelevant speculation about the psycho-social, historical origins of men's actual patterns of moral behavior. Deborin in this passage still retains, unexplained, an apparent distinction between 'social instincts' and 'moral laws resting upon them', which might have been influenced by Kautsky's similar distinction between social instincts and moral ideals. [77] That Deborin attempted no more detailed account of this crucial distinction is a measure of the superficiality of his thinking on the subject. He was by no means to be regarded as a moral philosopher; his primary philosophical interests were elsewhere. That he expressed himself in any detail at all publicly on these matters was apparently due to the circumstance of his falling into a polemic with Aksel'rod.

He was not left to contemplate his victory over Aksel'rod very long, however. Within a year his speculations about the evolution of 'moral laws' from 'social instincts' were the object of a sharp attack by M. Furščik, on the grounds that Deborin had identified human morality with that of the apes. Furščik denied that human morality could be viewed as a species of, or development from, social instincts in any sense of the term. [78]

In 1930 Novikov sprang to the vigorous defense of Deborin's view, but found it expedient to emphasize still more strongly the unexplained distinction between 'social instinct' and 'moral law'.

Precisely because morality is, in comparison with the social instinct of animals, a new quality, entirely a product of the socio-historical process, Deborin asserts that "morality doesn't exist in the animal kingdom".[79]

However Novikov, and also Razumovskij, argued that the concept of 'social instinct' was not to be discarded from Marxist social science as Furščik evidently intended.[80]

About this time Deborin's position as a Communist philosopher in favor with the young Soviet regime was being threatened. A particularly vicious and unprincipled form of politics invaded the philosophical arena, ultimately including the personal intervention of Stalin. Deborin was shortly deposed as head of the Communist Academy and a few months later, as editor of *Pod Znamenem Marksizma*.[81] The exchange of articles surrounding Deborin's ethical views in 1930 is illustrative of the general collapse of the necessary conditions for even modestly independent thought. Intellectual activity degenerated into a morass of vulgar diatribe, personal slander, and politically incriminating accusations whose consequences were potentially of the utmost seriousness.

The problems of ethical theory involved in the dispute were submerged, largely unresolved, in an escalating exchange of political incriminations by participants on both sides of the dispute. Deborin's view retained the advantage of a rough-hewn simplicity, reminiscent of the chapter on morality in Engels' *Anti-Dühring*.

Morality has neither an absolute nor a classless character (insofar as discussion concerns contemporary class society). All its norms, in terms of their content, are in essence subordinated to the interests of this or that class . . . .[82]

The significance of this episode in Soviet intellectual history has been variously interpreted by recent Soviet commentators. Gontarev and Xajkin have described the exchanges between Aksel'rod and Deborin as an argument over the relationship between simple universal norms of morality and class morality, in effect an earlier version of an argument which took place at the beginning of 1960's among contemporary Soviet writers on ethics.[83] Xarčev and Jakovlev have more recently criticized that interpretation as a 'modernization' of the original dispute affected by recent Soviet discussions.[84] These authors interpret the discussions (more accurately, polemics) of 1926–1930 as a crucial contribution to the development of ethical theory as a relatively autonomous subject of inquiry in Soviet thought, the primary accomplishment of which was to overcome the widespread influence of Kautsky's ethical theory in the Soviet Union and to eliminate certain extremely serious errors involved in his views.

The central issue in their view was the problem of how to construct Communist forms of upbringing (*vospitanie*), how to modify people's consciousnesses. The answers to these questions in turn depended upon the issue of whether people's moral consciousnesses were formed entirely by social conditions and socially-imposed patterns of individual upbringing, or whether some 'universal moral law' dwelled in a 'psychic substance' as a social instinct within each individual, placed there by evolutionary mechanisms originating in some ancestral forms of collective herd existence. This Darwinian bio-psychological conception of moral consciousness as a social instinct enjoyed wide popularity in the 1920's, primarily as a consequence of Kautsky's writings.[85] (Remember that Kautsky's two articles on social instinct in the animal and human worlds were published in Russian on three separate occasions).[86] The cardinal mistake of Kautsky's doctrine lay in its implication of an *unchanging* 'moral-phychological substance' which would have strictly limited the possibilities for a socialist transformation of human moral consciousness.

The series of exchanges described above served, in their view, to eliminate Kautsky's Darwinian conception. Deborin's critique of Aksel'rod correctly excluded the resurrection of the categorical imperative, an unchanging moral law based upon the Kautskian concept of an unchanging 'moral psychological substance' in human consciousness. However, in his critique, Deborin himself wished to rely on the notion of a 'general moral *feeling*' produced as a modification of these same Kautskian 'social instincts' of our biological ancestors.[87] Furščik then quite 'justly' attacked Deborin for recognizing a common moral feeling (in essence a common *content* of social instincts), claiming that Deborin's views lead to a restoration of Kautskianism in another form.[88] Later, Novikov and Razumovskij in separate articles properly criticized Furščik for attempting to eliminate the concept of 'social instinct' altogether as 'unscientific'. Summarizing the accomplishments of this period, Xarčev and Jakovlev claim that

Despite certain errors and the extremely sharp tone of the discussion, its scientific results were extremely significant. Soviet philosophers showed in the course of the discussion that moral consciousness is not genetically conditioned, produced by some pre-historical content; concepts and feelings of duty, conscience, etc., reflect the inter-relationships among people, the particularities of social existence. Simultaneously with the overcoming of Kautskian influence in ethics, nihilistic and simplistic-rationalistic conceptions in the understanding of morality put forward several years before the beginning of the discussion by Buxarin and Preobraženskij were decisively shattered. In the process of criticizing them, the relative autonomy and historical specificity of the moral form of consciousness, excluding the possibility of a rationalistic-organizational treatment of this particular sphere of the spiritual life of society, was demonstrated.[89]

Whatever the truth of this interpretation of the 'discussion' in question it would be difficult to believe that the participants themselves could have given such an account of the underlying issues and their aims at the time. That their exchanges might be seen in retrospect to have had some of the consequences attributed to them by Xarčev and Jakovlev is another matter.

In a further extension of their interpretation of this period, Xarčev and Jakovlev argue that the battle for the recognition of moral consciousness as a relatively autonomous sphere of social consciousness, meriting its own 'special' science (ethical theory) and exhibiting a linguistic vocabulary uniquely its own, was effectively won by 1935. In that year *Pod Znamenem Marksizma* published an editorial entitled 'Proletarian Humanism' criticizing attempts to eliminate references to 'humanity in general', 'humanism', etc., from Soviet Marxist literature in the name of a purely class viewpoint in morality. The editors argued that instead of seeing the resolution of universal human tasks in the practice of the proletariat, in proletarian but 'authentically socialist' culture, some people wished to restrict proletarian culture to precisely those qualities and characteristics to which the barbaric forms of capitalist production had condemned it.[90]

The 'leftist ethical nihilism' against which this editorial was directed according to Xarčev and Jakovlev stemmed above all from the 'pseudo-class demagoguery' begun by the *Proletkul't* (Proletarian Cultural and Educational Organization) and continued in part by the leaders of *RAPP* (Russian Association of Proletarian Writers), which strove to eliminate such terms as 'humanism' and 'universally human' from the Marxist vocabulary.[91] For the preservation of a broader conception of the humanist intent of the socialist revolution during this period, Makarenko and Gor'kij are given great credit.[92] Makarenko's writings on pedagogy and other subjects related to his work with orphaned and anti-social teenagers presented the first detailed analysis of the new Communist morality, and Gor'kij's numerous writings and speeches before and after the revolution continually stressed the theme of 'proletarian humanism' according to Xarčev and Jakovlev.

At any rate, after 1930, there were very few publications during the next two decades which could be unequivocally viewed as contributions to the development of a Soviet Marxist ethical theory. During the 1930's the works of Makarenko and the dispute over the notion of 'proletarian humanism', echoes of which could be heard at the first congress of the Union of Soviet Writers in 1934, appear to be more worthy of investigation than any other developments outside of purely literary ones, from the point of view of the construction of an ethical theory. The 1940's produced almost nothing of serious theoretical interest in this field, and while the following decade did witness the publication of several monographs on ethical theory, they were largely propagandistic in intent or presented a very low level of theoretical sophistication.[93]

CHAPTER FOUR

ETHICAL THEORY AND ITS OBJECT, MORALITY

1. MORALITY AS AN ASPECT OF SOCIAL CONSCIOUSNESS

A resurrection of interest in problems of formal ethical theory about 1960 in the Soviet Union led to a concern with more precise definitions of terms, and particularly to an attempt to characterize both *moral'* (morality), as a social phenomenon, and *etika* (ethics), as the science of morality, in a manner consistent with the general perspectives of dialectical and historical materialism.[1]

The Russian language contains two terms which are normally translated by 'morality': *moral'* and *nravstvennost'*. The second is based on a Slavic root meaning 'custom' or 'more', and hence can be regarded as a simply synonym of the first.[2] However the two terms provide a natural means for rendering Hegel's distinction between *'Moralität'* and *'Sittlichkeit'* in Russian, and are so used, *'Moralität'* being translated by *'moral"* and *'Sittlichkeit'* by *'nravstvennost"*.[3] Following Russian translations of Hegel, some Soviet authors have used *'moral"* to signify the subjectively moral, and *'nravstvennost"* to signify the objectively moral; others have used the terms in the reverse senses.[4] Still others have wanted to use *'moral"* as a form of consciousness and *'nravstvennost"* as a form of practical activity. The two terms have also been used to distinguish between the regulation of behavior by strict rules and external compulsion, versus voluntarily adopted, internal standards.[5] However the large majority of writers on ethical theory do not choose to make a systematic distinction between the uses of the two terms, and they are freely employed as synonyms in much Soviet philosophical literature.[6]

Because it is one of the clearly established categories of historical materialism, *morality* has long been thought of as one of the elements of social consciousness ranking along with politics, law, religion and art as a phenomenon fundamentally determined by social being. In other terms, it is one of the elements of the ideological superstructure and as such a product of the economic base. It shares all the standard properties of such superstructural phenomena, which were enumerated by one Soviet moral philosopher in part as follows: (1) it appears as a result of the reflection in people's heads of the material conditions of their social being; (2) its development is not autonomous, but produced, secondary, in relation to social being, and hence its

historical development is determined by the historical development of material social relations; (3) once arisen on this basis however, morality exhibits
a 'relative autonomy' in which it may fail to reflect the objective world adequately, and may also influence the development of the material (economic)
base itself, as well as that of other superstructural phenomena such as the
state, politics, culture, science, etc.[7]

The necessity of maintaining this fundamental Marxist distinction between
social consciousness and social being leads in this case, as in others, to a number of difficulties. It would appear difficult to provide an adequate account
of morality either exclusively in terms of 'social consciousness' or exclusively
in terms of 'social being'. As L. M. Arxangel'skij recently observed,

Morality is unquestionably one of the forms of social consciousness. But at the same
time it is also an essential aspect of social activity, inasmuch as the originating and
terminating point of all moral prescriptions is human deeds, behavior.[8]

Hence, "the distinction between moral consciousness and moral practice does
not signify their absolute opposition. Morality is a contradictory unity of the
spiritual and the practical . . .".[9]

This difficulty of reconciling the standard Marxist definition of morality as
an element of social consciousness (rather than of social being) with the
obvious truth that morality refers to certain types of *behavior*, and social
relations motivated by certain conscious projects, leads to a number of problems in defining 'morality'. Addressing himself to some of these difficulties,
O. G. Drobnickij maintained that the problem of identifying the constituent
elements of morality had not received adequate attention. Some authors, he
said, identified morality as a whole simply with *moral consciousness*. Others
included *moral action* and *moral relations* as constitutive elements. Drobnickij
himself defined 'morality' as constituted of all three elements: moral consciousness, moral action, and moral relations.[10]

In the most literal possible application of the Marxist categories, the *moral
relations* in question could be viewed as a component of the *social relations*
(*productive relations*) which together with the *forces of production* constitute
the *material basis* of society. *Moral consciousness* could then be viewed, in
one of the standard categories of Soviet philosophy, as a simple *reflection* of
the more basic *material, social relations*. This desire to describe morality in
accordance with the most fundamental concepts of Marxist sociology has led
writers such as G. D. Bandzeladze to posit some objective phenomenon which
could be viewed as the 'object' (and *basis*) of moral consciousness, such that
moral consciousness would obtain its own identity through being a reflection

of that object. Bandzeladze observed that "the basis of consciousness in general is the relation of an individual to the reality surrounding him", and argued that "consciousness can have no other content than a reflection of reality".[11] Accordingly he defined this reality of which moral consciousness is the reflection, as "the specific inter-relations with one another and society as a whole" in which people stand.[12] Judgments expressing these real relations are called "rules, norms and principles of behavior".[13] Moral consciousness, in turn, is defined as "the totality of people's views toward these rules of behavior and inter-relations of interests".[14] Bandzeladze concluded that moral consciousness as a rule is expressed in actions, hence morality includes not only moral consciousness but also "practical moral action".[15] The appeal to Soviet theorists of this particular strategy for defining 'morality' should be obvious.

In similar fashion, in an earlier work, Utkin described the distinguishing characteristic of morality as the fact that "it reflects norms of behavior of people objectively taking shape in society in such concepts as 'the good', 'honesty', 'conscience', 'justice', etc., which have an evaluative character".[16]

Criticizing the simple application of this distinction between social being and social consciousness, however, other writers such as Šiškin and Švarcman have complained of the tendency in Marxist literature to hold that moral concepts and judgments possess objective content to the extent that they reflect moral relations supposedly constituting an element of the productive relations, or a tendency to speak of the existence of ethical qualities of social reality similar to the objective properties of material objects existing independently of human beings. "Morality in this fashion is converted into the reflection of ethical or moral qualities of reality existing independently of people."[17] Amending this view, Šiškin and Švarcman claim that morality consists not merely in a reflection of some objective social relations, not merely in an element of consciousness, "but as a form of social practice, regulating the relations of people to each other and to society".[18] Ethical concepts, just as esthetic ones, reflect a "dialectical connection of the object and the subject". An evaluation always presupposes a clear position of the one who produces it — his conceptions of good and evil, which are connected with definite social views, ideals, etc. Hence these authors speak of the "impossibility of viewing moral relations as something existing independently of social consciousness, as something being formed 'without passing through consciousness' ".[19]

In her work *Theoretical Problems of Ethics*, Švarcman takes the view that morality can be characterized in terms of two concepts, 'moral consciousness' and 'moral relations', but doubts the usefulness of the concept 'moral action'. Other authors, such as Xarčev and Jakovlev, disagree; they insist that the concept 'moral action' cannot be discarded while the concept 'moral relations' is retained, on the grounds that 'social relations' and 'social action' are not only closely-related, but in some respects identical, concepts.[20]

The problem of defining 'moral relations' and relating that concept to the distinction between social consciousness and social being was pursued at a conference in Novosibirsk in 1969. Several participants undertook to defend the importance of 'moral relations' as a distinct component of morality. A. K. Uledov claimed that "moral relations, in our opinion, are neither partially nor completely related to the sphere of consciousness. They exist outside consciousness as real practical relations among people".[21] Nevertheless, in their formation, moral relations "pass through the moral consciousness of people".[22] N. A. Trofimov described moral relations as "morality itself in its real living manifestation", as "the most essential category of ethics".[23] G. E. Borisov claimed that "distinguishing moral relations from moral consciousness is both advisable and fruitful".[24]

Such views as these, emphasizing the concept of 'moral relations' as a distinct component of morality have come to represent the dominant view among Soviet moral philosophers on this question.[25] Consequently, some earlier, previously widely-reiterated definitions of 'morality' such as that in the *Philosophical Encyclopedia* ("a conjunction of principles, rules, norms by which people are guided in their behavior") have been criticized for their exclusively 'mentalistic' emphasis.[26]

Drobnickij and Bandzeladze have each pointed out a problem inherent in the most usual attempts to define morality in terms of certain types of relations obtaining in society: the types of relations in question are normally identified as *moral* relations, norms, principles, or ideals, producing an obvious definitional circle. Or where 'morality' is not defined in terms of *moral* norms and principles the latter are not then distinguished from legal, customary, and other norms. Hence in neither case can the definition be considered successful.[27]

The apparent agreement by a majority of Soviet ethical theorists to view *moral relations* as a distinct component of *morality* does not really resolve the issue of whether these moral relations are to be regarded in some sense as the 'real', 'objective' ('material') phenomenon of which moral consciousness is merely the reflection. A number of authors have argued that *moral relations* are dependent on *moral consciousness* for their identity, and not the other way around. Drobnickij, for example, objects to all forms of the strategy of

defining 'morality' in terms of some underlying reality of which moral consciousness could be said to be the reflection. The attempt to define 'moral
consciousness' in terms of some objective component of social relations is
defeated, according to him, because "moral consciousness does not have to
do with some particular sphere of social life".[28] He argues that

Moral behavior, the analysis of which must be placed at the basis of the construction of
a system of moral phenomena, cannot be empirically separated out as a fact immediately
distinguished from others: the concept of moral behavior is a theoretical abstraction,
selecting out a certain aspect of the complex phenomena of social life. Morality is not an
isolated sphere of human activity, or behavior, but a specific means of regulating it,
independent of the objective content of the action.[29]

Morality of course is not alone among the means of regulating social activity;
there are also material interests, legal norms, charters and arrangements of
particular organizations, decrees of the state and ideas of socio-political
doctrines as well, not to mention uninstitutionalized regulators of behavior
such as folk custom, national traditions, collective rituals and ceremonials,
canons of etiquette, and life-styles approved by various groups. Morality is
interwoven with all of these and "constitutes only some sort of aspect or side
but by no means an objectively isolated, empirically observable phenomenon".[30] If morality has any single distinguishing feature in comparison with
all these other means of regulation, it is perhaps in the role of "higher authority and judge, prescribing, founding, justifying, or condemning" reasons,
interests, or goals of action.

   From this perspective, Drobnickij rejected Bandzeladze's (and also Utkin's)
attempts to define 'morality'.[31] "As it turns out we are not in a position immediately to indicate that criterion by which it would be possible to separate
out moral actions and relations from the complex totality of other spheres of
social life and means of regulation."[32] Instead, Drobnickij suggests, only
'moral consciousness' can be separated out, distinguished from all other forms
of spiritual culture by means of a simple reference to moral norms, principles,
ideals, concepts of good and evil, conscience, honor, and justice known to
us.[33]

   In short, moral consciousness is not definable by reference to some object
— moral action or moral relations in society — of which it is the reflection;
rather moral action and moral relations are abstractions from social reality
which can be identified only by prior reference to well-established concepts
of 'moral consciousness' which has already historically produced its work of
abstraction, defining its own object in the process.[34]

Drobnickij is not alone in defending this more complex 'dialectical' view of the relation between moral consciousness and moral relations. Šiškin and Švarcman, Arxangel'skij, Titarenko, Ivanov and Rybakova, and Tugarinov, among others, have all emphasized one aspect or another of this view.[35] Their view appears to be that, although *moral relations* are a distinct aspect of *morality*, they are constituted only by passing through *moral consciousness*, another component of morality, and consequently the connection between morality and the productive basis of society is mediated through *moral consciousness* or a "moral-evaluative orientation".[36] This fact of course also entails that 'subjective, individual' factors as well as 'objective, social' factors must be considered in the definition of 'morality'.

In this way the attempt to define 'morality' has led a number of Soviet philosophers to focus their attention on 'moral consciousness' as opposed to 'moral relations' or 'moral action' in the belief that morality as a social phenomenon can only be defined after 'moral consciousness' has been successfully analyzed.

Drobnickij in particular devoted a large part of his attention to the analysis of 'moral consciousness' in the years 1968–73.[37] As an example of one of the most detailed treatments of 'moral consciousness' available in Soviet literature, Drobnickij's views will be briefly summarized here. Drobnickij believed that 'moral consciousness' possessed a stable *structure*, divided into three branches, each of which had evolved according to its own historical logic. By 'structure' he meant 'logical' or 'conceptual' structure; hence the analysis of the structure of moral consciousness for him entailed a study of the historical sequence of evolution of each of the groups of concepts or logical forms comprising a branch of moral consciousness. In addition to individual concepts, the 'logical forms' which he thought he could order in their sequence of historical development were primarily types of imperatival phrases. (This project was partly inspired by the work of two contemporary German philosophers who have had substantial influence upon Soviet ethical theory: F. Loeser and W. Eichhorn, both of whom have undertaken to distinguish and classify imperatival expressions according to logical form).[38]

In this analysis of the structure of moral consciousness Drobnickij distinguished three branches: 1. conceptual forms of moral consciousness expressing the demands of society toward the mass of individuals and to each individual separately (involving the concepts 'norm', 'moral code', 'forbidden', 'obligatory', 'good', 'evil', 'moral qualities', 'moral ideal', and 'moral principle'); 2. conceptual forms of moral consciousness directed to social reality (involving the concepts 'social ideal', 'social justice', 'meaning of life', and 'destiny of man'); and 3. conceptual forms expressing individual (subjective) moral demands (involving the concepts 'duty', 'responsibility', 'conscience', 'self-evaluation', 'honor', and 'dignity').[39]

The analysis of all these terms as well as of certain imperatival forms provided by Drobnickij relied primarily upon notions of logical simplicity and complexity. He assumed that the logically simpler (more basic) concepts and forms must have developed earlier, in historical terms, than logically more complex concepts and forms. In this manner he believed that the analysis of moral consciousness could be carried out equally well by relying *either* primarily on logical analysis, *or* primarily on anthropological, ethnographical and other historical data; if the general assumption were correct, either procedure should yield approximately the same results. Drobnickij himself relied mainly on an analysis of the simplicity or primitiveness of the terms in question, but did not hesitate to equate the results of his analysis with historical generalizations offering approximate dates for the evolution of each form in terms of Marxist socio-historical categories.

Confining his discussion initially to the first of the three supposed dimensions of 'moral consciousness', Drobnickij declared the simplest (most basic) form of moral demand to be 'You must immediately act thusly' or 'That act is evil', addressed to some particular individual under specific circumstances.[40] Such judgments need not be moral ones of course and become so only where the authority for the demand does not merely depend upon the will of the individual speaker making it, but proceeds from a rule which applies generally to all persons in the society. (This would be a necessary, but surely not a sufficient condition for a moral imperative). Such a rule would be a *norm*, which constitutes the simplest possible foundation for unique prescriptions in individual cases. The logical formula for norms expressing the general obligatoriness and impersonal nature of the demand would appear to be: 'All people must (must not) act in such-and-such fashion'.[41] Although the generalized norm was implicit in such moral judgments, Drobnickij points out that the actual prescriptions found in most ancient documents (such as the Bible) are of the form 'Do such and such' or 'You must . . .', which he attributes to the fact that such ancient forms of moral demand arose in the context of a religious consciousness in which moral duties were interpreted as commands of God to individual believers.[42] A collection of such norms together comprised the simplest form of *moral code*, which prescribed a form of life as a whole, rather than merely guiding conduct in a variety of special situations.

From this circumstance developed the most generalized (even tautological) form of prescription: 'Everyone must do what is obligatory, and refrain from what is forbidden'. The 'forbidden' and the 'obligatory' in this abstract sense are, Drobnickij claims, the simplest forms of the concepts *'good'* and *'evil'*.[43]

Supposedly the next major stage in the development of the first branch of moral consciousness was the appearance of the concept of *moral qualities* or *traits of character*, a development which Drobnickij believed to have taken place in late *gens* society, "when the individual for the first time becomes an independent bearer and personification of social morality possessing such distinguishing characteristics as bravery, endurance,' etc.[44] Such qualities were viewed as internal traits of character, and consequently one's character at this time came to be viewed as subject to training. In connection with the concept of moral qualities also appeared such concepts as 'self-education' (*samo-vospitanie*), 'courage', 'honesty', etc. The concept of 'trait of character' did not however include either the notion of an inner integrity or wholeness of the moral person, or the indefinitely great perfectibility of individual character, both of which notions are signified by the term 'moral ideal'. "The paradigm of moral perfectibility was conceived as the universal fulfillment of all possible accomplishments of humanity."[45] This concept of the 'moral ideal' arose together for the first time with the concept of 'humanity in general', as distinguished from membership in a particular culture or state, both developments taking place in the writings of the Stoics.

With the appearance of the moral ideal in the structure of moral consciousness as a whole, the contradiction between existing conditions of life and that which ought to be was greatly exacerbated.[46] With the appearance of the concept of membership in humanity as a whole rather than in some particular political order, there arose a need for some guidance in conduct which did not derive entirely from customs and traditions of a particular culture. This function was fulfilled by the development of *moral principles*, extremely widely formulated normative expressions fixing the 'essence' or 'significance' of humanity, revealing the meaning and general purpose of human activity. The development of such moral principles freed the individual to make his own moral decisions; hence the concept of autonomy of the moral individual appeared at the same time (in the period of 'late antiquity').[47]

The second dimension of moral consciousness hypothesized by Drobnickij arose when the moral consciousness of the autonomous individual, expressed in the form of moral principles, was succeeded by a new form of consciousness encompassing duties to *society as a whole, social ideals*, and *justice*. This dimension of moral consciousness Drobnickij regarded as a more or less distinct one, ultimately encompassing such things as norms expressing moral duties of society itself toward the individual. Such a consciousness arose in the context of extreme contrasts of poverty and luxury, oppression and power in society, giving rise to concepts of alternatives to the existing condition such as a golden age, the kingdom of God, or more recently the idea of social progress. All of these constitute social ideals, and each is founded on a still more complex concept of *social justice*. These two concepts, *social ideals* and *social justice*, constitute the nucleus of this dimension of moral consciousness. They are supplemented however by certain additional concepts such as the *meaning of life* and the *destiny of man*.[48]

The third dimension of moral consciousness identified by Drobnickij concerns individual (subjective) forms of moral demands. The concepts examined here include 'duty', 'responsibility', 'conscience', 'self-evaluation', 'honor', and 'individual dignity'; and as before, the historical appearance of each of these is roughly dated in terms of the Marxist scheme of sociohistorical stages, as part of the account of the origin and development of moral consciousness.[49]

Drobnickij's project of sketching in the logical structure of 'moral consciousness' as a history of the moralities of various cultures (in part a history of ethical theory) obviously owes something of its over-all conception to Hegel's *Phenomenology of Spirit*. Hegel's project of deriving the science of phenomenology from a study of the stages of natural consciousness, characterized in epistemological terms, is roughly paralleled by Drobnickij's attempt to derive ethical theory from a study of the stages of moral consciousness, characterized in terms of the evolution of the logical forms of norms and moral concepts. It proceeds by the method of a logical (speculative) reconstruction of the order and sequence of that evolution through an analysis of the present result of that historical process.

In some explicit remarks on the method of his own inquiry, Drobnickij cited the appearance of continuity and gradual development "which retrospectively presents itself as a completely logical and consistent development and concretization of concepts and ideas".[50] This appearance of completely logical and consistent development is possible "only due to the fact that several general lawful regularities of the development of society are crystallized in the structure of moral consciousness".[51] The moral consciousness resulting from this process grows by the accretion of concepts in various epochs, each of which may be incorporated into the structure of moral consciousness at a different time. Previously incorporated concepts may also be gradually modified in significance as a result of this evolutionary process. Given such a notion of moral consciousness, Drobnickij saw the essence of his method as lying in a certain 'correlation of the logical and the historical':

The problem arises of the inter-relation of the factual, empirical path of formation of morality in the actual historical process, and the 'logical' formation of the structure of moral consciousness — its lawfully-sequenced 'construction', its movement from the simple to the complex, the building up of ever more concretely-developed elements, etc. It appears that in some of the most general respects here it is possible to speak of a correlation of the logical and the historical. At the very least it is possible to establish parallels of a sort between the historical genesis and the theoretical consistency of the formation of the structure of moral consciousness.[52]

Notwithstanding this general 'coincidence' of logical and historical development, Drobnickij acknowledged that it could not be treated "in any sense categorically, let us say, tying the development of this or that element of morality to some chronological dates and concrete epochs", due to the lack of sufficient historical and ethnographical materials.[53] Consequently Drobnickij chose "the path of logical exposition and development of the structure as a whole in accordance with the way it appears in established form". He believed that such an approach nevertheless justified him in making observations about 'certain nodal points of causality' in the historical process of the development of moral consciousness.[54]

It might be argued that an enterprise which owes so much to the example of the method of Hegel's *Phenomenology of Spirit* would do well to give an explicit justification for borrowing elements of that method, most especially where the justifying assumptions inherent in the larger argument of Hegel's logic and metaphysics have been abandoned. As Drobnickij presents it, his method appears to lean indiscriminately on philosophical analysis, the study of social history and ethnography, the history of ethical theory, and Marxist philosophy of history.

Other theorists have undertaken similar approaches to the study of morality stressing one or the other of these various types of inquiry. A. I. Titarenko for example has stressed the necessity of drawing heavily on history and the social sciences in the analysis of the structure of morality; he speaks of the impossibility of resolving the problem by means of "abstract-speculative, purely terminological specifications and distinctions".[55] Titarenko undertakes an approach to the study of morality which emphasizes the role of emotions, feelings, and intuition in shaping the moral consciousness of each particular culture and epoch; the description he seeks of the moral consciousness of any culture would necessarily draw upon literary, artistic, and other materials constituting the particular history of that culture. He emphasizes the multitude of essentially unpredictable features which affect the development of particular moral cultures through history and insists that only the most detailed historical studies can resolve the question of the nature of moral consciousness.

At the other extreme, authors such as O. P. Celikova have stressed the necessity for close study of the language and logical forms of moral judgments, placing relatively less stress on the historical factors which Titarenko and Drobnickij advocated. Celikova pays particular attention to the possibility of distinguishing all normative judgments into a number of basic types, which could then be ordered into an analysis of all the forms of moral consciousness, an approach inspired partly by the two German philosophers mentioned above.[56]

Not every approach to the problem of defining morality found in Soviet literature has been presented here, but enough has been said to suggest the spectrum of approaches to be found. A recent Soviet textbook of ethics, commenting on this problem, simply declared that the structure of morality is a problem which remains poorly worked out.[57]

Notwithstanding the above-mentioned difficulties, the general intent of most Soviet definitions of 'morality' remains clear: to emphasize the *social* nature of morality and to interpret its development in accordance with *objective laws of history* as established by historical materialism. Morality is to be conceived as a *social* phenomenon in several very different respects. First of all, no ground for moral judgments or principles is to be located in non-naturalistic modes of judgment, or by references to a noumenal world, or by relation to a supra-historical frame of reference. Second, the authority for moral judgments is not to be ultimately located in an autonomous individual moral agent, but in the social collective, or perhaps 'history'. Third, inquiry into the *nature* of moral concepts and principles is to be satisfied primarily by the study of their *genesis* as part of the evolution of human social forms. In these respects Soviet ethical theory remains quite faithful to the views of Engels in *Anti-Dühring.*[58]

The assumption that the most important questions about moral concepts and principles are to be answered by an inquiry into their historical, social genesis has naturally led to an elaborate concern with a kind of ethnographical and anthropological speculation about the early history of morality and other forms of social regulation of conduct. Soviet authors are relatively more confident of their grounds in such discussions as these, but a certain range of disagreement persists. A number of authors have maintained that some form of morality as a means of regulating individual conduct in relation to the purposes of the group must have arisen simultaneously with socially-organized productive labor, in the earliest transition from forms of life governed by

animal instinct.[59] Others have argued that the problem of regulating the conflict between individual interests and group interests, or morality proper,
arose only comparatively recently in history when the self-conscious individual actively pursuing his own interests in opposition to those of the society
developed from a previous form of individual consciousness which was essentially communal in nature.[60] Though a substantial literature on such problems
can be found in Soviet publications, the issues involved will not be pursued
here.

A further dimension of the discussion of morality has developed in recent
years — the question of the *functions* of morality. The nucleus of a specialized
literature on this subject already exists and appears to be expanding.[61] Morality functions primarily, in the view of many Soviet authors, to regulate the
conduct of individuals in such a way as to harmonize individual and social
interests. For example Drobnickij unequivocally views the regulative function
as primary.[62] Arxangel'skii agrees that regulation constitutes the leading function of morality, but also discusses two others: its educational (*vospitatel'naja*)
function and its cognitive function.[63] T. S. Lapina as well as A. I. Titarenko
have linked the discussion of the functions of morality with the discussion of
its structure.[64] Lapina describes the 'value-orienting' function of morality as
dependent on the 'philosophical concepts of morality' (by which presumably
she refers to the 'world-view' implicit in any moral system, a point discussed
by several Soviet authors); the regulative function of morality as dependent
upon the 'prescriptive side of morality'; and the function of 'forming the
social subject' as dependent upon the basic forms of self-knowledge of the
subject such as "duty, conscience, responsibility, honesty and dignity, etc.".[65]
The most elaborate discussion of the problem has been provided by Titarenko,
who distinguishes no less than eight functions of morality: regulative, educational, cognitive, value-imperative, orientational, motivational, communica-
tive, and prognostic.[66] Interest in this topic among Soviet ethical theorists
appears to be growing, but as yet has not produced any especially striking
results.

2. THE SCIENCE OF ETHICS AND ITS OBJECT

The general intent of most Soviet definitions of 'ethics' as a science has been
clear for some time. S. Utkin stated that intent as succinctly as possible by
saying, "Ethics is the study of morality, its special characteristics, and laws
of development."[67] As described just above, 'morality' has yet to be defined

with any notable success; that difficulty aside however, most Soviet authors
are in close agreement that ethics is to be construed as a 'science' with 'morality' as its object of investigation.

One of the older, but most widely copied definitions of 'ethics' and its
object was given by A. F. Šiškin:

> Marxist-Leninist ethics is the science of the social essence and lawful regularities of
> development of morality as a particular form of social consciousness; of the lawful
> regularities of moral progress the result of which is Communist morality, a higher stage
> of the moral development of society and personality; of the lawful regularities of
> development of Communist morality, of its principles and norms, of its role in the
> struggle for Communism.[68]

More recently-offered definitions still adhere rather closely to this formula:

> Marxist ethics is the science of the essence, laws of origin and historical development of
> morality, of Communist morality in particular; of the specific functions of morality; of
> the moral values of social life.[69]

The language used in Soviet definitions of ethics usually suggests that the
relation between the science and the object investigated does not differ
fundamentally in ethics from that between any empirical science and its
object. That impression is usually qualified however by some discussion
of ethics as a 'philosophical science'. Acknowledging this ambivalence,
Bandzeladze remarks that,

> Insofar as morality is a social phenomenon, to that extent ethics is related to the class of
> social sciences. But on the other hand, morality is a form of consciousness, constituting
> part of humanity's world-views; for that reason ethics is related to the class of philo-
> sophical sciences, and is a part of philosophy.[70]

Not all Soviet authors agree to this dual characterization of ethics, however.
A very recent collective text *Marxist Ethics* observes that some authors consider ethics a division of philosophy, but others regard it as a special science
which, like psychology or mathematics, has already cut its ties with philosophy. The majority, however, like Bandzeladze above, "reject these extreme
conclusions".[71] This middle view shared by the majority in effect leaves the
matter in ambiguity: "ethics, although it is a philosophical science, has its
specific object of investigation, distinguishing it from other philosophical
sciences".[72] It is neither a pure philosophical inquiry, nor strictly speaking a
special science, but both. The existence of this 'compromise' view explains
much of the linguistic style characteristic of Soviet writing on ethical theory,
and certain common methodological assumptions as well.

This ambiguity appears in many discussions of the 'normative' nature of Soviet ethics. Bandzeladze explains that ethics studies moral norms and in that sense is a normative science. But it is not normative "in the sense that it supposedly itself formulates and establishes moral norms".

Ethics investigates the nature, essence, and prospects for development of moral norms already formed in the practice of social life. The object of ethics is the natural-historical necessity of the development of morality; for that reason ethics is a theoretical science.[73]

On the same subject, the text *Marxist Ethics* describes ethics as "called upon to reproduce morality ideally, *to scientifically ground its necessity, origin, essence, special characteristics, role in society, laws of development*".[74] Ethics is described as a *normative* science which does not merely represent morals, "but gives them a *critical-evaluative, party-committed analysis*".[75] Such a conception of ethics, in the view of these authors, avoids the two unacceptable extremes of ethics as purely normative or as positivistic-scientistic. "If ethics is limited to working out and formulating norms of conduct and values, it ceases to be a science, [and] is converted to didacticism, to moralization."[76] Hence the double conclusion that ethics is normative, "but its normativity is based on objective scientific analysis"; and is scientific, "but its scientific nature leads to the grounding of a definite moral ideal".[77]

A slightly different view of the relation between the science of ethics and its object, morality, can be found in the *Dictionary of Ethics*. The authors there, after noting the distinction between normative ethics and metaethics current in much non-Marxist ethical literature, interpret this distinction as meaning that in non-Marxist views, if ethics pretends to be a science, it must refrain from the task of formulating moral principles, or, if it remains 'practical philosophy', it must reject principles of scientific thinking.[78] (The authors ignore the problem of what they mean by 'science' and whether there is any univocal use of that term which renders their view coherent). In their view "only Marxist-Leninist ethical science correctly resolves the question of the relation of ethics to its object — morality".[79]

It proceeds from the fact that moral principles are not established by philosophers, but are worked out in the process of social practice. In them is reflected the enormous life experience of many generations. Ethics generalizes and systematizes these principles, and develops a theoretical understanding of their content.[80]

Marxist-Leninist ethical science turns out not to be quite so passive as this would suggest, however. After the emergence of a scientific theory of the development of society, revealing in part the laws of development of morality

(Marxism), ethics supposedly became capable of providing scientific grounding for moral principles, demonstrating the rationality of some and subjecting others to rational criticism.[81]

In this sense Soviet conceptions of the science of ethics move slightly closer to more usual non-Marxist conceptions of moral philosophy, as an inquiry aimed at justifying specific moral principles. However the canon of rationality to which the *Dictionary* appeals is evidently a special one: Marxist philosophy of history, the 'laws of development' of society and incidentally of morality. One of the most significant, and most elusive, features of Soviet ethical theory lies in the relation asserted between this specific theory of history and the moral principles which are viewed as a lawful product of that history. The relation in question is understood by many Soviet philosophers to *justify* or demonstrate the rationality of specific moral principles. Explaining precisely how this justification occurs could be viewed as the central task and challenge of Marxist-Leninist ethical theory.[82] It is obviously closely related to the problem pointed out in the previous section, of explaining the 'correlation between the logical and the historical' which is presupposed by the method of inquiry most typical of Soviet ethical studies.

In connection with this problem of defining the science of ethics, and its object, morality, Soviet writers have repeatedly emphasized a particular theme: that the terms 'good', 'duty', 'right', 'conscience', etc. must be understood to have one set of meanings when employed in ordinary moral discourse, or morality, and quite another when employed as 'categories' of the science of ethics.

A. G. Xarčev was one of the first to emphasize this distinction, in the concluding article of an extended discussion of problems of ethical theory organized by the editorial board of *Filosofskie nauki* between 1961 and 1965.[83] This series commenced with an article by L. M. Arxangel'skij on the categories of ethics, and later revolved about his book on the same subject. In his article, Xarčev objected to the view that the concepts of ethical theory were to be distinguished from those of ordinary moral discourse only by their greater systematization, a view implying that ethical theory is only the theoretical dimension of morality itself. Ethics, according to Xarčev, is a science of the essence and laws of development of morality relating not to the moral but to the scientific understanding of society.[84] Failure to maintain such a strict distinction between the concepts as employed in scientific ethical theory and the concepts employed in ordinary moral discourse constituted the primary shortcoming of Arxangel'skij's work in Xarčev's view.

The thesis of a systematic distinction between the meanings of terms employed in scientific ethics and the meanings of the same terms employed in ordinary moral discourse received further impetus from the discussion of Mil'ner-Irinin's writings on ethics.[85] In his major work on ethics Mil'ner-Irinin adopted an exhortatory style of writing in which each paragraph or group of paragraphs was numbered, and each based on some point or thesis expressed in imperatival form. In a formally-arranged discussion of Mil'ner-Irinin's work reported in *Voprosy Filosofii*, Drobnickij complained that

... many absurd and contradictory positions in the articles of Mil'ner-Irinin flow from the fact that the author confuses ethics and morality. Striving to create a theoretical work, he, however, thinks in the framework of a moral, and not a theoretical, consciousness, i.e., not as a theoretician, but as a moralist . . . .[86]

Drobnickij further accused Mil'ner-Irinin of mixing 'normative logic' with 'scientific-theoretical logic'.

In subsequent years this thesis of the distinction between the scientific or ethical, and the moral uses of terms has grown to the status of a well-established view of many Soviet theorists. Drobnickij, Xarčev, Jakovlev, Celikova have all continued to expand upon this theme.[87] A typical argument for this distinction can be found in Drobnickij's writings, where he defends the view that terms employed in the 'apparatus of categories of research' in scientific ethics signify "not at all those concepts with which moral consciousness operates".[88]

For example, moral consciousness thinks of 'duty' as that conduct which must be fulfilled by some concrete subject . . . . Here moral necessity is the immanent content of the thought . . . . Moral consciousness expresses obligation 'through itself', doesn't distinguish its representation of 'duty' from that which it is required to perform . . . . Besides, the general concept of duty is present here as a logical form, a deontological modality of thought and as a binding means of expression of will or motive to action, that is as a stratum of consciousness and experience of the moral subject. It is another matter when a theoretician considers moral duty. He subjects to analysis this normative logic of thought and phenomenology of feeling and will, describes them and reveals behind them those social relations of morality (appearing in the specific form of moral necessity) which found expression in them, shows the mechanism of motivation and performance of conduct, etc. The concept of duty for him is the sphere and structure of theoretical problems arising here, and not that stratum of thought and experience itself which would compel him personally to perform deeds or prescribe them to someone else. In other words, he regards the given form of consciousness 'from the side', while his own logic of investigation is extra-normative or even meta-normative . . . .[89]

Not every writer has been quite so convinced of the importance of such a distinction, however. Arxangel'skij for example recognizes a distinction between 'ethical categories' and 'moral concepts', but emphasizes their 'genetic and functional communality' and the fact that they 'are formed at the boundary between two forms of social consciousness: morality and science'.[90]

The insistence of many Soviet writers on this distinction between the 'categories of the science of ethics' and the 'concepts of moral consciousness' appears misplaced to the present writer. If one assumes with them, for the moment, that ethics constitutes, or ought to constitute, a 'strict science' (ignoring the great variety of senses in which this term may be used) along with the other Marxist sciences of society, there remains a substantial difficulty with the thesis. It appears to assume the existence of a special scientific language for ethical theory including a vocabulary of technical terms with precise meanings already distinguished from those implicit in other inquiries and forms of discourse in which these same terms might appear. Moreover, several writers speak as though use of a particular 'logic' unique to the science of ethics also constitutes a pre-condition of inquiry in this field. Such a 'logic' would amount to a developed theory of the phenomena in question, specifying, by implication, logical relations among the crucial terms of the technical vocabulary employed. The development of such a language and theory would however mark the maturity of any such special science and could only be the final product of, and never a pre-condition of, scientific inquiry into a particular field of phenomena. By stipulating that scientific ethics proceed only by the application of such a developed language, one in effect ignores the fact that no science can begin without the initial use of largely informal, inexact terminology borrowed from everyday language. The sharpening of such language, the introduction of special terms, and the development of precise logical relations among them are all marks of progress in the development of a science. In the beginning however, the view which Xarčev rejected must surely be correct: the terminology of ethical theory can be distinguished from that of ordinary moral discourse initially only by an aspiration to greater precision and systematization; ethical theory can only be 'the theoretical dimension of morality itself' in its early stages, regardless of what assumptions one harbors about its eventual attainment of the status of a mature 'science'.

As for the possibility that Soviet ethical theorists have already achieved such results for a science of ethics, it appears that the subject of the exact methods of the science of ethics has only just begun to be explored. A few authors have begun to use 'metaethics' as a synonym for the 'methodology' of the science of ethics. One author recently observed that "in Soviet litera-ture essentially no more-or-less definite and argued opinions relative to the possible constitution of metaethics have been expressed".[91] The author of this opinion pursues the possibility that 'metaethics' might be interpreted as the 'methodology' of ethics, and cites one other Soviet work of similar tendency in which metaethics is defined as containing four problems: 1. the foundation of ethics as a science, 2. the study of methods of ethical research, 3. problems connected with the justification of specific categories, concepts and terms of ethics, and 4. problems related to the study of the internal structure of ethical knowledge.[92] They refer to the work of the Polish Marxist M. Fritzhand as dealing with the problem of metaethics in far greater detail than any Soviet work to date. Hence the opinion that a Soviet science of ethics has already developed to maturity would seem to be difficult to defend.

The primary oddity about the general view of ethics just sketched remains the one pointed out at the beginning. Non-Marxist conceptions of metaethics are criticized for implying that if ethics pretends to be a science (metaethics) it must refrain from the task of formulating moral principles (setting aside the problem of the accuracy of this interpretation of non-Marxist metaethics). The Marxist-Leninist science of ethics on the other hand is meant to achieve the status of an exact science and yet at the same time provide the justification of specific principles of Communist morality. But that is possible only if 'science' can supply justifications for moral principles. The conception of science (and of the method of the science of ethics) which appears to supply this special requirement is termed 'the unity of the logical and the historical' and can probably be explained (but not necessarily defended in this form) by tracing its paternity to Hegel.

The principle of the unity of the logical and the historical is the true reference-point in the investigation of any moral phenomenon by means of its expression in definite thought forms. Transgression of the principle of historicism and abstract logical schemas created apart from it, always lead to sad consequences and unscientific conclusions.[93]

Celikova had in mind the most striking example of a departure from the standard conceptions of the nature of ethical theory to appear in print in the Soviet Union in many years — the view of Ja. A. Mil'ner-Irinin. Mil'ner-Irinin attempted to dispense with the usual element of empirical social science in Marxist-Leninist conceptions of ethics, and boldly declared that

... ethics is not at all a science of what is, was, or will be — granting even that present, past or future is characterized as a manifestation of that same moral consciousness — it is uniquely a science of that which, in accordance with the moral consciousness of humanity, ought to be, in principle, even granted that what is asserted by conscience as that which ought to be doesn't exist, didn't exist, and even never will exist in reality — in consequence of its lack of grounds.[94]

Carrying this thesis still further, he argued that

Since ethics is the science of that which ought to be, and not of that which is, it is evident that this or that phenomenon of moral consciousness, regarded as a fact of existence, is related, strictly speaking, not to ethics proper, not to the science of ethics as such, but to the history of moral views and ethical doctrines, or to sociology. Accordingly, this in the proper sense of that concept is not at all a science of what and why people in various times and in various cultures and in the capacity as representatives of these or those social classes perceived as moral, as morally obligatory, in one word, as that which ought to be — as that which in the light of their moral convictions ought to be, but the science of that which must be accepted as that which ought to be (morally obligatory) and of the grounds forcing (us) to count that as obligatory and not this.[95]

Mil'ner-Irinin's resolute view of the nature of ethics places him well outside any general consensus ascertainable from the mass of Soviet publications in ethical theory. His views were systematically criticized in a special conference convened to discuss an anthology in which they were published.[96] (However in the late sixties and early seventies, many Soviet moral philosophers informally regarded one of the most important divisions amongst themselves as that between opponents and supporters of Mil'ner-Irinin's views).[97]

Another rather special view of the nature of ethics was expressed by P. M. Egides in the same anthology as well as in other places. He observed that "almost all contemporary philosopher-Marxists writing on ethics term it a philosophical science". The majority do that, he said, "not noticing that neither from the definition of ethics which they give, nor from the content of morality exposited by them, does this follow".[98] He argued that ethics does constitute a 'philosophical science', but for a rather atypical reason. Philosophical science includes, in his view, only those inquiries which are not confined exclusively to the study of material objects, nature, or existence, and not confined exclusively to the study of the ideal, of thought or spirit. To philosophy belong "only those sciences which study the relations between spirit and being, consciousness and nature".[99]

Ethics qualifies as a philosophical science by this standard because the fundamental problem of all ethical theory is the *meaning of life*:

... precisely this problem is a problem of the relations of moral consciousness to being, to social and personal being, to the world as a whole; more precisely it is a problem of the relation of moral consciousness to the relation between humanity and the surrounding world. It is a question not simply of moral consciousness in itself, or moral norms, customs, behavior, moral relations, but a question which reads: 'why am I — a human being — in this world?'[100]

Egides' general approach to defining ethics has not received wide endorsement in Soviet literature; but on the other hand, a large number of Soviet moral philosophers do cite 'the meaning of life' among the scientific categories of ethics (along with, sometimes, 'happiness' and 'the destiny of man').

Touching finally on the *aims* of ethical theory as expressed by Soviet writers, one dramatic goal of their work emerges very clearly: the formation of a new type of human being: the Communist. Šiškin observes that in this process of forming people have operated such factors as the objective-historical order, and also subjective, spontaneous, uncontrolled processes, as well as consciously directed ones. Šiškin observes that

It is possible to see unequal development of moral consciousness in various spheres of life, for example, the social and personal; various levels and various 'tempos' of development of the new morality in various groups of the population; it is frequently possible to see in certain strata of workers the interweaving of demands of Communist morality with remnants of religious morality, collectivist principles with bourgeois-individualist traditions and habits, etc.[101]

However, taking into account all the complexities of this process, Šiškin urges that one thing not be forgotten:

... the formation of new people, of a new, Communist morality, takes place not haphazardly, not spontaneously, but under the direct influence of the organizational and educational (ideological) work of the Marxist party .... That means that the theory of Communist morality has as its basic object of study the experience of the education and self-education of the masses under the guidance of the Marxist party in the course of the struggle for a new society, in the course of the construction of a new society.[102]

This concern for the education (*vospitanie*) of the masses by the Communist Party and State as the proximate motive for the development of the science of ethics appears with great frequency in Soviet literature. Results from the study of ethics should enable those charged with the creation of a new humanity to intervene purposefully in the processes whereby the moral consciousness of the individual is formed and hence to influence the development of social consciousness as a whole. In the words of Drobnickij, the analysis of the conceptual apparatus of morality constitutes an "attempt to penetrate the 'internal laboratory' of moral convictions and feelings, concepts and manifestations of will" which operate according to their own specific laws in the ordinary consciousness of the individual moral agent.[103]

The purposeful intervention in these complex processes on the scale of society, or in the sphere of individual education, is unthinkable without a theoretical 'schema' – the conceptual system of moral consciousness – which has been adjusted and approved many times.[104]

If it is accurate to say that the central concern of the tradition of ethical theory which begins with Plato's Socratic dialogues and Aristotle's *Nicomachean Ethics* lies in assisting the individual who seriously desires to formulate clearly and justify the moral principles and ideals by which he lives, this could not be said to be the central focus of Soviet conceptions of the science of ethics. That inquiry is conceived fundamentally on the model of an ideal social science which provides the theoretical understanding of human social behavior necessary for the beneficent transformation of society by planners, leaders, and officials with the necessary authority. The seriousness of their commitment to this conception of the science of ethics and the management of social development which it is meant to facilitate is attested to by the enormous literature extant in Soviet publications on the subject of 'character education' (*vospitanie*). The subject of *vospitanie* merges with the science of ethics on one side, and with scientific pedagogy on the other, and constitutes a central practical concern and aim of both. The role of the science of ethics in Soviet conceptions as handmaiden to the social and political authorities will be further explored below in a discussion of some of the obvious parallels with social utilitarianism in eighteenth century French thought.[105]

3. UNIVERSAL NORMS AND CLASS NORMS OF MORALITY

When problems of ethical theory once again began to receive the attention of more capable Soviet theorists, it was very natural that one of the first topics on the agenda for discussion should be the problem of the admissibility or inadmissibility of 'simple moral norms' conceived as universally obligatory — a central issue in the disputes of 1926–1930, and implicit in the argument over 'proletarian humanism'. This dispute might potentially constitute a perennial one within Soviet Marxism save for such events as the official declaration in the 1961 Program of the Communist Party explicitly endorsing the notion of "fundamental all-human moral norms" as constituent elements of Communist morality.[106]

The best history of this entire problem can be found in an article by V. S. Štein in the anthology *Current Problems of Marxist Ethics* published in 1967.[107]

From a Marxist point of view, the dispute touches three crucial 'practical' issues: (1) the possibility of a sweeping dismissal of the moral claims by which the 'old' or 'bourgeois' world would condemn a revolutionary movement, (2) the integrity of historical materialism (in particular the scope and accuracy of a class analysis of socio-historical phenomena), and (3) the relative weight of conflicting claims of morality and political expediency on the revolutionary proletariat. In general Marxist opponents of the doctrine of universally obligatory moral norms or principles have felt more secure on all three counts in arguing that all moral norms are class-oriented, reflecting the interests of particular social classes. Their opponents have usually argued in one form or another that the denial of any universally obligatory moral principles comes at too high a price: extreme difficulty in providing any acceptable account of the grounds of moral obligation in general, and support to the foes of Marxism who frequently allude to the absence of any moral principles whatever in that world view which are logically immune from considerations of political expediency.

Marx's position on this issue is of course not very helpful. In the first charter of the International Brotherhood of Workers he appeared to endorse phrases referring to 'morality' and 'justice'. However in the letter to Engels mentioned above, he described these same phrases as in effect a harmless gesture to the Proudhonists. Similarly in the *Critique of the Gotha Program* he spoke of "ideological nonsense about right and other trash so common among the democrats and French socialists". The result has been a troublesome dilemma for Marxist ethical theory, and a running dispute over the extent of Marx's cynicism in his references to "simple norms of morality and justice". During the 1960's Soviet moral philosophers discussed the problem at length and found themselves divided.

Lenin's position is more helpful, in that he made a clearly uncynical reference to the "elementary rules of community" known to humanity for many centuries in his speech to the Third All-Union Congress of the Komsomol in 1919.

Apart from Engels, the remaining classical source on the problem is Plekhanov, and a reassessment of his position accompanied the recent reintroduction of discourse on ethical theory. Šiškin pointed out in 1961 (as Martov did in 1916) that if Plekhanov did interpret his simple laws of morality by analogy with Kant's categorical imperative, he thereby contradicted his own critique of Kantian ethics in his notes on *Ludwig Feuerbach* in 1905.[108] Martov's attack on Plekhanov was explicitly criticized in an article by Kus'minkov in 1964.[109] Most Soviet moral philosophers do interpret Plekhanov as having endorsed the Kantian categorical imperative, even as numbering it among his own "simple moral laws". However Štein argues at length that Plekhanov's mistake was not in his interpretation and acceptance of simple moral norms, but in his argument that the Allies should have been supported during World War I because Germany offended against simple laws of morality.[110]

To an outside observer, the amount of energy expended over this question during the 1960's in the Soviet Union may seem extraordinary. From the perspective of the participants however, what seems to have been at stake is nothing less than the admissibility of explicit judgments of ordinary moral obligation as an (at least 'relatively') autonomous sphere of discourse not grounded immediately in political considerations of 'revolutionary class consciousness' and *partijnost'* (party-mindedness or partisanship). It was part of the effort to secure a view of ethical theory and moral discourse as a distinct dimension of human activity, and to rescue them from the dissolution in politics and sociology which has been more typical of the Russian and Soviet *intelligenty* tradition since the 1840's. In this respect it should perhaps be linked to the discussions of 'proletariant humanism' in the early 1930's as described above.

The discussion was influenced very heavily in 1961 by a statement published in the new Party Program.

Communist morality includes the fundamental all-human moral norms which were worked out by the popular masses in the course of the thousands-of-years' struggle with social oppression and moral vices.[111]

For the most part this pronouncement settled the issue of the admissibility of moral norms conceived as universally obligatory for all humanity. Although the majority of professional philosophers in the USSR appear to accept this resolution, resistance in some quarters can still be found. The journal of literary criticism *Oktjabr'*, usually regarded as the most politically hard-line in the Soviet Union explicitly objected to the "resurrection of discourse about 'simple laws of morality' ", seeing in this "an abstract love of man in which there is no authentic love of mankind whatever, only much liberal-philanthropic jabber", preferring such formulae as Lenin's "Our morality is fully subordinated to the interests of the class struggle of the proletariat".[112] Similar reactions could be found in several issues of *Oktjabr'* during the 1960's, as well as occasionally in *Literaturnaja gazeta* and *Voprosy literatury*.[113] One woman, Larisa Krjačko, beginning in 1965, campaigned extensively in the columns of newspapers and journals against this sophistical opposition of morality to *partijnost'* by such self-designated revolutionary zealots.[114]

This particular argument, assuming an opposition between morality and *partijnost'*, the favorite of those who dispute the re-introduction of talk about

'laws of morality', shows a certain deficiency in logic if not in moral awareness: if the meaning and justification for the use of ethical terms cannot be
accounted for except by reference to political *partijnost'*, then in commend-
ing *partijnost'* with these same ethical terms, nothing of cognitive significance
is added. Morality has simply been reduced to politics.

The question of the nature of 'all-human' moral norms and of their basis
in a Marxist account of the development of morality has by no means been
entirely settled. One of the elder statesmen of Soviet ethics. A. F. Šiškin,
quite recently issued a general protest against claims to the effect that within
class society there exists, along with class morality, an 'all-human' morality
which is distinct from class morality but enters into 'dialectical interaction'
with it.[115] He attributes such views to a number of authors who wrote in the
much-discussed anthology *Current Problems of Marxist Ethics* and elsewhere.

The specific mistake which Šiškin identifies as the source of the general
error consists in positing an analogy between the 'all-human' norms of morality and the 'eternal truths' of science.

Not understanding the essence and social function of morality as a definite form of
social consciousness, as a particular ideological means of defense of class interests, some
comrades are inclined to see the 'all-human' in morality by analogy with science. Definite
moral demands are identified with eternal truths in the sphere of science; the development of morality is compared with the development of a concept through relative truth
to absolute truth, and the content of the truth does not depend on classes, but has an
all-human significance.[116]

Instead, Šiškin argues that however eternal the ideas of justice or good, duty
and conscience, virtue and vice be thought to be, the content of these concepts has "very substantially changed from people to people, from class to
class".[117] In general he considers it incorrect to speak of an 'all-human'
morality existing at the present time; such a morality "will become possible
when society is transformed into a single all-human association".[118]

The chief concern of most Soviet philosophers in discussing the question
of 'simple moral norms or laws' has been to distinguish the 'class' from the
'all-human' norms of morality, defining the latter in a 'non-metaphysical' or
'non *a priori*' way, and to provide a plausible account of how both elements
could arise in any particular moral order. Some have been concerned to
distinguish several types of simple moral norms or laws, and even to develop a
classification of them.

Štein defines the 'all-human' element of morality as, in the words of E. I.
Borodixina, "answering to the essential root interests of the majority of the
population in each given segment of historical development, coinciding with

the progressive in history . . ."[119] The empirical source of such 'simple norms of morality' he locates in

... those aspects of the conditions of labor, family relations and personal life, and of the elementary bases of social existence, with are not reducible to class relations, but are organically connected with the entire ensemble of conditions of the material life of society.[120]

Similarly, Bandzeladze, trying to account for the presence of all-human moral norms, argues that the class character of morality arose in the second, slave-owning stage of Marx's five stages of historical development, in the opposition between the life-outlooks of the slave class and the slave-owning class. Despite their opposing moral evaluations of many deeds and institutions in slave-owning society, "certain deeds and feelings were more or less identically moral both for the rich and for the poor (for example, love of country, respect for parents, etc.)".[121] In this fashion both class and all-human elements of morality could be conceived to exist together at each stage of social development (the position which Šiškin finds objectionable).

Apart from the specific dispute over the admissibility of talk about universal laws of morality, there has also been evidence of a self-conscious movement to reintroduce the *vocabulary* of ethical discourse into public currency. For example, in his path-breaking monograph on value theory in 1960, V. P. Tugarinov stated that,

... that psychological protest which the inclusion of the concepts of good and evil in Marxist ethics can call forth is fully understandable. However there is no theoretical basis for such a protest .... Without a Marxist understanding of good and evil there is no Marxist ethics as a science .... Incidentally the concept of conscience began to be used in our theoretical literature only in recent years, and the concept of good must still beat a path into our literature for itself, despite the fact that the classical authors of Marxism-Leninism used it widely.[122]

Štein also refers to calls in recent years appearing in the periodical press, and in theoretical and creative literature, to rehabilitate the term 'good'.[123]

A rather substantial literature on this subject, including several dissertations, with numerous points of contention, now exists in the Soviet Union; its details are perhaps unimportant for those convinced on other grounds of the propriety of the claims of ethical judgment as a distinct mode of discourse. It was in part the outcome of this discussion, however, which returned the attention of Soviet philosophers to the problems of ethical theory, to a recognition that moral discourse does have special implications which distinguish it from factual, descriptive discourse.

CHAPTER FIVE

DISCUSSIONS OF VALUE THEORY IN SOVIET MARXISM

1. THE ORIGINS OF THE DISCUSSION AND THE DISTINCTION OF VALUE FROM FACT

The discussion of value theory in the Soviet Union opened with the publication of V. P. Tugarinov's monograph *On the Values of Life and Culture*.[1] A conference on value theory convened in Tbilisi in 1965 provided a further impetus to the discussion.[2] In between these two events there appeared at least three articles and one book (in Ukrainian) devoted to the subject, and the Institute of Philosophy of the Academy of Sciences arranged two special meetings to consider the question of whether Marxist philosophy required any special theory of the nature of values.[3] The Leningrad philosophical *kafedra* of the Academy of Sciences also published a substantial anthology, *The Problem of Values in Philosophy*, in 1966.[4] These were the principal events in the context of which Soviet discussions of value theory developed.

Tugarinov's original work showed in many ways the author's conviction at the time that few of his compatriots would share his view of the relevance of value theory to Marxist philosophy. He refered to an opinion widespread among Soviet philosophers for many years that value theory was an unscientific inquiry pursued only by bourgeois philosophers. He claimed that such a view was a reaction to Kantian ethics and the struggle against the attempt by neo-Kantians to supply an ethical grounding for socialism. On the practical side, this rejection of value theory "flowed from the prior necessity to demonstrate the scientific character of the theory of socialism, and to prove that the October socialist revolution was historically lawful".[5] Taking the political offensive, Tugarinov alleged that the "rejection of values from neo-positivism" was to persuade people not to judge the negative phenomena of the capitalist social order "in whose conditions Carnap lives".[6]

Tugarinov described values as "those phenomena (or aspects of phenomena) of nature and society which occur as benefits of the life and culture of the people of a particular society or class, as something real or ideal".[7] He further claimed that Marxism counts as values only those phenomena which lead to progress or express progress.[8]

In defense of the objectivity of values, Tugarinov argued that all value categories are reflections of some objective phenomena or relations of social life in our consciousness. He acknowledged that values include a subjective dimension, since they are realized by persons who are guided by their own interests and views, but rejected the view he termed 'personal' or 'individual' subjectivism, i.e., the view that a judgment of value is no more than the personal opinion of each individual.

Such an individualist view on values fully liquidates the problem of values in general. If every man has his own morality, his own truth, etc., then all research on values becomes unneeded, as well as the concept (of value).[9]

In a further development of his theory of values. Turarinov seized on the concept of 'the good' as the 'single properly ethical concept', denying that any other categories could be related exclusively to the sphere of ethics and morality.[10] Good and evil are strictly social phenomena, he insisted; in nature there is neither good nor evil.[11] Within the social world of humanity, "Communist society will appear as the first realization in the history of mankind of human love and universal good".[12] Taking into account the problem of individual error in comprehending the good, he finally concluded that 'good' should be defined as such behavior as is carried out with the conscious goal of bringing actual benefit to society, i.e., benefit which facilitates social progress.[13]

Attempting to analyze the objectivity of value more deeply, Tugarinov resorted to Hegel. Inquiring whether the good exists objectively, "outside of us", he answers: in nature, no; but in society, yes. It exists objectively ('outside of us') not in the sense that something other than people creates it, but in the sense in which Hegel distinguished 'objective spirit' from 'subjective spirit'. Under 'subjective spirit', Hegel understood the spiritual life of the individual; under 'objective spirit', the spiritual life of society.

The objectivity of that latter 'spirit' signified for Hegel the fact that culture, the spiritual life of society, is created not by the individual alone, but by many generations of people; an individual can only perceive culture as something lying outside of and independent of himself; and if he is able, he may bring his contribution to it.[14]

Hence, he concludes, "good as a phenomenon of social life is objective", not only as a practical aspect of social life, but also as a social idea, as a form of social consciousness.[15]

The first step involved in developing a theory of values in the context of Soviet Marxism was, as Tugarinov suggested, winning acceptance of the idea that there were any special problems about the nature of value. Two meetings were convened at the Institute of Philosophy in Moscow, in effect, to assess this proposal. The questions on the agenda for both meetings were (1) is 'value' a philosophical concept, and (2) is a theory of values needed in Marxist philosophy? The basic point at issue was the significance of the distinction between factual and normative discourse: was it sufficiently important to warrant a separate investigation into the phenomena of values and evaluation? The majority of those attending were reported to have found the idea of a Marxist axiology 'far-fetched'.[16] F. V. Konstantinov, the influential general editor of the *Philosophical Encyclopedia*, attacked value theory as entirely a phenomenon of 'bourgeois' philosophy, having no role in Marxism. Two general positions developed in the discussion, one of which regarded 'value' as a sociological concept which "attempts to elucidate the social significance" of man's mastery over nature, and the other of which viewed it as an 'epistemological' concept.

Discussion of the 'epistemological' concept of value revolved about the notion of there being two 'approaches' to the study of, or the cognition of, phenomena − the 'scientific-theoretical' and the 'evaluative-practical'. The point at issue was whether these two approaches could be ultimately distinguished, and if so, whether the distinction was an important one. It was this proposed distinction, rather than Hume's distinction between fact and value, which preoccupied most discussants. Konstantinov and Švarcman were inclined to deny that the two modes of 'cognition' could be distinguished in practice and were opposed to the development of a Marxist theory of values. Šiškin agreed that these two modes of cognition were inextricably connected in practice, but saw no special difficulty in the path of working out a Marxist theory of values, within the context of Marxist 'epistemology'.

Various other reasons offered in support of the development of a Marxist theory of values were: (1) that one was needed in order to respond to 'bourgeois' discussions of the subject, (2) that it was needed for historical studies 'in order to evaluate the past in terms of the present', (3) that it was needed in order to be able to identify the social classes which bring good or evil to the world, and (4) that it was needed to strengthen 'spiritual' values. Despite the largely negative conclusions of this 'official' discussion, the major outcome appears to have been to underline the importance of the distinction between descriptive or 'scientific', and 'normative' discourse, and to have accelerated the wider discussion of the problem.

Awareness of the distinction between normative and descriptive discourse and of its importance developed simultaneously with interest in the problems of value theory. In a number of discussions of value theory after 1960 the distinction between fact and value was drawn quite generally, in contrast to previous practice in which 'Hume's guillotine' had been largely ignored. Some of the best contributions to this problem came from scholars well-versed in symbolic logic and the philosophy of logic.

A remarkably clear formulation of distinctions between descriptive and normative discourse could be found in D. P. Gorskij's article 'Truth and its Criteria', published in 1962.[17] From the perspective of epistemology Gorskij discussed the meaningfulness of several expressions:

(1)   All metals are electrical conductors
(2)   Metal
(3)   What time is it?
(4)   All the students must be disciplined

All these expressions he takes to be meaningful, but of the four, only the first is properly evaluated in terms of truth and falsity. The second is a word expressing a concept, not a judgment. In the language of modern logic, a concept can be employed in expressions such as 'x is a metal' where 'x' represents an individual variable. If 'iron' is substituted for 'x', then the resulting expression is, when asserted, true. But a concept examined out of context can be neither true nor false. The third expression, an interrogative, can also be neither true nor false. The fourth expression is a normative one:

That sort of proposition cannot be evaluated as objectively true or objectively false. Norms, demands are not reflections of facts or assertions of something given in the sense that the assertion "the sun rises in the East" is the reflection of an objective fact . . . . norms of social behavior are characterized from the perspective of their legitimacy or illegitimacy, effectiveness or ineffectiveness, timeliness or untimeliness, from the perspective of their usefulness or harm to society, for the realization of certain social demands and goals.

. . .

Thus, from the ranks of meaningful propositions it is only to declarative propositions (and also to propositions compounded from simple declarative propositions with the help of the logical connectives 'and', 'or', 'if . . . then', etc.) that the predicate of truth or falsity is applicable.[18]

Gorskij further distinguishes assertions about mental states from assertions of type (1).

Of them one may say that they are 'true' if the person describing his emotions, voluntary urges, etc., informs us of his real emotions, voluntary urges, etc. Observing his behavior we can establish whether he informed us truly or not. However, a proposition of this type is formulated not as a reflection of objective facts, and in that sense is distinguished from propositions of type (1).[19]

O. M. Bakuradze in Tbilisi formulated a similar distinction in somewhat different terms in a 1966 article entitled 'Truth and Value'.[20]

Truth exists in the form of true judgments. Therefore the explication of the nature of truth entails the explication of those conditions in which a judgment is true. A judgment is true if its content does not depend on the subject and is a reflection of objective reality. Such a judgment gives knowledge. Let us term it a cognitive judgment.

However the relation of man to reality has also another aspect – evaluative. In cognition facts are established in such a way that the relationship of the person to those facts is not evident . . . . In contrast, in evaluation the relation of the subject to the object is expressed. Here the main point consists in establishing what value the object represents for the subject . . . .

Let us term a judgment expressed by a subject, ascribing value to an object, a judgment of value.[21]

A true judgment constitutes a description of fact and accordingly is distinguished from a judgment of value, the function of which is to prescribe. The assertion 'x is valuable' is equivalent in meaning to 'x is good', that is 'that I approve of x'. "When a person terms something 'good', he does not simply assert a fact, but expresses a wish, that the phenomenon were present if it is absent, that it [continue to] be in the future if it is already present."[22]

Concluding his discussion, Bakuradze summarized:

. . . a judgment of value is essentially distinguished from a cognitive judgment in which a true content of our consciousness is expressed. The reduction of a cognitive judgment to a value judgment, or, conversely, the consideration of a value judgment as a description of facts is a result of an incorrect understanding of their nature.[23]

Bakuradze adopted an analysis of value strongly reminiscent of that given by the emotivist school of thought. He analyzed value judgments as having a descriptive aspect in addition to the emotive: a cognitive judgment is not only a necessary presupposition of a value judgment, but a part of its meaning. Apart from its slightly obscure epistemological terminology (e.g., contents of judgment "not depending on the subject" or "expressing the relation of the subject to the object") Bakuradze's treatment does not depart significantly from very familiar analyses of the distinction between fact and value encountered in Anglo-American and Western European philosophy. The significance of Bakuradze's article, as of Gorskij's, lies rather in the sharpness and clarity with which the distinction, and hence the potnetial problem for any account of the truth or objectivity of moral judgments, is put.

The precision with which Gorskij and Bakuradze discussed the problem was due in part to their familiarity with the recent history of formal logic, a background which few Soviet moral philosophers share. Little attention was paid to the development of formal systems of deontic logic, or logic of values, until quite recently, and most authors simply give favorable mention of such methods without actually adopting them.[24] In 1966 A. A. Ivin published a short but sophisticated summary of foreign work on deontic logic, commenting that this area had been almost completely ignored up to that time.[25] Two years later he published a second article summarizing work in foreign publications on value logic, and subsequently, a monograph on the same subject.[26]

According to Ivin, a simple analysis of the logical structure of evaluations can be made in terms of four elements: the subject who makes the evaluation, the object evaluated, the comparative or absolute character of the evaluation, and the basis of the evaluation. As subjects capable of making evaluations, Ivin mentions individuals and groups.[27] Drobnickij, in an interesting variant, describes moral evaluations in particular as made ultimately by humanity as a whole, thus accounting for their impersonal, universal character.[28] Xarčev and Jakovlev criticized Drobnickij's view as mistakenly identifying the "origin and content of a moral demand with the form of its expression and grounding in a series of historical types of morality" thereby exaggerating the universal, classless nature of moral judgments.[29] They consider the impersonality (*vnesub'ektnost'*) of moral judgments not to be a characteristic 'integrally present' in them. While no very generally agreed analysis of the logical structure of evaluative judgments or norms can be reported, the existence of a distinction between fact and value has been widely recognized, and, the possibility of a significant contribution to ethical theory by formal logic has been acknowledged.

Granting the widespread recognition of a distinction between fact and value, there remained a very wide spectrum of opinion as to the *importance* of the distinction, however. The following opinion regarding its importance was not atypical during the first several years of debate:

When contemporary positivists, following Hume, speak of the impossibility of a transition from factual judgments to 'prescriptive' or 'imperative' conclusions, they are correct so long as they remain within the framework of formal logical analysis. But formal logical analysis is neither the only nor the principal method of research. If social science does not remain on the level of mere description and classification of phenomena, but discovers laws and tendencies of social development, it creates the scientific basis for political slogans, expressed in imperative form, and also for specific moral demands, norms of behavior, evaluations, and so forth.[30]

The problem of how imperatives or value judgments may be reached as conclusions of Marxist social theory hinted at in this passage has troubled many commentators, Marxist as well as non-Marxist (recall the conclusion of Kautsky's *Ethics and the Materialist Conception of History*).[31] H. B. Acton held, for example, that "the Marxist can derive moral precepts from his social science only to the extent that they already form, because of the vocabulary used, a concealed and unacknowledged part of it".[32] Isaiah Berlin on the other hand wised to turn aside the objection that moral recommendations are illicitly derived from mere matters of fact in Marxist theory on the ground that "Marx, like Hegel, flatly rejected this distinction".[33] Whether or not Marx accepted the distinction (and there is considerable evidence to be cited that he did in fact make use of it), the distinction can be made, and has been accepted by Soviet followers of Marx in recent years. Along with acceptance of the distinction goes the problem just stated: how are value judgments derived and justified in the Soviet Marxist view?

2. ANALYSES OF VALUE

Soviet theories of value appear at first glance to fall into two different categories. In one category 'value' is analyzed simply as the property of a (social) object; in the other, as a concept relating persons to certain objects or states of affairs. In fact the first category turns out to be a sub-category of the second, for the concept of a 'social object' itself essentially involves the notion of a relation between individuals and the objects designated as 'social'. Hence there is a single basic type of value theory adopted by nearly all Soviet authors, and it is a relational one, seemingly belonging to the same group as a number of interest theories of value propounded by non-Marxist philosophers of the naturalist school as varied as Aristotle and Perry. At the same time however, Soviet philosophers are practically unanimous in rejecting 'the naturalist school of bourgeois theories of value', denying that their own views could be collected under this term. The adequacy of this claim will be examined below.[34]

Problems frequently discussed under both the headings of 'theory of value' and of 'metaethics' by English-speaking and Western European philosophers have been almost exclusively examined within discussions of value theory by Soviet writers. Here a 'metaethical' query has been relatively clearly put, as to whether values must be understood as (1) a property of the object itself, (2) the significance of that object for man, or (3) the relation of man to the object.[35] These three possibilities (assuming for the moment that they are

logically distinct) embrace all the analyses offered thus far in Soviet philosophical literature.

Drobnickij himself at one time proposed to analyze values as properties
of 'social objects'. The first task of any such analysis would of course be to
explicate the concept of 'social object' itself. This task in turn involves
stating some of the cosmological assumptions lying behind such analyses of
value, and Drobnickij's work went perhaps further than any other Soviet
theorist's in making these assumptions explicit. Not only the concept of
'social object' but also 'man' or 'person', the subject who makes evaluations,
must be explicated in terms of a specifically Marxist cosmology, as described
above.[36] Exploring this dimension of the problem, Drobnickij remarked that,

Marx distinguishes the natural and the social not as two spheres separated spatially and
in terms of objects, but as two 'interpenetrating' spheres, as two aspects of one and the
same reality. On the one hand, every object of nature is also a social object. Marx
indicates that "in society nature appears as the basis . . . of human existence proper"
and for that reason an object having a natural origin becomes for man a social object. On
the other hand, every object having a social origin, produced by man, is also a natural
phenomenon. A commodity is a natural body, although it is produced by labor. And
even labor itself, if it is considered as a 'metabolism', a transformation of energy and the
material form of objects, appears as a natural process, subject to natural laws. Marx says
that "man in the process of production can act only as nature itself acts, that is he can
change only the forms of things". Thus the natural and the social are not two different
types of objects, but two sides of one and the same object. A 'natural object' (thing,
phenomenon, process) is the natural substratum the bearer of that which we call the
'social object'.[37]

Borrowing from Marx's discussion of commodity value, Drobnickij points out
that any commodity is from one perspective a physical object, "a conjunction
of mechanical, physical, and chemical properties", etc. From another perspective it is an object introduced into the sphere of labor, someone's property,
consumer goods, an object of exchange, capital, etc.

In a similar fashion it is possible to analyze every object possessing value . . . . And in
every individual case the bearer of value will be not the natural object, but the object
in its social content. For example, the act of theft consists not in spatial transfer of an
object from one man to another, but in the illegal appropriation of property; i.e., for the
description of that act we use exclusively concepts which refer to specifically social phenomena. And precisely due to that social content a deed possesses positive or negative
moral worth.[38]

Drobnickij's attempt to go further in the definition of a social object unfortunately at this point trails off into metaphors:

In such fashion we have distinguished in things or phenomena a certain side which we can term 'the social object'. But what is that in essence? If we are speaking of a material object, then in it there remains, as Marx says, "not one grain of natural substance"; it is now not a body possessing chemical, biological characteristics, but an object of culture. It is a crystal, in the focus of which are reflected social relations; it is an intersection of social connections and dependencies, an object appearing under the most varied functions and definitions. This object moves in the world of social existence according to completely different laws than those of mechanics, physics, chemical reactions, and metabolism. But like an object of nature, it is relatively stable, discrete, capable of appearing in the most varied relations with other objects and yet retaining its inner unity, its identity with itself. Only in this sense is it an object, and not in the sense of the material-substantial substratum composing it. And only in relation to this social object is it possible to speak of value as its characteristic.[39]

In this analysis of value as a property of a social object, Drobnickij provided a conception reminiscent of Marx's cosmos. The obvious objection to be raised to this type of analysis of values would be that ultimately no special light has been shed upon the phenomenon of value until the cosmological doctrine of 'the sphere of social existence' has itself been illuminated more successfully. This last might turn out to be an extremely important feature of the cosmos, and a basic one in some sense; but it could scarcely be unanalyzably basic, and until such an analysis is provided it is doubtful that much has been contributed to the analysis of values.

Before proceeding with other Soviet accounts of the nature of value, a few linguistic observations are in order. The Russian language possesses two words which must be translated by the single English word 'good'. 'Good' in the sense of 'moral good' in Russian is translated *dobro*, a substantive form which is matched by an equally common adjectival form. 'Good' in all other senses must be translated by *xorošij*, an adjectival form with no proper matching substantive, and a word with no specifically moral connotations. Thus a 'morally good man' is a '*dobryj čelovek*' and a 'good man' is a '*xorošij čelovek*'. Certain equivalences which obtain in the English language do not obtain in Russian. To most English speakers the meanings of the following two questions are essentially the same: 'what is intrinsically valuable?' and 'what is intrinsically good?'. In Russian neither *dobro* alone nor *xorošee* alone can do the work of 'good' in this English usage.

Moreover the concept of *value* appears to differ subtly in Russian linguistic usage. Whereas the most common dictionary synonym of 'value' in English is 'worth', the two closest Russian synonyms of the Russian word for *value* are best translated as *importance* (*značenie*) and *significance* (*značimost'*). The latter term has been seized upon by many writers as the most appropriate for the purposes of a formal analysis of values and several accounts of value theory have been based upon it.

Tugarinov is one writer who objects to the definition of 'value' merely in terms of *'značimost''* which is offered by a number of his colleagues. He argued that 'significance' may be either valuable or harmful. "War, crime, and sickness have a great significance (*značimost'*) for society and the individual person, but no one terms these phenomena 'values'. . . . The concept of value is connected only with positive significance (*značenie*)."[40]

Tugarinov is of the opinion that no adequate synonym of 'value' (*cennost'*) exists in the Russian language, so he attempts to identify instances of value by means of certain 'indicators'. The most general of these indicators (or criteria) is that whatever is valuable satisfies human needs, requirements, or interests. ". . . not all values are pleasant. The useful and the pleasant in the majority of cases coincide, but not always. Not everything that is pleasant is also valuable."[41] Accordingly he offers the following definition of values:

Values are objects, phenomena and their properties, which are needed (necessary, useful, pleasant, etc.) to the people of a particular specific society or class and to individual persons, as a means of satisfying their needs and interests and also, ideas . . . in the capacity of norms, goals, or ideals.[42]

Tugarinov also locates his account of value theory within the context of Marxist 'epistemology' in which the concept of *praxis* (or *praktika*) is central. He improves somewhat on the standard claim that knowledge has two aspects: the theoretical and the practical. He points out that *praktika* is simply not a form of consciousness, and therefore not properly speaking a form of knowledge.

In reality, as was shown above, in social consciousness it is necessary to distinguish the cognitive and the evaluative aspects. The latter is the transitional link to *praktika*. In this manner a Marxist theory of values makes it possible to work out a more correct general formula for the concept of ideology.[43]

Thus in place of the standard distinction between the 'theoretical' and the 'practical' in knowledge, Tugarinov wishes to substitute 'theoretical-cognitive' and 'evaluative' attitudes in *consciousness*.

Continuing his analysis of values, Tugarinov finds it necessary to define "the *evaluative relation* of the subject to the object" as the central concept in his account. Placing the evaluative relation in the center of his analysis, he finds that all other aspects of the phenomena of values can be seen either as pre-conditions for the existence of this evaluative relation or as consequences of it in the 'epistemological process'. The pre-conditions he finds for the existence of evaluative relations are "needs, interests, and goals"; the epistemological process in question is described as "knowledge, evaluation, and *praktika*".

The evaluative relation itself issues in a mental act, *evaluation*, in which an object (or its property) is found to be useful, pleasant, morally good, beautiful, etc. "Evaluation therefore depends upon the properties of the evaluated object." The object of the evaluation may be "a phenomenon of the external world (object, thing, material substance, event, act) or mental fact (idea, image, scientific conception)".[44]

The needs which Tugarinov posits among the necessary pre-conditions of evaluative relations are those of the standard Marxist account. As living organisms all human beings have certain biological needs. Economic production in society is a social means of satisfying them. But as soon as humanity organizes itself into groups, and ultimately into societies, in order to satisfy these biological needs, *new* needs are created, not merely biological, but psychological, socio-political, and cultural. It is activity to satisfy these needs which constitutes the history of human society.

An *interest* is defined as the direction of thoughts and feelings of a person toward an object satisfying or capable of satisfying his needs. Thus for every need there corresponds an interest. "Directing his attention to objects of the external world with the aim of satisfying his needs and interests, man learns their properties and on this basis evaluates them as satisfying ... or not satisfying" these needs and interests.[45] "The character of the needs defines the direction of the interests."[46] But the direction of interests is determined not only by human biology, but also by the tasks of the society or class. "A huge group of class, national, and other interests are defined by social needs."[47]

Finally, concerning goals he argues: "a goal appears in the consciousness of a person as an ideal mental image of the value created".[48] "The goal, being the image of a value, as distinguished from a need or an interest, is a value, ... thought only a mental one."[49]

These then are the presuppositions of the occurrence of values. "Without needs and interests there would be no values." "An interest by itself is not a value. It only indicates the means for the satisfaction of a need ... the satisfaction of an interest is a value."[50]

Tugarinov offers several classifications of values, explicitly and implicitly. In his first work on value theory he divided all values into those of 'life' and those of 'culture'. In his second monograph he adopted the classification of 'material, socio-political, and cultural' at one point, and 'personal' and 'social' at another. He makes still another distinction between 'immediate sensuous' values experienced in the physical life of humanity, such as health, physical beauty, 'the joys of life', and those which are more indirectly experienced, primarily the socio-political and cultural. It is this distinction which Tugarinov employs to make some remarks about the relation between the assumption of historical *progress* and his account of values. Whereas he named 'usefulness' as the most general indicator of a thing's being a value, he must reconcile this with the Marxist assumption that the determined course of history defines what is progress and that this progress in turn defines what is (socially) valuable. Hence Tugarinov remarks, "In the sphere of socio-political and cultural values, the concept of utility must submit to the 'control' of a social criterion, namely the concept of social progress and the progress of the individual person".[51] He disputes other Soviet authors who would hold that 'progress' is itself the universal sign and criterion of value in general. The analysis of these 'immediately sensuous' values according to Tugarinov, does not allow any meaningful role for 'progress'. It is only in the case of socio-political and cultural values that progress serves as a criterion of value.[52]

Obviously for any Marxist except one who defines value as "whatever historical development appears to aim at", the logical relation between the account of historical progress and any further account of intrinsic values is going to present a number of awkward puzzles. Any account which offers a merely contingent connection between that which is valuable and that at which history aims will permit raising questions which, by assumption, cannot be raised within a Marxist philosophy of history. The as yet relatively small Soviet literature which confronts this dilemma explicitly will be examined separately below.[53]

Three Georgian philosophers, Bakuradze, Džioev, and Čavčavadze, offered a joint paper on value theory at the Tbilisi conference with certain differences of treatment representative of a number of Soviet theorists. Their general account falls within the context of Marxist 'epistemology' as did Tugarinov's, relying on a distinction between 'theoretical-cognitive assimilation' and 'evaluative assimilation' of the world. In the former, the real object always remains outside the mind, existing as something independent, precisely as long as the person is related to it only mentally, only theoretically. In the latter the phenomenon occurs as something having an essential relation to man, as something "capable of answering his feelings, needs, strivings, and wishes; it is revealed as a means of satisfying his needs or as a goal worthy of effort, i.e., as something possessing value".[54]

The authors rely on the concept of 'significance' to summarize this relation between the subject and the object in evaluation. In 'value consciousness' a person "judges the object not from the viewpoint of its factual existence, but from the viewpoint of its significance for the subject".[55] The object is viewed not from the viewpoint of its cause-and-effect connections but from the aspect of its suitability as a means or its worthiness as a goal.[56] The value of an object is perceived by a subject as a particular property of the object. "However the relation of the value to its bearer, the object, is fundamentally distinguished from the relation of its real, factual accidents to its substance".[57] ". . . however this does not mean that value in general is independent of the natural properties of its bearer; precisely the reverse: the particular value of any object is conditioned by its natural ontological particularity."[58]

The three authors recognize the distinction between instrumental and intrinsic values, which they term 'unconditioned value-goals, standing before men as categorical demands'. (This of course suggests a failure to distinguish between the analyses of value and of obligation, which is not confined to these authors alone).

The authors assume that without some assumption of the existence of objective values, it would be impossible to avoid a subjectivism which they find incompatible with Marxism. The task of accounting for this objectivity of 'unconditioned value-goals' they regard as the basic problem of a Marxist theory of values. Each of the authors sketches a different proposal for such an analysis. Bakuradze suggests that the criterion for a value is a norm. The content of the norm is defined by the content of the highest value-ideal. The ideal is a product of historical-social life, its reflection. The objectivity of the value has the nature of the objectivity of the ideal. This proposed 'solution' appears to offer a circular definition. A value is determined by a norm which is in turn determined by an ideal – which is another kind of value. The assertion that the ideal is an objective 'reflection' of historical social conditions seems to adapt Lenin's 'copy' theory of knowledge of physical objects by the individual consciousness to the metaphorical 'perception' of values in history by whole societies. The number of difficulties inherent in this suggestion is so great as a preclude taking it seriously without further elaboration.

Džioev observes that the value of something is its value for humanity. But the measure of value is not the individual person. Value is related to the *species*. 'Conditioned' values are founded upon that which empirically characterizes the species. Unconditioned values are those founded upon the *categorical* characteristics of human beings, flowing from their place in the world, their relationship to the world. A value is that which befits humanity's place in the world. By this last assertion Džioev intends to hint at a way of defining 'intrinsic' or 'unconditioned' values. Again, his view presupposes a knowledge of all important features of the cosmos before intrinsic values could be known. It also ignores a kind of 'partial' evidence that many thinkers have found most immediately relevant to the assessment of intrinsic value: the having of certain experiences which in themselves seem to the one experiencing them to be wholly good in and of themselves. It might well be that one estimates the major features of the human cosmos by inference from such experiences, not the converse.

Čavčavadze suggests that the root of all objectivity must be sought in ontological objectivity — in *existence* of one kind or another.

The goal-directed, obligatory character of values is a reflection in value consciousness of the trend, the directedness, of dialectically developing human existence. Building above nature a new social and cultural world, creating culture and himself, man is free in the choice of instruments, goals, and values; however his freedom is authentic and directed toward the realization of authentic values only when it is the recognition of necessity...[59]

This last claim seems at best self-contradictory. If man is truly free in the choice of values for the creation of society, from whence comes any 'necessity' to be recognized in the choice of values? If certain values are nevertheless 'necessary', no hint is given as to what kind of 'necessity' that could be. As for values being indicated by the 'directedness' of social evolution, this above all is what the non-Marxist would like the Marxist to explain, not take as self-evident.

One additional account of values should be cited for the sake of completeness, and for certain features it presents which are indicative of widespread tendencies in recent Soviet discussions of ethical theory. Vasilenko discusses values in cybernetic terms, defining 'value' as 'the significance of one system for the existence of another'. The stark simplicity of this conception eliminates any problem of qualitative differences among values, of course, and in the presumably less equivocal nature of survival, as opposed to happiness, it goes considerably beyond ethical hedonism in the simplification of ethical theory. The 'systems' Vasilenko refers to may be vital or inorganic, individuals, groups, classes, even historical periods. The system whose existence is being considered he terms the 'subject' and it of course defines what is valuable among the properties of the other system, the object of evaluation. Following the logic of his 'all-or-none' axiology, he takes it as axiomatic that the existence of a social group is a greater 'value' than the existence of any one of its individual members, and that the existence of a class is a greater 'value' than the existence of any of its individual groups. In this easily-adopted hierarchy of 'values', Vasilenko's position is directly reminiscent of Helvetius', for whom this particular axiom was a crucial component of his social utilitarian ethics.[60]

Speaking of persons, Vasilenko defines the subject (as bearer of value) not as 'consciousness' but 'man as a material and practically acting being', or 'a practically acting social being'.[61]

On the nature of values, Vasilenko thinks it important never to identify a value with a "value object, phenomenon, event, deed, etc., appearing in the role of a bearer of value". "Value is not a natural property of objects, as they are given immediately in nature, although it is directly connected with its bearer and unthinkable without it."[62]

As usual in Soviet accounts of value theory, value is identified as an essential relation between a subject and an object, but any suggestion that the value relation depends upon the subject's attitude, 'feelings, wishes, satisfactions, or decisions' is firmly rejected by Vasilenko. The value relation occurs only between objects possessing properties of certain sorts and individuals (as social creatures) or social groups who possess objectively given needs and interests.[63]

This account of values has one additional striking limitation to which its author confesses: "we cannot, without falling into a logical contradiction with ourselves speak of the value of something in itself, unrelated to some other thing".[64] A definition of value which logically eliminates the possibility of intrinsic value is a very limited tool indeed for the purposes of ethical theory, (assuming this is in fact a consequence of Vasilenko's system).

The severe limitations of this account are manifest; however it is instructive in several respects. First, it is unusually succinctly expressed for Soviet philosophical writing. Second, it is one of the earliest examples of the intrusion into Soviet ethical theory of essentially cybernetic terms of discussion and perspectives, which originated in theoretical discussions of the behavior of self-maintaining systems. In the late nineteen sixties, an essentially cybernetic perspective was often imported into discussions labelled 'ethical theory' thereby revealing the same direction of thought as that mainfest in the social utilitarianism of Helvetius and other theorists of the French Enlightenment: the problem of ethics is the problem of social control. The popularity of 'cybernetic' terminology seems more recently to have diminished in Soviet literature, as in our own, but for many Soviet theorists the problems of ethical theory are essentially those of the maintenance and control of society as a system, in particular the control of individual behavior as it affects the stability of the social system as a whole. (The special 'modernity' of the cybernetic approach seemed especially attractive to a number of Soviet ethical theorists, but a better knowledge of the history of ethical thought might have persuaded them that the aim of social control through the manipulation of moral beliefs is no newer than eighteenth century social utilitarianism).

3. VALUE JUDGMENTS AND TRUTH

One of the most direct and immediate consequences of any particular analysis of the nature of value should be its implication of the applicability or inapplicability of truth and falsity to value judgments (cognitivism or non-cognitivism). If values are conceived as properties ascribed to objects or types of experiences (whether natural, non-natural, or metaphysical; and whether simple or relational), then value judgments can be construed as susceptible of truth or falsity. If on the other hand value judgments are conceived not to refer to properties of any kind, they may be construed as expressing attitudes, prescribing, or some other allegedly 'non-cognitivist' function. In this light it would appear that discussions of the possible truth or falsity of value judgments could scarcely be separated from a general analysis of value, and indeed in most discussions of the theory of value, the question of truth or falsity would be treated as an integral part of that problem.

A slightly curious tendency has appeared in recent Soviet publications to treat this issue of whether 'true' and 'false' can be applied to value judgments as a separate one, to be pursued somewhat independently of the discussion of value theory. It has become known as the problem of 'the epistemology of morality' (*gnoseologii morali'*), and in the last several years has occasioned a growing body of literature. Although there are few prominent partisans of non-cognitivist analyses of value *per se* in Soviet literature who would defend the conclusion that truth and falsity are inapplicable to value judgments, there are a number of authors who do deny the applicability of truth and falsity to value judgments when this last issue is treated as an independent problem. The extent of disagreement over this last issue appears much wider than that over the logically implicated issue of the concept of value.

After the passage of a number of years, the article by Gorskij described above still remains one of the clearest statements of the non-cognitivist view of the inapplicability of truth and falsity to normative statements.[65] Apart from Gorskij, other Marxist authors cited by Soviet writers as endorsing the non-cognitivist position that "the property of truth is present only in assertive judgments" are usually from other socialist countries.[66]

A larger number of Soviet ethical theorists are usually cited as endorsing the cognitivist position, that is affirming the view that "there is no distinction in principle in the application of the criterion of truth to sentences independent of whether they are expressed in narrative-description, evaluative, or normative form".[67] Those claiming to take the cognitivist position however often turn out to have complex views of the problem which do not clearly qualify as 'cognitivist' in the most standard sense of the term.

Xarčev and Jakovlev speak of three 'aspects' of truth in morality: epistemological, pragmatic, and logical. By the 'epistemological' aspect, they refer simply to the fact that moral norms, evaluations, and principles are conditioned by facts of social existence, by objective social processes. By the 'pragmatic' aspect of truth in morality, they mean the correspondence of evaluations or norms to specific social interests and needs, which makes them obligatory or right.

The 'logical' aspect of the problem of truth in moral judgments refers to "the possibility of working out ways and means for establishing correspondence between evaluations and norms, on one hand, and 'objective facts' connected with them, on the other" — which is the problem normally treated under this heading by English-speaking philosophers.[68] Xarčev and Jakovlev have no doubt of "the applicability of the property of truth in the epistemological sense to morality under the materialist understanding of morality".[69] In the 'pragmatic' sense also, moral norms and evaluations are always "an expression and result of specific needs and interests belonging to historical subjects (social classes), the origin and activity of which is conditioned by the development of material production".

However these authors regard the proof of the applicability of truth to morality 'in the logical aspect' — which is the heart of the problem — as a more difficult matter. They refer to attempts by two other Soviet theorists to solve the problem. Tabunov introduces the notion of the 'situational context', only within which moral norms or evaluations can be analyzed. Outside of such contexts, the property of truth or falsity is inapplicable to them.[70] Tabunov's view would appear to concede so much to the non-cognitivist view as to qualify only very dubiously as a cognitivist account of value judgments. The same conclusion applies to the second account cited by Xarčev and Jakovlev. Kobljakov distinguishes "three levels of theoretical verification of the truth or falsity of moral norms: (1) empirical — "by comparing norms with descriptive sentences to establish their correspondence or non-correspondence with various practical needs", (2) logical — "by comparison of norms with other norms and principles operant in society to establish the consistency of the system of norms", (3) scientific-theoretical — "by comparing norms with scientific knowledge of the interests of the class and the tendencies of development of society as a whole".[71] This last criterion supposedly permits one to compare a norm with social practice as a whole, and to "define its place in the general chain of social and moral progress".[72] Though Kobljakov's view might turn out to be a species of cognitivism, he does not really address the central issue: If normative judgments are to be conceived as property-referring, precisely what is the nature of the properties involved? Until specific answers are supplied to this question, Kobljakov's view could only be described as 'aspiring' to cognitivism.

Švarcman likewise aspires to a cognitivist account of the applicability of truth and falsity to moral values, and like a number of other Soviet theorists, sees the answer in some sort of verification of the truth or falsity of moral norms in the context of a science of history.

Outside of history, outside of an elucidation of the interrelations of the wills of individuals, classes and historical necessity, we cannot establish criteria for evaluation of human acts, judgments and norms . . . . In order to establish the correctness, the truth of this or that system of morality in our time, it is necessary to compare it with the objective laws of developing social reality, with the interests of the class struggling for socialism.[73]

Arxangel'skij acknowledges that "normative judgments (judgments of the obligatory) are distinguished in principle from judgments of facts, with which science operates".[74] Whereas judgments of fact "establish the presence or absence of a connection between the object and a property characterizing it", normative judgments "speak not of facts . . . but express injunctions, commands, wishes ('Don't kill!')".[75] Nevertheless, since moral consciousness "reflects social being" we must "recognize the applicability of epistemological categories in ethics".[76]

To the extent that norms of morality reflect not only their immediate object (moral relations, behavior) but also social interests, it is appropriate to compare the results of moral reflection not only with the object of reflection, but also with the social position of the subject of reflection. The objectivity of moral norms and evaluations is guaranteed by their adequacy for social interests. The special characteristic of the truth of moral judgments and their verification is defined by this . . .[77]

Again, an implicit appeal to a science of history which would objectively define the true interests of classes is made, and the 'truth' of a moral judgment is defined as its 'adequacy' for these interests. The notion of 'adequacy' falls a long way short of making good the claim to a cognitivist analysis of values, but as with several other views surveyed above, it proclaims a clear aspiration to such an account.

In a slightly eccentric treatment of the same problem, Konovalova adopted a broad characterization of the entire history of ethical theory as falling into three types: normative, sociological, and epistemological theories of ethics. Normative ethics began with "later Greek and Roman ethics, in its doctrine of the virtues, and was then picked up by religious and idealistic philosophy, blossoming in the ethics of Kant".[78] Its main task is to create a system of moral precepts and work out the sum of demands satisfying a specific type of morality. Sociological ethics finds its origins in the 'brilliant guesses' of the ancient Greek materialists concerning the dependence of people's moral views and conduct on their social position, and in Aristotle's thesis of 'the connection of morality with politics'; it further proceeds through the doctrines of Hobbes and Locke to the ethics of the French materialists, and finally through the materialism of Feuerbach to Marx's doctrine of social being and social consciousness.[79] The principal task of sociological ethics is to understand the "objective source of morality, to see it in the social life of society, and to establish the real limits of the moral sphere . . . ."[80] The third type, epistemological ethics, develops only in the modern period, and its main concern lies with epistemological problems of ethics, such as "the truth and falsity of various positions in ethics, the question of the contents of moral judgments, of criteria of correctness of norms and precepts of morality, etc.".[81] In her view 'bourgeois ethics' has been almost entirely directed to the solution of these problems. She herself views the solution of such epistemological problems as essential if ethics is to have a "solid scientific base".[82] She divides the problem of the truth in moral judgments into two aspects, 'correctness' and 'truth'. 'Correctness' may be applied to the judgments of individuals within society, when those judgments correspond to the generally shared convictions as to what is moral and immoral. However the criterion of general acceptance by the majority is inadequate for the objective evaluation of the morality of a group, collective, or community.[83]

Conceptions of the good, the true, and what is moral for individual classes are submitted to the court of history and are evaluated in the light of objective criteria. In this light the morality of the progressive classes which in the greatest degree reflect the demands of historical necessity usually turn out to be objectively true.[84]

Once again, the problem of explicating the nature of moral judgments so as to show the relevance of truth and falsity to them has been relegated to the sphere of history, or rather to a special science of history which will accomplish that task.

Knovalova's rather exaggerated view of 'epistemological ethics' as a new type of ethical inquiry concerning itself with 'cognition in ethics' represents a fairly common attitude among Soviet theorists at the present time. This tendency itself however has not escaped criticism by other authors. Šiškin for example complained that "the emphasis on the cognitive function of morality as a common function for science and morality which has received rights of citizenship in our ethical literature" is inadmissible.[85] He claimed that from good intentions to demonstrate the real connection between knowledge and morality, an exaggeration of the cognitive function of morality was developing.[86]

4. GOOD AND EVIL

The concept of 'good' has received attention in a large number of Soviet publications, as the first among the list of so-called 'categories of ethics', the discussion of which has been a major preoccupation of Soviet writers since the renewal of their interest in the subject of ethics. This approach to ethical theory began with Arxangel'skij's 1961 article, and may have reached its climax in a national conference on the 'Categories of Marxist-Leninist Ethics' held in Novosibirsk in 1969.[87] In the first decade of renewed Soviet interest in ethical theory, the 'categories of ethics' constituted a major element of most discussions. More recently there is some evidence that this has been recognized as not an especially fruitful approach. Some of the most recent publications in ethical theory no longer pursue the topic, and others have submitted the entire approach to criticism. For example, Xarčev and Jakovlev comment that the entire literature on the ethical 'categories' — duty, conscience, responsibility, justice, honor, happiness, good — on the whole 'gives no one the right to speak of any serious theoretical achievements in that sphere'.[88] In the literature on the 'ethical categories', each of them is routinely examined in terms of "the interrelation of the objective and the subjective, the rational and the emotional, the external and the internal, the all-human and the class, the substantive and the formal, sides".[89] As a rule the whole of this literature suffers from a 'poverty of scientific argument', a 'passion for illustrativeness', and "an inability to distinguish banal 'passing' truths from really new approaches and to concentrate on the latter".[90]

Nevertheless the literature on the concept of 'good' retains some interest for non-Soviet readers since it does contain some of the clearest formulations of what Soviet writers take to be ultimate criteria of good.

According to Arxangel'skij 'good' is employed in at least five distinct senses in Marxist literature, which he lists as "(1) good as the objective moral quality (significance) of an act; (2) good as a general concept uniting the entire collection of positive principles and norms of a given morality, good as an ideal; (3) good as the moral goal of conduct, turning into (4) the motive of action; (5) good as virtue, the moral quality of a person".[91]

Ju. V. Sogomonov, in an unusually lucid and well-argued monograph on 'good' and 'evil', considered both consequentialist and deontological views of the nature of obligation (turning the discussion to the question of what determines moral right and wrong).[92] Inquiring what is more important, or, for what does a person bear responsibility, his intentions or the results of his actions, he rejected both the view that a person is responsible only for the consequences of his acts, and also the view that motives or intentions alone determine the moral quality of an act.

In this argument scientific ethics considers that moral evaluation must certainly be all-sided, summative. Its elements are the evaluation of the motives, goals, means, action itself, its results and remote consequences.

Evaluation only by motives and goals or exclusively by results is superficial, approximate, and very often mistaken.[93]

Unfortunately Sogomonov draws no distinction here between moral and non-moral uses of the term 'good' and does not distinguish therefore or attend to the difference between evaluating persons, groups, or traits of character on the one hand and non-personal objects, conditions, or events on the other. From the context it is clear however that his primary interest lies in assessing the moral worth of persons in reference to their voluntary actions, and his discussion remains focused on that problem.

Sogomonov's discussion of the objectivity of good and evil remains one of the most sophisticated to have appeared in Soviet literature up to the present despite a few oddities in his interpretations of non-Marxist ethical theories. He criticizes both the moral sense theories of the 18th century (which he describes as a variety of intuitivism) and the intuitivisms of the early twentieth century as 'subjectivism' on the grounds that both deny the deducibility of conclusions about good and evil from considerations of utility or pleasantness. He objects to the moral sense theorists' assertion that moral feelings (or a moral sense) are innate, given at birth as a component of some unchanging human nature. He does accept the view that one's moral feelings are an appropriate component of the process of making moral judgments.[94] "It is inadmissible to exaggerate either the rational aspect or the emotional aspect."[95] His central complaint against "the intuitivist negation of the objective nature of good and evil" concerns the threat of subjectivism or relativism:

... each person is a judge for himself; each is right in his own way; each must believe only in his own customs, flowing from his own form of life, each is right to justify his behavior only by an inner belief in its correctness.[96]

Sogmonov argues for the objectivity of good and evil, but "a different objectivity from the objectivity of existence unrelated to the subject".[97] He considers and rejects the view that if good and evil do not exist independently of people, then they cannot be objective. That only proves that the good does not possess substantial being, that it is not a thing, does not have a material bearer, that there is no object which has only the property of being good or evil.[98] Good and evil are characteristics, attributes. None of this proves the subjectivity of good, any more than it would prove the subjectivity of secondary qualities such as color or taste.

Good and evil are simultaneously objective and subjective, depending both on the properties of the object and on the evaluating subject. Sogomonov then goes on to cite the six varieties of ethical subjectivism described and criticized by Hegel, and endorses what he describes as Hegel's account of the objectivity of good and evil, namely that the state is a moral organism, and therefore the good of the state is the criterion of good and evil.[99] His only criticism of Hegel consists of the accusation that by 'state' Hegel meant the reactionary Prussian autocracy (surely a false reading of Hegel), and Sogomonov's own view seems to attempt a restatement of Hegel in cruder terminology:

The objectivity of good and evil consists in the fact that they exist prior to and independently of the consciousness of the separate individual. They exist as part of the ideals, conceptions, ideas of social consciousness, as a part of social psychology. It is necessary to remember that the consciousness of the separate individual, and in turn social consciousness, is not an arithmetic sum of the consciousness of all individuals, although it does not exist outside of subjects, only in their heads.[100]

Most Soviet authors treat the objectivity of good and evil in a more simplistic fashion, simply concluding that the good is the objective interest of society (especially in historical progress). For example, Arxangel'skij states that "loyalty to social interests is the most objective criterion of good and evil in its Communist meaning".[101] Or, the *Dictionary of Ethics* claims that,

In Communist morality the concept of 'good' is connected with the actual interests of people in contemporary historical conditions. And these interests in the final analysis coincide with the historical necessity of the victory of socialist over capitalist society, with the construction of Communism.[102]

In similarly broad and unqualified terms, Arxangel'skij describes the domination of private property as "the source and stimulus for all evil".[103]

5. CONCLUSION: SOVIET THEORIES OF VALUE AND METANORMATIVE NATURALISM

As described above (Sec. 3) the majority of Soviet philosophers addressing the issue of the applicability of truth or falsity to normative or value judgments profess a cognitivist account of the matter. Value judgments are analyzed as property-referring and hence susceptible of truth and falsity. It was also pointed out above that most of the 'cognitivist' analyses offered thus far contain serious difficulties possibly disqualifying them as variants of cognitivism.

More particularly, in the type of analysis most adopted by Soviet theorists, values are described as relations between an evaluating subject and a ('social') object constituting an interest for the evaluator. Tugarinov, for example, defined 'value' as 'the satisfaction of an interest'.[104] This would seem to place the most typical Soviet analysis of values squarely within the very traditional category of relational, interest theories of the naturalist school, similar to R. B. Perry, for instance.

However, Soviet authors universally reject naturalism (as well as non-naturalism), and counterpose their own analyses as an alternative to it. Despite the contrasts regularly drawn between 'naturalism' and their own positions by Soviet authors, the question may still be seriously put: do not most of the Soviet accounts turn out to be relational, interest theory versions of naturalism after all?

Many Soviet authors attempt to set up a contrast between their own views and something they term 'naturalism' in ethics by playing upon their own distinction between 'nature' and 'society', which they present as logically exhaustive. (For example in their criticism of intuitivism, Drobnickij and Kuz'mina remark, "But that which is non-natural in reality can only be social, relating to the world of social existence . . .").[105] 'Naturalism' in the *Dictionary of Ethics* is defined as a "methodological principle for the founding of morality" in which "moral demands are deduced . . . − from the laws of nature or from man's biological-psychological particularities".[106] The author of this article displays an awareness of the possibility that Marxist ethics also fall under this particular umbrella, when a different definition of 'naturalism' is employed, but rejects this definition as 'improper' (!)

In contemporary bourgeois ethics the term 'naturalism' is frequently improperly treated in a wider sense, and is used to signify all theories in which the categories of good and duty are defined by means of 'extra-moral concepts' – interests of man, natural or social or even supernatural laws, pleasure, happiness, and others. Such an interpretation comes from Moore. It numbers in the ranks of naturalist theories not only vulgar-materialistic, biological and psychological theories of ethics, but also certain religious moral doctrines, for example 'natural law' (*Neo-Thomism*), and occasionally even Marxist ethics as well. In reality Marxist ethics, founded on historical materialism, not only is not naturalistic, but also is the only theory in the history of ethical thought which subjects naturalism to criticism from a genuinely scientific position.[107]

This repudiation of naturalism by Soviet theorists often turns out to depend merely upon eccentric usages of the term, amid complaints about 'excessively broad' definitions of the term by non-Marxist scholars. A quite recent publication argues as follows:

Naturalism in ethics is occasionally understood extremely broadly – as any explanation of morality referring to facts of nature. In such an approach, tendencies of thought substantially distinguished from one another both by their theoretical content and by their historical significance, are united. It is more correct, so it seems to us and as already stated in the introduction, to understand under 'naturalistic' only those tendencies in ethics which proceed not from nature in general, but *from the nature of man.*[108]

This author then proceeds to discuss Konrad Lorenz's work on aggression in geese as a typical example of ethical naturalism in contemporary bourgeois thought, and prior to him, Herbert Spencer, complaining that "from naturalism, if one is somewhat consistent, it is impossible to derive social morality, the necessity of moral goodness and selflessness".[109]

The precise meaning of 'naturalism' in Western meta-ethics may indeed by subject to some ambiguity. Nevertheless a more thorough acquaintance of these authors with Western writings in ethical theory would have brought to their attention the following widely-used definition of 'naturalism' – (1) that ethical statements are statements about facts and are either true or false according as they describe these facts correctly or incorrectly, and (2) that the truth or falsity of these statements can be assessed by the methods of empirical science: observation and inductive reasoning.[110]

Each of the elements of the Soviet analysis of value would seem to submit to these conditions. That a man may be known to possess certain (social) interests regardless of the state of his own consciousness of them would appear to imply that such interests can be assessed 'objectively' by some (Marxist) science of society. Granted that the state of a man's interests can be established objectively, independently of his consciousness, his relation to objects, and their properties, can also be assessed by empirical science. Accepting these assumptions it is difficult to see how the Soviet analysis of value could escape the label of 'naturalism' as just defined.

The one obvious alternative to such a conclusion might be closer to the truth, but still less palatable to Soviet thinking. One might reply that the entire account of man's 'social interests' as provided by historical materialism is an instance of cosmological reasoning, and that historical materialism is not in fact an empirical science in any usual sense of the word, not dependent in any unequivocal way upon observation, and hence to 'assess' a man's social interests by means of historical materialism is not to engage in any recognizable form of empirical inquiry. Only upon such an interpretation of historical materialism as this would Soviet writers be correct in rejecting the label of 'naturalism' for their views of value theory.

CHAPTER SIX

SOCIETY AND THE INDIVIDUAL

1. SOCIAL UTILITARIANISM

When the recent Soviet discussions of ethics are examined from the perspective of the history of ethical theory as a whole, one of their more interesting general characteristics can be easily discerned: the framework and terms of these discussions, the problems posed, and the approaches taken toward their solution are remarkably similar to those of the 'social utilitarian' doctrines of the eighteenth century French Enlightenment. This is not so surprising when one remembers that Marx himself frequently drew attention to the doctrines of the 'French materialists', and more particularly, that Plekhanov wrote extensively on the eighteenth century French materialists. Russians who learned their Marxism through Plekhanov could scarcely fail to be highly conscious of these writers, even forgetting the special fascination which the *Philosophes* held for the nineteenth century Russian '*intelligenty*'. One of the earliest Soviet works on the history of ethical theory was an article on the 'social ethics' of Morelly and Mably, by a student of Deborin.[1]

For the eighteenth century social utilitarians, as for Soviet theorists now, the central problem of ethical theory was and is the maintenance of social order. One Soviet philosopher singled out the French materialists, the utopian socialists, and the Russian revolutionary democrats of the nineteenth century as the three principal groups who "firmly insisted on the idea that the social function of morality consists in the regulation of the interrelations between society and the individual".[2] The preservation of social order, more particularly the defense of social order against the threat posed by the egoistic individual preoccupied all these groups of ethical theorists.

One may distinguish three broad currents of ethical thought in eighteenth century France: (1) the traditional natural law theorists, including their distant cousins the moral sense theorists, and many of the Christian apologists, (2) the various schools of utilitarian thought, and (3) the Nihilists.[3] It is of course for the last two of these trends that the terms and limits of socialization of the egoistic individual constituted the chief preoccupation.

The egoistic individual, *bête noir* of so many Enlightenment thinkers, was a premise which began to take hold in the late seventeenth century, a product

136

of the confluence of many intellectual innovations, especially in cosmology, experimental science, and psychology. The collapse of the Medieval Christian cosmos, the astonishing successes of Newtonian mechanics, and the materialist sensationalist psychology which soon followed, all contributed directly to the conception of the hedonistically-motivated individual, that creature of nature whose motions could be reliably predicted by the universal 'law' (as well as 'Natural Right') of self-interest, just as the motions of physical bodies could be predicted by Newton's universal law of gravitation.

Utilitarianism developed in part as a response to the problem of how to integrate this hedonistically-motivated, self-seeking individual into a social order which would neither be destroyed by his activities nor destroy him in the process. Four different schools of utilitarian thought can be distinguished, according to which of four different 'solutions' were adopted to this problem of the potential clash between the self-interest of the egoistic individual and the social good: (1) the laissez-faire reasoning of Mandeville, Smith and the Physiocrats, (2) the 'social utilitarians' whose doctrines led to the argument for authoritarian control, (3) the argument for enlightened self-interest, which equated virtue with happiness, and (4) the supposition of a benevolent altruism which would outweigh self-interest.

Social utilitarianism began to emerge from the broader tradition of utilitarian thought when thinkers such as Morelly, Helvetius, and Mably began to stress the absolute right of the community to realize its own good, even at the expense of individual rights. The idea of the priority of the social benefit emerged gradually from the natural law tradition via the relatively easy assumption made by many thinkers both in France and England, that 'natural justice' required, and ultimately came to the same thing as, the social benefit. This 'easy' identification came about almost unnoticed in the works of a number of writers who were attracted to the relatively novel concept of the greatest happiness of the greatest number as the standard of right and wrong, and who strongly promoted the utilitarian standard, yet retained references to 'natural law' and 'justice' in such a way as to leave the impression that natural justice remained the ultimate criterion of right and wrong. Where a possible conflict between public utility and natural justice was not explicitly proposed, an equivalence between the two was very often assumed without hesitation.

The leader of the utilitarian movement in France was Helvetius, who was quite unequivocal in adopting a utilitarian concept of justice. He held that justice derives from positive law, and described the greatest happiness of the greatest number as "a principle which contains all of ethics and legislation".[4]

While retaining the language of natural rights, Helvetius constantly referred to self-interest as the basis for ethical judgments. His concept of self-interest was a three-tiered one: that of the individual, that of the group, and that of the whole community, where the last was the ultimate criterion of right and wrong. Society thus became the ultimate beneficiary of the 'natural right to self-preservation'.

Another group adopted positions quite similar to social utilitarianism, except that they insisted firmly upon the difference between justice and right on one hand, and utility on the other, thereby reaching nihilist conclusions. They insisted that utility was the only available criterion for action, that there was no ultimate right or wrong within human purview, and for this reason society was 'justified' in requiring anything it wished. Equally, the individual was 'justified' in the unrestrained pursuit of his own interest. The genuine problem was purely one of social order and control, for the maintenance of which any recourse was 'justifiable'. La Mettrie can be classified as a social utilitarian from this perspective. "Everything that is useful to society is [a virtue], the rest is its phantom".[5] The argument moved with equal ease to de Sade's unlimited license for the individual on one hand, to unlimited measures for the maintenance of social order under an authoritarian regime on the other. Thus when some thinkers began to distinguish the utilitarian criterion quite clearly from the concept of natural right, new and startling perspectives on moral discourse opened up. Society suddenly appeared to be the only arbiter of right and wrong in a cosmos where nothing was intrinsically either. Writers such as Helvetius and Rousseau earnestly advocated their new ethical theories as worthy of any respectable, morally serious person. Others such as La Mettrie, or in the extreme case de Sade, interpreted essentially the same assumptions of social utilitarianism as involving the denial of morality in any ordinary 'respectable' sense.

Contemporary Soviet theorists adopt arguments quite similar to those of the social utilitarian, transferring the locus of value and 'natural right' from the individual to the community, as in the works of Morelly, Helvetius, Mably, and Rousseau (with some reservations). It is characteristic of this view to 'dissolve' the individual into the community, treating him as an essentially social being whose identifying traits are simply instances of collective properties.[6]

With certain qualifications, Soviet authors can also be seen as sharing the assumption of the social utilitarians that nothing in the cosmos is intrinsically right or wrong. For example, Sogomonov argues as follows:

Let us begin with this question: can one find in the universe good and evil? An affirmative answer would be justified if the universe as a whole had some sort of pre-established goals. Then, everything which cooperated with these goals would be good, and everything which resisted, would be evil. But the point is that the world process does not exhibit a goal-directed character. It presents itself as a unity of ascending and descending lines.

It has no transcendent (*vnemirovoj*) goals, or strictly manifested directionality: it strives toward nothing and desires nothing. The universe does not gravitate toward perfection, nor to imperfection. It is a cause of itself; its movement, change is subordinated not to goals, but only to specific laws. And these laws are its own laws, and not external prescriptions. But since the universe has no goal, then there is no good and evil on the cosmic scale.[7]

The major qualification which must be added to most Soviet views of this sort concerns history. Whereas the universe as a whole may be viewed as exhibiting neither good nor evil, history of course does. And given the complexities of the relation between the natural and the social implicit in Soviet cosmology, to claim that history exhibits the properties of good and evil becomes tantamount to attributing them to the universe.

Common to all the eighteenth century French theorists of social utilitarianism was an extremely negative attitude toward humanity in its natural state. Each of them tended to view humanity untutored and unmolded by society with a degree of pessimism matched only by the nihilists. In the abbé de Mably's opinion, human beings are little better than animals.

It is these imbeciles who, by their number, by the stupidity of their brutal instinct and their physical force make reason tremble and exercise the most blind and violent tyranny in the world. We must spare their prejudices and fear to irritate them.[8]

Morelly too seems to have been horrified by human nature left unmolded by a strong government; it was the task of government to place the individual in a situation where it would be impossible for him to pursue his natural wicked inclinations. Rousseau of course depicted the individual in the 'original' state of nature as devoid of a moral or intellectual life. Helvetius saw humanity as ruled by inclinations, instinct, and appetites which were stronger than any alleged moral obligation, and he saw in coercion through education the only proper answer to the problem of human wickedness.

The chief redeeming virtue of the human species for each of the thinkers in this group was the malleability of its individual members. ". . . It is of little matter than men be vicious; it is enough that they be intelligent."[9] Mably's remarks on the malleability of man are still more graphic: speaking of the passions he inquires

Why couldn't you bring out how useful they would be in the hands of a skillful politician? ... If I play a certain key on a clavecin, I am sure of producing a certain sound. I believe, in truth, that it is the same with man .... Man would be happy if politics learned the springs of the heart well enough to move the passions at will, and to give them the extent, the activity, and the enthusiasm necessary to the success of its enterprises;...[10]

The object of education was not merely to secure social order; or rather, that goal should be seen as inextricably combined with another: to create a human being whose essential existence was social, who lived as a simple instantiation of the properties of the collective whole.

The one trait of this collective human being of greatest interest to these theorists was that he should see a complete identity of his own personal interests and those of the social collective. Helvetius, Morelly, Mably, and Rousseau all propose social arrangements within which all self-interest would be either identified with the good of the whole, or suppressed.

The chief agent for the reform of human nature was to be the state. Morelly set out in the *Code de la Nature* a detailed sketch of authoritarian social control, including the use of the technique of psychological conditioning for children. Similarly Mably in the *Principes de Morale* undertook the study of the psychology of children and adolescents in order to facilitate molding them by legislation, asserting that it was necessary to make the imbecilic multitude "the worthy instrument of the great men who make it act".[11] The legislator was to be the magician who brought about the identification of the personal and the social interest. Helvetius held that the entire art of the legislator consisted in forcing men to be just to each other out of a feeling of self-love. The state was to be not just the guardian of the social welfare, but creator and manipulator of society's morals as well. Rousseau's views on the essential role of the state in creating morals are too well known to require repetition.

The pronounced distrust of nature upon which social utilitarianism was based effectively removed nature as a potential resource for the social planner. Nature could be trusted only to supply disorder, egoism, and the war of all against all. Society had to rely above all upon reason and will to combat nature. As Crocker pointed out, each of these four theorists constantly made pious references to 'nature', claiming that his recommendations for the reconstruction of humanity within the confines of society included only what was 'natural', or at most, assisted what was virtuous in nature to realize its own. In truth theirs was a radical assault upon nature in the name of rationally ordered social convention masquerading as the 'natural'.[12]

The general constellation of views labelled here 'social utilitarianism' could be summarized from another perspective as the identification of ethics with politics, that simultaneous solution of the problems of individual virtue and social order which stems from Plato. It is assumed that morals grow properly out of law, not vice versa. The rational legislator of the eighteenth century, working in a cosmos without natural law, could be guided only by the interest of the whole. Where that ran counter to be individual's interest, there seemed to be no criterion available in the light of which the interest of the whole could be compromised. An essential arbitrariness, or rather, the dictates of power, lay just beneath the mantle of morality with which the social utilitarians attempted to cloak these arrangements.

This ultimate arbitrariness in the social utilitarian's doctrine of right — nothing is right or wrong save what society decrees — points to the perhaps surprisingly close relationship between the assumptions behind authoritarian social control and nihilism. They might be regarded as equally plausible responses to the one assumption that nothing is intrinsically right or wrong. The denial that anything is intrinsically right or wrong equally 'justifies' anarchist revolt and the ruthless repression of the individual.

The position just outlined as 'social utilitarianism' anticipates the general contours of Soviet ethical thought in several major respects. In Soviet theory too the 'social interest', conceived as distinct from the collective interests of individuals, serves as the ultimate criterion of right and wrong; the assumption of an inherent potential for conflict between personal and social interest is betrayed by the extent of hortatory literature arguing for the identity of the two, 'properly' understood. 'Egoism' is used as a synonym for 'immorality' and is one of the sharpest terms of moral condemnation.

For example, E. F. Petrov, in a substantial monograph entitled *Egoism*, relates egoism to evil:

The essence of egoism places it in the rank of ethical categories. In this sense it is very close to such a category of ethics as evil . . . .
 The question can arise, is the assertion true that egoism is a category derived from evil? With this aim let us compare the two categories with each other. If, with the help of the category of evil one may evaluate any negative act of the individual: unscrupulousness, dishonor, loss of dignity, including egoism, then the category of egoism evaluates specific acts of the individual . . . .
 Egoism is related to the category of evil approximately as Kepler's laws are related to the general law of universal gravity of Newton.[13]

The individual is viewed theoretically as a creation of society, his 'individual' traits as a product of social influences. As Petrov remarks,

From the interaction of the individual with society it follows that the human being is not born a civilized, moral being. If he were such from nature, then it would not be necessary to establish moral norms and rules of behavior, it would not be necessary for society to present demands to its members and strictly ensure their fulfillment.[14]

On the crucial question of the primacy of social over individual interests, Petrov quotes Lenin to the effect that "the interests of social development are higher than the interests of the proletariat".

In the formula asserting the coincidence of the interests of the individual and society in the conditions of socialism, primacy is always given to social interests. That is understandable, because "from the point of view of the basic ideas of Marxism", said V. I. Lenin, "the interests of social development are higher than the interests of the proletariat – the interests of the whole worker's movement in it as a whole are higher than the interests of a particular stratum of workers or a particular aspect of the movement."[15]

The development of a new morality is posited as part of the process of creating a new man within the crucible of society; the distrust of nature, while not positively affirmed, is implicit in the reliance upon reason ('science') as the guide to the construction of the new man.

The single greatest point of contrast between Soviet ethical theory and the 'social utilitarianism' of the Enlightenment concerns the agency for the reconstruction of humanity. Whereas the Enlightenment thinkers just considered were unanimous in attributing this agency to the state, in the form of the rational legislator, Soviet writers are unanimous in attributing this agency to History. History, or rather its handmaiden, the Communist party, is to be the agent for the formation of the new humanity. In this process however the party is to be guided by its scientific (Marxist-Leninist) knowledge of history's laws. In this may be seen the Soviet theorists' equivalent of their predecessors' claim that in reconstructing humanity within the confines of society, they were only following 'nature's' bidding. The inevitable 'laws of social development' have become the surrogate for Nature. The inevitability of the reconstruction of human nature as dictated by the 'laws of History' frees Soviet theorists of the problem of supplying a more detailed explanation of the 'necessity' for this reconstruction, and hence of revealing more explicitly a pessimistic contempt for unreconstructed humanity such as motivated Enlightenment thinkers of similar persuasion in ethical theory. On the contrary, Soviet authors constantly remind their readers and each other that 'optimism' is the watchword of the 'new' Marxist-Leninist ethical outlook. However, optimism about the *future* of humanity also characterized most of the Enlightenment thinkers just discussed here. The truly telling attitude, not explicitly expressed in Soviet literature, is that toward humanity *untutored* by the proposed socialist reconstruction. *This* attitude is the true test of one's basic opinion of humanity, and it is one in which social utilitarians merge with the nihilists. Despite the absence of any explicit acknowledgement of such an attitude in Soviet literature, a significant question remains: does not the general logic of social utilitarianism presuppose this attitude, whether expressed or not?

2. THE CONCEPT OF INTEREST

The concept of interest serves several crucial functions in Soviet ethical theory. As described above, the objectivity of value is defended in terms of the existence of objective interests, both individual and social, the satisfaction of which constitutes a value. Individuals, classes, and social orders are each viewed as possessing objective interests, and certain of these interests are conceived as manifesting historical progress, reflecting the development of humanity toward Communism.

Social needs and interests in this way serve as the chief links between the analysis of the structure of individual personality and Marxist historical sociology. Social needs are not derived from the interests of the individual:

[Social needs and class needs] must never be defined by starting out from the needs of individuals. Social interests are defined on their own basis by the needs of development of the productive forces.[16]

The evolutionary development of society's needs, as opposed to those of its constituent members, are among the main marks of the hypothesized social development central to Marxism. History is narrated in terms of successive configurations of the society-cosmos.

The development of society is a natural-historical process: the social existence of man is the movement of a certain whole, subject to objective laws. In the analysis of the content of these laws (the development of productive forces and economic relations, the historical process as a consecutive supercession of socio-economic formations, etc.) we get along without the concepts of subject and object.[17]

The individual in his uniqueness is logically superfluous in the sense that an essential description of his nature (all those aspects crucial to Marxist ethical theory) can be derived from the description of the society-cosmos at each point in its evolution. The individual, conceived as a creature of this society-cosmos, dependent for the (moral) essence of his nature upon it, is easily fitted into the schema by means of the assumption that his essence is in part constituted by, or rather identical with, the needs and interests of the society as a whole of which he is a part. As the society-cosmos evolves, so does individual nature. The assumption of an identity, or partial identity, of the needs and interests of society and those of the individual (1) constitutes part of the definition of the individual person, (2) links the description of the individual to the Marxist evolutionary schema, and (3) serves as a crucial assumption of ethical theory.

One is tempted to say that the usual Soviet conception of the individual person is that of an object produced by the society-cosmos in abstraction from his own individual will or consciousness. This would be considered a provocative over-simplification by most representatives of Soviet ethical theory; but in fact some Soviet authors have criticized many others for leaving themselves open to this very charge.

It can indeed be argued that to view the individual as a creature of society, defined in such a way that his essence consists of certain needs and interests which are attributes of the social whole at that point in its evolution, in no way uniquely dependent on the individual's will or consciousness, is just to make an object, not a subject in the usual sense, of the individual person.

This tendency to 'dissolve' the individual into the 'ensemble of social relations' of which he is supposedly constituted, has been criticized, for instance, by Igor Kon who argued that Marx's sixth thesis on Feuerbach is frequently misconstrued by Soviet philosophers and sociologists. Kon pointed out that Marx "clearly means not an individual person, but man as a generic concept. Man as a *type* actually coincides with the conjunction of social relations, with society".[18]

Other writers have voiced similar objections to this tendency in Soviet social theory to conflate sociological personality types with actual individuals. B. D. Parygin argues that the substitution of the sociological personality type for the concrete individual person 'deprives it completely of psychological properties' and reduces the concept of the person merely to "a simplistic personification of social forces".[19]

This problem has not been confronted very often in the literature on ethics, but one recent work does touch on it. Describing a 'debate' which took place in *Voprosy filosofii* between P. M. Egides and G. K. Gumnickij, Xarčev and Jakovlev took the opportunity to express themselves on the problem of the "interrelationship of social and individual values".[20]

Egides and Gumnickij were disputing the proper relationship between 'happiness' and 'the meaning of life' as ethical categories.[21] Gumnickij accused Egides of treating the personal happiness of the individual as without independent significance or meaning since Egides claimed that the meaning of life lay in service to society. Egides replied that one should never see only a kind of auxiliary value in personal life; it also has an independent value. The meaning of life lies not only in the achievement of social good, but in serving oneself, in striving for personal happiness.

Without settling the controversy, Xarčev and Jakovlev treated the exchange between Gumnickij and Egides as facilitating the resolution of the problem of the interrelationship of social and personal interests, and especially of the tendency to regard the individual as merely a 'cog' in the social mechanism, a mere instrument of social progress. Xarčev and Jakovlev describe this tendency as 'alien to Marxism' and observe that 'our party long ago subjected it to criticism', referring to some literature on 'man as the highest value', the problem of alienation, the correspondence of ends and means, etc.[22] The difficulty, of course, is that this same literature typically obscures rather than clarifies the very distinction between individual and social consciousness, or between individual and social interests. It may be that Xarčev and Jakovlev were offering a mild protest against what is in fact a deeply rooted problem in Soviet ethical theory, a solution to which might ultimately transgress the limits of Marxist sociology and social theory. For instance, despite Kon's objections to the dissolution of the individual into the social whole just discussed, he presents a well-established conclusion of Marxist social theory when he states that the individual himself "is not a pre-supposition of socialization, but its product".[23]

The importance attributed to this problem of the relation between the individual and the social interest in Soviet philosophy is in one sense very curious. It is possible to argue that within a consistently Marxist worldview the problem should be only peripheral. In a strictly Marxist cosmology one could argue that the problem of the identity of the individual and the social interest must remain a peripheral one for the very good reason that uniquely individual interests are themselves at best only peripheral, 'accidental' elements in the description of the individual. The properly Marxist approach is to *define* the individual person as constituted of certain 'social' needs and interests, regardless whether they are recognized as such by the individual. However, as betrayed in this formulation itself, the problem of the individual consciousness and will itself is not solved, merely ignored, for what is the entity which may or may not 'recognize' these social needs and interests which supposedly constitute his 'true' essence at a given point in history? If this difficulty in the Marxist conception of the individual person were not enough, Lenin's philosophical legacy tended to restore the traditional Cartesian distinction between the 'inner' consciousness and the 'outer' external world, and along with it, the traditional Cartesian implications as to the nature of the individual consciousness, as argued above.[24]

If one begins with the traditional Cartesian individual consciousness as the bearer of interests, then the traditional problem of the possible non-coincidence of the individual and the social interest is restored with all its usual vitality. However, the individual consciousness conceived in the traditional Cartesian manner as a thinking thing possessed of will, sensibility, etc., can be only dimly discerned in contemporary Soviet philosophy as a whole. Where the discussion explicitly concerns the 'Marxist' concept of the individual person, the definition of the individual in terms of social needs, interests and other social characteristics predominates. When, however, attention has been shifted to some other philosophical problem, the traditional language of 'inner' and 'outer' comes as naturally to Soviet philosophers as to any other. This vacillation between an implicit traditional philosophical psychology and an explicit philosophical sociology, or the attempt to have 'a psychology devoid of a psyche', leaves the entire problem of the conflict between individual and social interests in a state of philosophical obscurity.[25]

Obviously if no clear distinction between individual consciousness and social consciousness has been made, then *a fortiori* the more specific problem of the opposition or harmony of individual and social interests cannot be clearly formulated. There is nevertheless a rather large body of literature on the problem of individual and social interests.

In a relatively detailed discussion published in 1955, G. M. Gak acknowledged that the identity between social interests and individual interests could not be made in a simple fashion.[26] Quoting Rousseau, he inquired, "what does it mean to go to one's death for the sake of personal interest?"[27] More mundanely, "even family interest is not always personal interest . . .".[28]

To leave the matter at this point of course would make the coincidence between social and personal interests always a contingent matter, an unsatisfactory state of affairs for Marxist social theory. Gak secured the necessary definitional identity in another way. He distinguished 'personal interest' from 'the interest of the person'. 'Personal interest' is a phenomenon dependent upon the consciousness and will of the individual:

. . . determined by the needs of the individual connected with the preservation of his existence, with the development of his powers and capabilities, with the guaranteeing of his material needs and cultural interests, his freedom, etc.[29]

The 'interest of the person' on the other hand, like the 'social interest', does not derive from the individual will or consciousness, but from the nature of the collective whole.

Although the collectivity consists of people, it is a reality not reducible to a conjunction of the individuals composing it. The interest of the collectivity is given objectively as defined by its nature and conditions of existence . . . . And since every collectivity consists of people, its interests become objectively the interests of each of its members. Thus the class interest of the proletariat is objectively the interest of each individual proletarian.[30]

This 'interest of the person' which derives from class membership obtains regardless whether it is known by the individual and even when, under the influence of an alien class ideology, the individual struggles against it.

Gak introduces a number of terms into the discussion: 'the social interest', 'the general interest' (= 'class interest'), 'the interest of the person', and 'the personal interest', and he stipulates relations among all of these terms. At the conclusion his analysis turns out to be much simpler than the number of special terms would indicate.

First, the only clear distinction introduced between the 'social interest' and the 'general interest' (from which the 'interest of the person' is derived) is that the latter is attributed to *classes* and the former to *societies*. Where there are antagonistic classes comprising a society the social interest and the general interests of particular classes are not necessarily identical. However, where there are no antagonistic classes, no distinction between the social interest and the general interest is offered in the article. Therefore in socialist society one assumes the 'social interest' and the 'general interest' are identical.

Next comes the most crucial question of the relation between the 'social' (= 'general') interest and 'the interest of the person'. The definitions seem almost identical: each derives from the nature and conditions for the existence of some whole considered as a reality not reducible to the sum of its individual members; each exists 'objectively' whether or not it is recognized by the individual. The 'social interest' and its individual instantiation, 'the interest of the individual' are alike independent of the will and consciousness of the individual.

The 'personal interest', being dependent upon recognition by the individual consciousness for its existence, comes closest to what most theorists have intended by 'the individual interest'. Of its relationship to 'the interest of the person' Gak says only that it is 'included' in the latter. The 'interest of the person' is 'wider' than the 'personal interest'.[31]

Gak's 'solution' is thus ultimately no less simple than that of the Enlightenment *philosophes* whom he criticizes: he has merely introduced an unexplained *tertium quid*, 'the interest of the person', between the 'social interest' and the 'personal interest'. Since he offers no significant distinction between the last two (at least under socialism), he has in effect fallen back upon the familiar assertion of the identity of individual and social interest, adding only that there are some individual interests which may apparently conflict with the social. This is merely to re-state the original problem, not to solve it.

Gak's 1955 article was referred to in 1964 by one of the most highly regarded sociologists in the Soviet Union as the 'fullest treatment of *interest* in Soviet literature'. This second author published a short monograph of his own on the subject in that year, and it remained the most recent monograph on the subject to be cited in the *Filosofskaja enciklopedija* as of 1967.[32]

Zdravomyslov, the second author, pointed out that the founders of Marxism principally wished to distinguish 'interests' from 'ideas'; interests are something 'objective' by comparison to ideas.[33] The actual moving forces of history are *interests*; every idea is only a reflection of this or that interest, and the force of an idea in history depends upon how deeply it is connected with interests – the degree to which it expresses the general interest, or succeeds in representing the private interest in the guise of the general.[34] He quotes Plekhanov to the effect that interests are not a product of human will or consciousness, but are created by objective economic relations.[35]

Zdravomyslov himself speaks of an 'interest' as "a social position reflected in consciousness and moreover as consciousness issuing in action". In this notion he distinguishes four basic aspects of the logical structure of an interest: (1) the social position of the subject, or the conjunction of his practical connections with society; (2) the degree of recognition of the position, which can vary widely from non-understanding through clouded perception to clear recognition; (3) ideological motive forces, or motives for activity, directed at determinate objects of interest, and (4) action itself, which represents itself as an assertion of the subject in the objective world.[36]

On the troublesome question of the relation of coincidence or identity between individual and social interests, Zdravomyslov adopts the position that

... an individual ... or group interest is *social* if it binds the individual or group to the progressive tendencies of the age. Conversely a private interest locks the activity of the individual or community of people into a limited world of the everyday, directs the subject's consciousness toward himself, deprives human life of its historical content.[37]

In other words the relationship of identity holds between social and invididual interests if a certain other coincidence obtains: that between the individual and the *progressive*. In short Zdravomyslov's treatment of the concept of *interest* in relation to *value* also trails off into unexplained assumptions about a certain relationship between *value* and *historical progress*. This problem will be treated in the following chapter.

Finally, one further feature of the usual Soviet treatment of the concept of 'interest' is emphasized in Zdravomyslov's monograph and should be understood in relation to the definition of the individual in terms of social needs. Interests are interpreted as occurring by a certain kind of *necessity*.

... natural necessity, the properties of human existence, interest – that is what links the members of civil society to one another.[38]

Interest is described as 'a necessary property of human existence' (by which I assume it is meant that interests are logically involved in the definition of human nature). One consequence of insisting upon the necessary character of interests is to deflect attention from the distinction between the desired and the desirable. That in which one is *interested* in the sense used here is by definition also *desired*. The question of whether it, on reflection, is also considered *desirable* in a moral sense, or how desirable it is relative to some other goal, or whether it is intrinsically desirable, is not raised. Satisfaction of the interest is taken to be moral conduct, so long as the satisfaction of the interest is also in accord with social progress. If humanity is possessed of these interests by *necessity*, then inquiry into their desirability seems superfluous.

The appearance of necessity derives of course from the alleged dependence of these interests upon *needs*. It might appear that needs are determinable by empirical inquiry as a purely factual matter. On the contrary however, as Acton pointed out, the notion of 'need' in these circumstances conceals a moral assessment behind its apparently purely factual facade.

A man's needs may be understood in the sense of everything he desires. To satisfy his needs would then be to satisfy as many of his desires as possible. But what one man wants may conflict with what another man wants, and so the problem arises of deciding which wants of which men shall have precedence. It would be generally supposed that one man's desire to torture another one is a desire that ought not be fostered, and we generally take it for granted that social science should find means for satisfying, not any and every desire, but *legitimate* desires. If this is taken for granted, then the notion of a 'need' is not a purely empirical one based solely on 'sense [experience]'.[39]

Alternatively a 'need' may be taken in the sense of 'whatever man requires to maintain his existence', 'necessities' as opposed to 'luxuries'. It is a commonplace observation of course that the line between 'necessities' and 'luxuries' is a highly variable one. If by 'necessities' is meant that minimum which will prevent a man from dying biologically, then the denotata may be relatively constant. But if by 'necessities of life' we mean that which is necessary to maintain the standard of living customary to individuals in the society in question, then even this concept of 'need' may have a moral component. It may be considered *wrong* to force innocent citizens to live below this standard. Thus on the second definition as well, it is far from clear that 'need' is a purely descriptive or morally neutral concept.

By providing an analysis of values in terms of the satisfaction of interests, and viewing the occurrence of these interests as necessary, one appears to have given a complete outline of a major segment of ethical theory, which nowhere provides for an inquiry into the desirability or worth of generally accepted values. Far from constituting a valid theory of ethics, this is, from the viewpoint of most accounts of ethical theory, to stop short of raising a central ethical query.

Acton makes a very appropriate point when he remarks that for many thinkers

... Marxist social science has become morality, or rather has become a more desirable substitute for morality, in that it teaches how the basic wants and needs of men can and will be satisfied .... But an account of social policy in terms of wants or desires must suppose both that satisfaction is better than frustration and that some wants or desires are more worthy of satisfaction than others.[40]

Use of the term 'interest' in the context of ethical theory may easily convey the impression that some process of inquiry into the intrinsic worth of goals which are the object of the interest is presupposed; in fact no such inquiry is provided anywhere within the logic of standard Soviet accounts of Marxist ethics. The interests taken as crucial for the purposes of ethical theory are those given as 'necessary' in the course of history. Beyond this no ethical inquiry is proposed.

3. DUTY, RESPONSIBILITY, AND FREEDOM

Such views as these just discussed, which threaten to obscure any systematic distinction between individual interests and social interests, also affect discussions of a number of other fairly standard topics in Soviet literature. Duty, for instance, is one of the 'categories of ethics' which is thought to require a specifically Marxist treatment.

The *Dictionary of Ethics* simply defines 'duty' as "a social necessity expressed in moral demands in that form in which they appear before a specific individual".[41] The Marxist science of ethics views the question of duty as "part of the general problem of the origin and foundation of moral demands".

However people represented to themselves the origin of these demands, moral demands always in the final analysis reflected the laws of the objective process of social development . . . . The duty of each individual person in socialist society, founded in the last analysis on this historical necessity, takes an endless variety of forms depending on social conditions and changing situations, which a given individual encounters. Proceeding from that, Marxism resolves the problem of who is competent to specify the content of moral duty. Only society as a whole on the basis of the collective experience of the masses is capable of working out general moral demands.[42]

Duty in most Soviet discussions represents a concrete bond whereby the individual is incorporated into the social order. As 'moral demands' express the relationship of society to the individual, so 'duties' possessing the same content, express the relation of the individual to society.[43] Similarly, Sokolov, in a dissertation on the concept of *duty*, remarked that, "in the concept of duty is reflected the substantive connection of the individual with the motherland, with the class, with society, independent of accidental conditions".[44] 'Duty' he defines as "any morally obligatory action or relation conditioned on the one hand by objective necessity, external demands, and on the other, by internal convictions, the moral decisions of the individual".[45]

The source of the morally obligatory is the interests of the human community – of humanity, of the class, of the nation, of the family, of the worker collective – depending on the concrete forms of life-activity of people, conditioned by socio-historical necessity.[46]

Sokolov distinguishes three types of morally obligatory actions: (1) the most important group consists of morally necessary actions in response to urgent, pressing social or personal needs such as defense of the motherland, rescue of those in peril, fulfilling promises, and also to some degree labor activities and family duties; (2) a second category consists of 'morally-advisable' or 'socially-advisable' actions which are "founded on a knowledge of means and ends, on foreknowledge of the future", arising in scientific, organizational, pedagogical or working situations in which the individual himself has the possibility of chosing the moral goal and means for achieving it; and (3) 'morally valuable' actions having to do with the creation of values as in artistic creation, or invention, broadly construed, and is founded upon "an understanding of social and personal values".[47] Such a usage of the term 'duty' of course threatens to turn every possible morally good action into a moral duty, a

difficulty which the author does not address, and one which is often encountered in Soviet discussions of 'duty'. Another rather common difficulty
consists of the unnoticed shift from the use of 'duty' to refer to a category of
actions which a person may be morally required to perform, to the use of
'duty' to describe the *motive* out of which *any* morally required action is
performed by the individual. For example, Konovalova, arguing that 'duty'
constitutes the "central category of ethics" describes it as

. . . a concentrated form of morality as a whole, because in duty is expressed the most
essential quality of morality as such – the representation of the obligatory, of that
which ought to be, but has not yet today become an achievement of everyday moral
practice.[48]

Later she claims that "duty, in distinction from the good and the ideal, is
closely connected with the concrete behavior of the individual". "And from
this subjective, inner, psychological side duty also can be characterized as
the central category of ethics: duty is the most powerful motivational stimulus".[49] Discussions such as this, which slide from the concept of 'duty' as
morally requisite actions, to 'duty' as a description of the general motive for
right conduct in a particular type of ethical theory, acknowledging neither
the shift of meaning nor the commitment to a particular ethical theory, do
not contribute much to the clarification of the concept.

    Despite this sort of vagueness in some writings, the concentration on the
concept of duty is explicitly recognized by other authors as inspired by Kantian ethics, and Bandzeladze in particular provides a careful and substantial
discussion of 'duty' in this context, criticizing many Soviet philosophers
for dismissing Kant with "superficial and unconvincing arguments".[50]
Bandzeladze himself finally charges Kant's categorical imperative with
'formalism', endorsing Hegel's critique of it, but not before giving a fairly
careful summary of Kant's reasoning.[51]

    The general theme of most Soviet treatments of 'duty' also emerges in
Bandzeladze's discussion: "duty is the necessity to subordinate oneself to
the social will".[52] In a lengthy description of the "moral duty of the builder
of Communism", Bandzeladze claims that not only the Soviet people, "but
also citizens of the other countries of the socialist camp" are guided by the
principles of Communist morality.[53] He describes the main condition defining the moral community of workers in the socialist countries as their political
unity.[54]

    In order to speak of the moral duty of Soviet man, says Bandzeladze, it
is necessary first of all to define his highest moral ideal, sense of life, and

purpose. That highest 'sense of life' for Soviet man consists in the struggle for the victory of Communism.[55] Accordingly his highest ideal is the struggle for the well-being and happiness of society.[56]

But if my ideal is service to society, then personal happiness is defined by the happiness of society, and the relation to oneself is transformed into a relation to another, to society; the concept of the ideal is transformed into the concept of duty.[57]

The Soviet citizen sees the highest aim of his life in the happiness of society, and that does not mean that he considers concern for the happiness of society a means to achieve personal happiness. If my highest ideal is the happiness of society, then that is my goal, and not means .... The recognition of society as a goal implies regarding myself as a means. Moral duty requires the subordination of personal interests to society. In relation to society, the individual cannot fail to regard himself as a means. The social nature of humanity consists precisely in the fact that whoever is deprived of such a social nature is deprived of humanity.[58]

Speaking of the essential harmony of interests of the individual and society under Soviet society, Bandzeladze inquires (somewhat rhetorically),

Is not the principle of harmony of interests transgressed when the moral duty of a Soviet individual requires him to sacrifice his personal interests? To the extent that I am compelled to reject personal benefit, to refuse food, an apartment, clothes, amusements, health, or finally, sacrifice life itself, to that extent the harmony of interests of course is transgressed, and personal interests are subordinated to social. But to the extent that this subordination of interests is not external, but internal, free, voluntary, that is (not) the demand of moral duty but concern for the realization of the latter, my highest goal and the basic content of my personal interests, to that extent the harmony is not transgressed.[59]

Bandzeladze concludes this discussion by claiming that Soviet society, in actuality and in theory, excludes any such opposition of personal and social interests.[60]

The concept of 'responsibility' serves as a bridge between the concepts of 'duty' and 'freedom'. According to the *Dictionary of Ethics,*

... if the *duty* of a person consists in recognizing, applying to the concrete situation in which he finds himself, and practically realizing, moral demands, then the question of the degree to which this task is fulfilled or the degree to which this person is guilty in its non-fulfillment, that is the problem of personal responsibility.[61]

At bottom, the problem of responsibility according to these authors is the problem of the actual moral freedom of the person.[62] The *Dictionary of Ethics* treats the question of responsibility in a manner very similar to that of Sogomonov, arguing that one's moral responsibility extends both to the motives for which one acts, and the consequences of one's actions as well, rejecting either an exclusively deontological or exclusively teleological account of moral responsibility.[63]

The concept of moral responsibility is often treated in conjunction with several other varieties of responsibility such as 'economic', 'political', 'legal' and 'professional'.[64] Plaxotnyj describes 'social responsibility' as structured by three phenomena: the socially-significant behavior of the individual, free will, and measures of social influence on the individual.[65] Concerning 'free will' he remarks only that

Free will as an element of responsibility is a process of interaction of the will of the individual and the will of society, where the will of society appears as a tendency in an enormous variety of voluntary activities of individuals.[66]

Plaxotnyj defines 'moral responsibility' as a constituent element of the other forms and aspects of social responsibility, fundamentally a free recognition by the individual (social group, collective, etc.) of social necessity, and a conviction of the correctness of the moral demands made by society.[67] Among the other varieties of responsibility commonly discussed, 'political responsibility' was described in the following terms by Plaxotnyj:

... a socially necessary relation of the individual or social group to class, national, state and other political interests, a free realization of the political ideology. Political responsibility manifests itself in the sphere of class, party, national, state, and inter-state relations.[68]

In an article entitled 'The Category of Free Will in Ethics' V. E. Dolja remarked that the traditional philosophical and ethical category of free will was comparatively little developed in Soviet ethics.[69] In place of the traditional term, free will, a number of related terms have been employed: 'ethical freedom' has been ranked along with 'political freedom', 'legal freedom', or 'religious freedom'; more particularly, 'freedom of choice' has frequently been discussed as one of the preconditions of moral responsibility, as has been 'internal freedom'.[70] However, the notion of *free will* as a characteristic belonging to rational human beings as such, and a precondition of moral responsibility is usually dismissed as a feature of religious or idealistic philosophy.

Marxist ethics, on the contrary, examines human freedom concretely and historically, as a condition of a human being achieved only in specific conditions, as the result of his social and cultural development.[71]

More specifically, an objective precondition for 'moral freedom' is the "overcoming of the contradiction between the individual and society".[72]

The more full and all-sided becomes the unity of individual and social interests in the process of the construction of Communist society, the more does the individual become capable of freely realizing his moral activity .... A condition of full freedom occurs when recognized necessity develops into a personal moral *inclination*, becomes an internal need of the individual, for whom the interests of society are indistinguishable from his own.[73]

By comparison with standard texts on ethical theory familiar to English-speaking readers, Soviet works on ethics frequently de-emphasize the entire problem of free will and moral responsibility. Bandzeladze for example discusses it only briefly under the general heading of 'duty'. It was not among Arxangel'skij's original list of 'ethical categories'; he also discussed it only in connection with duty. Among the major early texts in the recent revival of ethical theory in the Soviet Union, Šiškin treated the topic of 'freedom and necessity' at greater length than most. He objected to the accusation that Marxism leaves "not the slightest freedom of action" to the individual, and went on to discuss the traditional problem of determinism and indeterminism, siding firmly with the determinists. The necessity he recognized as determining human actions was not natural necessity however, but *historical* necessity which "is discovered in the actions of people who establish themselves specific goals, strive for the realization of their desires, etc.".[74] "But these goals and strivings by themselves still do not signify genuine freedom, since here there is no recognition of necessity."[75] The choice of the individual is genuinely free "only when it is based on the recognition of objective necessity to act one way and not another".[76] Šiškin's discussion, like a number of others in Soviet literature, stresses the "inter-relation of freedom and necessity" in a manner not unlike many non-Soviet publications on the same subject, objecting to fatalism but insisting on the lawful character of human actions.

In terms of the quantity of attention devoted to the subject, however, it is clear that most Soviet moral philosophers are more comfortable discussing the specific nature of society's moral demands on the individual, rather than exploring the various facets of individual moral freedom in detail. For Soviet authors an especially prominent category of demands on the individual arises in connection with patriotism.

4. PATRIOTISM

Although calls for the 'defense of the socialist fatherland' were sounded as early as March, 1918, the notion of partiotism was regarded with extreme suspicion by the Bolsheviks after their success in establishing political control over practically the same territory as the Russian tsarist empire, and it continued to be regarded as a sign of reactionary bourgeois ideology until the early 1930's.[77] The prevailing attitude toward patriotism during the 1920's was summarized by the jurist P. Stučka who remarked that "in our times patriotism plays the role of the most reactionary ideology, whose function it is to justify imperialist bestiality and to deaden the class consciousness of the proletariat, by setting impassable boundaries to its struggle for liberation".[78] This contempt for the feeling of patriotism was thought to be required and justified by the Marxist expectation of an international proletarian revolution in which the brotherly unity of all working peoples everywhere would be asserted against the various bourgeois-capitalist-dominated nation states. Such attitudes toward traditional symbols of the life of the nation state did not begin to change decisively in the Soviet Union until the years 1933–34, when in a series of speeches and declarations by Stalin, and in an abrupt shift of attitude in the official press toward the concept of patriotism and 'Soviet' nationalism, the moral virtue of patriotism was strongly re-asserted.[79]

The term 'motherland' (*rodina*) which traditionally held much stronger emotional associations than the term 'fatherland' (*otečestvo*), and had been systematically eliminated from official Soviet publications, suddenly reappeared in the title of a *Pravda* editorial in July, 1934.[80] Since this period of Soviet history, and above all, since the development of nationalist political symbols in the Soviet Union which took place during 'the Great Patriotic [Fatherland-*otečestvennaja*] War', patriotism in the sense of 'love for the socialist motherland' has played a prominent role in political ideology of the country, and now also plays an explicit role in 'official' ethics. For example among the twelve points of the 'Moral Code for Builders of Communism' promulgated in 1961, 'love of the socialist motherland' occurs in the first.[81] A number of the large monographs on ethical theory, in particular those of Šiškin and Bandzeladze, contain substantial chapters discussing 'love of the motherland' as an essential component of Communist morality.

Šiškin describes patriotism as "an integral characteristic of the moral makeup of the Soviet people", and "the moral feeling of a person who strives to be a worthy citizen of his fatherland".[82] Patriotism, according to Šiškin consists not only in loving the language, culture, and natural beauty of one's native country, but especially in loving its people.

To the extent that the individual through patriotic feeling binds himself to the interests of his people, lives by these interests, proceeds to a great deed and self-sacrifice in the name of the Motherland, it, this feeling, possesses a deeply moral character.[83]

Insisting on the inspirational moral power of the feeling of patriotism, Šiškin recalls Joan of Arc, Hector, Odysseus, the works of Dante, Shakespeare, Goethe and Pushkin, as well as of Saltykov-Ščedrin, as examples of the patriotic feeling he finds worthy of admiration.

Dealing perfunctorily with Marx's claim that the worker has no fatherland, Šiškin interprets this phrase as meaning simply that the working class cannot tolerate the power of capital in its fatherland, that together with the workers of other countries, he fights against this power, and cites a letter from Lenin to Inessa Armand to support this rather shaky conclusion.[84] Rejecting in general any suggestion of opposition between Soviet patriotism and the interests of humanity at large, he simply asserts that "Marxism all-sidedly developed the idea of the unity of the interests of the Motherland and humanity".[85] In particular he rejects any suggestion of conflict between Soviet patriotism and the interests of the other socialist countries, as well as of the workers of all countries.

Still more particularly, Šiškin refers favorably to *Russian* patriotism as a basis of Soviet patriotism:

In Soviet patriotism are fulfilled the best traditions of the patriotism of the popular masses of Russia, struggling for the freedom and independence of their fatherland. But Soviet patriotism cannot be reduced to these traditions.[86]

The Georgian philosopher Bandzeladze's discussion of the same theme provides an interesting counterpoint to the Russian Šiškin's. Bandzeladze remarks that although the Soviet patriot takes pride in all the peoples building Communism, loves and respects the culture and traditions of all socialist countries, "the strength of love toward the national culture cannot be identical in relation to all nations". Each citizen loves more his own nation and culture.

The possibility is not excluded that for example some Ukranians, Georgians, or Armenians might love Russian culture more than Ukranian, Georgian, or Armenian. Love is not related to the sphere of compulsion, and each has the legal and political right to love the culture of that nation which he likes best. But that in no way undermines the feeling of national pride. In the first place, the feeling of national pride cannot be based on the fact that representatives of another nation respect the culture of that nation. On the other hand, love for another nation makes sense when the representatives of that nation itself love it.[87]

Apart from this rather interesting digression into the complex reactions produced by a strong emphasis on patriotism in a multi-national political unit like the Soviet Union, Bandzeladze's fundamental concept of patriotism does not differ significantly from Šiškin's:

Thus patriotism is that moral feeling which manifests itself in the striving of the individual to subordinate all his activity to the interests of the fatherland.[88]

The moral duty of the individual to subordinate his interests to those of social progress, the conclusion reached by nearly all Soviet ethical theorists, is reinforced by the superimposition of this second form of duty, patriotism, on the first, in effect producing a conflation of duties to society with duties to the state as guardian of the motherland.

CHAPTER SEVEN

HISTORICAL PROGRESS AND INTRINSIC VALUE

1. THE PROBLEM OF A CRITERION OF PROGRESS IN SOVIET PHILOSOPHY

At numerous points in their expositions of various aspects of a Marxist ethical theory, Soviet authors refer to a 'science of history' which supposedly provides the ultimate foundation for many of their claims concerning the nature of value and moral norms. This science of history is thought to provide an objective account of the relations between the laws of historical development, the historically determined succession of interests characterizing each social formation and class, and the values represented by the satisfaction of such interests. More particularly, the majority of Soviet accounts of the objectivity of value resort in the end to the claim that this science of history demonstrates which social interests, values, and moral norms are progressive, and which not. Ethical theory, the method of which is commonly characterized as 'the unity of the logical and the historical', in several respects rests on this underlying science of history.

The question of historical (social) progress, and more particularly, of 'moral progress', constitutes the central issue here. What is the criterion of progress in history generally, and in morality particularly? If a criterion is to accomplish its function, does it not have to be acknowledged to be an intrinsic value or good, or derived from one, and if so on what grounds is such a claim to be justified? And if it is justified on any grounds other than the mere fact that it *appeared*, as a product of history itself, has not the science of history as the allegedly ultimate source of all objective judgments of value been transcended? Or if one refuses to give any extra-historical account of the criterion of progress, does not 'progress' itself simply become an intrinsic value? But can the meaning of this last claim be explicated in any way without explicitly naming some *further criterion* of progress, and hence some intrinsic value, the realization of which is said to constitute progress?

All these dilemmas threaten to break out into the open whenever an opinion is ventured as to 'the highest good', 'the intrinsically valuable', 'the criterion of moral progress', 'the highest ideal', etc., in Soviet discussions of ethical theory. Equally, most attempts to provide an account of the objectivity of

159

value judgments lead to some reference to what is 'historically progressive' in some objective sense supposedly established by the science of history, and hence to the same problem.

As examples of this last problem one may cite several authors from the preceding pages. Bakuradze attempted to explain 'intrinsic values' as determined by 'norms' which were themselves determined by 'ideals', which were in turn 'products of historical-social life' ascertainable by Marxist-Leninist historical science.[1] Kobljakov argued that values could be validated by "comparing norms with scientific knowledge of the interests of the class and the tendencies of development of society as a whole".[2] Švarcman maintained that in order to establish the truth of a particular system of morality, "It is necessary to compare it with the objective laws of developing social reality, with the interests of the class struggling for socialism".[3] Konovalova claimed that conceptions of the good could only be "submitted to the court of history" and "evaluated in the light of objective criteria".[4] Examples of such views could be multiplied almost indefinitely from Soviet literature.

Discussions of the nature of intrinsic value, as well as accounts of the objectivity of value, or of the justification of value judgments, contain few specific answers of the familiar sort. Instead there is near unanimity of conviction that 'history' indicates what is ultimately valuable, that 'history' demonstrates what is 'progressive', and that value judgments are objective to the extent they accurately reflect the historically-determined, progressive interests of society. In short, to most Soviet philosophers it seems possible only to make the very general observation that intrinsic values are identical with whatever is ultimately progressive in history, and to discover what this is, we must study history from the viewpoint of Marxism-Leninism.

However it should be obvious that this formula provides no answer to the question of what is intrinsically valuable. The point is of course that 'history' cannot be declared to exhibit progress unless we have available to us a logically prior set of judgments as to what is intrinsically valuable, and therefore some standard or criterion by which to make the assessment of progress. In the absence of such a set of judgments it is logically impossible to make any pronouncement as to whether history exhibits progress at all. Conversely, if one claims that history does exhibit progress, then by implication one has already committed oneself to some set of judgments as to what is intrinsically valuable. A certain uneasiness concerning these difficulties has affected many Soviet discussions of the problem.

Šiškin's original monograph on Marxist ethics contained the simplest possible 'answer' to the problem of a general 'criterion of morality':

The movement toward Communism, the struggle for Communism, is the *objective* measure of evaluation of human actions, that is, the necessary, general basis which does not depend on the consciousness of this or that person. It permits one to clearly distinguish true morality from false.[5]

There are a number of problems with such a 'criterion' however. First, and most obviously, it does not appear to be a plausible candidate for an *intrinsic* value; rather it appears to be an extrinsic good, i.e., a means to a good end. One could conceivably claim that 'Communism' just *means* 'a just distribution of goods', and argue that the latter is an intrinsic value. It is not clear that Šiškin's use of the term 'Communism' is restricted to any sense which could be plausibly defended as an intrinsic value, however. Furthermore it is possible to argue, as for example William Frankena does, that nothing counts as an intrinsic value which cannot be the direct *experience* of some person.[6] For example it would not be Communism itself which counted as an intrinsic good, but the *experience* of Communism. The awkwardness of this last locution suggests that numerous difficulties stand in the way of making 'Communism' a plausible candidate for intrinsic value. More particularly, an intrinsic value would be something which is taken as good in itself, and not simply because of its consequences. But Šiškin himself appears to defend the value of Communism not in terms of its intrinsic properties, but in terms of its consequences, specifically the "all-sided development of the human personality".[7] One could perhaps argue that this is part of the meaning of 'Communism' and not simply a consequence of its occurrence, but in the absence of such detailed explications of the term, the plausibility of 'Communism' as an intrinsic value must remain in doubt.

Other authors attempted to supply more precise formulations of 'the objective criterion of moral progress'. Kamyšan for instance argued that in principle, since morality is a superstructural phenomenon reflecting objective productive relations, to determine what constitutes progress in morality it would only be necessary to determine which productive relations are reflected in a given morality, and then observe whether those productive relations are progressive or regressive at the present time.[8] Amending this a bit later, he acknowledged that

... if we say that Communist morality is more progressive than bourgeois only because it facilitates the strengthening and development of a higher type of productive relations, then we add essentially nothing new to the idea of the economic superiority of socialism over capitalism.[9]

Therefore, Kamyšan concludes, a 'relatively independent criterion' of specifically moral progress is still required. Seeking such a criterion, he makes a distinction between the spheres of the political and the moral: the sphere of the political is that of relations between social groups, classes, states, and nations: and the sphere of morality is that of relations between the individual and society.

From this it logically follows that the objectively real content of moral progress is progress in the interrelations of the individual and society in social reality itself, conditioned in the last analysis by economic causes. The degree of that objectively real progress, reflected by morality in each stage of its development, the active, reverse contribution of morality as superstructure to that lawful historical change is the objective criterion of moral progress [sic].[10]

Apart from the ambiguity apparent in Kamyšan's definition of the criterion for objective moral progress, it also appears to suffer from simple circularity: "The degree of that objectively real progress . . . is the objective criterion of moral progress". Whatever these difficulties, Kamyšan intended to define moral progress (progress in the interrelation between the individual and society) in terms of two aspects: "the subordination of the activity of the individual person to the interests of society" and "the harmonization of social progress with the progress of each individual as a person, with the growth of objective social possibilities for the free development of the individual as a person".[11] Once again, the more general criterion of "the free development of the individual" appears as the explanation of what is meant by 'moral progress'.

The inadequacy of such attempts as Kamyšan's to define 'moral progress' was accurately diagnosed by Kulikova and Gumnickij. They pointed out that the most frequently encountered criterion of morality in Soviet literature was simply 'that which facilitates historical progress', leading to the conclusion that the struggle for Communism constitutes the basic criterion of morality in our epoch, the position which Šiškin, among others, elaborated.[12] But this claim must always encounter the question, 'Is Communism progressive because it is the outcome of history, or does history exhibit progress because it tends toward Communism?'. In other words no criterion has been supplied until this further question has been satisfactorily answered. Kulikova and Gumnickij observe that this 'criterion' is useless, even for Marxists, when applied to the past; that it is too general; and that when applied specifically to morality, not always true. For example the transition from primitive-communal to class society was historically progressive, but it involved a regress in the moral sphere.[13] Moreover, the criterion in question does nothing to explain why Communist morality in particular is 'authentically human'.[14] "On the contrary it establishes no difference between it and bourgeois morality of that period when it facilitated the development of society. Both moral systems turn out to be equally valuable."[15] Obviously a criterion of moral progress will also have to be a specifically moral one, one which distinguishes progressive morality from progressive politics, progressive economics, progressive art, etc.[16]

Kulikova and Gumnickij concentrate first of all on the charge that Marxism entails moral relativism. On Engels' famous, thoroughly ambiguous formulation in the *Anti-Dühring* concerning the possibility of objective moral progress, they assert that he "absolutely unambiguously referred to the truly human, and that means absolute, elements in such moral systems as the feudal, the bourgeois, and the proletarian, and observed that 'in morality, as in all other branches of human knowledge, progress is generally observed' ".[17] The authors argue that no such general progress could be identified if there were not some common element in all the moral systems of history in terms of which progress could be measured. That common element, which they define as the principal characteristic of morality itself, is *the subordination of individual interests to those of the collective.*

As was remarked above, the primary meaning, the very character of morality consists in the subordination of the individual to the interests of the collective, in the preservation of the community by means of such a subordination . . . .
  Guaranteeing the interests of society by means of the subordination of individual interests to social, is the basic law of moral conduct.[18]

  The benefit of the individual cannot be a fundamental, absolutely independent moral value.[19]

The criterion of moral progress is "connected with the perfection of the inter-relations between society and the individual, with the achievement of that individual conduct which most fully responds to the demands of social development".[20] Hence, apart from offering an appropriate critique of Kamyšan's 'solution' to the problem, these two authors accomplish little more than he. They too go on to discuss an 'increase in moral freedom' and 'the gradual development of human-ness' as characteristics of moral progress, but offer no definition of moral progress beyond "increasing the degree of subordination of the individual to the social interest".

A. I. Titarenko has devoted more effort to defining 'moral progress' than any other Soviet philosopher. In a long series of publications beginning about 1966, he has discussed the history of the concepts of social progress and of moral progress in particular, criticizing non-Marxist views of both, and in his doctoral dissertation and subsequent writings, defended a criterion of moral progress which, according to him, overcomes the difficulties in the way of stating a Marxist position on this problem.[21]

Within certain limits, Titarenko confronted the fundamental difficulty facing most Marxist definitions of an ultimate or intrinsic good (which could also serve as a criterion of moral progress), namely how to retain the historicist, relativist tendency of historical materialism, and at the same time defend the claim of objective progress applied to human history as a whole. Titarenko confronts this difficulty as "the problem of the 'circle' in the definition of measures of moral progress".[22] This circle he describes in a number of ways, first as the fact that "historical progress cannot be 'a criterion for the sphere of the obligatory', because it itself requires moral justification".

[But] On the other hand, a moral criterion can be defined only through the historical process, which is impossible, because the development of the 'obligatory' is not reducible to the development of social existence.[23]

The circle can be reiterated as follows: the criterion of social-moral progress must be derived from progress itself, and at the same time to discover progress is possible only when in possession of a ready criterion. In still broader terms, "progress is defined as ascending historical development, and, on the other hand, historical development is viewed as progressive".[24] Titarenko concludes that "from the point of view of formal logic such definitions are inadmissible".[25]

To escape this series of logical circles and paradoxes, Titarenko resorts to the dialectic, observing, in a memorable phrase (which might serve as a motto for many such discussions!), "there where the metaphysician sees a logical dead-end, and the sceptic, material for paradoxes, it is necessary to seek the dialectic".[26] The definition of concepts in terms of each other, the circle,

... is logically justified only in that case when it not only reflects the inner mutually-conditioned oppositions of a single object, but also examines that mutual conditioning as a process of self-development.[27]

Titarenko acknowledges that in any judgment of moral progress "are included such evaluations, norms, ideals which are directed to the future and the genuine historical significance of which is impossible to discover by means of simple empirical observation".[28] The science of Marxism-Leninism is equipped to make such judgments, in his view, with no sacrifice of scientific objectivity.

The Marxist-Leninist worldview, being a strict system of scientifically expressed facts, is deeply logical. The normative, evaluative aspect in that worldview is no merely subsidiary principle located outside of this logic, but a *profoundly internal aspect of the entire system.*[29]

In this claim Titarenko appears to revive one of the major aspirations of the neo-Kantian socialists to provide a philosophical system within which the moral judgments of Marxism could be equally firmly grounded as its sociological conclusions in an over-arching philosophical system. The difference is of course that Titarenko turns, much more plausibly, to Hegel rather than to Kant for the 'solution' he requires.

Consequently, a circle in the definition of the fundamental concepts of each science from the viewpoint of dialectical methodology is the beginning of self-movement, and not an immovable paradox. In this sense the circle of definitions is not so much a circle (if one resorts to superficial comparisons) as it is a spiral.[30]

Finally terming his view a species of historicism, Titarenko claims that "historicism lies in the very foundation of the mutual conditioning of moral progress and its criterion".[31] "Accordingly, the historical process itself produces a certain 'winnowing' of the accidental from the necessary in the sphere of norms, ideals and evaluations. That *creates the objective preconditions* for revealing the criterion of moral progress."[32]

Following all of these methodological considerations, Titarenko finally provided his own summary of the criterion of morality:

The general historical criterion of moral progress is the level of humanization of the interaction, collision, and resolution of the oppositions of good and evil, of the interrelation of the individual and society, the degree of broadening of objective possibilities for morally positive choice in conduct, the maturity of moral self-knowledge and the emotional-moral richness of the person, the operation of norms and voluntariness in following them, the correctness of evaluation of the morality of social existence.[33]

According to Titarenko, the basic indicator in this complex criterion is the "level of humanization of the interrelation, collision, and resolution of the oppositions of good and evil"; it constitutes a *substantive* criterion, subordinating all other aspects and indicators of moral progress to itself. His criterion permits one to "avoid the onesidedness and simplification of ethical evolutionism" and also to reject ethical relativism and the sceptical negation of moral progress, "because it is a historically substantive indicator permitting one objectively, truly to demonstrate and normatively define the superiority of one level of moral relations over another".[34] In a later work Titarenko acknowledged that his criterion in a certain sense 'simplified' the history of morals and recommended much more detailed investigation of the prevailing moralities in a great variety of historical periods and cultures.[35] Still insisting on his underlying notion, however, he described moral progress, beginning with Communist society, as the 'moral perfection of humanity' proceeding on

the basis of "a further humanization of social relations".[36] To this extent
however we are still in the land of circles: Moral progress . . . is the moral
perfection of humanity. Once again, too, the vague notion of the 'humanization' of social relations turns out to be perhaps the most fundamental crite-
tion, but again it is not elaborated as such.

Although Titarenko wrestled with the inherent difficulties in the usual
Soviet view of the relation between progress and intrinsic value more earnestly than most, the fundamental problems still remain. On one hand, one of the
most universal concerns of Soviet philosophers is to maintain a type of historicism in which no basis for a 'trans-historical' perspective for the evaluation
of social change is conceivable. On the other hand, this motive cuts across an
equally strong and different motive to regard the course of history as a whole
as an objectively determined *progress*. But to articulate any intrinsic value in
terms of which the latter appears plausible, threatens to violate the historicism
as interpreted by most Soviet philosophers. This fundamental ambivalence
toward any explicitly-stated intrinsic value, or any discussion of the intrinsic
good in 'extra-historical' terms, manifests itself in a practically irresistible
temptation to substitute 'historical' evaluation using historical terms such as
'progressive' and 'reactionary' for 'moral' evaluation of human conduct using
such terms as 'right', 'wrong', 'good', 'evil', or at a minimum, making the
'historical' the determinant of the 'moral'.

The distinction made here between 'historical' and 'moral' evaluation is an
attempt to recall Hegel's distinction between the prevailing moralities of
particular cultures in history which may have forbidden certain types of acts,
and the 'higher' interest of the development of spirit which sometimes required the commission of these very deeds. But as was argued in Chapter One,
Hegel did not make such a distinction with regard to the present, much less
the future. His 'criticism' of the limited perspectives of prevailing moralities
in history, his 'justification' of the deeds of world-historical individuals who
transgressed these moralities, was always *retrospective*. With regard to the
present, Hegel argued that the only morally justified course of action was to
live as an obedient citizen of one's own state (using that term in his sense),
fulfilling the duties attached to one's station.

Hegel's reticence in criticizing the prevailing morality of one's own social
order was by no means shared by Marx. Marx was prepared to criticize prevailing morality from the perspective of the 'higher' interest of historical
progress. It is clear that this notion of a 'higher' framework for the evaluation
of human conduct is derived from Hegel's philosophy of history, but by
presuming to apply it to the present, Marx obtained what could never have

been available for Hegel, an alternative framework for the evaluation of human conduct which appears to replace, or transcend, morality in any ordinary sense. More particularly, this apparent alternative framework for the evaluation of human conduct appeared to supercede ordinary morality in the eyes of many Bolsheviks, providing an alternative basis for the justification of, above all, political action. Moreover, it was very natural for them to regard all human conduct from the political perspective.

Given this fascination with the possibility of an alternative framework for the evaluation of human conduct transcending morality, the most crucial point of all is often overlooked in the interpretation of Hegel: 'historical' evaluation and moral evaluation for Hegel were not ultimately distinct. There were not two independent frameworks of evaluative discourse in this sphere, one moral and another transcending morality. His defense of the duty of obedience to the laws and obligations of one's present state and society rested ultimately on his conviction that "insofar as dialectic abrogates moral determinations, we must have confidence in reason that it will know how to restore them again, but restore them in their truth and in the consciousness of their right, though also of their limitations".[37]

Soviet Marxists, who are by and large extremely reluctant to abandon the distinction between 'historical' and moral evaluation, are at the same time faced with the necessity of justifying their conception of 'moral progress'; the latter would seem to be impossible without referring explicitly to some intrinsic value, but as soon as an intrinsic value is identified, one would appear to have the necessary foundations for making moral evaluations in the strict sense, moral evaluations which might justify the individual in rejecting the demands of 'social progress' in specific circumstances. In short, it is not clear how a Marxist can defend his philosophy of historical progress without re-establishing a degree of universality to moral claims which far exceeds that usually admitted within Marxist philosophy. Also at stake in this issue is the justifiability of the continued use of the framework of 'historical' evaluation ('progressive' and 'reactionary') as transcending that of any ordinary morality.

2. THE CRITERION OF PROGRESS IN MARX'S PHILOSOPHY OF HISTORY

The task of identifying Marx's criterion of progress and elucidating the role it plays in his philosophy of history has no simple solution, and perhaps no unambiguous one at all. It may be that Marx's thought never achieved complete coherence and consistency on this particular problem. A number of points concerning his notion of progress can be made however.

One common hypothesis which must be considered is that Marx's implicit criterion of progress was 'the realization of authentic human nature'. It is this notion which appears to lie behind the many Soviet references to greater 'humanization' as a criterion of moral progress. In the early writings Marx made many pronouncements which could be taken together as a theory of 'authentic human nature', i.e., human nature unafflicted by alienation and developed to some threshold of 'self-realization' or maturity. His discussion of human nature takes place primarily in terms of *needs*, among which are the need for the free and creative development of human personality; the need for creative labor as an end in itself rather than a mere means for satisfying other, especially physical, needs; and the need to exercise all of one's capacities, both intellectual and physical in one's work. The condition of alienation, in all of its forms, represents the diminution of one's true humanity, the frustration of truly human needs:

... the worker does not affirm himself in his work but denies himself, feels miserable and unhappy, develops no free physical and mental energy but mortifies his flesh and ruins his mind. The worker, therefore feels at ease only outside work, and during work he is outside himself. He is at home when he is not working and when he is working he is not at home.[38]

Needs themselves are distinguished by Marx into these two categories: authentic and alienated. The alienated needs are *real* ones, but only under conditions of alienated existence.

Within the system of private property ... Every man speculates upon creating a *new* need in another in order to force him to a new sacrifice, to place him in a new dependence, and to entice him into a new kind of pleasure and thereby into economic ruin. Everyone tries to establish over others an alien power in order to find there the satisfaction of his own egoistic need.[39]

Such egoistic needs are a manifestation of alienation:

The less you eat, drink, buy books, go to the theatre or to balls, or to the publishing house, and the less you think, love, theorize, sing, paint, fence, etc., the more you will be able to save and the greater will become your treasure which neither moth nor rust will corrupt – your *capital*. The less you *are*, the less you express your life, the more you *have*, the greater is your *alienated* life and the greater is the saving of your alienated being.[40]

The question arises, upon what basis does Marx identify one set of needs as those of alienated humanity, and another as those of authentic humanity?

That the 'alienated' needs are real enough is attested to by Marx's own observations. One obvious answer would be that Marx distinguished these two
types of needs on moral grounds: avarice, for instance, is identified as a need
of alienated humanity because it is immoral, 'egoistic'. If the principle for
identifying alienated and authentic needs is a moral one, then Marx's conception of authentic human nature may be regarded as a set of value judgments,
perhaps that set of values by which the course of history is evaluated. This
may be too simple a way of regarding the matter, but the question remains,
what is the status of Marx's own prouncements as to 'authentic human nature' within historical materialism? Upon what grounds does he declare the
nature of 'true humanity'? Since by hypothesis the conditions of unalienated
human existence had yet to be realized in history, Marx's conception of authentic human nature must be hypothetical in some sense.

The remarks on authentic human nature could be regarded as inferences
from the observation of the frustration of human needs under existing social
conditions. But that would not by itself warrant the conclusion that the
frustrated nature was 'authentic' in some way transcending the conditions of
particular socio-economic formations and classes. The claim that one particular conception of human nature somehow takes precedence over all other
possible conceptions as 'authentic' would require some additional assumptions to be justified. One such assumption might be that human nature is in
some underlying sense always the same, merely capable of being frustrated
or hindered in development under certain conditions. But Marx strenuously
objected to the idea that there was any fixed 'human essence', and in fact
supplied an alternative conception of progress which was discussed above.[41]

In that conception the intrinsic value which serves as a measure of progress
would be 'the development of all human powers as such', leading to 'the full
development of human mastery over the forces of nature, those of so-called
nature as well as of humanity's own nature'. Marx specifically insisted that by
the development of all human powers as such, he did not mean a fixed concept of human nature 'as measured on a pre-determined yardstick'. To possess
such a fixed concept of human nature would place it within the sphere where
'closed shapes, forms, and given limits are sought for'. Such a possibility of
'satisfaction from a limited standpoint' Marx thought unworthy of humanity.

As was argued above, this determination to specify no human essence, to
apply no pre-determined yardstick to it, or to history, threatened to defeat
any attempt to establish a structure or logic of history. But in fact, Marx
does commit himself to one defining feature of authentic humanity sufficient
to ensure the possibility of a philosophy of history: it is a defining trait of

authentic human nature to possess mastery over itself and the rest of nature, to freely develop its own creative potentialities "with no presupposition other than the previous historic development". From this perspective a dialectical logic of history can be developed; its constitutive event, though not its culmination, must be humanity's development of self-conscious mastery over itself and nature, in effect the achievement of rational planning and control over its own subsequent history.

As was also argued above, this conception implies that Communism, a particular form of social organization, cannot be regarded as the end in itself by which the course of history is to be measured. At most it could only be an indicator of the more fundamental value, humanity's development of mastery over its own situation, implying the full development of all human powers.

In order to clarify the actual role of assumptions concerning intrinsic value and progress in Marx's philosophy of history, it is instructive to consider a few points involved in the logic of such philosophies generally. Marx's philosophy of history can be classified as an instance of the linear variant of the 'law of history' type, in the classifications of Mandelbaum and Dray.[42] All philosophies of history may be described as an attempt to discover some 'meaning' within the whole of human history, established through the discovery of some ultimate explanatory principle supposedly operative throughout the course of history.[43] Some such explanatory factor accounting for or determining historical change, is then shown to be intrinsically connected to some set of human values such that the course of history and its outcome are revealed to be not only intelligible but also necessarily culminating in the realization of these values. One major type of such philosophies of history treats this ultimate explanatory principle as a developmental *law* (or set of laws) of history which serves to explain the ultimate direction of historical change. It is this type which concerns us insofar as we are dealing with Marx.

The other crucial component of such theories, the criterion of value or progress, identifies the values in terms of which historical change is to be evaluated. Within the philosophy of history, the standard of evaluation and the ultimate principle of explanation cannot be made logically independent. If they were, the theory could not 'show' what it purports to show, that the ultimate principle of historical change which 'explains' history also renders it 'meaningful'. The explication of Marx's conception of progress therefore requires an examination of the connection between his explanatory principle (or principles) for historical change, and his criterion of progress or evaluation. The latter must be derivable from the former if the theory is to fulfill its function in a coherent manner.

The most usual explanation of historical change in Marx refers to a 'conflict' between the material forces of production in a society and the relations of production within which these forces are applied.

At a certain stage of their development, the material [economic] forces of production in society come in conflict with the existing relations of production, ... From forms of development of the forces of production these relations turn into their fetters. Then occurs a period of social revolution. With the change of the economic foundation the entire immense superstructure is more or less rapidly transformed.[44]

It is, approximately speaking, the autonomous evolution of the forces of production (technology) which causes changes to come about in the socio-economic formations (societies) of which history is the record. Every pattern of relations of production is, at the time of its inception, appropriate to the prevailing technology or productive forces. At some point however, the productive forces evolve into new forms, creating an ever-growing conflict between the productive forces and the relations of production until a change in the latter is brought about, synonymous with a change of socio-economic formations (societies).

The question to be raised here concerns the relation between this explanatory principle for historical change, and Marx's criterion of historical progress. Can the features necessary to the positively evaluated outcome of history be shown to be necessarily inherent in the course of history as determined by the ultimate explanatory principle? The answer to this question depends upon which of the two accounts of the criterion of progress offered above we accept.

Suppose we adopt the conception of 'authentic human nature' as the criterion for progress. How then does it happen on Marx's account that the self-determined evolution of the mode of production (in accordance with objective 'laws of development') necessarily issues in 'authentic human nature'? How does it come about that humanity is produced in the image of 'authenticity' and not, for example, in the image of contented automata relating to each other only through machines, and experiencing no frustration? Marx's argument in *Capital* underlines the significance of this question. The de-humanization of the individual, rather than the reverse, would seem to be the most natural outcome of the autonomous development of the forces of economic production. Strictly speaking, in the terms of the materialist theory of history alone, the fact that the actual forces determining the course of history (the evolution of productive economic forces) happen in the end to produce the conditions for the realization of 'authentic human nature' must be regarded as a cosmic coincidence. There appears to be no way of demonstrating that the evolution of economic forces must necessarily create authentic humanity. The logical link can only be established if we suppose that 'authentic human nature', experienced in terms of actual needs, can be attributed to individual human actors throughout history, in such a way that the frustration of these same 'authentic' needs could be an actual motive force in the developmental activities of humanity. But the concept of human nature as identical *merely* with the essence of productive relations at each stage of history cannot be reconciled with the assumption that 'authentic human nature' has determined the evolution from the beginning. In order to make such an assumption, numerous passages expressing the central thesis of historical materialism would have to be dismissed as seriously inadequate:

As individuals express their life, so they are. What they are, therefore, coincides with their production, with *what* they produce and with how they produce it. What individuals are, therefore, depends on the material [economic] conditions of their production.[45]

Yet nothing would preserve the logical relevance of this explanation of historical change and human development to Marx's criterion of progress short of a demonstration that the appearance of fortuitious coincidence is an illusion, and that some deeper logic does after all connect the actual motive force of history with the 'authentic' nature of humanity. If this view of the criterion of progress is to be defended, it may prove possible only if it is recognized that the materialist conception of history alone is inadequate to supply the necessary connection with the criterion of progress. If this connection is to be supplied, it can only be through the supplement of some further component of a philosophy of history to be discovered in Marx's writings.

Thus, adopting the conception of 'authentic human nature' as the criterion of progress for Marx appears to require supplementing the materialist theory of history with some further doctrine without which it seems impossible to give an account of the meaningfulness of human history. In terms of the original inquiry which led to this discussion, it appears that Marx's theory is possibly incoherent on the very point which is crucial for the most usual Soviet view of the nature of intrinsic value. The connection between this conception of intrinsic value and historical change seems highly obscure in the absence of some further, as yet unstated, assumptions of the philosophy of history.

What becomes of the problem if we adopt the alternative conception of progress described above? Suppose we adopt the conception of 'the development of all human powers as such' as our criterion of progress. How does this affect the difficulties outlined just above? In general, the problem remains the same: how can this criterion of progress be shown to be derivable from the ultimate explanatory principle of historical change? If we could modify the materialist conception of history somewhat, and simply declare that the fundamental motive force of historical change has been and is humanity's desire for self-development; then the necessary logical connection would have been demonstrated, and this conception of progress successfully defended in the context of Marx's theory. But to do so would entail discarding a large part of the materialist conception of history. Marx explicitly constructed his account of the motives of the economic actors responsible for socio-economic development in terms of their desire merely to *reproduce* the conditions for their existence. Beginning with the primitive communal forms of socio-economic organization, the activities of individuals have always been directed specifically to the reproduction of the conditions necessary to maintain the established forms and activities of communal existence. But this attempt at mere *reproduction*, Marx explained, unwittingly resulted in *production* of new needs, new activities to satisfy these needs, new forms of socio-economic organization to accomodate these new activities, and, ultimately, new forms of human nature.[46] To view all of these developments as foreseen and planned by the agents would be to discard the materialist theory of history. Hence it will not do to assume that the fundamental motive force of history has been the desire of humanity to develop itself. On the other hand, this account of the motive force of history suits Marx's theory perfectly *after* the realization of Communism, *after* humanity has achieved fully self-conscious mastery of its own destiny.

In summary, on this conception of human progress, too, Marx's materialist conception of history appears inadequate to account for the meaningfulness of human history. For the solution to this problem of the connection between the principles of historical change and the criterion of progress, one must seek a further dimension of Marx's philosophy of history, his evolutionist cosmology.

3. PHILOSOPHY OF HISTORY AND COSMOLOGY IN MARX

The fundamental assumptions on which Marx's conception of progress in history rests constitute a *cosmology* in a particular sense of that term – an attempt to describe the structural elements of the *human* world, or of the world *for humanity*, the best paradigm for which is perhaps offered by the original neo-Platonists. One might also speak of Marx as offering a cosmogony, an account of the coming to be of a cosmos from a prior condition which might be compared to an original chaos. Speaking more accurately, one should say that Marx proposed an *evolutionary cosmology*.

As was argued in Chapter Two, the central concept of Marx's philosophy of history, the basic entity in terms of which it is constructed, is the socio-economic formation (society), a succession of which constitutes history.

This conception of history depends on our ability to expound the real processes of production, starting out from the material [economic] production of life itself, and to comprehend the form of intercourse connected with this and created by this mode of production (i.e., civil society in its various stages), as the basis of all history.[47]

'Society' as a term in this Marxian discourse carries a rather special burden of meanings acquired in Marx's discussions of *nature* and *society*. *Nature* is of course bifurcated in Marx's conception of it, into 'virgin' or 'untransformed' nature on one hand, and 'transformed' or 'produced' nature on the other. The first, untransformed nature, especially in the early writings, held no interest for Marxian social theory; it was 'the kind of nature which preceded human history', "the nature which no longer exists anywhere except perhaps on a few Australian coral islands of recent origin".[48]

The nature which did interest Marx was that 'actual objective world' which human activity established through the productive process, through the trans-formation of virgin nature. Ultimately the distinction between this transform-ed nature and society was to disappear: "Thus society is the completed, essential unity of man with nature, the true resurrection of nature, the ful-filled naturalism of man and humanism of nature".[49] The creation of human society is another name for the process whereby virgin nature is gradually appropriated and reproduced in a reflection of human needs as transformed nature, as nature-humanized-and-man-naturalized.

Nature developing in human history − the creation of human society − is the actual nature of man; hence nature as it develops through industry, though in an *alienated* form, is truly *anthropological* nature.[50]

This process of the transformation of nature which is also the history of humanity's creation of itself, constitutes the subject matter of historical materialism, the outcome of which is Communism. The completion of the historical process of the realization of Communism signifies much more: the realization of rational control by humanity over the process of its own devel-opment. Prior to the realization of Communism humanity is in a sense the unwitting object of the operation of these laws of historical development; after it, humanity is capable of directing its own development; rational control replaces victimization. In this sense also, the realization of Communism marks the realization of the society-cosmos in the sense of the eradication of the distinction between nature and society.

At the level of cosmological discourse, these passages must be interpreted as an account of the evolutionary formation of the cosmos itself, the world *for humanity*, in a literal sense, because the completion of this process also represents the completion of the process of the transformation of virgin nature. Communist society as humanity-naturalized-and-nature-humanized refers to *all there is* for humanity (speaking for the moment only of the early writings), the whole of its world, hence the cosmos.[51]

It has often been remarked that Marx's theory of history entails that all events occurring up to the international Communist revolution are in one sense *pre-history*. Only after this unique event is humanity in possession of the freedom to make a fully rational disposition of its social institutions. What has been observed less clearly is the significant sense in which these events prior to the realization of Communism are not merely pre-historical, but *pre-cosmic* in the literal sense, by analogy with ancient Greek cosmologists who provided accounts of the formation of the cosmos from chaos. 'Pre-cosmic' would refer to any occurrence between the original condition of a chaos, structured only by the assumption of differentiable elements inherent in it, to the completion of the cosmos as comprehended by the same cosmology. It is to this period, for example, that the activities of Plato's Demiurge are related. One can argue that pre-cosmic 'time' in Marx has been superimposed upon historical time. Two radically different varieties of discourse have been conflated, and a number of crucial terms in Marx seemingly refer to concepts in both the cosmological and the ordinary historical narratives simultaneously. Much that is arresting in Marx's thought owes its power to this subtle inter-play of evolutionist cosmology and the empirical, descriptive elements of the materialist theory of history.

As an example of this ambiguity of reference to two concepts belonging, respectively, to the cosmological and the historical narratives, the concept of 'humanity' is of interest. There is a constantly reiterated theme in Marx that 'humanity produces itself'. The humanity which creates itself, in the image of 'authentic human nature' is humanity as species-being, collective humanity. There is a second sense of the term however in which humanity is a by-product of the evolution of the society-cosmos which takes place in accordance with objective laws operating independently of human consciousness.

Humanity as the collective being which 'produces itself' fits quite coherently into the cosmological narrative in a role literally analogous to the Platonic Demiurge. Humanity-Demiurge is active precisely in the period of the formation of the cosmos, realizing itself as humanity-naturalized-and-nature-humanized. Since this latter concept is equivalent to the cosmos (at least in Marx's early writings, one can argue), this process is analogous to the activity of the Platonic Demiurge in creating the cosmos. He occupies the interval between the initial chaos and the completion of the cosmos. This god-like conception of humanity's role in its own creation lies at the heart of Marx's conception of human freedom and dignity.[52]

The 'empirical' human being, the individual, who properly inhabits the historical narrative alone, is humanity as 'produced by circumstances'. This human being is externally-determined, alienated, and suffering, a victim of that same society of which he is destined to become ultimate master in the cosmological narrative. It is extremely difficult to see in this second concept of humanity either dignity or freedom. Empirical humanity has freedom and dignity *conferred* on it (from the cosmological narrative) only at the consummation of history, when humanity as Demiurge and empirical humanity are merged, ostensibly as an event within the historical narrative alone.

A second example of ambiguity in Marx's analysis, when understood, contributes to a clearer realization of the place of the cosmological narrative in the theory as a whole. This second instance of ambiguity concerns the term 'nature'. Untransformed nature, which 'precedes human history' can be understood as the original state of things analogous to the condition of chaos in ancient Greek accounts, the original condition out of which the structure of all there is emerges. What emerges from the chaos (Marx would probably say 'blindness') of untransformed nature is of course a cosmos, a conception of the world as a whole for humanity. In this way Marx attempts the grafting of a cosmos onto blind, untransformed nature, describing the whole as a single evolutionary process.

In effect we have been discussing Marx's account of the relation of spirit to nature, an account which was meant to replace the Hegelian one. As we have seen, in the early Marx the original term of the problem, virgin nature, tends to drop out altogether, to be replaced by 'transformed' nature, which can also be ultimately identified with 'society'. This would constitute a shrinking of the dimensions of nature to something entirely susceptible of appropriation, or humanization. This, at least, is the view seemingly inherent in the early works. In the mature work of Marx however an important qualification was added to this account: a perpetual role for untransformed nature is discovered which has great significance for human existence.[53] In this discovery of a perpetual role for untransformed nature, what was described above as the 'society-cosmos' acquires an ambiguous 'other' which tended to drop from view in the earlier writings, an other which it cannot appropriate to itself, and hence a perpetual opposition of subject and object which is never transcended. But this implies that society can no longer be equated with the cosmos. The cosmos must be redefined to incorporate untransformed nature as an irreducible, crucial element. If the early works and the mature works of Marx are to be distinguished in a fundamental way, this modification in conceptions of the cosmos may be one of the most important.

This modification of the original conception came about when Marx developed the nation of the 'metabolism of nature'.

The labor-process, resolved as above into its simple elementary factors, is human action with a view to the production of use-values, appropriation of natural substances to human requirements; it is the necessary condition for effecting exchange of matter [metabolism] between man and Nature; it is the everlasting Nature-imposed condition of human existence, and therefore is independent of every social phase of that existence, or rather, is common to every such phase.[54]

Untransformed nature remains a crucial element in human existence for the reason that once its materials have been appropriated, transformed into use values for human consumption, they do not remain in this form.

A machine which does not serve the purposes of labor is useless. In addition, it falls a prey to the destructive influence of natural forces. Iron rusts and wood rots. Yarn with which we neither weave nor knit, is cotton wasted.[55]

The homely truth that iron rusts, thereby shedding its condition as transformed or appropriated nature and reverting to its previous status, entails that 'society' can never be fully identified with the cosmos after all; the metabolism of nature itself confronts humanity with the necessity for perpetual labor, with the impossibility of ever 'completing' the cosmos in the form of wholly appropriated nature.

These are some of the fundamental cosmological terms within which Marx's conception of historical progress must be understood. At least one Soviet ethical theorist, Drobnickij, has addressed himself to these concepts, discussing the distinction between the natural and the social, and developing his own view of them:

Of course no one would go so far as to deny that contemporary man is a creature who is not only social but also natural (although, let us notice by the way, the negation of this would logically flow from the principle of division mentioned: if man – in his physical constitution – is a product of labor, his specific morphology, distinguishing him from the animals, is a purely social formation).[56]

The problem posed by Drobnickij has two parts: the natural and the social must be distinguished not only as two phases in the development of humanity, but also as phenomena and laws co-existing in time, inter-acting throughout the whole of human history. In other words, the cosmos is at all times conceived to be distinguishable into the social and the natural; Marx's early tendency to identify the cosmos with society is implicitly rejected.

Searching for a distinction between the social and the natural, Drobnickij considered the most usual one: the social is whatever results from human labor, and the natural, whatever is of natural origin. This distinction he rejects on the grounds that it draws a line merely between 'virgin nature' and 'produced or artificial nature'. If this distinction is extended to embrace human nature, then the natural, in contradistinction to the social, is understood as an *extra-historical* foundation for human existence which, once *Homo sapiens* developed, remained fixed, given, according to Drobnickij. All human development takes place within the social realm of produced objects. The laws of human development would in this case be exclusively social laws, distinguished from the laws of biological evolution. However, if we suppose that development of the human brain does take place after primitive man formed social groups, then this further biological development must be regarded as a mysterious form of teleology [sic] whose contribution just happens coincidentally to facilitate the development of humanity's social nature. This alternative Drobnickij finds unacceptable. On the other hand, assuming a fixed contribution to the human constitution, one might assume that all progress in manipulative and cognitive activity takes place exclusively as a result of social organization. But in this case the particular organization of the human brain and hands would have to be regarded as an accident having no significance in principle [sic].[57] This implication Drobnickij also rejects as unpalatable. Thus, finding a dilemma on either interpretation of the usual Marxist distinction between the natural and the social, Drobnickij rejects it as unworkable. If the natural and the social aspects of human nature are to be comprehended as interacting and participating simultaneously in a progressive development of human nature, then the line between the natural and the social cannot be drawn temporally, and their interaction must be presumed, and investigated, *within* history, within any segment of it, including the present.

But in this conclusion Drobnickij may have made a false step. If the development of nature in both senses, and that of society, are to be conceived as events occuring only *within* history, then 'history' no longer has any of its usual senses; it now means 'the evolution of the cosmos'. But this use of the term 'history' in an equivocal way, as a term of cosmological discourse on one hand, and a term of philosophy of history in the usual sense on the other, also tends to obscure the boundaries between society and any other element of the cosmos, because 'history' in its normal usage refers to *social* events.

To reinforce this new assumption, Drobnickij cited yet another reason why the distinction between nature and society cannot be drawn between the naturally-occurring or the 'virgin' and the 'produced'. The point is that, in the 'artificial nature' produced by human beings, the same laws of nature continue to operate.[58] The manufacture of new objects directed to socially-created human needs obeys, indeed necessarily depends upon, those same laws of nature which appear to operate quite independently of humanity's purposes. Indeed it is the social institution of science which seems to multiply ever-increasingly the number of natural laws known. The production of purely synthetic substances first requires the discovery of, and then the application of, previously unknown laws of nature. At this point Drobnickij concluded that the boundary between nature and society must be understood as a 'relative' one, and cited the well-known phrase from Marx and Engels as support: nature in its original state, preceding all human activity "no longer exists anywhere except possibly on individual Australian coral islands of the newest origin".[59] He concludes,

Neither does man exist outside of nature, nor can nature in its original state be strictly distinguished from man acting in it . . . . The natural and the social to a significant degree interpenetrate each other, and nowhere – neither in space nor in time – is there an absolute, strictly unambiguous border between them.[60]

The attitude toward nature expressed by Drobnickij appears significantly different from that of Marx.

On the one hand, the world as a whole, including also virgin nature, is the sphere of man's life activity, which "converts all nature into his *inorganic* body" [Marx and Engels, *Iz rannyx proizvedenii*, p. 565]

. . . That very act of appropriation by man of natural material presupposes that nature as an object of the activity of people is unlimited, inexhaustible, infinite in space, and from the point of view of the possibilities of transformation hidden in it . . . . The natural world as a whole is given to man in his practice as an inexhaustible reservoir of material and energy, formative forces and plastic forms, an inexhaustible means for creation, and a source of inert obstacles to human 'arbitrariness'. It is unimportant which phenomena and dependencies man has not yet encountered factually; at every moment he enters into a practical relation with them, and must foresee what will be uncovered in the future and what will be the individual results of his interference in the 'natural course of things'. That future silently lurks in every present process of interrelation of man with nature, threatening implacable consequences in the event that it is not sufficiently taken into account. For that reason man is compelled to plan not only every separate act of labor, but also his historical development in the far distant future, the farthest 'expansion' of production in the realm of up-to-now virgin and uncognized nature.[61]

The 'mastery' of humanity over nature here appears to be more of a compulsion than an opportunity. The vision of humanity's relation to nature here is that of an anxious, even fearful demiurge, capable of appropriating nature bit by bit to its own purposes, but constantly overawed by the nature it confronts, effectively hostile in its limitless immensity. This vision seems light-years away from the quietly confident, bourgeois Victorian world of Marx in which untamed nature, if it existed at all, was to be found only on a few newly-created coral reefs.

Finally, Drobnickij characterized the relation of humanity to nature in the following way. In each separate act of production, it sees consciously or unconsciously, an element of the universal task — the transformation of nature as a whole.

Thanks to this universal-historical relation to himself, man also relates to nature as to a whole, to something universal, not limited to that part which he uses or even transforms at a given moment. Appearing before man as a sphere of unlimited possibilities for himself, nature becomes for man something limitless, absolute, inexhaustible, in a word, *objectively* given.[62]

Far from following the early Marx, rejecting the concept of nature unincorporated into human activity as of no interest, Drobnickij proposes that humanity's relation is to 'virgin' nature as a whole *before* its material transformation. However the obscurity mentioned above still remains: Drobnickij proposed to examine the relation between virgin nature and society as occurring entirely *within history*, thereby implying, but not really examining, some very special cosmological assumptions. But since 'history' is used to refer to that which develops, progresses, in the Marxist worldview, Drobnickij's conception would appear to place the determinants of that progress, now conceived to incorporate untransformed nature as well as society (and transformed nature), still further from view. For an elucidation of the basic problem we must look in another direction.

4. COSMOS AND VALUE, SOCIETY AND PROGRESS

The set of claims typically made by Soviet moral philosophers concerning the relations between intrinsic value and historical progress can be profitably examined in the light of the foregoing discussions.

The first claim discussed above, that historical progress is the only genuine indicator of intrinsic value was dismissed at the outset as logically inadmissible. The very judgment that history exhibits progress at all presupposes some logically prior set of value judgments as to what would constitute historical progress. It was also argued that Marx committed himself to an independently stateable criterion of value, the development of all human powers as such, as a standard of reference by which progress or regress in history was to be assessed.

The remainder of the discussion was devoted to a further set of related claims to the effect that the values by which the course of history is to be assessed are nevertheless themselves *historically produced* in some significant sense, and could only be so; that they occur as part of the general evolution of humanity as described by the materialist theory of history; and finally that because history determines what is intrinsically valuable, we as individuals or even as individual social classes never 'choose' or 'decide' what is intrinsically valuable or desirable, but only *learn* what is so 'objectively' from the observation of historical change.

As an instance of such a view, the following quotation from Drobnickij is typical:

Historical materialism contains nothing in itself other than scientific knowledge, requires no value-supplement, because the goals of people here are included in the structure of the historical process itself. The interpretation of history by its participants (even if it occurs in the evaluational form of ideals, conceptions of good and evil, etc.) is conditioned by the laws of social development, and itself constitutes an aspect of it, and is not imported into it from somewhere outside.[63]

If one claims to be evaluating the course of history relative to some chosen standard of value in the ordinary understanding of 'evaluate', it would be legitimate to infer that one is selecting, from among a list of possible relations between the course of history and the standard of value, that one which appears actually to obtain. But this (standard) act of evaluation would be beside the point, or distinctly peculiar, in the situation where, on the description of history which one gives, it is not logically possible that any of several values may or may not result, but on the contrary there is a necessary connection between the uniquely possible outcome of history on one's description of it and a particular evaluation of it.

As argued above, the materialist theory of history which supposedly shows objectively what constitutes progress, is itself embedded in an evolutionary cosmology which, if accepted, in effect eliminates all alternatives to the assumption of evolutionary development. That history exhibits progress is not 'scientifically discovered' by the materialist conception of history, but posited as an implication of the evolutionist cosmology it presupposes. One does not accept the materialist theory of history and the evolutionary cosmology it presupposes, and then as a distinct act, 'evaluate' the course of history as *progressive*. The latter act is not logically distinct from the former. But committing oneself to an evolutionist cosmology is not an act of scientific observation; it is rather a choice among metaphysical hypotheses which requires explicit discussion and justification.

Hence the oddity of talk about 'evaluating' the course of history within the context of a philosophy of history as discussed here. In the analysis developed above, it is evident that one's standard of evaluation is adopted prior to the elaboration of the universal history; it is one of the principles guiding the construction of the historical narrative, guiding the selection of relevant data to be included in the narrative. However, once the narrative has been constructed, the standard of evaluation will be 'inherent' in it as logically 'implied' by the sequence of events narrated. 'History' will then 'demonstrate' that these values are 'objectively real'.

Granting that in the materialist theory of history only one outcome relative to the standard of evaluation is conceivable, then the assertion 'history exhibits progress' is merely a tautology. It is a tautology of course so long as 'history' means 'history as described by the theory', i.e., the materialist theory of history (hereafter History$_{MT}$). The only significant empirical assertion one could make would be that 'History$_A$ (history in some alternative or more general interpretation not based on this particular evolutionist cosmology) exhibits progress in relation to some stipulated standard of value' (let us say, that of the original theory). But for a Marxist the statement 'History$_A$ exhibits progress' could not be a statement in his theory; only a statement *about* it. It would be part of a claim that History$_{MT}$ is a true account; but this claim would be appropriate only in a context where at least the possibility of an alternative interpretation (History$_A$) has been implicitly admitted. Otherwise one could only be engaging in the pointless exercise of repeating 'History$_{MT}$ exhibits progress' as though one were performing an evaluation in some significant sense, whereas this utterance is necessarily true in the theory. At most one would be only reaffirming that history inevitably must exhibit progress on one's description of it. If the apparent evaluation is to have significance in an empirical sense, it must be History$_A$ which is referred to. Most Soviet appeals to the conclusion that 'History exhibits progress', supposedly derived from the materialist conception of history as an 'objective science', offer merely a pseudo-evaluation masquerading as a genuine one.

Another difficulty in the usual Soviet view of the relation between historical progress and value lies in certain determinist assumptions behind it. In Drobnickij's view quoted above, for example, the evaluation of history by its participants is itself conditioned by the laws of social development. By this remark Drobnickij appears to claim that one aspect of the total (economically determined) historical process is the criterion of value used to evaluate its course. The role of the individual in 'evaluating' the course of history would be restricted to the rather empty one of accepting the value yard-stick supplied by history as a part of the over-all determined process, applying it to some other aspect of this single, determined process, and reporting the (pre-determined) result as an 'evaluation'.

The Georgian philosopher Džioev has examined the concept of historical determination implicit in the usual Soviet view of 'the laws of history' and on the basis of his own view, objects to this conception of the evaluation of history, in particular to the superfluousness of the operation and hence of the individual's role in performing it.

Marxism doesn't at all understand the historical process as though on the one hand there is historical necessity, and on the other, human goals and strivings defined by it, in such a way that it only remains for people to harness themselves in the yoke of historical necessity and drag behind them the two-wheeled cart of history.[64]

Without the recognition of the independent role of values it is impossible to understand the role of the individual person in history. Marxism has always protested against the reduction of the person to the mouthpiece of a social movement.[65]

Džioev based his objections to the usual Soviet conception of historical necessity on an explicit examination of some of the cosmological assumptions behind it, and proposed his own conception of the 'world' (cosmos) and 'man's place in it' as an alternative. He concluded that the existence of the individual cannot be conceived entirely as an aspect of some evolving society-cosmos.

Existence is not only the bustle of the day, and not only a given social order; that is, human existence does not consist only in that he, man, is a member of a given society. The place of man in the world also comprises his existence. As we explained in the preceding chapter, universal human values 'flow out of' this existence of man.[66]

Values, in Džioev's analysis, depend upon the place of man in this larger
'world' which is synonymous neither with an evolving society-cosmos nor with
an inexhaustible untransformed nature, but contains both as components.

An (unconditional) value is that which is worthy of man, that which suits the place of
man in the world. Marx proceeds from such an understanding of value when he characterizes Communist society as a society in which the conditions most adequate to and
worthy of human nature will be created.[67]

Man is a part of nature, he is one of the sons of the earth, but he is not like any of her
other sons. Man is a part of nature, but also more than nature.[68]

The similarity of these remarks to those of the young Marx quoted above
should not be overlooked.[69] Džioev lifts the problem of evaluating the course
of history out of the context of historical determinism and necessity, and
places it in the context of human subjects who are capable of adopting values
to some extent independently of the course of history.

The problem of the meaning of history, evidently, consists not in whether there is
lawlike regularity in history. The question of meaning is a question of values, of the
evaluation of the lawlike course of history .... It will have meaning if it facilitates the
realization of human values. The problem of the meaning of history is the problem of
the realizability of values, in the final analysis, of universally human values. In order that
history have meaning it is necessary that it be not only a lawlike process, but that it also
lead to moral progress.[70]

Džioev himself adopts an analysis of historical change and its relation to
intrinsic value similar to one described above.[71] He locates the motive force
of history in the dissatisfaction and frustration of individuals who encounter
their true nature stifled and distorted under existing social conditions and
exert themselves in an intelligent way to realize conditions more congenial to
their desires. His is, in effect, the view that 'authentic human nature', or 'the
determination of humanity to develop all of its potential powers' is not
merely an *outcome* of history, but one of its determinants or motive forces,
from the beginning.

If one is to summarize the distinction between natural-historical necessity and natural
[necessity], it will be the participation of ideas in the determination of history. The
point is not that material [economic] interests often take the form of ideological motive
forces, but that these ideological motives are not entirely conditioned by circumstances.
... Human activity depends, mainly (in very large measure), on circumstances, but it
also depends on ideals, values, which cannot be reduced to concrete-historical conditions, for the criterion of the particular is the universal, and in the final analysis, the
universally human.[72]

In a second book continuing the argument of the one just quoted, Džioev issued a broader and more sustained attack upon the 'sociologism' and 'absolute historicism' prevailing among many Marxists (he chose Western European Marxists to bear the brunt of his critique). His criticism is aimed at those who see in activity of the individual historical subject 'only an illustration of the action of unvarying laws'.

We are convinced that investigation of the uniqueness of historical necessity and its realization has contemporary significance due to the importance of the problem itself, and also due to the fact that in Marxist philosophical literature to the present time the view which ignores this uniqueness and disparages the role of human activity in the process of realizing historical necessity remains current.[73]

Džioev defends a conception of individual human beings as active subjects, rather than mere objects of history, possessing their own strivings, ideals, and values which may be creatively applied under various social conditions. "The socialness of man cannot be reduced to the ensemble of given social relations, or, more precisely, the social relations characteristic of a particular social order."[74]

Ignoring the moment of creativity, regarding human freedom as an illusion, brings the structuralists to the negation of humanity as the subject of history. Such a position creates insuperable difficulties in comprehending the process of transition from one social system to another.[75]

Still more interestingly, Džioev states flatly that the fundamental issues involved in the discussion are not empirical ones.

The question of who is the authentic subject of history cannot be decided on a purely empirical level, by reference to the fact that it is none other than people who extract ore and till fields, that they pronounce speeches in parliaments and hold conferences in colleges, write and criticize poetry, etc. These facts are not denied by those who do not consider humanity the subject of history. People make history, but they could turn out to be blind instruments by means of which history is made.[76]

He insists that to approach the study of social phenomena purely on the basis of a conception of causality adopted without modification from the study of the physical universe cannot lead to an adequate understanding of the former. To ignore the difference in appropriate conceptions of causality "leads to a diminishing of the significance of the philosophical investigation of social life and fundamental tendencies of humanity".[77]

Although Džioev would not agree that the materialist conception of history is an inadequate basis upon which to explicate the concept of progress, his insistence that an adequate account of historical valuation can only be given on the basis of an explicit discussion of the philosophical issues involved in effect meets the objections voiced above to the views of other Soviet philosophers. It was argued that references to the materialist conception of history as a 'science' which supplies the only correct criterion of value could not satisfy an inquiry into the problem of progress, that only an explicit defense of the cosmological assumptions behind the materialist conception of history would be appropriate to that inquiry.

In the absence of any detailed discussion of these issues in the writings of the vast majority of Soviet ethical theorists, a substantial gap remains in the center of most of their accounts of normative value.

CHAPTER EIGHT

SOVIET CRITICISMS OF 'BOURGEOIS' ETHICAL THEORY

1. KANTIAN ETHICS AND SOVIET DEONTOLOGICAL THEORIES

In a sense the ambition of the neo-Kantian Marxists at the turn of the century to marry Kantian ethics with Marxian social theory was realized sixty years later in the work of one of the most original, noteworthy, and unorthodox moral philosophers to have participated in the recent rebirth of interest in ethical theory in the Soviet Union, Ja. A. Mil'ner-Irinin. In a monograph entitled *Ethics, or the Principles of True Humanity* Mil'ner-Irinin developed a denotological ethics inspired in a number of respects by Kant's practical philosophy, but also influenced by Hegel, and of course Marx.[1] His writings on ethics also contain some treatments of metaphysical issues which reflect his interest in Spinoza.[2] In Mil'ner-Irinin's own view his *Ethics* constitutes the first truly substantial and successful attempt to develop Kantian ethics in the light of the materialist conception of history, to construct a deontological ethical theory which accomodates the insights of Marx. He describes his own ethical system as a deontological one, or an 'ethics of principle', which he distinguishes from 'normative ethics' or an 'ethic of negatives'.[3]

It is difficult to assess the position and influence of Mil'ner-Irinin's views within the Soviet philosophical community, especially from the published record alone, because his major work was not published in the usual sense, but printed in a few dozen copies for the purpose of a discussion and decision within the Academy of Sciences as to whether it should be published, the outcome of which was negative.[4]

On the other hand a number of the most prominent moral philosophers in the Soviet Union look upon Mil'ner-Irinin's work as a valuable contribution to the development of a Marxist ethics, and lament the semi-official resistance his work has encountered. To be sure none of those who consider themselves supporters of Mil'ner-Irinin's work adopt quite the same style of writing or argument, and most of their published views do not reflect many of the details of his ethics and metaphysics. As a distinguishing characteristic of this group however, one might point to a great seriousness of interest in Kantian ethics, and a more detailed consideration of it as a prelude to the exposition of their own views.[5]

Mil'ner-Irinin's ethical system can be described as deontological in the sense that a doctrine of *conscience* supplies all of its normative principles; each principle is regarded as a dimension of conscience. There are ten such principles, and correspondingly ten chapters of his *Ethics*, each providing an exposition of one principle, building upon the previously established principles. The ten principles of true humanity which together comprise *conscience* are as follows:

1. The principle of conscience, which prescribes that every human being preserve his or her conscience.[6]
2. The principle of self-perfection, which requires that one make a person of oneself, "for a person is not born such, but forms himself through the whole of life".[7]
3. The principle of good, which commands one to create good, that is, a world both social and natural in which truth, justice, and beauty converge in an ideal synthesis.[8]
4. The principle of social property, which commands one to struggle for and to cherish social property as a means of production.[9]
5. The principle of labor, which commands one to labor because only socially useful, productive labor creates human beings, and only the laborer is a genuine creator of history.[10]
6. The principle of freedom, which requires of human beings the preservation of an inner, spiritual freedom "for there is no more vile crime against the human conscience than spiritual (moral) slavery".[11]
7. The principle of nobility, which requires that one seek an appropriately moral, harmonious combination of ends and means, and that a person pursue only worthy ends in life through the use of worthy means.[12]
8. The principle of gratitude, which obliges one to be filled with a feeling of thankfulness to others for a mutual enrichment of human nature.[13]
9. The principle of wisdom, which directs one "to have faith in humanity, and in its high historical destiny, in the invincible power of its reason, the inexhaustible treasury of its conscience, and in the boundless creative power of its revolutionary, creating and transforming capability; to trust in the ultimate triumph of good – truth, justice and beauty; to love life in all its inexhaustible charms".[14]
10. The principle of action, which teaches how one ought to conduct oneself in each individual situation, and of the obligating meaning of death.[15]

This last principle obliges one always to act in accordance with conscience, and Mil'ner-Irinin asserts in rather Platonic fashion that it is absolutely impossible for a truly wise person to act other than according to conscience.

He insists that these ten principles are to be taken as mutually equivalent: for example there is no way to fulfill the first principle (to preserve one's conscience) other than by fulfilling the tenth (following the dictates of conscience in each individual deed). There is no hierarchy of subordination; to transgress one principle is to diminish or destroy one's conscience to that extent, and hence to transgress all of the principles which comprise it.[16]

The heart of Mil'ner-Irinin's 'transformation' of Kantian ethics is to be found in his re-definition of the ethical subject or agent. Whereas Kant described the foundations of moral reasoning for *rational* beings, Mil'ner-Irinin undertakes to supply an ethic for *social* beings, conceived essentially as laboring beings:

the function of labor is the fundamental and all-determining function of humanity as a social being, to the extent that the concept of a social being and a laboring being completely coincide in their content and identically characterize the human essence.[17]

More precisely, in the first chapter of *Ethics* Mil'ner-Irinin describes *reason* as a characteristic only of *social* beings:

66. Reason, in the proper sense of the term, as developed, like consciousness and like self-consciousness, is present uniquely to a person as a social being, a laboring being, and conscience is the inner inspiration of reason, its highest triumph.[18]

The theme of labor as a defining trait of humanity is elaborated by Mil'ner-Irinin to its ultimate consequence: that humanity, by virtue of its social, laboring nature, stands as creator and revolutionary transformer of the world.

64. Humanity and revolutionary are synonyms, like the synonyms conscience and humanity, like the synonyms laborer and human being.[19]

Humanity according to Mil'ner-Irinin has a mission "entirely determined by its objective social and laboring nature, its creative-transforming and revolutionary nature", to resolve the contradiction between that which is and that which ought to be in nature, in society, and in himself.

Mil'ner-Irinin's concept of nature, exclusive of humanity which appears as its revolutionary transformer and creator appears to be influenced by Spinoza as well as by Hegel:

141. The essence of nature consists in the fact that it is cause of itself, that is, cause and act of itself, that it exists in itself and require no external forces for its existence and action. Nature is absolute self-sufficiency. Due to its essence as cause of itself, nature possesses absolutely infinite (eternal) existence, in other words, absolutely infinite capability for existence.[20]

The appearance of humanity in nature was one of "the most important boundary markers" along the path of eternal self-definition of nature.[21] The development of the organic world led to a new quality: humanity. Prior to the appearance of humanity, blind necessity prevailed everywhere without exception in nature, a necessity recognized by no one for there was no one to become conscious of it.

With the appearance of human beings, together with the history of humanity, together with social development, the recognition of this necessity of nature in the process of material-labor activity of people begins, and only with humanity, in humanity, nature begins to become conscious of itself: the process of the self-definition of nature (in the respect of human interests) came to an end in principle, and the process of self-definition of humanity began. More precisely: the process of self-definition of nature henceforth takes place as the process of self-definition of humanity; in humanity's creative-transforming activity nature reveals . . . its absolutely infinite capability for renewal.[22]

Mil'ner-Irinin argues that the mere fact of being born a human being does not constitute the source of one's human dignity. On the contrary, the fact of one's origin as a product of blind accidents of nature in which one as an individual plays no role constitutes an insult to one's moral dignity.

179. All your life must be directed to 'overcoming' (in quotation marks, of course) the accidental (accidental-necessary) character of your appearance in the universe – in activity serving the moral perfection of yourself and your surroundings. In other words all your life must be a practical demonstration that you were not born a human being in vain. Precisely in this will consist your actual service, as much before yourself as before humanity as a whole, in this will consist the fulfillment of the commands of your conscience, in this also consists your true dignity as a human being.[23]

This conscience whose commands a human being must fulfill to realize his dignity is at one and the same time individual and universal. Ethics, as the study of the dictates of an ideal, abstract conscience (not the actual conscience of some particular group or individual in history), or the principles of true humanity, is no merely individual phenomenon:

It is directed to the whole of humanity, independently of the country and society in which people live, for wherever and in whatever circumstances a person lives, he must realize himself as a human being, realize his most profound essence as a revolutionary transformer of that which exists on the principles of the good as an ideal; [he] is obliged to fulfill his human duty; [he] must follow the commands of his own conscience – the conscience of all humanity, if he does not wish to punish himself with a genuine misfortune – his own defectiveness as a human.[24]

This doctrine of the universality of conscience Mil'ner-Irinin explicates with the aid of Hegel's doctrine of the universal, the particular, and the individual moments of the notion.

In this fashion the all-human character of morality is fulfilled in its class-revolutionary character, which in its turn is fulfilled in the individual consciousness of each separate, morally reasoning human being. And here, as everywhere, the relation of the universal, the particular, and the individual has a fully dialectical character: the first, the second, and the third coincide in that same thing – in conscience. The latter at one and the same time is both all-human and class-revolutionary and intimately personal. [25]

Mil'ner-Irinin's mixture of Spinozistic, Hegelian, and Marxist influences exhibits a fundamentally Kantian tendency in another respect. While Mil'ner-Irinin does not endorse Kant's categorical imperative as such, his entire doctrine of *conscience* (the ten principles of true humanity) is intended to be taken as a single moral law expressing categorical demands. Mil'ner-Irinin refers to them variously as 'categorical demands'.[26] and 'unconditional commands',[27] which are to be fulfilled in a spirit of 'strictest rigorism'.[28] It is an ethics of duty which he presents, not of utility.

In this respect Mil'ner-Irinin tends to oppose the spirit, if not the letter, of much writing on ethical theory in the Soviet Union, for among the various features which characterize the more typical views, there is a constantly-repeated reference to a moral duty to do whatever serves the revolution, or whatever serves the building of Communism, which is of course a teleological conception of duty. Plekhanov explicitly criticized Kant's rejection of utilitarian ethics, claiming that Kant had misunderstood the utilitarian principle simply as 'self-love', whereas in fact morality is founded "on the striving not for personal happiness but for the happiness of the whole: the clan, the people, the class, humanity".[29] Plekhanov's preference for a teleological ethical theory has found more followers than Kantian deontology in the Soviet Union, but this observation must be qualified in several respects.

Drobnickij describes Soviet philosophers as divided on this question, somewhat along the lines of the traditional dispute between deontologists and teleologists in the history of ethical theory. There is a group of ethical theorists who focus attention first of all upon the defining role of interests, both social and individual, in their conception of moral duty, emphasizing above all those in which the individual and the social coincide. From this perspective theorists such as Banzeladze, Samsonova, and Selivanov conclude that moral duty is to be defined in terms of benefits resulting from actions, or the good.[30] Other theorists, such as Xarčev, stress that morality arises in society precisely because of the conflict between the interests of the individual and those of society, and that morality, for that reason, is above all a limitation on the assertion of the interests of the individual, a constraint on his will which is regulated by means of a system of prescriptions and prohibitions.

Drobnickij himself, in a rather complex two-stage analysis of moral duty, adopts a deontological description of the duty of the individual moral agent, and a teleological description of the historical process which defines these duties, in effect thus dividing his allegiance between Kant and Hegel, one might say. The question of moral duty is determined, according to Drobnickij, not by 'thinking humanity', but by "real historical humanity uncovering for itself the 'meaning of humanity' through practical experience".[31] It is not 'thinking humanity' which proposes moral norms as expressions of a goal-directed will; rather it is historically developing humanity which made certain moral norms necessary, as a condition of further development.

Thus on the level of the socio-historical subjects of moral consciousness and action, moral demands appear above all as obligations, as stipulating and compelling, and not as simple expressions of will.[31]

Going over the same ground in more specific terms, Drobnickij poses the question: "what lies at the *foundation* of moral demands to an individual?"; and replies that in the final analysis moral demands reflect the objective needs of social existence, thereby pointing toward a teleological conception of duty. However, in the same paragraph he cites Kant's view that in fulfilling his duty, an individual must 'abstract himself from any goal', that is, act from duty itself, and not something else. "In this lies the distinction between the moral 'categorical' imperative and the 'hypothetical', by means of which the individual chooses the means for the achievement of the goal pursued by him."[32] "In some sense", concludes Drobnickij, "Kant is obviously correct".[33]

In the concrete situation the individual, from the point of view of morality, must above all fulfill his duty, submit both his goals and means for achieving them to the demands of morality. It has come to be that in concrete situations an individual behaves morally, acting not by the principle of simple purposefulness, but by the laws of obligation.[34]

Reiterating the same point in still more specific terms, Drobnickij again poses 'a more fundamental question': "does not the concept of goal (and benefit) lie in the foundation of morality as a whole?".[35] Rephrasing the question yet again he asks, "which category — obligation or purpose, benefit — is the fundamental one in moral consciousness?".[36] He answers this last question unambiguously, that even if in some sense morality gives expression to some purpose, recognized or subjectively desired by the individual, "morality *prescribes* these goals to the individual, *imposes* them on him, grounds them as appropriate to humanity, i.e., as obligatory. Hence in morality the very category of purpose is defined through obligation."[37] The same reasoning applies both to *interests* and to the *good* according to him.[38]

> ... from the point of view of morality, the individual must act not according to the principle of maximum results and effectiveness, but in accordance with that norm which in the given situation must be fulfilled.[39]

Thus at the level of individual moral reasoning and conduct, Drobnickij must be placed among the deontologists.

The discussion of Kantian ethics is not confined to those writing primarily in ethical theory, of course. Kant has naturally received much attention from specialists in the history of philosophy, and the range of writing available on this subject is quite wide. V. F. Asmus, one of the most respected commentators on the history of philosophy, discussed Kant's ethics at some length in a recent commentary on Kant's philosophy as a whole, providing a sample of some of the more sophisticated Soviet writing on Kantian ethics. Asmus views Kant as having rendered two great services in his practical philosophy: first by insisting on the autonomy of morality with respect to religion, and second, by subordinating the ethics of personal happiness to the ethics of duty.[40]

Not surprisingly Asmus congratulates Kant on pursuing Hume's point that morality stands in no need of religious sanctions, but criticizes Kant for failing to remove God wholly from his conception of the moral life, in the following sense:

> Thus Kant did not carry through to the end his idea of the autonomy of ethics. He only limited the authority of religion, but by no means rejected religious belief. The God of Kant, to be sure, is not the legislator of morality, not the source of the moral law, does not proclaim that law directly. But he is the cause of moral order in the world. Without that order the moral form of conduct, and felicity, would remain uncoordinated.[41]

As do many commentators on the categorical imperative, Asmus complains that it remains a completely formal principle which "says nothing and can say nothing concerning the problem of which substantive principles should guide behavior".[42] He also complains that Kant's doctrine of human nature is painted in "gloomy, pessimistic tones, completely in the spirit of the ideology of Protestantism" which left an imprint of its doctrine of original sin on Kant.[43] This pessimism concerning human nature, and the formalism of the moral law as well, are traced to sociological causes in the circumstances of Kant's life. As a member of the economically weak and feudally backward German burgher society at the end of the eighteenth century, Kant's perspective suffered from the absence of a social class capable of becoming the represent-

ative of the German people, who were suffering under feudalism and absolutism, or capable of leading the struggle against the institutions of the feudal
order.

In the consciousness of German philosophers practical activity itself acquires the appearance of ideal activity. It is conceived not as a material, object-oriented activity of social
man, as member of an actual society, but first of all and primarily as the activity of
moral consciousness, of 'practical' reason. Real practical activity is transformed into the
concept of the 'good will'.[44]

In this of course Asmus endorses a well-established Marxian attitude toward
Kantian philosophy which charged the 'powerless German burghers' with
having got "only so far as the 'good will' ".[45] This analysis of the influence of
Kant's historical circumstances on his philosophy has been a standard one in
Soviet literature since Vinogradskaja's article on the subject in 1924.[46] In
that article, for example, Vinogradskaja argued that Germany of Kant's day
remained in the first stage of the process of the emancipation of the bourgeoisie from the feudal order, in a period when the bourgeoisie was still too
weak to challenge the Church and the aristocracy in any but mystified philosophical writings, whereas England and France had already long entered the
second stage of either outright victory for the bourgeoisie or a successful
forcing of compromises by the old order.[47]

Kant himself came from a petty-bourgeois environment. On one hand, he had to formulate in the head-breaking' (*kopfzerbrechende*) and foggy language of his philosophy the
general socio-political strivings of the leading elements of his time; on the other, he could
not fail to include in part in his philosophy, what was dictated to him by his class origins,
his native surroundings, and finally, the impressions of childhood and youth as the son
of a Koenigsburg saddle-maker.[48]

Despite these various criticisms, Asmus believes that Kant's notion of the
unconditional worth of each person, the necessity of treating each individual
as an end in himself (a doctrine in which Kant was influenced by Rousseau),
constituted a major progressive development in the history of philosophy.[49]

For Asmus the most interesting feature in the whole of Kant's ethics was
his concept of the freedom of the rational being as a thing-in-itself.[50] Faced
with the necessity of accounting for the autonomy of the will which was a
presupposition of the moral law on the one hand, and with his thesis of
universal causal determinism concerning any event (appearance) occurring
within the temporal sphere on the other, Kant could account for the freedom
of the rational being only by relying upon his doctrine of the ideality of time,
and the distinction between appearances and things-in-themselves.

Only if, besides appearances, there are 'things-in-themselves', and only if time is ideal, in other words, there is no definition of things as they exist in themselves, is freedom possible. One who does not distinguish 'appearances' and 'things-in-themselves', and also rejects the ideality of time, is incapable, according to Kant, of avoiding Spinozism.[51]

Asmus stresses the 'deep connection' between Kant's theory of knowledge as provided in the first *Critique* and the ethics of the second *Critique*, above all the reliance of the ethics on the doctrine of the ideality of space and time.[52]

In some respects the most interesting part of Asmus' commentary lies in the connections he makes between Kant's doctrine of freedom in the ethics, and his philosophy of history.

Since the historical process is an empirical process proceeding in time, and since any event or action taking place in time is located beyond the power of the one who performs those actions, because it is determined by preceding events and itself determines what follows, the sphere of history, according to Kant, turns out to be a sphere in which there is no place for freedom.

It is true that Kant strove with all his might, as has already been shown, to avoid fatalistic conclusions from his doctrine of the total determination of the psychological process and of the determination of its causes . . . . Kant wanted to develop his philosophy as a doctrine which nowhere entered into conflict with the principle of determinism, embracing the entire circle of sensory appearances of the empirical world, and would have 'rescued' in Kant's own expression, the possibility of freedom in human conduct.[53]

However, concludes Asmus, in the final analysis Kant's doctrine of freedom "is not a doctrine of the philosophy of history or sociology, but only the metaphysical and dualistic hypothesis of a moralist".[54]

Freedom turns out to be an achievement of man not as the subject of real historical practice and the class struggle in real society, but as the subject of the moral will, transcendent in relation to the real world. The entire specific content of socio-historical life was reduced, in this manner, to the narrowly individual framework of the struggle between the sensual nature of the human being and moral obligation, going back to its basis in the suprasensuous and supraempirical world.[55]

Thus insofar as a person is really free as an 'intelligible' subject of the suprasensuous world, he cannot be the subject of history; and conversely, insofar as a person is the subject of history, he cannot be free.[56] "In vain therefore Kant flattered himself with the hope that his 'critical' philosophy might overcome the 'fatalism' of Spinoza."[57] Asmus goes on to consider Schopenhauer's and Hegel's criticisms of Kant, largely dismissing the former and endorsing the latter.[58] In this respect he is typical of a large number of Soviet commentators on Kantian ethics.[59]

2. THE INFLUENCE OF HEGEL ON SOVIET ETHICAL THEORY

The influence of Hegel, being much more pervasive and at the same time more diffuse than that of Kant, and also not always explicitly acknowledged when it is present, presents a much greater challenge to the would-be summarizer. As was argued in Chapter Two, Hegel's work must be understood as a presupposition of much of Soviet thought, even where that presupposition is only ambiguously acknowledged. The full measure of that ambiguity can be seen in one possible interpretation of Šinkaruk's conception of the relation of Hegel's system to dialectical materialism, as discussed above.[60] Succinctly stated, that relation might be characterized by the claim that the 'laws' of the Hegelian dialectic (as formulated by Engels) can be discovered to operate in the processes of nature and history, through scientific investigation. That process of scientific investigation seems to be regarded by some as an essentially empirical one. Thus, in effect, on this interpretation of Šinkaruk's views, taking them as typical of many Soviet philosophers, a number of the assumptions and conclusions of Hegel's system can be taken as established for the purposes of Soviet philosophy. They are not necessarily established 'philosophically', through a well-argued defense of the metaphysical assumptions involved, rather 'scientifically' by some sort of evidence provided by the study of natural and social processes in dialectical-materialist terms. In this way many separate elements of Hegel's system are presumed to be available for philosophical use, in the absence of any special justification or defense of that use.

Specifically in terms of ethical theory, the method of the 'science of ethics' has been described by numerous Soviet authors, with good reason, as "the principle of the unity of the logical and the historical".[61] That methodological assumption appears strongly influenced by, if not explicitly identified with, the outlines of Hegel's method of inquiry in the *Phenomenology of Spirit*. The 'science of ethics' as presented by a number of Soviet philosophers depends directly on that 'unity of the logical and the historical'; the 'science of history' is also required to justify the claim to objective validity of certain moral norms and values.[62]

Drobnickij's analysis of the structure of moral consciousness provides a specific illustration of the 'methodological unity of the logical and the historical'. In that study he supposed that the (logical) structure of moral consciousness could be adequately grasped only through a reconstruction of the historical evolution of logical forms in which moral imperatives and values were expressed. To supply this historical reconstruction however, he argued that it was sufficient to carry out a *logical* reconstruction, subsequent to an analysis of the various logical forms exhibited in contemporary moral consciousness, and a classification of them in terms of a continuum of simplicity and complexity. As was argued above, his procedure seems to have been inspired by that of Hegel's *Phenomenology*, but he does not discuss or defend it in these terms, contenting himself with the assertion that such a "correlation of the logical and the historical" obtains.[63]

The influence of Hegel's ethical theory itself, as opposed to his general methods, can be explicitly seen in the work of other Soviet ethical theorists. For instance, both Tugarinov and Sogomonov make explicit references to Hegel's philosophy in order to explicate their conceptions of the objectivity of values.[64] Both of them rely upon the distinction between subjective spirit and objective spirit in Hegel's work to give an account of what they mean by the 'objectivity' of value.

In another feature of Soviet ethical theory which appears to be Hegel-inspired, if not directly adopted from Hegel, most authors attempting to explain the sense in which value judgments may be construed as susceptible of truth or falsity resort ultimately to some reference to the 'court of history' as supplying, in some (often obscure) fashion, a criterion of truth or falsity for value judgments. A number of accounts of the truth and falsity of value judgments described above shared some such assumption.[65] Similarly, *interests* were said to be assessable as objective or not on the basis of a knowledge of what is historically progressive.[66]

In another unambiguous if implicit dependence upon Hegel, a number of authors employ the concept of dialectical negation, or some other feature of the dialectic, to resolve problems which otherwise appear insoluble. For instance, Titarenko explicitly relies upon the dialectic to 'solve' the problem of formulating an 'objective' criterion of moral progress in history, without transcending an historicist perspective.[67] Mil'ner-Irinin and a number of other ethical theorists, employ Hegel's three moments of the notion – the universal, the particular, and the individual – in order to explicate puzzling assertions concerning the identity of the universal and the individual.[68]

The broadest and most significant Hegelian theme manifest in Soviet discussions of ethical theory does not necessarily require explicit references to Hegel. As has been argued above (especially in Chapters One and Seven) the interplay between two competing conceptual frameworks for the evaluation of human conduct, which have been termed here the 'historical' and the moral, arguably constitutes the most important Hegelian influence upon Soviet ethical thought.

It is the intersection of Hegel's philosophy of history with his account of morality (*Moralität*) which holds the most potent key to the estimation of Hegel's influence on Marx's and Soviet Marxists' writings in ethical theory. The suggestion, drawn from Hegel's philosophy of history, that there is an interest, that of the development of spirit, superior to the demands of morality in any particular historical epoch, has tempted legions of thinkers since to suppose that merely moral demands at all times and in all places must be seen as liable to be transcended by those of historical progress, or in crude terms, of revolutionary politics. It is this assumption which stands behind the nearly universal tendency of Soviet ethical theorists to subordinate the demands of morality to those of 'historical progress', indeed to attempt ·in certain respects to *base* the former on the latter. The refusal in the end to treat moral principles as autonomous, in most cases can be traced to this Marxian reading of Hegel.

Drobnickij provides an interesting example of the view in question which in fact does attribute a degree of autonomy to moral principles, an autonomy which is explained however primarily by human ignorance, and the absence until the modern period of a science of history which would supply knowledge of the full consequences of the adoption of some particular moral principle, deontologically conceived. In effect, according to Drobnickij, the institution of morality in which right and wrong are conceived deontologically, developed *faute de mieux*; he implies that a mature science of history which explained all of the consequences for humanity dependent on the adoption of a particular moral principle would supply a rational grounding of the deepest kind for moral principles. Such a grounding was not available until the most recent period of human history however. Prior to the development of Marxism there was no conception of historical method adequate for such a science of history, and even given the method, the investigations required to supply all the relevant information still exceeded practical possibilities. Moreover, it is only the intellectuals who might come into possession of such a science of history, and hence of the rational grounds for moral norms; 'the wide masses of workers and laborers' would continue to grasp their essential interests in moral rather than scientific-historical terms.[69]

Drobnickij's conception of moral duty was intended to answer a question which recurred as a kind of *leitmotif* in his work over a number of years: what is the *source* of authority behind moral obligations? He answered this question, both early and late, by claiming that the authority behind all moral obligations is a subject "transcending the limitations of the existing individual, group, class, or even the society existing at a given moment"; that subject is humanity as a whole.[70] Despite resistance to this view from other Soviet philosophers, Drobnickij retained it in his last work:

On the socio-historical plane, moral commands and evaluations are expressed in the last analysis 'for the whole of humanity' and 'in the name of humanity'.[71]

He was consistent in his view that the authority of moral demands comes ultimately from humanity as a whole; but in what sense did he understand 'humanity' as the source of moral obligation? We have already seen above that on the level of individual moral reasoning, he subscribed to a deontology in which the consequences of individual action do not affect its moral worth, and the individual's purposes are relevant to the assessment of his action in the first instance simply as an indication of whether he acted out of duty. The will of the individual, to the extent that it is moral, is *determined* by or *defined* by, his objectively given moral duty. And yet, in some sense the ultimate justification for any moral principle lies in a demonstration of its 'expediency' (*celesoobraznost'*) or usefulness to humanity as a whole. Drobnickij's account of the form of an ultimate justification of, or demonstration of the rationality of, any moral principle occurs in the following passage:

Any time when moral consciousness undertakes the attempt (in ethical theory or in life, for the self-clarification of the significance of practical activity) to demonstrate to itself the expediency [*celesoobraznost'*] of some principle, concept, norm, it in the end, explicitly or implicitly, resorts to a certain 'destiny' of humanity, which still must be realized in life, in social practice, in history. And something is recognized as a good for a human being not simply because he desires or is interested in it, but also because such is his 'true', 'authentic' (i.e., obligatory, speaking in specifically moral language) nature, or the 'essence' of social life (such as it necessarily must be). Accordingly, even when moral consciousness begins to recognize the expediency and usefulness of specific principles for the existence of human society (almost always in some specific form, i.e., from this or that class position), this rationally comprehended connection is, in its turn, inscribed in a wider conception of the 'destiny' of society and humanity, of what ought to be, and what is appropriate to it.[72]

It is this conception of the rational defense of moral principles that justifies Drobnickij's claim that all moral judgments are made 'in the name of humanity'. However, in his view it remains at least equally important in the explanation of his deontological conception of moral norms, that such demonstrations of the rationality of a moral norm are almost never within our grasp, and were certainly unavailable in the historical periods which produced the major moral principles which have governed human communities into the modern period. 'Thinking humanity' cannot be construed as giving the moral law to itself "for in the conditions of social antagonisms, the struggle of interests and positions, only particular subjects are actually represented".[73] "Each of them outlines for itself a conception of 'humanity' as it ought to be."[74] The 'meaning of history' and appropriate moral norms are produced only through the contest for social positions and a recognition of the consequences of that struggle, in limited fashion, by the participants involved; 'humanity' has no over-all grasp of its situation, of the consequences of the competition, or of the (moral) rules evolved to govern that competition.

Drobnickij conceives of a moral norm as a condensation or crystallization of the enormous historical experience of many generations; hence the task of analyzing its total social significance far transcends the capabilities of any single individual. Moral norms must necessarily arise under conditions of relative ignorance: the consequences of adopting a particular moral norm cannot be known in advance, and it often turns out that action in accordance with the demands of morality promises little likelihood of successful consequences from some other point of view. Even under such circumstances, the individual may be obliged to act according to the moral principle "to demonstrate by the same his faithfulness to the moral principle, to the idea of humanity, justice, etc.".[75]

In these conditions, when moral consciousness only dimly guesses the prospects or possibilities of historical change, but does not recognize the real practical presuppositions for the realization of these demands, it presents them in the form of obligation.[76]

In Drobnickij's view, the deontological nature of moral norms represents, in effect, a confession of and concession to human ignorance: "From this point of view it is possible to criticize the limitation ('impracticality') of a purely moral orientation of the individual in the social world . . .".[77] Morality is only one aspect of the socio-historical, practical activity of people, and it can be distinguished as a separate sphere of investigation only by means of theoretical abstraction; it is not equivalent to a 'scientific-theoretical or philosophico-historical' investigation and does not pretend to a grasp of the inner mechanisms and objective laws of the socio-historical process.[78]

Next Drobnickij considers a view of moral obligation toward which his own analysis tends, but one which he ultimately rejects: a rule utilitarianism in which individual acts are viewed as falling under a deontological principle, but the principle itself is justified in terms of the goodness of its consequences. (As we have seen this is in effect Drobnickij's view of the justification of moral principles with one crucial exception: we are almost never in a position as individual moral agents to obtain the necessary knowledge of historical consequences). Drobnickij examines this general conception not as rule utilitarianism, but as a version of the 'social contract', the logic of which could be construed as equivalent to that of rule utilitarianism for this purpose. The notion of the social contract has two presuppositions according to Drobnickij. First, the general good is assumed to be a simple summative product of the interests of the multitude of separate individuals composing the society. Second, both on the social plane and the individual plane, general norms are formulated on the basis of a rational understanding of the situation being created, a comprehension of the social causes and consequences, and a recognition by everyone of their mutual social needs.[79] Neither of these suppositions stands up to historical confirmation, he claims.

First of all, the socio-historical significance of moral norms is not at all exhausted by the fact of how they affect the interests of that individual or group subject, which works them out.[80]

In this he appears to take a stand with the social utilitarians as described above.[81] Moreover, he argues, there are no social situations in which the individual's interests would genuinely be served at all times by obeying such generally-agreed rules; and such rules have often developed in history long before the individuals affected by them could have accurately assayed their own interests in them.[82]

Second, in the conditions under which certain fundamental universal moral norms were formulated, "people by no means thought them out rationally to such a degree that they could understand 'why it is necessary' that people act this way and not that, or still less, explain the origin and social significance of social norms".[83] As a consequence of all this Drobnickij maintains that neither the science of ethics nor the science of history is yet in a position to provide an analysis of the origin and formation of such norms. Considering the actual origins of one moral norm — the obligation to fulfill promises — Drobnickij concludes that it arises "absolutely spontaneously, by means of a purely practical selection and strengthening of the rules of mutual relations".[84]

In attempting to explain the origin of such a norm, Drobnickij reverted on one hand to the Kantian-sounding argument that social life would have been simply impossible without it, and on the other, to the faint suggestion of a Darwinian natural selection of moral principles. In general people are unable to comprehend the expediency or usefulness of moral norms in the circumstances under which they develop, and it is this fact which entails that moral norms be viewed in deontological rather than teleological terms.

This absence of a rational demonstration of the historical benefit or 'expediency' of moral norms constitutes a limitation of moral consciousness by comparison with 'scientific historical thought' at the present time. In other words, historical science is capable of supplying the rational justification for moral norms which moral consciousness alone is not. This apparent defect of moral consciousness turns out to have been an advantage for most of human history. The point is that historical science arose only a century ago. Moral consciousness, which was incapable of grasping the actual justification for moral norms, and could only conceive them deontologically, was able to *compensate* for the limitations, or the absence, of rational historical understanding for most of human history.

The deontological form of thought permitted one to compensate for the limitation of rational-practical thought, occurring right up to the modern period in rather limited bounds; it permitted moral consciousness to reflect the social need before it received rational-theoretical representation; before the concept of causal relations between the mass actions of people and their socially significant consequences; before objective social necessity found adequate expression in the subjectively recognized interests and the voluntary strivings of the corresponding social groups and individuals.[85]

Even after the development of a science of history adequate to grasp all of these relations for which the deontological reasoning of morality was a primitive substitute, moral consciousness still retains a crucial role in enabling the

wide masses of workers and laborers still unacquainted with scientific historical theory to recognize their particular class interests in the form of 'authentically human' (obligatory) interests and relate them in such fashion to the prospects for the universal development of human society as a whole.[86]

It turns out that the justification of each individual moral norm involves demonstrating that "without it society would have been simply impossible".[87] Hence the ultimate justification for moral norms is teleological.

Morality fulfills 'useful' functions in society, but these functions by no means appear evident in that form in which moral demands are prescribed to individuals in the ordinary circumstances of life. . . . The non-coincidence (or even opposition) of the sense of a moral demand and the demand of social expediency is an empirical fact. That fact however in no way refutes the socio-historical origin, foundation, and significance of the moral norm.[88]

On the whole it might appear more appropriate to classify Drobnickij's conception of moral norms primarily as evidence of the continued influence of Kant in Soviet ethical theory, if we overlook Drobnickij's own originality for the moment. There are however some deeper implications of his position, which he does not explore in much detail himself, which also point to the strong influence of Hegel in the end. In Drobnickij's view it turns out that morality is an historically crucial, but nevertheless in certain respects inferior, substitute for a science of history. It should be clear from the role he attributes to this science of history that it is conceived as a source of *justifications* for certain patterns of human conduct. Moreover, since the science of history matured, it is apparently the preferable (rational) conceptual framework within which to make judgments concerning the requirements of human action in the present. It is the intellectual instrument with which we will construct the future of 'authentic humanity'. The justification of moral principles then is not a task of ethical theory, but of the science of history (or else the two are simply identical). What Drobnickij does not explore at all, is the question of upon what criteria is the science of history to *justify* moral principles? He mentions in various places, almost randomly, notions such as 'the benefit of humanity', 'authentic humanity', 'humanity, justice, and honesty', and 'usefulness'; the principal notion to which he referred was *expediency* [*celesoobraznost'*]. Although the usual English translation of this term probably does not do justice to Drobnickij's use of it, in the absence of any further discussion of the criteria in terms of which the science of history is to justify or demonstrate the rationality of moral principles, one might argue that his account of the meaning and justification of moral terms is seriously incomplete. Nor does he explain the sense in which a science of history could *justify* moral principles as opposed to establishing some of the social conditions under which they arose, or perhaps some of their consequences. He seems implicitly to assume that a science of history could discover some *necessity* about the origins of each moral principle, but the nature of that necessity is not explained. At first glance it is not obvious that such necessity could be an object of empirical history.

That Drobnickij could have regarded this account as a relatively comprehensive outline of the problem of justifying the authority of moral norms suggests that the competition between 'historical' evaluation and moral evaluation still thrives in Drobnickij's conception. This in itself would constitute evidence for the continued strong influence of Hegel's philosophy of history and ethical theory. It also suggests that the debt to Hegel has yet to be repaid.

Only one monograph devoted specifically to Hegel's ethical theory has been published in the Soviet Union, and that one, by Kissel' and Emdin, appeared in 1966.[89] The authors provide a rather casual summary of the three main parts of Hegel's *Philosophy of Right*, with critical commentary on certain portions of it. Their commentary suggests that at least during the

1960's, any Soviet discussion of the major theses of Hegel's ethical theory
was still heavily under the influence of the earlier sweeping dismissals of
Hegel's political philosophy as an apology for the reactionary Prussian
monarchy. Toward the end of their discussion of Hegel's philosophy of the
state, the authors engage in an explicit dispute over this issue, criticizing other
Soviet and East European commentators for adopting an 'antihistorical
approach' to the interpretation of Hegel. They object to any approach "based
on the conception that this or that theory can be reactionary 'in general' or
progressive 'in general' without reference to place, time, and conditions".[90]
They also suggest that many other commentators have ignored the general
principles and fundamental conception of the *Philosophy of Right* and based
their evaluations only on some particular doctrines in it. In general they
counteract such interpretations by arguing that Hegel's views were progressive
for a person of his historical and social situation.

   Nevertheless their own approach to Hegel relies heavily at various points
upon sociological explanations deriving from the observation that Hegel was
"above all an ideologue of the German bourgeoisie of his time".[91] More specifically they explain that Hegel was "an ideologue of the cowardly German
bourgeoisie, craving compromise with the ruling feudal estate of Prussia".[92]
In such passages they seem not to diverge very far from the sort of commentary they themselves subject to criticism in other passages.

   Kissel' and Emdin describe Hegel as "relocating the ethical problematic on
the plane of the socio-historical: not individual moral quests but the movement of universal history itself overcomes all contradictions of moral consciousness and leads to the identity of reason and justice on earth".[93] The
authors stress the limitations which Hegel placed upon the possibility of
philosophical knowledge of the history of the spirit, quoting the famous 'owl
of Minerva' passage from the Preface. In this connection they observe,

Thus the philosophy of right (ethics) can give reliable knowledge only of the past, of
that which has been fully realized in human society, regardless of whether it continues
to exist, or has already sunk in oblivion.[94]

Not surprisingly they regard the principal defect of Hegel's conception of
ethics to be his "rejection of the transforming role of progressive moral ideas
in social development".[95] They fully endorse Plekhanov's complaint that

... if, according to Hegel, philosophy grasps in the present only that which has outlived
its time, it becomes impossible to understand why it cannot grasp in existence its other,
necessary, actual side, i.e., the novel, which is beginning and developing, and on that
basis foresee the future and assist its realization.[96]

It is in effect the original complaint of the Young Hegelians against their master, transmitted through Feuerbach, Marx, and Plekhanov, which appears here as the central objection of Kissel' and Emdin to Hegelian ethics.[97] Equally predictably, Kissel' and Emdin find Hegel's treatment of private property as a necessary condition of freedom to be a stumbling block to the acceptance of his ethical theory.[98] Marx's critique of Hegel's doctrine of the state makes this aspect of the theory also impossible to accept. On the other hand, Kissel' and Emdin assert that Hegel's critique of Kantian ethics "to a certain extent can be used by us even now in the struggle against contemporary bourgeois, opportunistic and revisionistic ethics".[99]

Above all, Kissel' and Emdin see as the most useful aspect of Hegel's ethical theory his extraordinary sensitivity to the concrete dialectical process of development of morality through history. They quote with great approval Engel's observation that throughout Hegel's works his manificent understanding of history runs like a red thread.[100]

Given difficulties such as these indicated by Kissel' and Emdin in the acceptance by Soviet Marxists of many of the major elements of Hegel's ethical theory, the comparative dearth of literature on the subject is less surprising. This relative inattention to the explicit details of Hegel's theory however must always be considered in the context of the implicit Hegelian influences of a much more general character which can be discerned in Soviet moral philosophy.

3. THE CRITIQUE OF NEOPOSITIVIST ETHICAL THEORY

The literature on 'bourgeois' ethical theory which has appeared in the Soviet Union contains, in addition to large numbers of journal articles and chapters of monographs on the subject, several full-length monographs devoted entirely to bourgeois ethical theories.[101] The typology of contemporary bourgeois ethical theories which emerges from that literature coincides on the whole with the most familiar histories of ethical theory in the English language. Švarcman exemplifies the most common Soviet Marxist view in distinguishing pragmatist, intuitivist, neopositivist, existentialist, Freudian, and neo-Thomist ethical theories. Drobnickij and Kuz'mina adopt a similar typology, except that they employ the two generic categories of 'formalism' (intuitivism, neopositivism, linguistic analysis) and 'irrationalism' (existentialism and neo-Protestantism). An alternative, and less usual typology was adopted by Kissel', who distinguished three basic tendencies in contemporary bourgeois ethical theory: 1. religious ethics (neo-Thomist, phenomenalist, Bergsonian, and the religious variant of existentialism); 2. the ethics of personalist humanism (atheistic existentialism, Fromm's neo-Freudianism, and personalism); 3. 'the ethics of bourgeois loyalty' (intuitivism, emotivism, linguistic ethics, American neorealism, and pragmatism).[102]

As should be expected, the later works on the history of 'bourgeois' ethical theory tend to differentiate more sensitively the various identifiable 'schools' of ethical thought in twentieth century philosophy. For example, in Švarcman's book, no very definite distinction is made between the views of the very early emotivists such as Ogden and Richards, members of the Vienna Circle in the 1930's, and post-war ethical theorists such as Patrick Nowell-Smith, R. M. Hare, and Stephen Toulmin, whom she identifies simply as the 'Oxford group' within the neopositivist school. Slightly later works, such as that by Drobnickij and Kuz'mina, distinguish these groups rather carefully and competently, both in terms of chronology and in terms of the positions they defended.

'Neopositivism' in particular has received a great deal of attention from various Soviet commentators, and there are several relatively competent surveys of the emotivist theory of moral judgments associated with it. The emotivist thesis presents a metaethical doctrine concerning the meaning and justification of ethical terms and judgments; however many Soviet commentators reject either the distinction between metaethics and normative ethics, or some of its most commonly accepted implications. Drobnickij and Kuz'miina reveal this tendency in one of the first comments they make concerning the neopositivists.

Neopositivists characterize their theory of morality as 'metaethics' and regard it as the sphere of problems beginning on the far side of moral reasoning, where questions of good and evil lose all meaning. The metaethical approach to the analysis of morality in effect implies the complete indifference of the theorist to the 'vital' problems of morality, puts him outside of any moral position whatever.[103]

Since so many 'Western' ethical theorists operate comfortably with this distinction between meta- and normative ethics, it is significant that most Soviet commentators tend to reject it or severely qualify it. Objecting to the claims of Reichenbach and Ayer to have given a 'purely logical' analysis of moral judgments, Drobnickij and Kuz'mina quote Reichenbach to the effect that one must not inquire of the philosopher what is to be done, rather one must listen to the voice of one's own will and attempt to unify it with the wills of others, because there is no other aim and no other meaning in the world, other than the one you place there. This statement of Reichenbach and other similar ones by Ayer, "completely overturn their conceptions and intentions relative to the character of metaethics".[104]

First, the 'strictly scientific' approach to morality, from the point of view of which moral ideas are represented as utterly opposite to scientific reasoning, inevitably leads to an irrationalist interpetation of morality. Second, the supposedly 'neutral' metaethics, it turns out, supplies the basis for a very specific moral position – a position of individual arbitrariness and a nihilistic attitude toward moral principles.[105]

In similar fashion Gusejnov complains that although the neopositivists claimed to have developed an approach to ethical theory which was confined entirely to 'logical analysis', abstracted from all issues of metaphysics or 'general worldviews', in fact they attributed the significance of a 'general worldview' to their 'logical analysis', a significance which culminated in "scepticism, relativism, and nihilism".[106]

The survey of neopositivist writings on ethical theory by Drobnickij and Kuz'mina offers a very detailed and accurate history of that subject, probably the best which has appeared in Soviet publications. They provide an account of the sociological theories of morality found in Durkheim, Lévy-Bruhl, Sumner, Mannheim, and Pareto in the early twentieth century, in which moral beliefs were regarded as sociological facts to be recorded, possessing no special claims to 'authority' beyond the fact of being shared by some existing social group.[107] In similarly thorough fashion, they survey the 'psychological theories of morality' (moral sense theories) from their origins in the writings of Smith, Shaftesbury, Hutcheson and Hume, to the subjectivist ethics of Westermarck, and 'affective-volitional' theories of value of W. M. Urban and D. W. Prall. These influences are then pursued into the value theories of C. I. Lewis and J. B. Pratt.

Concentrating particularly on Carnap and Ayer, Drobnickij and Kuz'mina describe the central point of the emotivist theory in its original form as the verificationist analysis of the meaning of ethical terms and judgments which "are devoid of meaning in the literal sense".[108] They focus especially on Ayer's famous argument from *Language, Truth and Logic* that all meaningful propositions are either synthetic or analytic, and that moral judgments are neither, hence without cognitive content.

In criticism of this thesis, Drobnickij and Kuz'mina discuss the judgment 'murder is wrong', arguing first that the judgment does not submit to empirical verification simply because it has to do not with a natural phenomenon, but with a social phenomenon. The phenomenon of killing could for example be observed in purely empirical fashion as a natural event. But since 'murder' refers to a social event, its 'verification' must consist in an explication of the social consequences of the action, again, not in the immediate consequences of some unique instance of murder, but in the *usual* consequences for social life of this type of action. It is in this sense that the judgment 'murder is wrong' must be explicated, and such a judgment contains the fruits of enormous historical experience accumulated by humanity through the social processes of many generations.[109]

Second, they argue that it is incorrect to claim that the predicate 'is wrong' adds nothing to the identification of the act as an instance of murder, because the predicate expresses the fact of appropriateness or inappropriateness of the act in question for social practice as a whole.

Third, they deny that the predicate 'is wrong' is logically unconnected with the subject 'murder'. The very concept of murder is not a purely descriptive one, but implicitly presents the act as wrong; in this concept is expressed the negative attitude of people to this action.

The authors agree that Ayer is right to some degree when he observes. ". . . if I say to someone: 'You acted badly when you stole that money', I say no more than if I simply said: 'You stole that money'. In adding that the act in question is bad, I have said nothing new."[110]

But he is correct only in the case that the description 'That is stealing' already contains an evaluation of the act, and does not simply state the factual content of the act. By his discussion Ayer has proven only one thing: that a moral phenomenon is something more than an empirical 'fact', and its designation in moral language is not a purely descriptive term.[111]

In conclusion they argue that the theoretical apparatus with which the emotivists analyzed moral language is absolutely inappropriate for such an analysis.

Turning to a discussion of the expressivist thesis of the function of moral terms, Drobnickij and Kuz'mina deny that the 'rational-informative' and the 'emotive' aspects of linguistic communication can be conceived as two types of language. Rather, they insist, these are two aspects involved simultaneously in all verbal communication.[112] Pursuing the emotivist account of the expressive function of moral language, Drobnickij and Kuz'mina argue that on this account of the use of moral language, the only criterion for the correctness of moral judgments, and a sufficient criterion, is simply the profound conviction of the speaker in the rightness of his position. This 'voluntaristic' conception of moral judgment they trace to Luther and Kant, and reject it as a wholly inadequate account of the moral life, because it converts what is essentially a question of social requirements and demands into a question of individual psychology.[113]

The authors conclude their discussion of the emotivist account of moral language with an analysis of the 'hidden social motives' of such an analysis.[114] In the negative, critical part of their theory the emotivists "express the strivings of that part of the bourgeois scientific intelligentsia which pretends to an independence from 'all' ideology and strives to screen itself off in the world of 'pure science' from anything connected with 'politics' ".[115] But of course, they argue, such a liberation from ideology is impossible for a theorist occupied with the problems of morality. The liberation from ideology claimed by the emotivists depends entirely upon the success of their claimed distinction of metaethical inquiry from normative ethics. Drobnickij and Kuz'mina argue that the myth of the 'neutrality' of metaethics was revealed by the reception given these views by their intended audience. That response showed that many people were 'shocked by the cynicism of this theory', a response which proved that the 'subjective intentions of the emotivists' were contradicted by the 'objective significance of the doctrine', and that the alleged distinction between metaethics and normative ethics cannot be maintained.

As for the 'positive' part of the emotivist theory of moral language, Drobnickij and Kuz'mina conclude that it treats morality as a sphere of politics, or of propaganda. Referring in particular to Stevenson's discussion of the *persuasive* function of moral language, they conclude that the emotivist thesis in the end supports an ideological manipulation of mass consciousness in the service of the existing elites in bourgeois society.

A definite role here was played by the 'neutrality' of metaethics, i.e., the absence in it of any sort of moral position: it considers only means of ideological influence, with the help of which it is possible to inculcate *any content*. For this reason metaethics, regarded as a purely philosophical science is easily transformed into an applied discipline pursuing methods of the manipulation of mass consciousness.[116]

The most commonly shared focus of criticism of emotivism among Soviet commentators is its claim concerning the non-cognitive status of moral judgments, and hence the impossibility of providing a 'scientific' basis for moral judgments. For example Švarcman reveals a view of science in terms of which it is understood to supply judgments of moral and non-moral value, and she criticizes emotivists for failing to present either science or morality in this light.[117]

In their history of 'bourgeois ethical theory' Drobnickij and Kuz'mina offer a fairly detailed account of the development of ethical theory in the hands of the 'linguistic analysts', in whose ranks they include Nowell-Smith, Toulmin, Hare, Montefiore, and Aiken. They present the views of the linguistic analysts on ethical theory as a modification of emotivism, in terms of which moral judgments were regarded as rationally defensible after all. They point out that the 'analysts' provided a more sophisticated account of the functions of moral discourse, noting that it may be used to express commands, recommendations, advice, desires, approval, evaluations, etc., and that the cognitive content of any such use of language can only be assessed within the context of utterance.[118]

Regarding the rationality of moral judgments, the analysts are described as holding two characteristic doctrines:

First, the analysts recognize that moral utterances are comprehensible judgments possessing a specific thought content. Second, the possibility of providing a foundation for these judgments is admitted. "... in any event in one specific sense," says Montefiore, "value judgments can be called rational; it will always be right to require a foundation for them." (p. 64, *A Modern Introduction to Moral Philosophy*) The foundation for these moral utterances, according to the analysts, can be of two sorts – empirical, by means of reference to corresponding facts, and logical, by means of references to more general moral principles. ... Finally, third, the analysts connect moral ideas with social practice, referring to the fact of their being socially conditioned. Such are the three nodal problems of the ethical theory of linguistic analysis, comprising its basic content.[119]

However, following a rather careful and detailed summary of the views of the above-mentioned moral philosophers, Drobnickij and Kuz'mina conclude that their program for the creation of an ethics having a 'practical character', overcoming the absence of content in emotivist metaethics, turns out to be an empty declaration.[120] In support of this conclusion they cite Toulmin's discussion in *The Place of Reason in Ethics* of the possible role of religion in the choice of moral principles as proving the ultimate irrationality of his views, and Montefiore's observation that "the Marxist cannot derive value judgments from judgments of fact just as the capitalist or bourgeois cannot" as evidence of the disguised commitment of linguistic analysis to a particular ideology. (Montefiore argued that to employ the term 'class struggle' was not merely an exercise in scientific theory, but a commitment to certain political and social values).[121]

4. THE CRITIQUE OF EXISTENTIALIST ETHICAL THEORY

Existentialist writings on ethical theory have also received especially great attention from Soviet commentators. On that subject as well a standard summary and set of criticisms has developed which can be found in a variety of sources, based upon a composite 'existentialism' derived from several different philosophers.[122]

In abbreviated form, that summary usually begins with the observation that problems of morality occupy a peculiarly prominent, even central place in the writings of most existentialists, including those who describe themselves as religious (Jaspers, Marcel, Berdjaev, Shestov) and those who describe themselves as atheists (Heidegger, Sartre, Camus, de Beauvoir).

Moreover, the treatment of moral obligation acquires an unusual ontological dimension in most existentialist writings through the doctrine of 'authentic being'. Since authenticity of being is not a given fact, but rather a certain task, an 'intention', a 'choice', a 'project', it also constitutes a type of obligation.[123] Quoting Drobnickij and Kuz'mina, "Morality is represented by the existentialist as a means for the manifestation of the real ontological structure of 'authentic' being, as a means for the affirmation of the individual as such".[124] The distinction between authentic and inauthentic existence has crucial implications for social and moral philosophy. First of all, actual, or existing morality belongs to the sphere of inauthentic being, since it is a social phenomenon. The morality society would impose is simply another of the manipulations of the empirical self encountered in the social world. "Social morality with its substantive, specific norms forces the person to act in accordance with a prescribed role ...".[125] Drobnickij and Kuz'mina quoted Tillich as claiming that within contemporary society the individual is transformed into a screw in an enormous machine to which he must accomodate himself. This gives rise to a feeling of emptiness and meaninglessness, dehumanization and alienation. The individual ceases to encounter reality as filled with meaning. They also cite Camus' use of the myth of Sisyphus in this connection. From such claims as these, the existentialists reach the conclusion that the sphere of social being of the individual is his 'inauthentic' existence, dwelling as *man* or *on* in which the individual is depersonalized, deprived of individuality, and acts 'like the others', fulfilling the roles assigned to him, etc. 'Authentic' being, according to the existentialists, is found outside the social activity of the individual; it is found by the individual 'despite' society.[126]

Gusejnov speaks of two concepts of morality within existentialism, the prevailing morality of society which belongs to the sphere of inauthentic being, and the personal morality of the individual who strives for authentic being or *Existenz*.

If the morality which realizes social demands, functions as a social norm, turns out inauthentic, then morality in the existentialist interpretation ('authentic morality') cannot appear as a universally significant social demand. Social morality is 'inauthentic' and 'authentic' morality is extra-social. The conflict between the individual person and society appears in existentialism in an extremely sharpened form: the position of the individual and of society in morality turn out to be absolutely incompatible, contradictory.[127]

The upshot of this, in Gusejnov's view is a "militant moral relativism which logically must lead to the rejection of ethics as a normative science".[128] Still greater difficulties lie in the fact that although morality is something intrinsically asocial in the existentialist view, it is nevertheless called upon to orient the individual in the social world.

The doctrine of authentic existence, or *Existenz*, in which the individual is conceived to exist independently of any natural or social determination, obviously depends upon a radical conception of freedom. According to Švarcman, that concept of freedom is derived from Kierkegaard, among other things, as an explicit rejection of the Hegelian concept of freedom as 'the recognition of necessity'.

From the point of view of Kierkegaard freedom is an internal action expressed above all in the decisions of the subject. When a person has taken a definite decision (even though it cannot be manifested in action), he by that fact already acts. That decision is primary in the definition of the ethical essence of the person. The ethical, according to Kierkegaard, is not connected with necessity; it cannot transcend the boundaries of internal decisions of the person.[129]

Following Kierkegaard, the existentialists also objected to regarding the individual person as something conditioned by external relations. "The individual person, according to the existentialists, can be understood only as absolutely free existence, as *Existenz*."[130] She quotes Sartre as saying that "Existence has neither cause, nor reason, nor necessity".[131]

This radical freedom in which the individual has no previously fixed essence or nature ('existence precedes essence') has two important consequences. It entails that the individual has an equally radical responsibility for defining his own essence through the choices he makes, and this radical freedom and its attendant responsibility are experienced as *Angst*, dread, or anxiety in the face of the threat of non-existence, or of nothingness, or of death.[132]

Drobnickij and Kuz'mina emphasize particularly the insignificance of the results of moral action, from the existentialist perspective:

For the existentialist, in this fashion, the question of the practical result of the moral action of the subject, of which morality he wanted to assert, is absolutely unimportant.[133]

They argue that the morality which the existentialists want to represent as the manifestation of the pure, intimate 'selfhood' of the individual is unreal in essence, even for them.

It is limited only to the sphere of possibility (and even that in consciousness – as an ideal, unrealizable possibility) and factually reduces itself to a Stoic acceptance of defeats, a recognition of the collapse of all attempts of the individual to establish his ideal of morality. The moral 'passion' of the individual is pronounced 'useless' by Sartre and morality is regarded in the final analysis as the 'free' acceptance of this futility of his moral pretention.[134]

Drobnickij and Kuz'mina conclude that the ontology of existentialism is only a mystified form of social psychology in which the strivings, attitudes, and illusions widely shared in contemporary capitalist society are described. Like Švarcman and like Gusejnov, Drobnickij and Kuz'mina conclude that the 'exaggerated' interest in morality typical of most existentialists in fact disguises the destruction of its very possibility.

The problem is not that ethics as an independent discipline is impossible to distinguish from existentialist ontology, and not even that the 'ontologization' of morality makes a mystery of its actual social nature. The whole problem is that ethics in existentialism loses its object as a theoretical discipline, and morality becomes logically impossible.[135]

Thus in existentialist ethics the question of the distinction between that which is and that which ought to be is entirely removed. The conception of that which ought to be ceases to serve as the basis for the accomplishment of moral action. On the contrary, the accomplishment of action turns out to be the basis for calling it what ought to be.[136]

They argue that under these assumptions it turns out to be impossible for the individual to commit wrong.[137] On the one hand the existentialist account of morality can be interpreted as a negation of bourgeois morality; but on the other it seems to deny the very possibility of an alternative society or morality, and by that fact lends support of a kind to bourgeois morality.[138] This last conclusion is endorsed in one form or another by all the other commentators mentioned here.

There are in Soviet philosophical literature some detailed studies of individual existentialist thinkers which would be more profitably pursued by one who wished to assess the impact of existentialist thought on Soviet culture; however within the Soviet literature on the history of 'bourgeois' ethical theory, the summary just given of a 'composite' existentialism reproduces the most commonly presented view of it.

CHAPTER NINE

CONCLUSIONS

The discussion up to now has largely ignored considerations of political philosophy and national differences of historical perspective, except where these were immediately relevant to some specific point of doctrine in Soviet moral philosophy. The intent has been so far as possible, to consider Soviet writings in ethical theory as contributions to an abstract philosophical inquiry transcending national political boundaries and social conditions. Such an approach must of course to some degree misrepresent a discussion in which most participants presuppose as established beyond question a Marxist sociology of knowledge, which, moreover, is frequently applied in a very sweeping way to produce 'explanatory' generalizations of a very simplistic sort.

Nevertheless there are some general differences of national perspective, determined partly by Marxist-Leninist political ideology itself, partly by the unique historical experiences of the Russian and Soviet people in the twentieth century, and partly by differences of cultural heritage, which must be taken into account, however sketchily, in any general assessment of Soviet perspectives in ethical theory. Some of these factors can only be suggested, not documented, here, and hence our conclusions can be only tentative; but their relevance and significance for the inquiry, if true, should be self-evident.

The preceding chapter offered a very brief overview of Soviet writings on 'bourgeois' ethical theory, in which contemporary non-Marxist-Leninist ethical perspectives are criticized and dismissed, as rooted in 'idealism' and as products of the ideology of the bourgeois ruling class during the process of the collapse of capitalism. That chapter did not accurately convey or represent the sheer quantity of such material, at every level of sophistication and naiveté, which appears in Soviet publications. One is occasionally reminded of the anxieties of the early Fathers of the Christian church who were tempted to make use of the splendors of Hellenic philosophy for the elaboration of their own new insight into the truth of the human situation, and were at the same time extremely anxious lest some pagan influence unwittingly find its way into the exposition of their own doctrines. One cannot read very much of the Soviet literature without becoming convinced of the sincerity (if not the persuasiveness) of many of its authors. The dismissal of all alternatives to the Marxist-Leninist viewpoint in ethics appears motivated by the prior and more general historical conviction that the October revolution indeed constituted a radical turning-point in human history. As argued above, the deeper cosmological implications of this view suggest that all historical events prior to the revolution (pre-history) were in effect pre-cosmic as well, contributing to the formation of a cosmos the actual existence of which commences only with the revolution.[1] The consequence of this event with greatest import for moral philosophy is of course the supposed creation of a new type of individual – the Communist – possessed of a qualitatively new relation to society, and hence a new morality. The constant reiteration of this claim by Soviet ethical theorists has been noted above.[2] If one accepts such claims at face value, then one must accept the further implication that the world at present is inhabited by at least two types of humanity, one a product of the civilization produced by the October revolution and centered on the Soviet Union, and the other produced by the various bourgeois revolutions and centered on the collapsing capitalist socio-economic formation.

It would of course be unjustified to suggest that all members of the Soviet intelligentsia contributing to the development of Marxist-Leninist ethical theory necessarily share the view just stated in any simple form. A philosophical literature produced under conditions of state censorship cannot be automatically accepted as a literal record of its authors' views. However, on the whole, the evidence is overwhelming that a substantial number of Soviet intellectuals do share some form of this conviction that the socialist order of Soviet society has produced, or is producing, a morally new type of human being. The socialist revolution was expected to usher in a number of qualitatively new features of social and political, as well as moral, order. It was expected to bring about a great increase in efficiency of production based upon a new, rational organization of economic activity; it was also expected to initiate a process in which the state as an instrument of coercion for political purposes would wither away; it was expected to eliminate crime; etc. Even if none of these supposed consequences has occurred (or perhaps especially *because* they have not occurred), it is nevertheless still possible (necessary?) to regard the revolution has having had enormous *moral* consequences for the history of humanity, as creating a new and morally superior type of human being.

It is when non-Soviet and non-Marxist observers confront this last claim that skepticism, if not incredulity, tends to become the dominant reaction. The events of the twentieth century, beginning with the insane carnage of the Great War, followed by an economic depression seemingly beyond our power

to control, the military conflicts of the 1930's which culminated in World
War II, the evidence of millions of lives destroyed in the Soviet collectivization, industrialization, and purges; World War II and the holocaust, and the
seemingly endless continuation of savage military conflicts since, have tended
to put beyond possibility of renewal any of the Victorian pieties about the
moral perfectibility of the human race.

The impact of the first of these events on the Western literary imagination,
the Great War, which has to some extent remained a paradigm of modern
experience, has been persuasively documented in a recent work by Paul
Fussell.[3] He argues that "the Great War was perhaps the last to be conceived
as taking place within a seamless, purposeful 'history' involving a coherent
stream of time running from past through present to future".[4] As a consequence of the Great War, in part, the very possibility of an underlying 'meaning' of historical experience was irretrievably lost for many thinkers.

Fussell argues that the Great War has become the archetype for the subsequent violence with which the twentieth century has been filled, that our
poetry since 1918 has been filled with recognition scenes which return us to
the horror of those events, and that what we recognize in that literature is a
part of our own buried lives a generation and more later.[5]

One need not dwell on such considerations at length to suggest their significance for Western reactions to Soviet claims concerning the moral perfect-
ability of the human race. They are after all commonplaces of 20th century
historical commentary as well as literature and literary criticism. At the same
time, the extent to which these historical experiences, which have shaped the
reactions of many Western thinkers to claims of human perfectibility, have
been shared by the Soviet authors of such claims, is less often considered in
an imaginative way. It must be remembered first of all that, although Russia's
participation in the Great War was in many respects as deep and as painful as
that of Western Europe, its images have probably not so permanently scarred
the memories, actual or literary, of succeeding generations for the reason that
its historical significance was immediately overwhelmed in ideological terms
by the February and October revolutions and by the extraordinarily bloody
and savage civil war which followed. Literary images of this last experience
do indeed haunt the memories of succeeding Soviet generations. However it
must be borne in mind that the shape of Soviet images of this civil war can
hardly fail to have been affected by decades of continuous hammering into
the ideological simplicities of 'revolutionary-anti-revolutionary', 'progressive-
reactionary', 'good-evil' which attend the Bolshevik interpretation of these
events. Moreover, once the revolution had occurred, and the civil war had

been won, the ideology which triumphed as a result of these events immediately relegated World War I, including Russia's participation in it, into the category of pre-history, an event taking place in the previous historical epoch, and not a determining one for the new epoch.

One might argue that if the experiences of World War I and the Civil War did not have the impact on Soviet collective memory that the first event did for Western Europe, then surely the unique horrors of Stalin's collectivization campaign, industrialization process, and purges, to which the Soviet population was subjected, should have supplied a similar fund of memories of peculiarly senseless mass violence. But of course this is by no means obvious. The 'senselessness' of these events depended entirely upon how one understood them, what one knew of them, and upon one's assumptions about the larger possibilities of history.

More particularly, even when one has condemned the purges as 'senseless', as having no relation to the larger historical purpose of the Soviet socialist order, as many Soviet intellectuals evidently have done, the implications are not necessarily those which might be expected by an external observer. In this connection one should recall the recent Soviet discussions of the 'criterion of moral progress' in history. Titarenko made a rather obscure proposal (which has been endorsed by other Soviet moral philosophers) according to which the "general historical criterion of moral progress is the level of humanization of the interaction, collision, and resolution of the oppositions of good and evil".[6] It is not fanciful to suggest that Titarenko's notion of a *changing level of humanization* is employed in part to deal with such problems as the 'excesses' and 'mistakes' of Stalin's period. It is interesting that Titarenko does not argue that there will be any diminution in the oppositions of good and evil in history, or that any such diminution could be adopted as the criterion of moral progress. Instead he simply argues that the opposition of good and evil will occur on a higher plane of 'humanization'. Implicit in his view seems to be a doctrine of *qualitative differences* in evil, such that the evils inflicted upon the Soviet population by Stalin in the name of the Communist Party could, *regardless of their extent*, be viewed as qualitatively different from the evils inflicted upon the populations of the bourgeois capitalist world by their leaders. Titarenko does not draw these conclusions explicitly himself, but similar ones are frequently encountered in various Soviet apologies for the 'excesses' of Stalin.

Following the same line of argument, it can be seen that the Soviet experience of World War II, which for them was the Great (Patriotic) War, not World War I, would not necessarily contain the same lessons for them as it did for the Western allies even in this connection. The holocaust which accompanied the second war could be regarded simply as one more evidence of the essential insanity and ultimate fitness for extinction of the bourgeois capitalist world. Its moral implications for Soviet expectations of the future need not have paralleled those which often prevail among Western thinkers.

Obviously the complexity and scope of these considerations far exceed the limits of this book. The suggestions made here are merely that; documentation or criticism of them would fall within the spheres of historical or literary scholarship. They have been presented for only one purpose, to suggest that the task of assessing the sincerity of Soviet ethical theorists' beliefs in the genuine perfectibility of humanity (or at least socialist humanity) is, if possible, still more complex than is frequently supposed. And such considerations serve to underline still more strongly the dependence of Soviet ethical doctrines upon a particular philosophy of history.

The most commonly encountered doctrines of Soviet ethical theory have been shown to depend upon the prior adoption of the particular philosophy of history contained in Marxism-Leninism. The implicit competition between this philosophy of history and the demands of a fully comprehensive and explicitly stated ethical theory has been shown to affect a number of discussions. There are two areas in which this competition has very significant consequences for the possibility of a coherent ethical theory within Marxism. First, the adoption of the philosophy of history introduces a substantial confusion into the discussion of the nature of moral progress, as was described in Chapter Seven. The claim that history exhibits progress appears to be one of the most distinctive assumptions of Soviet ethical theory. However the attempt to explain precisely what is meant by this claim, and what its grounds are, runs afoul of the equally prominent assertion of radical historicism, and Soviet discussions up to this time could not be said to have clarified the matter very far. Second, the assumption that progress is somehow an intrinsic feature of the historical process, combined with the assumption that the process is objectively determined by laws which are not subject to manipulation, leads to a great reticence about identifying the intrinsic value or values in terms of which moral good and duty are to be assessed on one hand, and in terms of which history is to be judged to exhibit progress on the other.[7] But this might be regarded as a crucial requirement which any adequate ethical theory must satisfy; to remain vague about the nature of intrinsic value, the moral good, and the grounds of moral duty is to fail to produce a satisfactory ethical theory.

The heart of the problem can be seen to lie in the combination of an 'objectivist' view of the determination of historical change and of a 'scientism' in the account of those 'laws' of historical change or 'social development', which are characteristic of Soviet Marxism-Leninism.

The objectivist view of historical determination is illustrated by the claim that "the interpretation of history by its participants (even if it occurs in the evaluational form of ideals, conceptions of good and evil, etc.) is conditioned by the laws of social development, and itself constitutes an aspect of it, and is not imported into it from somewhere outside".[8] The scientism is evident, in part, in the claim that "historical materialism contains nothing in itself other than scientific knowledge, requires no value-supplement, because the goals of people here are included in the historical process itself".[9]

The scientism consists first in the claim that 'science' alone supplies generalizations concerning the nature of historical progress, without the addition of any 'extraneous' concept of intrinsic value, and more particularly in the peculiar knowledge status claimed for such generalizations. These generalizations are not treated as relatively well-confirmed empirical hypotheses which are nevertheless subject to subsequent refutation should some contradictory generalization or alternative theory prove more successful. Instead, certain 'findings' of Marxist-Leninist historical science are treated as certainties, beyond any liability to disconfirmation or refutation. In this respect their status could be more accurately compared to metaphysical first premises, or to axioms in a deductive system, than to findings of any empirical science.

The general point to be made concerns a systematic confusion about, or misrepresentation of, the status of 'Marxist-Leninist historical science'. It is not clearly an empirical 'science' in any settled sense of the term with which we are dealing, but more accurately a philosophy of history. In general, the claim that history exhibits progress could be either a generalization resulting from empirical inquiry, or a premise of a philosophy of history. Its epistemological status would be very different, of course, depending upon which of the two alternatives were adopted. It is conceivable that as a matter of contingent fact, history does exhibit progress. For such a generalization to be established (even as partially confirmed) by empirical investigation would require a number of steps. First, 'progress' would have to be empirically defined. That would entail among other things offering an explicit definition of the value or values to be realized, a definition such that an increase of the value in question could be empirically assessed. Then some set of categories for collecting data concerning historical change would have to be established, and these categories would have to be neutral with respect to the value in question. Next, assuming the data were collectible in practice, the hypothesis concerning

the occurrence of progress could be examined in the light of the data collected, and found to be supported or not supported. Whatever the outcome of
this investigation at any particular point in history, it is not clear how any
guarantee could be given that the finding would not be reversed in some future development of this putative 'historical science'. Without claiming that
this simple sketch actually represents any feasible historical investigation, it
does at least serve to point out, in however crude a fashion, the epistemological status which any such empirical generalization would necessarily have.

The epistemological status of the generalization that history exhibits
progress would of course be very different if it were regarded as a premise in
a philosophy of history. The particular assumption that history exhibits a
meaningful progress toward the realization of some value such as 'authentic
humanity', in the words of William Dray, "clearly transcends historical or
scientific concerns and becomes part of metaphysics, ethics, and religion" and
such philosophies of history as a whole "cannot be finally assessed without
considering the total world views on which they rest".[10] In the case of Marx,
this of course requires an assessment of his evolutionist cosmology as described above.[11] If it is clearly recognized that the generalization in question functions as a conclusion in an evolutionist cosmology and hence as an assumption
in the philosophy of history which presupposes that cosmology, then its
epistemological status, if not free of philosophical puzzles, at least could not
be confused with that of a generalization provided by an empirical science of
history.

In fact however, there is a very widespread reluctance among Soviet philosophers to confront this issue explicitly. The authority of 'science' is continually invoked to support this crucial generalization, and at the same time it is
treated as being beyond empirical refutation. This introduces a fundamental
ambiguity into most Soviet claims to the effect that "Marxist-Leninist historical science demonstrates that certain values, as determined by objective laws
of social development, are being realized in the succession of socio-economic
formations which comprise history". If this claim were put forward on a
genuinely empirical foundation, one would expect to find Soviet theorists
carefully and explicitly defining the value or values in terms of which history
is supposed to exhibit progress, and marshalling data concerning contingent
historical events to support the hypothesis. Instead one finds in the works of
a great variety of Soviet theorists a casual profusion of references to various
values which are supposedly proven to be inherent in the historical process by
Marxist-Leninist historical science. Almost nowhere does one find a careful
stipulation of intrinsic values in terms of which the question of historical

progress could be assessed as a contingent empirical matter. This surely indi-cates that the occurrence of historical progress is an assumption embedded in a philosophy of history accepted by most Soviet philosophers, and its status as such could only be obscured by a particularly egregious scientism.

The objectivist view of the determination of historical change which com-plements this scientism has long been a characteristic of Russian Marxism, beginning with Plekhanov's interpretation of Marxian historical determinism in the late nineteenth century. The scientism just described is not likely to change significantly unless this objectivist view of historical change is also altered. There is, most recently, some evidence of a rethinking of this doctrine by individual Soviet philosophers.[12]

Clearing away both these obstacles to a clear recognition of the status of 'Marxist-Leninist historical science' as a philosophy of history presupposing a specific evolutionist cosmology, and hence not an empirical (scientific), but a metaphysical (philosophical) theory would constitute a large step in the direction of a more coherent ethical theory.

The combination of these two deficiences produces the more general obstacle hindering the construction of a fully adequate ethical theory, in the present writer's view: the failure to deal explicitly with the consequences of the implicit competition between the philosophy of history and an ethical theory as the ultimately authoritative framework for the evaluation of human conduct. So long as the conflict between the 'historical' assessment of human conduct as 'progressive' or 'reactionary' and the moral assessment of that con-duct as 'right' or 'wrong' has not been resolved, Soviet ethical theorists will continue to leave their fundamental assumptions about the nature of intrinsic value obscured in the foundations of that philosophy of history, and ethical theory will suffer from a consequent lack of clarity in its central concepts. Hegel recognized this difficulty and provided at least the outlines of a recon-ciliation of the claims of these two perspectives. It remains unclear whether Marx recognized the same difficulty. His Soviet followers have yet to provide an adequate solution for it.

REFERENCES

PREFACE

[1] See for example, Maximilien Rubel, *Karl Marx, Pages Choisies Pour une Ethique Socialiste* (Paris, Librairie Marcel Rivière et Cie, 1948); and Svetozar Stojanović, *Between Ideals and Reality* (New York, Oxford University Press, 1973).

[2] See for example, Donald Clark Hodges, *Socialist Humanism, The Outcome of Classical European Morality* (St. Louis, Warren H. Green, Inc., 1974).

[3] Jean Jaurès, *De primis socialismi Germanici lineamentis apud Luterum, Kant, Fichte, et Hegel* (Tolosae, Chauvin, 1891).

[4] Jaurès, p. 35f, cited in Karl Vorländer, *Kant und der Sozialismus* (Berlin, Verlag von Reuther & Reichard, 1900), p. 41.

[5] Eduard Bernstein, *Die Voraussetzungen des Sozialismus und die Aufgaben der Sozialdemokratie*, 1899, translated as *Evolutionary Socialism, A Criticism and Affirmation* by Edith C. Harvey (New York, Schocken Books, 1961).

[6] *Kierkegaard's Concluding Unscientific Postscript*, trans. by David F. Swenson and Walter Lowrie (Princeton, Princeton University Press, for the American-Scandinavian Foundation, 1941), pp. 108–109.

[7] *Ibid*. p. 272n.

[8] Maximilien Rubel, *Karl Marx, Pages Choisies*, p. lx.

[9] *Ibid*. p. xxvii.

[10] Stojanović, *Between Ideals and Reality*, p. 137.

[11] *Ibid*. p. 138.

[12] *Ibid*. p. 142.

[13] *Ibid*. p. 152.

[14] *Loc. cit.*

[15] *Myśl Etyczna Młodego Marksa* (Warsaw, 1961); cited by Stojanović, p. 142.

[16] Stojanović, p. 155.

[17] Hodges, *Socialist Humanism*, p. 155.

[18] *Ibid*. p. 115.

[19] For an excellent survey and discussion of Soviet work in ethical theory up to 1971 see Peter Ehlen, *Die philosophische Ethik in der Sowjetunion, Analyse und Diskussion* (Munich, Anton Pustet, 1972).

CHAPTER ONE

[1] Karl Marx, Frederick Engels, *Collected Works* (London, Lawrence & Wishart, 1975–; and New York: International Publishers, 1975–), vol. 1, p. 26. (Hereafter referred to as *Works*).

[2] Marx, Engels, *Works*, vol. 3, p. 4.

³ *Ibid*. p. 230.

⁴ *Ibid*. vol. 5, p. 20.

⁵ Karl Marx, *Grundrisse: Foundations of the Critique of Political Economy* (*Rough Draft*), trans. Martin Nicolaus (Great Britain, Penguin Books, Ltd., 1973), p. 7n. See also David McLellan, ed., *Karl Marx, Early Texts* (New York, Barnes & Noble, 1972) for dates of appearance of translations in the major European languages.

⁶ Charles Taylor, *Hegel* (Cambridge, England, Cambridge University Press, 1975), p. 537.

⁷ Frederick Engels, *Ludwig Feuerbach and the End* [*Ausgang*] *of Classical German Philosophy*, in Karl Marx and Frederick Engels, *Basic Writings on Politics and Philosophy*, ed. Lewis S. Feuer (Garden City, N.Y., Doubleday & Company, Inc. Anchor Books, 1959), p. 205.

⁸ *Ibid*. p. 219.

⁹ *Ibid*. p. 224.

¹⁰ For example, see David McLellan, *The Young Hegelians and Karl Marx* (New York, Frederick A. Praeger, 1969), pp. 101–116.

¹¹ *Works*, vol. 1, p. 3 and p. 8.

¹² Pico della Mirandola, *Oration on the Dignity of Man*, trans. E. L. Forbes in *The Renaissance Philosophy of Man*, ed. Ernst Cassirer *et al.* (Chicago, University of Chicago Press, 1948), p. 225.

¹³ Karl Marx, *Economic and Philosophic Manuscripts*, in Loyd D. Easton and Kurt H. Guddat, eds. and trans., *Writings of the Young Marx on Philosophy and Society* (Garden City, N.Y., Doubleday & Company, Anchor Book, 1967), p. 314. For references to Pelagianism by Feuerbach see *The Essence of Christianity*, 'Introduction,' in *The Fiery Brook: Selected Writings of Ludwig Feuerbach*, trans. and ed. Zawar Hanfi (Garden City, N.Y., Doubleday & Company, Anchor Book, 1972), pp. 126–127 and pp. 132–133. For a recent Soviet discussion of Pelagianism see Lev N. Mitroxin, 'Problema ličnosti v protestantizme' (The Problem of the Individual in Protestantism) in the anthology *Ličnost' v buržuaznom obščestve i socialističeskom obščestve* (*Individuality in Bourgeois Society and Socialist Society*), (Moscow, 1966), pp. 59–86.

¹⁴ Taylor, chap. 1 and pp. 76–80.

¹⁵ Hanfi, p. 119.

¹⁶ *Ibid*. p. 120.

¹⁷ *Ibid*. p. 111.

¹⁸ *Ibid*. p. 119.

¹⁹ *Ibid*. pp. 123–124.

²⁰ *Ibid*. p. 124. Compare with Marx's *Economic and Philosophic Manuscripts* in Easton and Guddat, pp. 289–90.

²¹ Feuerbach, 'Introduction' to *The Essence of Christianity* in Hanfi, p. 97.

²² *Ibid*. p. 98. For other examples of Feuerbach's application of this principle see Hanfi pp. 125ff and pp. 182–83.

²³ *Ibid*. p. 99.

²⁴ *Ibid*. p. 121.

²⁵ *Ibid*. p. 109.

²⁶ Feuerbach, *Principles of the Philosophy of the Future*, in Hanfi, p. 244 (para. 59).

²⁷ *Loc. cit.* (para. 60).

²⁸ Marx, *Economic and Philosophic Manuscripts*, in Easton and Guddat, p. 298.

²⁹ *Ibid*. p. 296.

[30] *Ibid.* p. 294.

[31] *Ibid.* pp. 294–95.

[32] Karl Marx, *Grundrisse*, trans. Martin Nicolaus, p. 488.

[33] "In speaking of Right [*Recht*, i.e., *jus*] in this book, we mean not merely what is generally understood by the word, namely civil law, but also morality, ethical life, and world-history; these belong just as much to our topic, because the concept brings thoughts together into a true system." *Hegel's Philosophy of Right*, trans. T. M. Knox (Oxford, Clarendon Press, 1952), addition to Para. 33, p. 233.

[34] Marx, *Economic and Philosophic Manuscripts* in Easton and Guddat, p. 314.

[35] William K. Frankena, *Ethics* (Englewood Cliffs, N.J., Prentice-Hall, 1963), p. 10.

[36] For a contrary view, see George L. Kline, 'Leszek Kolakowski and the Revision of Marxism', in Kline, ed., *European Philosophy Today* (Chicago, Quadrangle Books, 1965), pp. 128–29.

[37] Friedrich A. Lange, *Geschichte des Materialismus und Kritik seiner Bedeutung in der Gegenwart* (Iserlohn, J. Baedeker, 1866).

[38] Frederick Engels, *Herr Eugen Dühring's Revolution in Science (Anti-Dühring)* trans. Emile Burns, ed. C. P. Dutt (New York, International Publishers, 1939, 1966), p. 104.

[39] *Ibid.* p. 105.

[40] Karl Kautsky, 'Die sozialen Triebe in der Tierwelt', *Neue Zeit* 1883, 1, 67ff.; and 'Die sozialen Triebe in der Menschenwelt', *Neue Zeit* 1884, 2, 13ff., 49ff., 118ff.

[41] Franz Mehring, 'Allerlei Ethik', *Neue Zeit* 1892–93, vol. 11, pt. 1, 265–70; Tönnies, 'Offenen Brief', *Deutsche Worte* January, 1893; Mehring, 'Ethik und Klassenkampf', *Neue Zeit* 1892–93, vol. 11, pt. 1, 700–02; Barth, *Neue Zeit* 1892–93, vol. 11, pt. 1, 449; Tönnies, Mehring, and editor, 'Noch Einiges über Ethik', *Neue Zeit* 1892–93, vol. 11, pt. 2, 103–16. For more detailed views of the defenders of the German Society for Ethical Culture, see the journal *Deutsche Worte* for the same period.

[42] Eduard Bernstein, *Die Voraussetzungen des Sozialismus und die Aufgaben der Sozialdemokratie* (Stuttgart, J. H. W. Dietz, 1899).

[43] F. W. Foerster, 'Soziale Demokratie und Ethik – ein neues Kapitel aus dem englischen Munizipalsozialismus', *Soziale Praxis* 1901, vol. 10, no. 4; Kautsky, 'Klassenkampf und Ethik', *Neue Zeit* 1900–1901, vol. 19, pt. 1, 233ff.; Foerster, 'Klassenkampf und Ethik', *ibid.* pp. 438ff.; Kautsky, 'Nochmals Klassenkampf und Ethik', *ibid*, pp. 468ff.

[44] Karl Kautsky, *Ethik und materialistische Geschichtsauffassung* (Stuttgart, J. H. W. Dietz, 1906); available in English as *Ethics and the Materialist Conception of History*, trans. John B. Askew, 4th ed., rev., (Chicago, Charles H. Kerr & Company, 1918); Kautsky, 'Leben, Wissenschaft, und Ethik', *Neue Zeit* 1905–06, vol. 24, pt. 2, 516–20 (reply to Otto Bauer, 'Marxismus und Ethik', *ibid.* pp. 485ff.); Kautsky, 'Der Ursprung der Moral', *Neue Zeit* 1906–07, vol. 25, pt. 1, 213–17 and 252–58.

[45] George Lichtheim, *Marxism, An Historical and Critical Study*, 2nd ed., rev. (New York, Frederick A. Praeger, 1965), p. 295.

[46] Kautsky, *Ethics and the Materialist Conception of History*, p. 5.

[47] Karl Vorländer, *Kant und der Sozialismus* (Berlin, Verlag von Reuther & Reichard, 1900); and *idem, Kant und Marx* (Tübingen, Verlag von J. C. B. Mohr (Paul Siebeck), 1911).

[48] Hermann Cohen, *Kants Begründung der Ethik* (Berlin, F. Dümmler, Harrwitz und Gossman, 1877).

[49] Vorländer, *Kant und Marx*, p. 122.

[50] *Idem, Kant und der Sozialismus*, pp. 6–7.

[51] Immanuel Kant, *Groundwork of the Metaphysic of Morals*, trans. H. J. Paton in *The Moral Law* (London, Hutchinson University Library, 1948), p. 98n. See also Vorländer, *Kant und der Sozialismus*, p. 7.

[52] Paton, *The Moral Law*, p. 93; Vorländer, *Kant und der Sozialismus*, p. 7.

[53] Vorländer, *loc. cit.*

[54] Hermann Cohen, 'Einleitung mit kritischem Nachtrag' to the 5th German edition of Lange, *Geschichte des Materialismus* (Leipzig, J. Baedeker, 1896), p. LXV; quoted by Vorländer, *Kant und Marx*, p. 124; also by Max Adler, *Marxistische Probleme* (Stuttgart, Verlag von I. B. W. Dietz Nachf.G.m.b.H., 1913), p. 143.

[55] Hermann Cohen, *Ethik des reinen Willens* 3rd. ed. (Berlin, B. Cassirer, 1921). Vorländer's references are to the 2nd rev. ed. (Berlin, B. Cassirer, 1907).

[56] Vorländer, *Kant und Marx*, p. 126.

[57] *Loc. cit.*

[58] Cohen, *Ethik des reinen Willens*, pp. 313–15 (pp. 311–13 2nd ed.).

[59] *Ibid.* p. 314 (p. 312 2nd. ed.)

[60] *Loc. cit.*

[61] *Ibid.* p. 311 (p. 309 2nd. ed.)

[62] *Ibid.* pp. 315–16 (p. 313 2nd ed.)

[63] *Ibid.* pp. 314–15 (p. 312 2nd ed.)

[64] *Ibid.* p. 315 (p. 313 2nd ed.)

[65] *Ibid.* p. 322 (p. 320 2nd ed.)

[66] Kautsky, *Ethics and the Materialist Conception of History*, pp. 57–58.

[67] Vorländer, *Kant und der Sozialismus*, p. 13.

[68] [Franz Mehring], 'Kant und der Sozialismus', *Neue Zeit*, 18, pt. 2 (1899–1900), p. 2.

[69] Conrad Schmidt, 'Sozialismus und Ethik', *Sozialistische Monatshefte* 4 (Sept., 1900): 525. (Vorländer's note number 219 in *Kant und Marx* misidentifies the year as 1908).

[70] Vorländer, *Kant und Marx*, p. 161.

[71] *Loc. cit.*

[72] Schmidt, pp. 525–26.

[73] Vorländer, *Kant und Marx*, p. 161.

[74] Schmidt describes morality in part as "doing away with the double standard, so that man has to submit to the same thing that he demands of others, and that he will bear the disadvantages that will accrue to him because of the general law he has approved of." Schmidt, p. 526.

[75] *Ibid.* p. 527; see Vorländer, *Kant und Marx*, p. 162.

[76] In an article appearing in the newspaper *Vorwärts*, February 12, 1904, cited in Vorländer, *Kant und Marx*, p. 167.

[77] Vorländer, *Kant und Marx*, p. 167.

[78] Ludwig Woltmann, *System des moralischen Bewusstseins mit besonderer Darlegung des Verhältnisses der kritischen Philosophie zu Darwinismus und Sozialismus* (Düsseldorf, H. Michel, 1898); *idem, Die Darwinische theorie und der Sozialismus* (Düsseldorf, H. Michels, 1899); *idem, Der historische Materialismus* (Düsseldorf, H. Michels, 1900).

[79] Vorländer, *Kant und der Sozialismus*, p. 57.

[80] Woltmann, *Der historische Materialismus*, pp. v–vi.

[81] *Ibid.* p. 64; see also Vorländer, *Kant und der Sozialismus*, p. 59.

[82] Woltmann, *Der historische Materialismus*, pp. 66–67; see also Vorländer, *loc. cit.*

[83] Lichtheim, *Marxism*, p. 265.

[84] Kautsky, *Ethics and the Materialist Conception of History*, p. 70.

[85] Ralph B. Perry, *Philosophy of the Recent Past* (New York, Charles Scribner's Sons, 1926), pp. 5–6, and pt. II.

[86] Kautsky, *Ethics and the Materialist Conception of History*, pp. 11–12.

[87] *Ibid*. pp. 14–18.

[88] *Ibid*. pp. 16–17.

[89] *Ibid*. p. 17.

[90] *Ibid*. p. 28.

[91] *Ibid*. p. 31.

[92] *Ibid*. p. 38.

[93] *Ibid*. p. 39.

[94] *Ibid*. p. 41.

[95] *Ibid*. p. 47.

[96] *Ibid*. p. 49.

[97] *Ibid*. p. 53.

[98] *Ibid*. pp. 53–55.

[99] *Ibid*. pp. 55–56.

[100] *Ibid*. pp. 60–61.

[101] *Ibid*. p. 60.

[102] *Ibid*. p. 61.

[103] *Ibid*. p. 71.

[104] *Ibid*. p. 94.

[105] *Ibid*. p. 95.

[106] *Ibid*. p. 96.

[107] *Ibid*. p. 97.

[108] Thomas H. Huxley, 'Evolution and Ethics', Romanes Lecture, 1893, reprinted in Thomas H. Huxley and Julian Huxley, *Touchstone for Ethics, 1893–1943* (New York, Harper & Brothers, 1947), p. 87.

[109] Edward O. Wilson, *Sociobiology: the New Synthesis* (Cambridge, Mass., Belknap Press of Harvard University Press, 1975).

[110] For a contemporary analogue of this controversy see Wilson's work, and also, for example, C. H. Waddington's review of it, 'Mindless Societies', *New York Review of Books*, August 7, 1975, p. 30; Donald Griffin, 'A Possible Window on the Minds of Animals', *American Scientist* 64 (Sept.–Oct., 1976), 530–35; and John Terrell, 'Animals are Human, Too', in the *Field Museum of Natural History Bulletin* 48 (March, 1977).

[111] Kautsky, *Ethics and the Materialist Conception of History*, p. 97.

[112] *Ibid*. p. 98.

[113] *Ibid*. p. 103.

[114] *Ibid*. p. 178.

[115] *Ibid*. pp. 178–79.

[116] *Loc. cit.*

[117] *Ibid*. p. 195.

[118] *Ibid*. p. 201.

[119] *Ibid*. pp. 202–03.

[120] See Vorländer, *Kant und Marx*, p. 253.

[121] *Loc. cit.*

[122] *Ibid.* p. 255.

[123] Max Adler, *Kausalität und Teleologie im Streite um die Wissenschaft*, in *Marx-Studien, Blätter zur Theorie und Politik des wissenschaftlichen Sozialismus* Published by Dr. Max Adler and Rudolf Hilferding (Vienna, Wiener Volksbuchhandlung, 1904), p. 415.

[124] *Loc. cit.*; see also Vorländer, *Kant und Marx*, pp. 255–56.

[125] Adler, p. 416; Vorländer, p. 256.

[126] Vorländer, p. 256.

[127] *Loc. cit.*

[128] *Loc. cit.*

[129] Adler, p. 431; Vorländer, p. 256.

[130] Adler, *Loc. cit.*

[131] *Ibid.* p. 432n.

[132] *Ibid.* p. 432f.

[133] *Ibid.* p. 433; Vorländer, p. 258.

[134] Max Adler, [review of Kautsky's *Ethics and the Materialist Conception of History*] in the *Wiener Arbeiterzeitung*, April, 1906, cited in Vorländer, *Kant und Marx*, p. 259. Adler's article was unavailable to this author; however, judging from Vorländer's quotations from it, the article must have been incorporated verbatim into Adler's *Marxistische Probleme*, pp. 106–07.

[135] Vorländer, p. 260; Adler, p. 107.

[136] Adler, p. 108.

[137] Quoted from Vorländer, p. 260.

[138] Vorländer, pp. 260–61.

[139] Max Adler, *Marxistische Probleme*, (see above note 54).

[140] *Ibid.* p. 142.

[141] *Ibid.* p. 147.

[142] *Loc. cit.*

[143] *Ibid.* p. 148.

[144] *Ibid.* p. 144.

[145] See below pp. 79ff. and pp. 187–95.

[146] Vorländer, *Kant und der Sozialismus*, p. 64.

[147] Hegel, *The Philosophy of History*, trans. J. Sibree (New York, Dover Publications, 1956). p. 67.

[148] Hegel, *The Science of Logic*, trans. A. V. Miller, Foreword by J. N. Findlay (London, Allen & Unwin, 1969), p. 832.

[149] Hegel, *Philosophy of Right*; see above note 33.

[150] Hegel, *Philoscphy of History*, p. 143.

[151] "But if a good heart, a good intention, a subjective conviction are set forth as the sources from which conduct derives its worth, then there is no longer any hypocrisy or immorality at all; for whatever a man does, he can always justify by the reflection on it of good intentions and motives, and by the influence of that conviction it is good." Hegel, *Philosophy of Right*, Remark appended to para. 139, p. 99.

[152] *Ibid.* translator's note, p. 319.

[153] *Ibid.* Remark appended to para. 141, p. 104.

[154] *Ibid.* p. 105.

[155] Hegel, *Philosophy of History*, p. 63.

[156] *Ibid.* p. 64.

[157] *Loc. cit.*
[158] *Ibid.* pp. 63–64.
[159] *Ibid.* p. 28.
[160] *Ibid.* p. 29.
[161] *Ibid.* p. 33.
[162] *Ibid.* p. 21.
[163] Shlomo Avineri, ed., *Karl Marx on Colonialism and Modernization* (Garden City, N.Y., Doubleday & Co., 1968), p. 131.
[164] Hegel, *Philosophy of History*, p. 66.
[165] *Ibid.* pp. 66–67.
[166] Hegel, *Science of Logic*; see note 148 above.
[167] Marx, article in *New York Daily Tribune*, June 25, 1853; quoted in Avineri, p. 89.
[168] Marx, article in *New York Daily Tribune*, August 8, 1853; quoted in Avineri, p. 125.
[169] Marx, article in *New York Daily Tribune*, June 25, 1853; quoted in Avineri, p. 88.
[170] *Ibid.* p. 89.
[171] Eugene Kamenka, *The Ethical Foundations of Marxism* (New York, Frederick A. Praeger, 1962), p. 38.
[172] George L. Kline, 'Was Marx an Ethical Humanist?' *Studies in Soviet Thought* 9 (1969), 91–103.
[173] *Ibid.* p. 100.
[174] Kamenka, p. 99.
[175] *Ibid.* p. 38.

CHAPTER TWO

[1] G. V. Plekhanov, *In Defence of Materialism: the Development of the Monist View of History*, trans. A. Rothstein (London, Lawrence & Wishart, 1947), pp. 27–28; and *idem*, *Essays in the History of Materialism*, trans. R. Fox (New York, Howard Fertig, 1967), p. 3.
[2] V. I. Lenin, *Philosophical Notebooks*, in vol. 38 of the *Collected Works*, 4th ed. (Moscow, Foreign Languages Publishing House, 1963), p. 276.
[3] Ludwig Feuerbach, 'Principles of the Philosophy of the Future', p. 203; and 'Towards a Critique of Hegel's Philosophy', p. 61; in *The Fiery Brook: Selected Writings of Ludwig Feuerbach*, trans. Zawar Hanfi (Garden City, N.Y., Doubleday & Company Anchor Books, 1972).
[4] Feuerbach, 'Towards a Critique of Hegel's Philosophy', *ibid.* p. 58 and p. 68.
[5] Karl Löwith, *From Hegel to Nietzsche*, trans. D. E. Green (Garden City, N.Y., Doubleday & Company Anchor Books, 1967), p. 71.
[6] Feuerbach, 'Towards a Critique of Hegel's Philosophy', in Hanfi, ed., p. 59.
[7] *Ibid.* p. 61.
[8] *Ibid.* p. 56.
[9] *Ibid.* p. 66.
[10] *Ibid.* p. 67.
[11] *Ibid.* p. 68.
[12] Feuerbach, 'Principles of the Philosophy of the Future', p. 204.
[13] *Ibid.* p. 215.

[14] *Ibid.* pp. 221–222.

[15] K. Marx, 'Toward the Critique of Hegel's Philosophy of Law: Introduction', in L. D. Easton and K. H. Guddat, trans. and eds., *Writings of the Young Marx on Philosophy and Society* (Garden City, N.Y., Doubleday & Company Anchor Books, 1967), p. 256.

[16] V. I. Lenin, *Materialism and Empirio-Criticism* (Moscow, Cooperative Publishing Soviet of Foreign Workers in the U.S.S.R., 1937), pp. 226–27.

[17] "The Hegelian philosophy is the resolution of the contradiction between thinking and being as, in particular, expressed by Kant; but, *nota bene*, the resolution of the contradiction still remains *within the contradiction*; i.e., within one element – *thought*. *Thought* is *being* in Hegel; i.e., *thought* is the *subject, being* the *predicate*." (Feuerbach, 'Preliminary Theses on the Reform of Philosophy', in Hanfi, ed., p. 167).

[18] Marx refers in particular to the 'Preliminary Theses on the Reform of Philosophy' and 'Principles of the Philosophy of the Future'.

[19] Feuerbach, 'Principles of the Philosophy of the Future', in Hanfi, ed., p. 224.

[20] *Ibid.* p. 227 and p. 241.

[21] Feuerbach, 'Towards a Critique of Hegel's Philosophy', *ibid.* p. 54.

[22] Feuerbach, 'Principles of the Philosophy of the Future,' *ibid.* p. 238.

[23] *Loc. cit.*

[24] *Loc. cit.*

[25] *Loc. cit.*

[26] *Ibid.* p. 226.

[27] *Ibid.* p. 227.

[28] *Ibid.* p. 244.

[29] *Ibid.* p. 231.

[30] Marx, 'Economic and Philosophic Manuscripts', in Easton and Guddat, eds., p. 316.

[31] *Ibid.* p. 326. (Compare with Feuerbach, 'Preliminary Theses on the Reform of Philosophy', in Hanfi, ed., p. 163).

[32] *Loc. cit.*

[33] *Ibid.* p. 323.

[34] *Ibid.* p. 324.

[35] *Ibid.* p. 325.

[36] *Ibid.* p. 324.

[37] *Ibid.* p. 325.

[38] *Ibid.* p. 333.

[39] *Ibid.* pp. 333–34.

[40] *Ibid.* p. 335.

[41] *Ibid.* p. 336.

[42] Marx and Engels, 'The German Ideology', in Easton and Guddat, eds., p. 418.

[43] Marx, 'Economic and Philosophic Manuscripts', in Easton and Guddat, eds., p. 325.

[44] Marx, 'The German Ideology', in Easton and Guddat, eds., p. 418.

[45] L. Kołakowski, 'Karl Marx and the Classical Definition of Truth', in *idem, Toward a Marxist Humanism*, trans. J. Z. Peel (New York, Grove Press, Inc., 1968), pp. 42–51.

[46] Marx, 'Economic and Philosophic Manuscripts', Easton and Guddat, eds., p. 311.

[47] *Ibid.* p. 306.

[48] A. Schmidt, *The Concept of Nature in Marx*, trans. B. Fowkes (Atlantic Highlands, N.J., Humanities Press, 1972), p. 29.

[49] See the article by O. G. Drobnickij in I. F. Balakina, *et al., Problema čeloveka v*

sovremennoj filosofii (*The Problem of Man in Contemporary Philosophy*), (Moscow, 'Nauka', 1969), for a discussion of the distinction between 'virgin nature' and 'artificial or produced nature' by a Soviet author.

⁵⁰ Marx, 'The Holy Family', in Easton and Guddat, eds., p. 391.

⁵¹ J. N. Findlay, Foreword to *Hegel's Philosophy of Nature*, trans. A. V. Miller (Oxford, Clarendon Press, 1970), p. xiii. Findlay continues "And it is arguable that if one wants to call one's absolutism a 'dialectical materialism', then such a 'dialectical materialism' is to be found in a more coherent and intelligibly worked-out form in Hegel's Philosophy of Nature and Spirit than in the imperfectly coherent 'dialectics' of Marx, Engels, and the Marxists generally."

⁵² L. Oken, *Lehrbuch der Naturphilosophie*, 3rd. ed. (Zürich, F. Schulthess, 1843); translated by A. Tulk as *Elements of Physiophilosophy* (London, The Ray Society, 1847). One of Oken's readers was of course Hegel, who objected that while it was perfectly possible to arrange the various species of the animal kingdom, for example, into the terms of a series, and that there was great intellectual benefit to be had in the order so produced, this benefit consisted in an increased insight into the differentiations of the notion, and not in any evolutionist hypothesis according to which the various terms of the series (species) were regarded as actually producing each other. (Hegel, *Philosophy of Nature*, remarks appended to para. 249, p. 21).

⁵³ His *Lehrbuch der Naturphilosophie* went through three editions (1809–11, 1831, and 1843). On this subject see J. T. Merz, *European Thought in the Nineteenth Century*, vol. 2 (Edinburgh, William Blackwood and Sons, 1903), p. 354, footnote 1.

⁵⁴ Without claiming that Marx or Feuerbach were directly influenced by the work of Oken, it is worth pointing out that the final, most substantial edition of Oken's *Lehrbuch der Naturphilosophie* appeared in 1843, the same period in which Marx was most concerned with these questions. On the other hand, Engels explicitly defended the work of Oken in *Anti-Dühring* (p. 16, footnote).

⁵⁵ N. Lobkowicz, 'Materialism and Matter in Marxism-Leninism', in *The Concept of Matter*, ed. Ernan McMullin (Notre Dame, University of Notre Dame, 1963), p. 464.

⁵⁶ F. Engels, *Herr Eugen Dühring's Revolution in Science* (*Anti-Dühring*) (New York, International Publishers, 1939, 1966), p. 13. However one should bear in mind Z. A. Jordan's observations on the state of Marx's health and other distractions at the time, which should cast some doubt on the significance to be attributed to Engels' statement. See Z. A. Jordan, *The Evolution of Dialectical Materialism* (New York, St. Martin's Press, 1967), pp. 10–11.

⁵⁷ Engels, *Anti-Dühring*, p. 15.

⁵⁸ *Ibid.* p. 16.

⁵⁹ *Ibid.* pp. 42–43.

⁶⁰ *Ibid.* p. 29.

⁶¹ *Ibid.* p. 30; see also p. 21.

⁶² *Ibid.* p. 29.

⁶³ *Ibid.* p. 154.

⁶⁴ See for example Z. A. Jordan, *The Evolution of Dialectical Materialism*; L. Kołakowsi, 'Karl Marx and the Classical Definition of Truth'; A. Schmidt, *The Concept of Nature in Marx*; and N. Levine, *The Tragic Deception: Marx contra Engels*, in the Twentieth Century Series, L. H. Letgers, ed., (Oxford, Clio Books, 1975).

⁶⁵ Plekhanov, *Essays in the History of Materialism*, Preface, p. vi.

[66] *Ibid*. pp. 87ff.

[67] *Ibid*. p. 6 and p. 191.

[68] *Ibid*. pp. 174–75.

[69] Plekhanov, *In Defense of Materialism*, p. 28; and *Essays in the History of Materialism*, pp. 189ff.

[70] Lenin, *Materialism and Empirio-Criticism*, p. 247.

[71] *Ibid*. p. 263.

[72] See Richard T. DeGeorge, *Patterns of Soviet Thought* (Ann Arbor, Univ. of Michigan Press, 1966), pp. 147–51.

[73] Lenin, *Materialism and Empirio-Criticism*, p. 246.

[74] K. Korsch, *Marxism and Philosophy*, trans. and intro. F. Halliday (New York, Modern Reader, 1970), pp. 68–69.

[75] *Ibid*. pp. 86–87.

[76] *Ibid*. pp. 87–88.

[77] Korsch, 'The Present State of the Problem of 'Marxism and Philosophy' ', *ibid*. pp. 131–32.

[78] *Ibid*. p. 133.

[79] Source: Lenin, *Collected Works*, 4th ed. (English translation) vol. 38, p. 13.

[80] *Ibid*. p. 141.

[81] *Ibid*. p. 104.

[82] *Ibid*. p. 146.

[83] *Ibid*. p. 147.

[84] *Ibid*. p. 223.

[85] *Ibid*. p. 109.

[86] *Ibid*. p. 211.

[87] *Ibid*. p. 199.

[88] *Ibid*. p. 289.

[89] *Ibid*. p. 287.

[90] *Ibid*. p. 285.

[91] *Ibid*. p. 196.

[92] *Loc. cit*.

[93] *Loc. cit*.

[94] *Loc. cit*.

[95] *Ibid*. p. 180.

[96] *Ibid*. p. 266.

[97] *Ibid*. p. 362.

[98] *Ibid*. See pp. 175, 182, 192, 223, 234, 319.

[99] *Ibid*. p. 234.

[100] (L. N. Suvorov), 'Gegel' i filosofskie diskussii 20–x godov' (Hegel and the Philosophical Discussions of the Twenties), in *Filosofija Gegelja i sovremennost'* (The Philosophy of Hegel and the Present), L. N. Suvorov, *et al*., eds. (Moscow, Mysl', 1973), p. 289.

[101] For the most detailed account available in English of the development of Soviet philosophy in the 1920's, see David Joravsky, *Soviet Marxism and Natural Science, 1917–1932* (London, Routledge and Kegan Paul, 1961), esp. pp. 93–106.

[102] *Ibid*. pp. 104–06.

[103] See the account of these events given by Deborin himself in 1960 in A. M. Deborin,

Filosofija i politika (Moscow, Izd. AN SSSR, 1961), pp. 3–19; see also the collection of his essays from the period in question (partly revised) in the same volume.
[104] See *Bolshevik*, 1925, Nos. 5, 6.
[105] Lenin, *Philosophical Notebooks*, pp. 359-60.
[106] *Ibid*. p. 361.
[107] *Ibid*. p. 362.
[108] Deborin, 'Gegel' i dialektičeskij materialism' (Hegel and Dialectical Materialism), in *Filosofija i politika*, p. 530.
[109] *Ibid*., pp. 563–64.
[110] Lenin, *Philosophical Notebooks*, p. 180.
[111] At the October, 1930, Conference of the Presidium of the Communist Academy. See Joravsky, p. 259.
[112] L. N. Suvorov, p. 304.
[113] (B. V. Bogdanov), 'Iz istorii issledovanija filosofii gegelja v sovetskoj filosofskoj nauke' (From the History of the Study of Hegelian Philosophy in Soviet Philosophical Science), in L. N. Suvorov, *et al.*, p. 309.
[114] *Loc cit.*
[115] *Gegel' i dialektičeskij materialism: Sbornik statej k 100-letiju so dnja smerti Gegelja*, (Hegel and Dialectical Materialism: A Collection of Articles for the 100th Anniversary of the Death of Hegel), Institut filosofii, Kommunist, Kommunističeskaja Akademija (Moscow, Partijnoe Izdat., 1932).
[116] Bogdanov, *op. cit.*, p. 310.
[117] *Loc. cit.*
[118] *Ibid*. p. 311.
[119] *Loc. cit.*
[120] *Loc. cit.*
[121] *Ibid*. pp. 312–18. In the same volume see the bibliography of Soviet publications on Hegel for the years 1960–1970, pp. 397–414.
[122] K. S. Bakradze, *Sistema i metod filosofii Gegelja* (The System and the Method of the Philosophy of Hegel), (Tbilisi, Izd. Tbilisskogo Universiteta, 1958); reprinted as vol. 2 of the *Izbrannye filosofskie trudy* (Selected Philosophical Works), (Tbilisi, Izd. Tbilisskogo Universiteta, 1973); see especially pp. 140–75.
[123] Bogdanov, *op. cit.* p. 315.
[124] Bakradze, *op. cit.* p. 174.
[125] V. I. Šinkaruk, *Logika, dialektika, i teorija poznanija Gegelja* (Hegel's Logic, Dialectic, and Theory of Knowledge), (Kiev, Izd. Kievskogo Universiteta, 1964).
[126] *Ibid*. p. 290.
[127] *Ibid*. p. 289. For a detailed discussion of this problem see T. J. Blakeley, *Soviet Theory of Knowledge* (Dordrecht-Holland, D. Reidel Publishing Company, 1964), pp. 18–27.
[128] Šinkaruk, *op. cit.*, p. 291.
[129] *Loc. cit.*
[130] *Ibid*. p. 293.

CHAPTER THREE

[1] See p. 14 above.
[2] For these essays See G. V. Plekhanov, *Sočinenija* (Works), ed. D. Rjazanov (Moscow,

Gos. Izd., 1923), vol. 11.
³ *Ibid*. p. 115.
⁴ *Ibid*. pp. 130–31.
⁵ F. Engels, *Ljudvig Fejerbax i konec klassičeskoj nemeckoj filosofii* (Ludwig Feuerbach and the End of Classical German Philosophy), trans. and ed. G. V. Plekhanov, 2nd. ed. (Geneva, 1905); quoted in G. V. Plekhanov, *Selected Philosophical Works* (London, Lawrence & Wishart, 1961), vol. 1, which contains the notes to both the 1892 and the 1905 editions.
⁶ *Ibid*. p. 527.
⁷ *Ibid*. p. 528.
⁸ *Loc. cit.*
⁹ Nikolai Berdiajew, 'Fredrich Albert Lange und die kritische Philosophie in ihren Beziehungen zum Sozialismus', *Neue Zeit*, vol. 28, tome 2 (1899–1900), pp. 132–40, 164–74, 196–207. See p. 207.
¹⁰ *Ibid*. p. 136.
¹¹ *Loc. cit.*
¹² *Ibid*. pp. 168–69.
¹³ *Ibid*. p. 205. (For Vorländer's sceptical reaction to this aspect of Berdjaev's thought see his *Kant und Marx*, p. 201).
¹⁴ *Ibid*. p. 169.
¹⁵ *Ibid*. p. 197.
¹⁶ *Loc. cit.*
¹⁷ N. Berdjaev, *Sub'ektivizm i individualizm v obščestvennoj filosofii* (St. Petersburg, 1901).
¹⁸ Quoted in the translation by A. E. Moorhouse in *Russian Philosophy*, James M. Edie, *et al.*, eds. (Chicago, Quadrangle Books, Inc., 1965, 1969), vol. 3, p. 151.
¹⁹ *Ibid*. p. 149.
²⁰ *Ibid*. p. 150.
²¹ *Ibid*. p. 153.
²² *Loc. cit.*
²³ *Loc. cit.*
²⁴ *Ibid*. p. 154.
²⁵ *Ibid*. p. 155.
²⁶ Vorländer, *Kant und Marx*, p. 199; George L. Kline, 'Theoretische Ethik im Russischen Frühmarxismus', *Forschungen zur Osteuropäischen Geschichte*, vol. 9, p. 273.
²⁷ Evgenij Lozinskij, 'Neo-Kantianskoe tečenie v marksizme' (The Neo-Kantian Tendency in Marxism), *Žizn': literaturnyj, naučnyj, i političeskij žurnal'*, (St. Petersburg), vol. 12 (December, 1900), pp. 132–54.
²⁸ Available in L. Aksel'rod, *Filosofskie Očerki: otvet filosofskim kritikam istoričeskogo materializma* (Philosophical Essays: an answer to philosophical critics of historical materialism), (St. Petersburg, Izd. M. M. Družininoj, 1906), pp. 93–129.
²⁹ *Ibid*. p. 116.
³⁰ *Loc. cit.*
³¹ *Ibid*. p. 121 (quotation translated from Russian).
³² *Loc. cit.*
³³ Peter von Struve, 'Die Marxsche Theorie der sozialen Entwicklung', *Archiv für Soziale Gesetzgebung und Statistik*, vol. 14 (1899), pp. 658ff.

[34] I. Kant, *Critique of Pure Reason*, trans. Norman Kemp Smith (London, Macmillan & Co., Ltd., 1963), p. 231; for Vorländer's approving comments, see his *Kant und Marx*, p. 203.

[35] Struve, *op. cit.* pp. 702–03.

[36] These articles are reprinted in vol. 11 of Plekhanov's *Sočinenie*.

[37] M. Tugan-Baranovskij, *Sovremennyj socializm v svoem istoričeskom razvitii* (St. Petersburg, 1906); German edition: *Der moderne Sozialismus in seiner geschichtlichen Entwicklung* (Leipzig, 1908); quoted here from the English edition: *Modern Socialism in its Historical Development*, trans. M. I. Redmount (London, Swan Sonnenschein & Co., Ltd., 1910), p. 9.

[38] *Ibid.* p. 10.

[39] *Ibid.* p. 11.

[40] Karl Forlender, *Kant i Marks: Očerki etičeskago socializma* (Kant and Marx: essays on ethical socialism), trans. B. I. Elkin, foreword by M. I. Tugan-Baranovskij (St. Petersburg, 1909); quoted in the review by A. Deborin, *Sovremennyj mir*, vol. 9 (1909), 115–17.

[41] Vorländer, *Kant und Marx*, p. 217.

[42] K. Forlender, *Kant i socializm* (Kant and Socialism), (Moscow, Pul's Žizni, 1906); *idem, Neokantianskoe dvizenie v socializme* (The Neo-Kantian Movement in Socialism), (Moscow, Pul's Žizni, 1907); *idem, Sovremennyj socializm i filosofskaja etika* (Contemporary Socialism and Philosophical Ethics), (Moscow, Pul's Žizni, 1907).

[43] See note 37 above.

[44] Ljudvig Vol'tman, *Sistema moral'nogo soznanija v svjazi s otnošeniem kritičeskoj filosofii k darvinizmy i socializmy* (The System of Moral Consciousness in Connection with the Relationship of Critical Philosophy to Darwinism and Socialism), (St. Petersburg, 1901); *idem, Teorija Darvina i socializm* (Darwinian Theory and Socialism) (1900); *idem, Istoričeskij materializm: Izloženie i kritika marksistskogo mirosozercanija* (Historical Materialism: Exposition and Critique of the Marxist Worldview), (1901).

[45] K. Kautskij, *Obščestvennye instinkty v mire životnyx i ljudej* (The Social Instinct in the World of Animals and of Humans), (Petrograd, Izd. Kommunističeskoj universiteta Zinov'eva, 1922); also printed in the journal *Severnyj Vestnik*, vol. 9 (1890); also printed in *idem, Očerki i etjudy* (Essays and Studies), 4th ed. (St. Petersburg, G. L'vovica, 1907).

[46] K. Kautskij, *Proisxoždenie morali* (*Polemika s Kvesselem*) (The Origin of Morality: A Polemic with Quessel), (St. Petersburg, Izd. Dviženie, 1907).

[47] K. Kautskij, *Očerednye problemy meždunarodnogo socializma* (Current Problems of International Socialism), (Moscow, Izd. Kommunist, 1918).

[48] K. Kautskij, *Etika i materialističeskoe ponimanie istorii* (Ethics and the Materialist Conception of History). See Ja. S. Rozanov, ed., *Marksizm i etika*, 2nd ed., (Xar'kov, Gos. Izd. Ukrainy, 1925), pp. 437–38 for a bibliographical listing of the separate editions, reproduced in the Appendix of this work.

[49] See Appendix for the Rozanov bibliography.

[50] See George L. Kline, 'Changing Attitudes Toward the Individual', in C. E. Black, ed., *The Transformation of Russian Society* (Cambridge, Harvard University Press, 1960), pp. 606–25, esp. pp. 618–25; *idem,* 'Theoretische Ethik im Russischen Frühmarxismus'; and *idem,* 'Leszek Kołakowski and the Revision of Marxism', in George L. Kline, ed., *European Philosophy Today* (Chicago, Quadrangle Books, 1965), esp. pp. 127–40.

[51] Kline, 'Changing Attitudes . . .', p. 619.

[52] S. Vol'skij, *Filosofija bor'by: opyt postroenija etiki marksizma* (The Philosophy of Struggle: an essay in the construction of a Marxist ethics), (Moscow, 1909); quoted in Kline, *ibid.*, p. 620.

[53] Kline, 'Changing Attitudes . . .', p. 620.

[54] *Ibid.* p. 621.

[55] *Ibid.* p. 622.

[56] *Ibid.* pp. 622–23.

[57] A. Deborin, review of Forlender, *Kant i Marks, Sovremennyj mir*, vol. 9 (1909), p. 117. (See above note 40).

[58] *De Profundis* (Moscow, 1918); reprinted in Paris, 1967. Source: 'Introduction' by Max Hayward to *From Under the Rubble*, by A. Solzhenitsyn, *et al.*, trans. M. Scammell *et al.* (Boston, Little, Brown and Company, 1975). The latter collection of essays itself represents a renewal of this critical discussion.

[59] S. Frank, *Nravstvennyj vodorazdel v russkoj revoljucii* (The Moral Watershed in the Russian Revolution), (Moscow, 1917), pp. 10–11, quoted in A. G. Xarčev and B. D. Jakovlev, *Očerki istorii marksistsko-leninskoj etiki v SSSR* (Essays on the History of Marxist-Leninist Ethics in the USSR), (Leningrad, Izd. 'Nauka', 1972), p. 63.

[60] *Loc. cit.*

[61] *Ibid.* pp. 64–65.

[62] E. Radlov, *Etika* (Petrograd, 1921), p. 80; quoted in Xarčev and Jakovlev, p. 67.

[63] N. Berdjaev, *Smysl istorii* (The Meaning of History), (Berlin, 1923); *idem, Novoe srednevekov'e: Razmyšlenie o sud'be Rossii i Evropy* (The New Middle Ages: Thoughts on the Fate of Russia and Europe), (Berlin, 1924); *idem, Xristianstvo i klassovaja bor'ba* (Christianity and the Class Struggle), (Paris, 1931).

[64] For a more detailed treatment see Xarčev and Jakovlev; and V. I. Klusin, *Bor'ba za istoričeskij materializm v Leningradskom gosudarstvennom universitete (1918–1925 gody)* (The Struggle for Historical Materialism in Leningrad State University, 1918–1925), (Leningrad, Izd. Leningradskogo Gos. Universiteta, 1970).

[65] G. V. Plekhanov, *O vojne* (On the War), (Petrograd, Knigoizdat. vo byvš. M. V. Popova, 1915); excerpt reprinted in Ja. S. Rozanov, pp. 203–06.

[66] G. V. Plekhanov, *Ešče o vojne* (Once Again on the War); excerpt reprinted in Rozanov, ed., pp. 207–10. Quotation from p. 209.

[67] L. Martov, 'Kant s Gindenburgom, Marks s Kantom' (Kant with Hindenburg, Marx with Kant), *Letopis'*, 1916, No. 3; reprinted in Rozanov, ed., pp. 211–18; quotation from p. 211.

[68] Marx to Engels, 4 November, 1864; also printed in Rozanov, ed., pp. 200–02.

[69] L. Aksel'rod, 'Prostye zakony nravstvennosti i prava' (Simple Laws of Morality and Right), *Delo*, 1916, No. 1; reprinted in Rozanov, pp. 219–31; quotation from p. 227.

[70] *Loc. cit.* p. 223.

[71] L. Martov, 'Prostota xuže vorovstva' (A Simplicity Worse than Theft); reprinted in Rozanov, ed., pp. 233–56.

[72] L. Aksel'rod, *Dialektika v prirode* (The Dialectic in Nature), No. 2, p. 303; quoted in A. M. Deborin, 'Revizionizm pod maskoj ortodoksii' (Revisionizm under the Guise of Orthodoxy), Part 2, *Pod znamenem marksizma*, 1927, No. 12, p. 10.

[73] Deborin, *op. cit.* p. 13.

[74] Deborin, 'Revizionizm pod maskoj ortodoksii', Part 3, *Pod znamenem marksizma*, 1928, No. 1, p. 7.

[75] *Ibid.* p. 13.

[76] *Ibid.* p. 12.

[77] See above pp. 26ff.

[78] Furščik, 'O liberal'nom i marksistskom ponimanii etiki' (On the Liberal and the Marxist Understanding of Ethics), *Bolshevik*, 1930, No. 6. (See also *Bezbožnik*, 1930, No. 22).

[79] S. Novikov, 'O liberal'no-men'šivistskom i marksistsko-bol'ševistskom ponimanii etiki' (On the Liberal-Menshevik and the Marxist-Bolshevik Understanding of Ethics), *Pod znamenem marksizma*, 1930, No. 5, p. 152.

[80] I. Razumovskij, 'O marksistskom i eklektičeskom ponimanii etiki' (On the Marxist and the Eclectic Understanding of Ethics), *Pod znamenem marksizma*, 1930, No. 5, pp. 187–221.

[81] See above p. 62.

[82] Deborin, 'Revizionizm pod maskoj ortodoksii', Part 3, p. 27.

[83] G. A. Gontarev and A. L. Xajkin, 'Razvitie marksistskoj etičeskoi mysli v SSSR' (The Development of Marxist Ethical Thought in the USSR), *Filosofskie nauki*, 1967, No. 5.

[84] Xarčev and Jakovlev, pp. 121–30 and pp. 214–15.

[85] *Ibid.* p. 123.

[86] See above note 45.

[87] Xarčev and Jakovlev, pp. 125–26.

[88] *Ibid.* p. 126.

[89] *Loc. cit.*

[90] *Ibid.* p. 146.

[91] *Ibid.* pp. 145–46. For a description of the *Proletkul't* and *RAPP* see E. J. Brown, *Russian Literature Since the Revolution* (New York, Collier Books, 1963).

[92] Xarčev and Jakovlev, pp. 130–46.

[93] *Ibid.* pp. 149–52.

CHAPTER FOUR

[1] As evidence of the sudden growth of interest in ethical theory, Xarčev and Jakovlev report that in the three years from 1966–69 there were approximately 500 publications on ethics, one and a half times the total number in the twenty years from 1917 to 1937. (*Očerki istorii marksistsko-leninskoj etiki v SSSR*) (Essays on the History of Marxist-Leninist Ethics in the USSR), p. 154.

[2] O. G. Drobnickij and I. S. Kon, *Slovar' po etike* (Dictionary of Ethics), 2nd ed. (Moscow, Izd. Polit. Literatury, 1970), 'Nravstvennost'' (Morality), p. 203.

[3] See above Chap. One, pp. 32ff.

[4] Bandzeladze, *Opyt izloženija sistemy marksistskoj etiki* (An Essay in the Exposition of the System of Marxist Ethics), both editions, pp. 62–63.

[5] Drobnickij and Kon, *Slovar' po etiki*, p. 203.

[6] The authors of the 'Nravstvennost'' article in the *Slovar' po etike* as well as Bandzeladze endorse this practice.

[7] T. V. Samsonova, *Teoretičeskie problemy etiki* (Theoretical Problems of Ethics), (Moscow, Izd. Moskovskogo universiteta, 1966), pp. 14–15.

[8] L. M. Arxangel'skij, *Kurs lekcij po marksistsko-leninskoj etiki* (A Course of Lectures in Marxist-Leninist Ethics), (Moscow, Vysšaja škola, 1974), p. 46.

[9] *Ibid.* p. 47.

[10] O. G. Drobnickij, 'Priroda moral'nogo soznanija' (The Nature of Moral Consciousness), *Voprosy filosofii* 1968, 2, 26–37. (See especially pp. 26–30 and ftnt. 1, p. 29). See also the article on 'Moral" (Morality) in the *Slovar' po etike*, 2nd ed., p. 171.

[11] Bandzeladze, *Opyt izloženija* . . . , 1st ed. p. 20 (2nd ed. p. 21).

[12] *Ibid.* 1st ed. pp. 20–21. (2nd ed. pp. 21–22).

[13] *Ibid.* 1st ed. p. 21. (2nd ed. p. 22).

[14] *Loc. cit.*

[15] *Ibid.* 1st ed. p. 22. (2nd ed. pp. 22–23).

[16] S. Utkin, *Očerki po marksistsko-leninskoj etike* (Essays in Marxist-Leninist Ethics), (Moscow, Izd. Social'no-ekonomičeskoj literatury, 1963), pp. 78–79.

[17] A. F. Šiškin and K. A. Švarcman, *XX vek i moral'nye cennosti čelovečestva* (The 20th Century and Moral Values of Humanity), (Moscow, Izd. 'Mysl'", 1968), p. 26. They refer to F. A. Selivanov as committing this error: "That which we term 'just', 'good', or that which which fills us with indignation, exists without possessing for itself or in itself our feelings, our concepts." *Etika: očerki* (Ethics: essays), (Tomsk, Izd. Tomskogo universiteta, 1961), p. 34.

[18] Šiškin and Švarcman, *op. cit.* p. 29.

[19] *Ibid.* p. 31.

[20] Xarčev and Jakovlev, *Očerki istorii* . . . , p. 167. They refer to K. A. Švarcman, *Teoretičeskie problemy etiki* (Moscow, Vysšaja škola, 1969), p. 7.

[21] A. K. Uledov, 'Moral'nye otnošenija kak sociologičeskaja i etičeskaja kategorija' (Moral Relations as a Sociological and an Ethical Category), in *Problemy kategorii marksistsko-leninskoj etiki* (Problems of the Categories of Marxist-Leninist Ethics), Institut Filosofii, AN SSSR and Novosibirskaja vysšaja partijnaja škola (Novosibirsk, 1969), p. 88. Also cited in Xarčev and Jakovlev, p. 167.

[22] Uledov, p. 87.

[23] N. A. Trofimov, 'Nravstvennye otnošenija – najbolee suščestvennaja kategorija etiki' (Moral Relations – the Most Essential Category of Ethics), in the same anthology, p. 93.

[24] G. E. Borisov, 'O kategorii nravstvennyx otnošenij' (On the Category of Moral Relations) in the same anthology, p. 91.

[25] See for example Xarčev and Jakovlev, p. 168.

[26] Definition taken from the *Filosofskaja enciklopedija*, vol. 3, p. 499.

[27] Drobnickij, 'Priroda moral'nogo soznanija', *Voprosy filosofii* 1968, 2, 30 and ftnt. 1; Bandzeladze, *Opyt izloženija* . . . , 1st ed., ftnt. 1, pp. 21–22. (2nd ed. pp. 22–23).

[28] Drobnickij, *op. cit.* p. 27.

[29] *Loc. cit.*

[30] *Ibid.* pp. 27–28. For a similar view see also Arxangel'skij, *Kurs lekcij* . . . , p. 21.

[31] Drobnickij, *op. cit.* p. 28, ftnt. 1.

[32] *Ibid*, p. 29.

[33] *Loc. cit.*

[34] *Loc. cit.*

[35] See the discussion of this point in Xarčev and Jakovlev, p. 168–69.

[36] *Ibid.* p. 168.

[37] Apart from his unpublished doctoral dissertation Drobnickij's views are developed in three articles appearing in *Voprosy filosofii*: 'Priroda moral'nogo soznanija', 1968, 2, 26–37; 'Moral'noe soznanie i ego struktura' (Moral Consciousness and its Structure),

238 REFERENCES

1972, 2, 31—42; 'Struktura moral'nogo soznanija' (The Structure of Moral Consciousness), 1972, 6, 51—62; and in his *Poṇjatie morali* (The Concept of Morality), (Moscow, 'Nauka', 1974).
[38] F. Loeser, *Deontik* (Berlin, VEB Deutscher Verlag Der Wissenschaften, 1966) and W. Eichhorn, *Wie ist Ethik als Wissenschaft möglich*? (Berlin, VEB Deutscher Verlag der Wissenschaften, 1965).
[39] This analysis of the structure of moral consciousness is provided in the two articles appearing in *Voprosy filosofii*, 1972, numbers 2 and 6. See note 37 above.
[40] Drobnickij, 'Moral'noe soznanie i ego struktura', *Voprosy filosofii* 1972, 2, 36.
[41] *Loc. cit.*
[42] *Ibid.* p. 37.
[43] *Ibid.* p. 38.
[44] *Ibid.* p. 39.
[45] *Ibid.* p. 40.
[46] *Ibid.* p. 41.
[47] *Ibid.* p. 42.
[48] Drobnickij, 'Struktura moral'nogo soznanija', *Voprosy filosofii*, 1972, 6, 54.
[49] *Ibid.* p. 55.
[50] Drobnickij, 'Moral'noe soznanie i ego struktura', p. 33.
[51] *Loc. cit.*
[52] *Loc. cit.*
[53] *Loc. cit.*
[54] *Loc. cit.*
[55] A. I. Titarenko, 'Specifika i struktura morali' (Specific Features and Structure of Morality), in *Moral' i etičeskaja teorija* (Morality and Ethical Theory), ed. O. P. Celikova, Institut Filosofii, AN SSSR (Moscow, 'Nauka', 1974), p. 49.
[56] For references to the two German philosophers' works see note 38 above. For Celikova's views see 'Osobennosti vyraženija v jazyke moral'no-etičeskogo soderžanija' (Peculiarities in the Linguistic Expression of Moral-Ethical Contents), in Celikova, ed., *Moral' i etičeskaja teorija*, pp. 151—53. See also Arxangel'skij, *Kurs lekcij . . .*, pp. 68ff.
[57] Arxangel'skij, p. 46.
[58] See above Chap. One, p. 13.
[59] See Xarčev and Jakovlev, p. 175.
[60] *Ibid.* pp. 176—77.
[61] See for example Drobnickij, *Ponjatie morali*, Chaps. Four and Five; T. S. Lapina, 'Social'nye funkcii morali' (The Social Functions of Morality), in Celikova, ed., *Moral' i etičeskaja teorija*; L. M. Arxangel'skij, *Kurs lekcii po marksistsko-leninskoj etike*, Chap. One; A. I. Titarenko, ed., *Marksistskaja etika* (Marxist Ethics), Chap. Three.
[62] Drobnickij, *Ponjatie morali*, pp. 228—54.
[63] Arxangel'skij, *Kurs lekcii . . .*, pp. 37—46.
[64] See references in note 61.
[65] Lapina, 'Social'nye funkcii morali', p. 62.
[66] Titarenko, ed., *Marksistskaja etika*, Chap. Three, p. 93ff.
[67] Utkin, *Očerki po marksistsko-leninskoj etike*, p. 9.
[68] Šiškin, *Osnovy marksistskoj etike* (Foundations of Marxist Ethics), p. 43. For a practically identical formulation of this definition see Utkin, p. 28.
[69] Arxangel'skij, *Kurs lekcii . . .*, p. 25.

[70] Bandzeladze, *Opyt izloženija* . . . , 1st ed. p. 8.

[71] A. I. Titarenko, ed., *Marksistskaja etika* (Moscow, Politizdat, 1976), p. 10.

[72] *Loc. cit.*

[73] Bandzeladze, *Opyt izloženija* . . . , p. 58.

[74] Titarenko, *op. cit.* p. 10.

[75] *Ibid.* p. 11.

[76] *Ibid.* p. 12.

[77] *Loc. cit.*

[78] *Slovar' po etike*, p. 378.

[79] *Loc. cit.*

[80] *Loc. cit.*

[81] *Ibid.* p. 379.

[82] See below Chap. Seven.

[83] This discussion was initiated by L. M. Arxangel'skij's article 'Suščnost' etičeskix kategorij' (The Essence of Ethical Categories), (*Filosofskie nauki*, 1961, 3) which was then expanded into his monograph *Kategorii marksistskoj etiki* (Moscow, Socekgiz, 1963).

[84] A. G. Xarčev, 'K itogam diskussii o kategorijax etike' (On the Results of the Discussion of Ethical Categories), *Filosofskie nauki* 1965, 2; see also Xarčev and Jakovlev, pp. 155–56.

[85] Ja. A. Mil'ner-Irinin's major work *Etika, ili principy istinnoj čelovečnosti* (Ethics, or the Principles of True Humanity) was printed in a very limited edition of about 60 copies for the purpose of discussion within the Academy of Sciences in 1963. An article by him, 'Etika – nauka o dolžnom' (Ethics – the Science of that which Ought to Be) and an excerpt from the larger work both appeared in Bandzeladze, ed., *Aktual'nye problemy marksistskoj etiki* (Current Problems of Marxist Ethics), (Tbilisi, Izd. Tbilisskogo gos. universiteta, 1967).

[86] 'Za naučnost' i konkretnost' v razrabotke problem etiki' (For Science and Concreteness in the Resolution of Problems in Ethics), *Voprosy filosofii* 1968, 8, 152.

[87] Drobnickij, 'Moral'noe soznanie i ego struktura', *Voprosy filosofii* 1972, 2, 31–32; Xarčev and Jakovlev, pp. 155–56; Celikova, 'Osobennosti vyraženija v jazyke moral'no-etičeskogo socerzanija', in Celikova, ed., *Moral' i etičeskaja teorija*, pp. 164–82; and Celikova, 'Kategorii i ponjatija etiki' (Categories and Concepts of Ethics), *ibid.* pp. 195–218.

[88] Drobnickij, 'Moral'noe soznanie i ego struktura', p. 31.

[89] *Ibid.* pp. 31–32.

[90] Arxangel'skij, *Kurs lekcij* . . . , p. 152.

[91] R. V. Petropavlovskij, 'Metodologičeskie problemy etiki' (Methodological Problems of Ethics), in Celikova, ed., *Moral' i etičeskaja teorija*, p. 229.

[92] *Loc. cit.* ftnt. 6; the reference is to V. P. Kobljakov and L. V. Konovalova, *Predmet i sistema etiki* (The Object and the System of Ethics), (Moscow and Sofia, 1973), p. 224.

[93] Celikova, ed., *Moral' i etičeskaja teorija*, p. 183.

[94] Mil'ner-Irinin, 'Etika – nauka o dolžnom', in Bandzeladze, ed., *Aktual'nye problemy*, p. 15.

[95] *Ibid.* p. 17.

[96] See N. A. Golovko and V. S. Markov, 'Za naučnost' i konkretnost' v razrabotke problem etiki', *Voprosy filosofii* 1968, 8, 148–55.

[97] Based on the author's personal conversations with a large number of Soviet ethical

240   REFERENCES

theorists in those years.

[98] P. M. Egides, 'Osnovnoj vopros etiki kak filosofskoj nauki i problema nravstvennogo otčuždenija' (The Fundamental Problem of Ethics as a Philosophical Science and the Problem of Moral Alienation), in Bandzeladze, ed., *Aktual'nye problemy*, p. 59.

[99] *Ibid.* p. 69.

[100] *Ibid.* p. 71.

[101] Šiškin, *Osnovy marksistskoj etiki*, p. 45.

[102] *Loc. cit.* See also very similar remarks in his article 'O nekotoryx voprosov issledovatel'skoj raboty v oblasti etiki' (Concerning Several Questions of Research Work in the Area of Ethics), *Voprosy filosofii* 1973, 1, 21.

[103] Drobnickij, 'Struktura moral'nogo soznanija', p. 62.

[104] *Loc. cit.*

[105] See below Chap. Six.

[106] See below p. 108.

[107] V. S. Štein, 'Problema prostyx norm nravstvennosti i spravedlivosti v marksistsko-leninskoj etike' (The Problem of Simple Moral Norms of Morality and Justice in Marxist-Leninist Ethics), in Bandzeladze, ed., *Aktual'nye problemy*, pp. 124–82.

[108] A. F. Šiškin, *Osnovy marksistskoj etiki* (Moscow, Izd. Institut Meždunarodnyx Otnošenij, 1961), p. 430.

[109] M. I. Kus'minkov, 'Kommunističeskaja moral' i obščestvennye normy nravstvennosti' (Communist Morality and Social Norms of Morality), *Kommunist* 1964, 1.

[110] Štein, p. 136.

[111] *Program of the Communist Party of the Soviet Union*, reprinted in *The U.S.S.R. and the Future*, ed. Leonard Schapiro (New York, Frederick A. Praeger, 1963), p. 304.

[112] See for example G. Brovman in 'Klub Oktjabrja', *Oktjabr'* 1966, 7, 208; and 'Glašataj abstraktnoj čelovečnosti' (Herald of Abstract Humanity), *Oktjabr'* 1963, 5, 200–01; cited by Štein, p. 179.

[113] See for example D. Starikov, 'Real'naja nravstvennosti" (Real Morality), *Voprosy literatury* 1964, 7, 26–31.

[114] Štein, pp. 178–79.

[115] Šiškin, 'O nekotoryx voprosov issledovatel'skoj raboty', pp. 14–26; esp. p. 15.

[116] *Ibid.* p. 17.

[117] *Ibid.* p. 19.

[118] *Loc. cit.*

[119] Štein, p. 146.

[120] *Ibid.* p. 166 and ftnt.

[121] Bandzeladze, *Opyt izloženija* . . . , 1st ed. p. 86.

[122] V. P. Tugarinov, *O cennostjax žizni i kul'tury* (On the Values of Life and Culture), (Leningrad, Izd. Leningradskogo universiteta, 1960), pp. 120–21.

[123] See for example F. Vigdorova, 'Dobrota? Za čem ona?" (Goodness? For What?), *Literaturnaja gazeta*, 29 March, 1960; cited by Štein, p. 176.

CHAPTER FIVE

[1] V. P. Tugarinov, *O cennostjax žizni i kul'tury* (On the Values of Life and Culture), (Leningrad, Izd. LGU, 1960).

[2] 'Simpozium po teorii cennostej: doklady i soobščenija' (Symposium on the Theory of Values: Reports and Communications), (Tbilisi: October, 1965), (unpublished); and 'Simpozium po probleme cennostej' (Symposium on the Problem of Values), *Filosofskie nauki* 1966, 2, 139–45.

[3] I. F. Balakina, 'Probleme cennostej – vnimanie issledovatelej' (The Problem of Values – Attention Researchers), *Voprosy filosofii* 1965, 9.

[4] A. G. Xarčev, ed., *Problema cennosti v filosofii* (The Problem of Value in Philosophy), (Leningrad, 'Nauka', 1966).

[5] Tugarinov, *op. cit.* p. 6.

[6] *Loc. cit.*

[7] *Ibid.* p. 3.

[8] *Ibid.* p. 4.

[9] *Ibid.* p. 25.

[10] *Ibid.* p. 120.

[11] *Ibid.* p. 121.

[12] *Ibid.* p. 123.

[13] *Ibid.* p. 125.

[14] *Ibid.* p. 131.

[15] *Ibid.* p. 132.

[16] Balakina, *op. cit.* p. 154.

[17] D. P. Gorskij, 'Istina i ee kriterij' (Truth and its Criterion), *Voprosy filosofii* 1962, 2, 121–33.

[18] *Ibid.* p. 128.

[19] *Loc. cit.*

[20] O. M. Bakuradze, 'Istina i cennost" (Truth and Value), *Voprosy filosofii* 1966, 7, 45–48.

[21] *Ibid.* p. 45.

[22] *Ibid.* p. 47.

[23] *Ibid.* p. 48.

[24] See for example, V. E. Ermolaeva, 'Etika i logika' (Ethics and Logic), *Voprosy filosofii* 1968, 11, 78–83.

[25] A. A. Ivin, 'Deontičeskaja logika' (Deontic Logic), *Voprosy filosofii* 1966, 12, 160–71; see also *idem*, 'Nekotorye problemy teorii deontičeskix modal'nostej' (Some Problems of the Theory of Deontic Modalities), in *Logičeskaja semantika i modal'naja logika* (Logical Semantics and Modal Logic), (Moscow, 'Nauka', 1967).

[26] A. A. Ivin, 'O logike ocenok' (On the Logic of Values), *Voprosy filosofii* 1968, 8, 53–63; and *idem, Osnovanija logiki ocenok* (Foundations of the Logic of Values), (Moscow, 1970).

[27] Ivin, 'O logike ocenok', p. 55.

[28] Drobnickij, 'Priroda moral'nogo soznanija', p. 34.

[29] Xarčev and Jakovlev, p. 200.

[30] Šiškin and Švarcman, *XX vek i moral'nye cennosti čelovečestva* (The 20th Century and the Moral Values of Humanity), pp. 20–21n.

[31] See above p. 27.

[32] H. B. Acton, *The Illusion of the Epoch* (London, Cohen & West, Ltd., 1955), p. 190.

[33] Isaiah Berlin, *Karl Marx* (London, Oxford University Press, 1948), p. 140.

[34] See below pp. 133–35.

[35] O. G. Drobnickij, 'Nekotorye aspekty problemy cennostej' (Some Aspects of the Problem of Values), in A. G. Xarčev, ed., *Problema cennosti v filosofii*, p. 26.

[36] See above pp. 49ff.

[37] Drobnickij, *op. cit.* in Xarčev, ed., *Problema cennosti*, pp. 36–37.

[38] *Loc. cit.*

[39] *Ibid.* pp. 37–38.

[40] V. P. Tugarinov, *Teorija cennostej v marksizme* (Theory of Values in Marxism), (Leningrad, Izd. Leningradskogo universiteta, 1968), p. 11.

[41] *Loc. cit.*

[42] *Loc. cit.*

[43] *Ibid.* p. 25.

[44] *Ibid.* p. 13.

[45] *Ibid.* p. 16.

[46] *Ibid.* p. 17.

[47] *Ibid.* p. 18.

[48] *Loc. cit.*

[49] *Ibid.* p. 19.

[50] *Loc. cit.*

[51] *Ibid.* pp. 34–35.

[52] *Ibid.* p. 35.

[53] See below pp. 159–60.

[54] *Simpozium po teroii cennostej: doklady i soobščenija* (Tbilisi, 1965), unpublished, p. 15.

[55] *Loc. cit.*

[56] *Loc. cit.*

[57] *Loc. cit.*

[58] *Ibid.* p. 16.

[59] Čavčavadze, in *Simpozium po teorii cennostej.*

[60] See below p. 138.

[61] V. A. Vasilenko, 'Cennosti i cennostnye otnošenija' (Values and Value Relations), in A. G. Xarčev, ed., *Problema cennosti*, p. 45.

[62] *Ibid.* p. 46.

[63] *Ibid.* p. 47.

[64] *Loc. cit.*

[65] See above p. 114.

[66] V. P. Kobljakov lists O. Vajnberger (Czechoslovakia), G. Klaus (GDR), D. P. Gorskij (SSSR), V. Eichhorn (GDR) as non-cognitivists; and F. Loeser (GDR), A. F. Šiškin (SSSR), and N. N. Mokrousov (SSSR) as cognitivists, in his article 'Ob istinnosti moral'nyx suždenij' (On the Truth of Moral Judgments), *Voprosy filosofii* 1958, 5, 61–62. Xarčev and Jakovlev (p. 204) and Arxangel'skij (*Kurs lekcij . . .* , p. 63) also cite the East Germans Klaus and Eichhorn as well as Gorskij, as the most prominent defenders of non-cognitivism.

[67] Xarčev and Jakovlev, pp. 201–02.

[68] *Ibid.* p. 202.

[69] *Loc. cit.*

[70] N. D. Tabunov, 'Istina i dobro' (Truth and the Good), in *Problemy kategorij marksistsko-leninskoj etiki*, p. 47; Xarčev and Jakovlev, p. 202–03.

[71] Kobljakov, 'Ob istinnosti moral'nyx suždenij', pp. 69–70; Xarčev and Jakovlev, pp. 203–04.

[72] Xarčev and Jakovlev, *loc. cit.*

[73] K. A. Švarcman, *Teoretičeskie problemy etiki*, p. 37; cited by Xarčev and Jakovlev, pp. 204–05.

[74] Arxangel'skij, *Kurs lekcij* . . . , p. 62.

[75] *Loc. cit.*

[76] *Ibid.*, p. 63.

[77] *Loc. cit.*

[78] L. V. Konovalova, 'Problema istiny v morali' (The Problem of Truth in Morality), in *Nasuščnye voprosy etiki* (Moscow, Institut Filosofii, AN SSSR, 1971), p. 87.

[79] *Ibid.* pp. 87–88.

[80] *Ibid.* p. 88.

[81] *Loc. cit.*

[82] *Ibid.* p. 90.

[83] *Ibid.* p. 103.

[84] *Loc. cit.*

[85] A. F. Šiškin, 'O nekotoryx voprosax issledovatel'skoj raboty v oblasti etiki' (Concerning Several Questions of Research Work in the Area of Ethics), *Voprosy filosofii* 1973, 1, 17.

[86] *Ibid.* pp. 17–18.

[87] L. M. Arxangel'skij, 'Šušcnost' etičeskix kategorij' (The Essence of Ethical Categories), *Filosofskie nauki* 1961, 3; and *Problemy kategorij marksistsko-leninskoj etiki* (Novosibirsk, 1969).

[88] Xarčev and Jakovlev, p. 191.

[89] *Loc. cit.*

[90] *Loc. cit.*

[91] Arxangel'skij, *Kurs lekcij* . . . , p. 184.

[92] Ju. V. Sogomonov, *Dobro i zlo* (Good and Evil), (Moscow, Izd. Političeskoj literatury, 1965).

[93] *Ibid.* p. 76.

[94] *Ibid.* pp. 52–54.

[95] *Ibid.* p. 94.

[96] *Loc. cit.*

[97] *Ibid.* p. 55.

[98] *Loc. cit.*

[99] For Hegel's discussion of subjectivity see *Hegel's Philosophy of Right*, trans. T. M. Knox (Oxford, Clarendon Press, 1952, 1967), the Remark following Para. 140, pp. 94–103.

[100] Sogomonov, *Dobro i zlo, op. cit.* p. 58.

[101] Arxangel'skij, *Kurs lekcij* . . . , p. 186.

[102] Drobnickij and Kon, *Slovar' po etike*, p. 73.

[103] Arxangel'skij, *Kurs lekcij* . . . , p. 194.

[104] See above p. 121. Soviet discussions of the notion of 'interest' are to be examined in the next chapter.

[105] O. G. Drobnickij and T. A. Kuz'mina, *Kritika sovremennoj buržuaznoj etiki* (Critique of Contemporary Bourgeois Ethics), (Moscow, 'Vysšaja škola', 1966), p. 107.

[106] Drobnickij and Kon, *Slovar' po etike*, p. 190.

[107] *Ibid.* pp. 190–91.

[108] A. I. Titarenko, ed., *Marksistskaja etika*, p. 307.

[109] *Ibid.* p. 308.

[110] R. B. Brandt, *Ethical Theory* (Englewood Cliffs, N. J., Prentice-Hall, Inc., 1959), p. 152.

CHAPTER SIX

[1] I. Luppol, 'Social'naja etika Mabli i Morelli' (The Social Ethics of Mably and Morelly), *Trudy Instituta Krasnoj Professury*, vol. 1, pp. 42–58 (Giz., 1923).

[2] M. A. Kamyšan, 'Ob ob'ektivnom kriterii nravstvennogo progressa' (On an Objective Criterion of Moral Progress), *Filosofskie nauki* 1962, 5, 90–97.

[3] For an excellent survey of ethical thought in the French Enlightenment, see L. G. Crocker, *An Age of Crisis* (Baltimore, The Johns Hopkins Press, 1959); and *idem, Nature and Culture: Ethical Thought in the French Enlightenment* (Baltimore, The Johns Hopkins Press, 1964).

[4] Helvetius, *De l'Esprit*, quoted in Crocker, *Nature and Culture*, p. 263.

[5] La Mettrie, *Discours sur le bonheur, Oeuvres* (Paris, Charles Tutot, 1796), p. 171; quoted in Crocker, *Nature and Culture*, p. 259.

[6] See below pp. 143–46.

[7] Sogomonov, *Dobro i zlo* (Good and Evil), p. 45.

[8] De Mably, *De la superstition*; quoted in Crocker, *Nature and Culture*, p. 479.

[9] Helvetius, *De l'Homme*, quoted in Charles Frankel, *The Faith of Reason* (New York, King's Crown Press, 1948), p. 58, ftnt. 4.

[10] De Mably, *Principes de Morale, Oeuvres*, vol. X; quoted in Crocker, *Nature and Culture*, p. 479.

[11] Crocker, *ibid.* p. 480.

[12] *Ibid.* p. 463.

[13] E. F. Petrov, *Egoizm: filosofsko-etičeskij očerk* (Egoism: a Philosophico-Ethical Essay), (Moscow, 'Nauka', 1969), pp. 60–61.

[14] *Ibid.* p. 49.

[15] *Ibid.* p. 196.

[16] G. M. Gak, 'Obščestvennye i ličnye interesy i ix otnošenija pri socializme' (Social and Individual Interests and their Relations Under Socialism), *Voprosy filosofii* 1955, 4, 21.

[17] Drobnickij, in Xarčev, ed., *Problema cennosti*, p. 33.

[18] I. S. Kon, *Sociologija ličnosti* (Sociology of the Individual), (Moscow, Izd. političeskoj literatury, 1967), p. 9.

[19] B. D. Parygin, *Social'naja psixologija kak nauka* (Social Psychology as a Science), (Leningrad, Izd. Leningradskogo universiteta, 1965), p. 117.

[20] Xarčev and Jakovlev, pp. 194–95.

[21] P. M. Egides, 'Marksistskaja etika o smysle žizni' (Marxist Ethics on the Meaning of Life), *Voprosy filosofii* 1963, 8; and G. K. Gumnickij, 'Smysl žizni, sčast'e, moral'' (The Meaning of Life, Happiness, Morality), *Voprosy filosofii* 1967, 5.

[22] Xarčev and Jakovlev, p. 195.

[23] Kon, *Sociologija ličnosti*, p. 94.

[24] See above pp. 56–57.

[25] The phrase is Gustav Wetter's, quoted by N. Lobkowicz, 'Materialism and Matter in Marxism-Leninism' in Ernan McMullin, ed., *The Concept of Matter*, p. 463.

[26] G. M. Gak, 'Obščestvennye i ličnye interesy i ix otnošenija pri socializme', *Voprosy filosofii* 1955, 4.

[27] *Ibid.* p. 20.

[28] *Loc. cit.*

[29] *Ibid.* p. 19.

[30] *Ibid.* p. 21.

[31] *Ibid.* p. 20.

[32] A. G. Zdravomyslov, *Problema interesa v sociologičeskoj teorii* (The Problem of Interest in Sociological Theory), (Leningrad, Izd. Leningradskogo universiteta, 1964). See A. Ajzikovič, 'Obščestvennye interesy' (Social Interests), in *Filosofskaja enciklopedija* vol. 4, pp. 116–17.

[33] *Ibid.* p. 26.

[34] *Ibid.* p. 24.

[35] *Ibid.* p. 27.

[36] *Ibid.* pp. 29–30.

[37] *Ibid.* p. 32.

[38] *Ibid.* p. 24.

[39] H. B. Acton, *The Illusion of the Epoch* (London, Cohen and West, Ltd., 1955), pp. 112–13.

[40] *Ibid.* pp. 189–90.

[41] Drobnickij and Kon, eds., *Slovar' po etike*, 'Dolg' (Duty), p. 77.

[42] *Ibid.* pp. 78–79.

[43] *Ibid.* p. 77.

[44] E. V. Sokolov, *Nravstvennyj dolg i ego rol' v obščestvennoj žizni (aftoreferat)* (Moral Duty and its Role in Social Life – Author's Summary), (Leningrad, 1964), p. 13.

[45] *Loc. cit.*

[46] *Loc. cit.*

[47] *Ibid.* pp. 14–15.

[48] L. V. Konovalova, 'Dolg – central'naja kategorija etiki' (Duty – the Central Category of Ethics), in *Problemy kategorij marksistsko-leninskoj etiki*, p. 165.

[49] *Loc. cit.*

[50] Bandzeladze, *Etika*, 2nd ed., pp. 216f.

[51] *Ibid.* pp. 209–16.

[52] *Ibid.* p. 199.

[53] *Ibid.* p. 227.

[54] *Loc. cit.*

[55] *Ibid.* p. 228.

[56] *Ibid.* pp. 228–29.

[57] *Ibid.* p. 229.

[58] *Ibid.* pp. 229–30.

[59] *Ibid.* p. 236.

[60] *Ibid.* pp. 237–42.

[61] Drobnickij and Kon, eds., *Slovar' po etike*, 'Otvetstvennost'' (Responsibility), p. 214.

[62] *Ibid.* p. 215.

[63] For Sogomonov's argument, see above pp. 131–32.

[64] See for example, A. F. Plaxotnyj, 'Struktura i formy social'noj otvetstvennosti' (The Structure and Forms of Social Responsibility), in *Problemy kategorij marksistsko-leninskoj etiki*, pp. 182–86; and A. I. Orexovskij, 'O strukture kategorii otvetstvennosti' (On the Structure of the Category of Responsibility), *ibid*. pp. 192–97.

[65] Plaxotnyj, pp. 182–83.

[66] *Ibid*. p. 183.

[67] *Ibid*. p. 185.

[68] *Loc. cit.*

[69] V. E. Dolja, 'Kategorija svobody voli v etike' (The Category of Freedom of the Will in Ethics), *ibid*. p. 200.

[70] *Ibid*. pp. 200–01.

[71] Drobnickij and Kon, *Slovar' po etike*, 'Svoboda nravstvennaja' (Moral Freedom), p. 280.

[72] *Loc. cit.*

[73] *Ibid*. pp. 280–81.

[74] Šiškin, *Osnovy marksistskoj etiki* (Foundations of Marxist Ethics), p. 171.

[75] *Loc. cit.*

[76] *Ibid*. p. 173.

[77] F. G. Barghoorn, *Soviet Russian Nationalism* (New York, Oxford University Press, 1956), pp. 12–13.

[78] P. Stučka, 'Patriotizm' (Patriotism), in the *Enciklopedija gosudarstva i prava* (Encyclopedia of the State and Law), (Moscow, 1926–27, 3 vols.), vol. 3, pp. 252–54; quoted in Barghoorn, *loc. cit.*

[79] Barghoorn, p. 16.

[80] *Loc. cit.*

[81] For a detailed discussion of the Moral Code for the Builders of Communism, see R. T. DeGeorge, *Soviet Ethics and Morality* (Ann Arbor, University of Michigan Press, Ann Arbor Paperbacks, 1969). For the phrase quoted, see p. 83.

[82] Šiškin, *Osnovy marksistskoj etike*, pp. 277 and 263.

[83] *Ibid*. p. 259.

[84] *Ibid*. p. 265.

[85] *Ibid*. p. 266.

[86] *Ibid*. p. 273.

[87] Bandzeladze, *Etika*, 2nd ed., p. 358.

[88] *Ibid*. pp. 362–63.

CHAPTER SEVEN

[1] See above p. 123.

[2] See above pp. 127–28.

[3] See above p. 128.

[4] See above p. 129.

[5] Šiškin, *Osnovy marksistskoj etiki* (Foundations of Marxist Ethics), p. 185.

[6] W. Frankena, *Ethics*, p. 73.

[7] Šiškin, *Osnovy marksistskoj etiki*, p. 181.

[8] M. A. Kamyšan, 'Ob ob'ektivnom kriterii nravstvennogo progressa' (On the Objective Criterion of Moral Progress), *Filosofskie nauki* 1962, 5, 91.

[9] *Ibid.* p. 92.

[10] *Loc. cit.*

[11] *Loc. cit.*

[12] N. N. Kulikova and G. K. Gumnickij, 'K probleme kriterija nravstvennogo progressa' (On the Problem of the Criterion of Moral Progress), *Vestnik Moskovskogo Universiteta* 1965, 2, 35.

[13] *Loc. cit.*

[14] *Loc. cit.*

[15] *Loc. cit.*

[16] *Ibid.* p. 36.

[17] *Loc. cit.*

[18] *Ibid.* p. 38.

[19] *Ibid.* p. 39.

[20] *Loc. cit.*

[21] See A. I. Titarenko, *Kriterij nravstvennogo progressa* (The Criterion of Moral Progress), (Moscow, 'Mysl' , 1967); and *idem, Nravstvennyj progress* (Moral Progress), (Moscow, Izd. Moskovskogo universiteta, 1969).

[22] Titarenko, *Kriterij nravstvennogo progressa*, pp. 82–95.

[23] *Ibid.* p. 83.

[24] *Loc. cit.*

[25] *Loc. cit.*

[26] *Ibid.* p. 93.

[27] *Ibid.* p. 89.

[28] *Ibid.* p. 90.

[29] *Ibid.* p. 93.

[30] *Ibid.* pp. 93–94.

[31] *Ibid.* p. 94.

[32] *Loc. cit.*

[33] *Ibid.* p. 157.

[34] A. I. Titarenko, *Problema kriterija nravstvennogo progressa i nekotorye anglo-amerikanskie idealističeskie filosofsko-etičkeskie koncepcii (aftoreferat)* (The Problem of the Criterion of Moral Progress and Some Anglo-American Idealist Philosophico-Ethical Conceptions – author's summary), (Moscow, Izd. Moskovskogo universiteta, 1968), pp. 20–21.

[35] Titarenko, *Nravstvennyj progress*, pp. 172–73.

[36] *Ibid.* p. 174.

[37] *Hegel's Science of Logic*, trans. A. V. Miller, p. 832.

[38] Easton and Guddat, *Writings of the Young Marx on Philosophy and Society*, p. 292.

[39] T. B. Bottomore, trans. and ed., *Karl Marx, Early Writings* (New York, McGraw-Hill Book Company, 1964), p. 168.

[40] *Ibid.* p. 171.

[41] See above pp. 8–10.

[42] See M. Mandelbaum, 'Some Neglected Philosophic Problems Regarding History', *Journal of Philosophy*, XLIX (1952), 10, 317–28; and W. H. Dray, *Philosophy of History* (Englewood Cliffs, N. J., Prentice-Hall, Inc., 1964).

[43] Mandelbaum, p. 318.

[44] Marx, *Preface to the Critique of Political Economy*, excerpted in L. W. Feuer, ed., *Marx & Engels: Basic Writings on Politics & Philosophy* (Garden City, N. Y., Doubleday & Company Anchor Books, 1959), pp. 43–44.

[45] Marx and Engels, *The German Ideology*, ed. C. J. Arthur (London, Lawrence & Wishart, 1970), p. 32.

[46] Marx, *Grundrisse*, trans. Martin Nicolaus, pp. 493–95.

[47] Marx and Engels, *The German Ideology*, p. 50.

[48] See above p. 48.

[49] See above p. 50.

[50] See above p. 50.

[51] This claim is qualified somewhat below: see pp. 176ff.

[52] See above pp. 3–4.

[53] See A. Schmidt, *The Concept of Nature in Marx*, trans. B. Fowkes (Atlantic Highlands, N. J., Humanities Press, 1972), pp. 73–93.

[54] K. Marx, *Capital*, ed. F. Engels (New York, International Publishers, 1967), vol. 1, pp. 183–84.

[55] *Ibid*. p. 183.

[56] See Drobnickij's article in the anthology *Problema čeloveka v sovremennoj filosofii* (The Problem of Man in Contemporary Philosophy), ed. I. F. Balakina, *et. al.* (Moscow, 'Nauka', 1969), p. 193.

[57] *Loc. cit.*

[58] *Ibid*. p. 195.

[59] See above, Chapter Two, Footnote 43.

[60] Drobnickij, in Balakina, *Problema čeloveka*, p. 197.

[61] *Loc. cit.*

[62] *Ibid*. p. 198.

[63] Drobnickij, 'Problema cennosti i marksistskaja filosofija' (The Problem of Value and Marxist Philosophy), *Voprosy filosofii* 1966, 7, 40.

[64] O. I. Džioev, *Priroda istoričeskoj neobxodimosti* (The Nature of Historical Necessity), (Tbilisi, Izd. 'Mecniereba', 1967), p. 97.

[65] *Ibid*. p. 101.

[66] *Ibid*. p. 121.

[67] *Ibid*. p. 95.

[68] *Ibid*. p. 94.

[69] See above pp. 3–4.

[70] Džioev, p. 132.

[71] See above pp. 171ff.

[72] Džioev, pp. 134–35.

[73] O. I. Džioev, *Materialističeskoe ponimanie istorii i buržuaznaja filosofija* (The Materialist Conception of History and Bourgeois Philosophy), (Tbilisi, Izd. 'Mecniereba', 1974), p. 114.

[74] *Ibid*. p. 111.

[75] *Ibid*. p. 109.

[76] *Ibid*. p. 108.

[77] *Ibid*. p. 115.

CHAPTER EIGHT

[1] Ja. A. Mil'ner-Irinin, *Etika, ili Principy istinnoj čelovečnosti* (Ethics, or the Principles of True Humanity), (Moscow, 1963), manuscript. The first chapter of this work, slightly revised, was reprinted in Bandzeladze, ed., *Aktual'nye problemy marksistskoj etiki* (Current Problems of Marxist Ethics), pp. 253–302. See also the article by Mil'ner-Irinin, 'Etika – nauka o dolžnom' (Ethics – Science of that which Ought to Be), in the same volume, pp. 15–58.

[2] See his earlier work, *B. Spinoza* (Moscow, 1940).

[3] From personal conversation with the author.

[4] See above p. 239, note 86, for criticism of his works.

[5] For example see Bandzeladze's praise of Mil'ner-Irinin's *Etika* in the introductory pages of *Aktual'nye problemy*, p. 11; see also his discussion of Kant in his own *Etika*, 2nd ed., esp. pp. 209–19.

[6] Mil'ner-Irinin, 'Etika – nauka o dolžnom', p. 43.

[7] *Ibid*. p. 45.

[8] *Loc. cit.*

[9] *Ibid*. p. 47.

[10] *Ibid*. p. 48.

[11] *Ibid*. p. 49.

[12] *Ibid*. p. 50.

[13] *Ibid*. p. 51.

[14] *Ibid*. p. 52.

[15] *Ibid*. p. 53.

[16] *Ibid*. p. 54.

[17] *Ibid*. p. 48.

[18] Mil'ner-Irinin, 'Etika, ili Principy istinnoj čelovečnosti (princip sovesti)', in Bandzeladze, ed., *Aktual'nye problemy*, 269.

[19] *Loc. cit.*

[20] *Ibid*. p. 289.

[21] *Ibid*. p. 297, para. 169.

[22] *Ibid*. p. 298, para. 172.

[23] *Ibid*. p. 300.

[24] Mil'ner-Irinin, 'Etika – nauka o dolžnom', p. 22.

[25] *Ibid*. p. 37.

[26] *Ibid*. p. 15.

[27] *Ibid*. p. 19.

[28] *Ibid*. p. 44.

[29] See above p. 69.

[30] Quoted in Drobnickij, *Ponjatie morali, Istoriko-kritičeskij očerk* (The Concept of Morality, an Historico-Critical Essay), (Moscow, 'Nauka', 1974), p. 354, ftnt. 6. The references are to Bandzeladze, *Opyt izloženija sistemy markskstskoj etike* (Essay in the Exposition of the System of Marxist Ethics), p. 52; Samsonova, *Teoretičeskie problemy etiki* (Theoretical Problems of Ethics), pp. 21–22, 24, 26; Selivanov, *Etika, Očerk* (Ethics, An Essay), (Tomsk, 1961), p. 3. For the opposite view see A. G. Xarčev, *Leninizm i aktual'nye problemy morali* (Leninism and Current Problems of Morality), (Moscow, 1970), p. 538.

[31] Drobnickij, *op. cit*. p. 355.
[32] *Ibid*. p. 356.
[33] *Loc. cit*.
[34] *Ibid*. p. 357.
[35] *Loc. cit*.
[36] *Loc. cit*.
[37] *Loc. cit*.
[38] *Ibid*. pp. 357–58.
[39] *Ibid*. p. 359.
[40] V. F. Asmus, *Immanuil Kant* (Moscow, 'Nauka', 1973), p. 374.
[41] *Ibid*. p. 321.
[42] *Ibid*. p. 327.
[43] *Ibid*. p. 321.
[44] *Ibid*. pp. 322–23.
[45] K. Marks i F. Engel's, *Sočinenija* (Works), vol. 3, p. 182.
[46] N. Vinogradskaja, 'Etika Kanta s točki zrenija istoričeskogo materializma' (The Ethics of Kant from the Point of View of Historical Materialism), *Pod znamenem marksizma* 1924, nos. 4 and 5.
[47] *Ibid*. no. 4, p. 83.
[48] *Ibid*. p. 67.
[49] Asmus, *op. cit*. pp. 334–35.
[50] *Ibid*. pp. 337–42.
[51] *Ibid*. p. 342.
[52] *Ibid*. pp. 342–43.
[53] *Ibid*. p. 358.
[54] *Ibid*. p. 359.
[55] *Ibid*. p. 360.
[56] *Ibid*. p. 360–61.
[57] *Ibid*. p. 361.
[58] *Ibid*. pp. 374–78.
[59] See for example Kissel' and Emdin, below p. 205.
[60] See above pp. 65–67.
[61] See above p. 103.
[62] See above pp. 97–100.
[63] See above pp. 94–95.
[64] See above pp. 112 and 132.
[65] See above pp. 127–30.
[66] See above pp. 148–49.
[67] See above pp. 164–65.
[68] See above p. 191.
[69] Drobnickij, *Ponjatie morali*, p. 373.
[70] Drobnickij, 'Priroda moral'nogo soznanija' (The Nature of Moral Consciousness), *Voprosy filosofii* 1968, 2, 33.
[71] Drobnickij, *Ponjatie morali*, p. 346.
[72] *Ibid*. p. 372.
[73] *Ibid*. p. 355.
[74] *Loc. cit*.

[75] *Ibid.* p. 360.
[76] *Ibid.* p. 361.
[77] *Loc. cit.*
[78] *Ibid.* p. 365.
[79] *Ibid.* p. 367.
[80] *Loc. cit.*
[81] See above pp. 137ff.
[82] Drobnickij, *ibid.* p. 367.
[83] *Ibid.* p. 368.
[84] *Ibid.* p. 371.
[85] *Ibid.* p. 373.
[86] *Loc. cit.*
[87] *Loc. cit.*
[88] *Ibid.* p. 374.
[89] M. A. Kissel' and M. V. Emdin, *Etika Gegelja i krizis sovremennoj buržuaznoj etiki* (The Ethics of Hegel and the Crisis of Contemporary Bourgeois Ethics), (Leningrad, Izd. Leningradskogo universiteta, 1966).
[90] *Ibid.* p. 77.
[91] *Ibid.* p. 12.
[92] *Ibid.* p. 66.
[93] *Ibid.* p. 4.
[94] *Ibid.* pp. 16–17.
[95] *Ibid.* p. 17.
[96] *Loc. cit.*; Plekhanov quoted from his *Izbrannye filosofskie proizvedenija* (Selected Philosophical Works), (Moscow, 1956), vol. 1, p. 441.
[97] See above, esp. p. 44.
[98] Kissel' and Emdin, pp. 28ff.
[99] *Ibid.* p. 43.
[100] *Ibid.* p. 27.
[101] See for example K. A. Švarcman, *Etika . . . bez morali, Kritika sovremennyx buržuaznyx etičeskix teorij* (Ethics . . . Without Morality, A Critique of Contemporary Bourgeois Ethical Theories), (Moscow, 'Mysl'', 1964); O. G. Drobnickij and T. A. Kuz'mina, *Kritika sovremennyx buržuaznyx etičeskix koncepcij* (A Critique of Contemporary Bourgeois Ethical Conceptions), (Moscow, 'Vysšaja škola', 1967); and M. A. Kissel', *Očerk istorii etiki* (An Essay in the History of Ethics), (Moscow, 1969).
[102] Kissel', *Očerk istorii etiki*, chap. XIII, sec. 5; quoted in Titarenko, ed., *Marksistskaja etika*, chap. six, 'Kritika sovremennoj buržuaznoj etiki' (A Critique of Contemporary Bourgeois Ethics), (Gusejnov), p. 287.
[103] Drobnickij and Kuz'mina, *op. cit.* p. 148.
[104] *Ibid.* p. 196.
[105] *Loc. cit.*
[106] Gusejnov, *op. cit.* p. 296.
[107] Drobnickij and Kuz'mina, *op. cit.* pp. 149–58.
[108] Ayer, *Language, Truth and Logic*, p. 150; quoted in Drobnickij and Kuz'mina, *op. cit.* p. 190.
[109] Drobnickij and Kuz'mina, *op. cit.* p. 192.
[110] Ayer, *op. cit.* p. 158; quoted in Drobnickij and Kuz'mina, *op. cit.* p. 193.

[111] Drobnickij and Kuz'mina, *op. cit.*, p. 193.

[112] *Ibid.* p. 197.

[113] *Ibid.* p. 200–07.

[114] *Ibid.* p. 209.

[115] *Ibid.* p. 212.

[116] *Ibid.* p. 218.

[117] Švarcman, *Etika . . . bez morali*, pp. 116–25; see also Drobnickij and Kuz'mina, *op. cit.* pp. 183ff.

[118] Drobnickij and Kuz'mina, *op. cit.* p. 226.

[119] *Ibid.* p. 227.

[120] *Ibid.* p. 256.

[121] *Ibid.* pp. 256–60.

[122] See sources listed in note 101 above; plus P. Gajdenko, 'Ekzistencializm' (Existentialism) in *Filosofskaja enciklopedija*, vol. 5, pp. 538–42.

[123] Gusejnov, *op. cit.* p. 289.

[124] Drobnickij and Kuz'mina, *op. cit.* p. 273.

[125] Gusejnov, *op. cit.* p. 289.

[126] Drobnickij and Kuz'mina, *op. cit.* p. 269.

[127] Gusejnov, *op. cit.* p. 289; compare with Drobnickij and Kuz'mina, *op. cit.* p. 277.

[128] Gusejnov, *op. cit.* p. 290.

[129] Švarcman, *op. cit.* pp. 152–53.

[130] *Ibid.* p. 153.

[131] Sartre, *L'Etre et le Néant*, (Paris, 1943), p. 713; quoted in Švarcman, *op. cit.* p. 153.

[132] See for example Drobnickij and Kuz'mina, *op. cit.* pp. 283–88.

[133] *Ibid.* p. 298.

[134] *Ibid.* p. 306.

[135] *Ibid.* p. 307.

[136] *Ibid.* pp. 308–09.

[137] *Ibid.* p. 311.

[138] *Ibid.* p. 318.

CHAPTER NINE

[1] See above pp. 175ff.

[2] See above pp. 105ff.

[3] Paul Fussell, *The Great War and Modern Memory* (New York, Oxford University Press, 1975).

[4] *Ibid.* p. 21.

[5] *Ibid.* pp. 324–25, 335.

[6] See above p. 165.

[7] See above pp. 159–67.

[8] See above p. 181.

[9] See above p. 181.

[10] William Dray, 'Philosophy of History', in *The Encyclopedia of Philosophy*, P. Edwards, ed., vol. 6, p. 253.

[11] See above pp. 173ff.

[12] See above pp. 183–86.

APPENDIX

The following is the 'Bibliography on Ethics' which appeared in the second edition of *Marksizm i etika*, Ja. S. Rozanov, ed., Xar'kov, Gosudarstvennoe izdatel'stvo Ukrainy, 1925, 442p. A few corrections have been made in some entries, and further bibliographical data supplied where available.

Aksel'rod, A. (Ortodoks). *Počemy my ne xotim itti nazad*? (Why Don't We Want to Go Back?). In her *Filosofskie očerki* (Philosophical Essays), Giz., 1923, pp. 111–117. (Critique of Kantian ethics).

Aksel'rod, A. (Ortodoks). *O problemax idealizma* (Problems of Idealism), 2nd ed., Odessa, 1905. Reprinted in the anthology *Protiv idealizma* (Against Idealism), Giz., 1922, pp. 7–43.

Aksel'rod, A. (Ortodoks). 'Problema etiki v sovremennom osveščenii' (The Problem of Ethics in the Present Light), *Sovremennyj Mir*, 1907, nos. IX and X; located also in the book *Etika i materialističeskoe ponimanie istorii* (Ethics and the Materialist Conception of History), by K. Kautskij, Giz., Moscow, 1922, pp. 151–91; also included in this anthology.

Aksel'rod, A. (Ortodoks). 'Prostye zakony prava i nravstvennosti' (Simple Laws of Right and Morality), *Delo*, 1916, 1, 44–55. (See Martov's answer in his article 'Prostota xyže vorovstva').

Bazarov, V., 'Avtoritarnaja metafizika i avtonomnaja ličnost' (Authoritarian Metaphysics and the Autonomous Individual). In the anthology *Očerki realističeskogo mirovozzrenija* (Essays on a Realist Worldview), St. Petersburg, Izd. S. Dorovatovskogo i A. Čarušnikova, 1904, pp. 183–278.

Bogdanov, A., 'Celi i normy žizni' (Goals and Norms of Life), *Obrazovanie*, 1905, 7. Reprinted in his anthology *Novyj mir* (New World), Moscow, Izd. 'Kommunist', 1918, pp. 38–89.

Bauer, O., 'Marksizm i etika' (Marxism and Ethics), in the anthology *Etičeskaja problema v istoričeskom materializme* (The Ethical Problem in Historical Materialism), Moscow, Izd. 'Pul's žizni', 1907. Also included in this anthology. (Bauer defends the Kantian viewpoint).

Dembskij, D., *Pravo i nravstvennost' s točki zrenija istoričeskogo materializma* (Law and Morality from the Viewpoint of Historical Materialism); see his *Filosofija prava i nravstvennosti L. Petražickogo* (The Philosophy of Law and Morality of L. Petražickij), Xar'kov, 1909.

Dembskij, D., *Nravstvennost' i pravo s točki zrenija istoričeskogo materializma* (Morality and Law from the Viewpoint of Historical Materialism), Izd. 'Proletarij', 1925, 91p.

Dicgen, I., 'Moral' social-demokratii' (The Morality of Social Democracy), in his anthology *Filosofija social-demokratii* (The Philosophy of Social Democracy).

Engel's, F., *Ljudvig Fejerbax* (Ludwig Feuerbach) translated with a foreword and notes by G. V. Plekhanov, Moscow, Izd. 'Krasnaja Nov', 1923; see pp. 51–59.

Engel's, F., *Anti-Djuring* (*Filosofija, političeskaja ekonomija i socializm*), (Anti-Dühring – Philosophy, Political Economy and Socialism), St. Petersburg 1904. See Chapter 7, 'Nravstvennost' i pravo. Večnye istiny' (Morality and Law. Eternal Truths); Chapter 8, 'Nravstvennost' i pravo. Ravenstvo' (Morality and Law. Equality); Chapter 9, 'Nravstvennost' i pravo. Svoboda i neobxodimost' (Morality and Law. Freedom and Necessity); pp. 48–75 in the edition by 'Moskovskie Rabočie'.

Etičeskaja problema v istoričeskom materializme (The Ethical Problem in Historical Materialism), an anthology of articles with a foreword by Morkovnikov, trans. by Ja. Lindenberg, Moscow, Izd. 'Pul's Žizni', 1907. Contents: Kautskij, 'Razbor 'Učenija o nravstvennosti' Mengera' (A Review of Menger's 'Doctrine of Morality'); Ioffe, 'K etike Mandevillja i 'socializmu' Kanta' (Toward Mandeville's Ethics and the 'Socialism' of Kant); Bauer, 'Marksizm i etika' (Marxism and Ethics); Kautskij, 'Žizn', nauka, i etika' (Life, Science, and Ethics).

Forlender, K., *Kant i Marks, Očerki etičeskago socializma* (Kant and Marx, Essays in Ethical Socialism), translated by B. I. El'kin with a foreword by Prof. Tugan-Baranovskij, St. Petersburg, 1909. See the review by Deborin in *Sovremennyj Mir*, 1909, 9, pp. 115–17.

Forlender, K., *Kant i socializm* (Kant and Socialism), Moscow, Izd. 'Pul's Žizni', 1906, 80p.

Forlender, K., *Neokantianskoe divženie v socializme* The Neo–Kantian Movement in Socialism), Moscow, 'Pul's Žizni', 1907.

Forlender, K., *Sovremennyj socializm i filosofskaja etika* (Contemporary Socialism and Philosophical Ethics), translated from German, Moscow, Izd. 'Pul's Žizni', 1907. (Defends the Kantian viewpoint).

Gil'debrand, R., 'Evoljucija prava i nravov' (The Evolution of Law and Morals), *Naučnoe Obozrenie* (Science Survey), 1898, 2. Also in the journal *Obrazovanie*, 1896, 12. Presents a condensed exposition of the work. Concerning this work see the review in *Naučnoe Obozrenie*, 1899, 10.

Hildebrand, R., *Recht und Sitte auf dem verschiedenen wirtschaftlichen Kulturstufen*, 2nd ed., Jena, 1907. (1st ed., 1896).

Gorter, G., *Istoričeskij materializm* (Historical Materializm), Petrograd, Izd. 'Kommunist', 1919. See the chapter 'Nravy i nravstvennost'' (Morals and Morality), pp. 75–100.

Gofman, K., *Desjat' zapovedej pravjaščix klassov* (The Ten Commandments of the Ruling Class), translated from German. St. Petersburg, Izd. 'Mysl'', 1906.

Gofman, K., *Egoizm i socializm ili 'ja' i obščestvo* (Egoism and Socialism or 'I' and Society), translated from German by P. Gurevich, St. Petersburg, Izd. 'Mir', 1906.

Gurevich, G., *Pravo i nravstvennost' s točki zrenija materialističeskogo ponimanija istorii* (Law and Morality from the Viewpoint of the Materialist Conception of History), *Trudy Belorusskogo Gosudarstvennogo Universiteta*, vol. 1, Minsk, 1922. Also Izd. Socialističeskoj Akademii, Moscow, 1924, 46p.

Ioffe, A., *Ob etike Mandevillja i socializme Kanta* (On the Ethics of Mandeville and the Socialism of Kant), included in this anthology and in the anthology *Etičeskaja problema v istoričeskom materializme*.

Kautskij, K., *Obščestvennye instinkty v mire životnyx i ljudej* (The Social Instinct in the Animal and the Human Worlds), Petrograd, Izd. Kommunističeskogo Universiteta Zinov'eva, 1922, 90p. See 'Obščestvennye instinkty u ljudej' (The Social Instinct in Humans) printed also in the journal *Severnyj Vestnik*, 1890, 9. Also in his *Očerki i etjudy* (Essays and Studies), 4th ed., St. Petersburg, G. L'vovica, 1907.

Kautskij, K., 'Proisxoždenie morali' (Polemika s Kvesselem), (The Origin of Morality – A Polemic with Quessel). St. Petersburg, Izd. 'Dviženie', 1907.

Kautskij, K., 'Klassovaja bor'ba i etika' (The Class Struggle and Ethics). Appeared in his anthology *Očerednye problemy meždunarodnogo socializma* (Current Problems of International Socialism), Moscow, Izd. 'Kommunist', 1918.

Kautskij, K., 'Ešče ob etike' (Polemika s Bartom), (Once Again on Ethics – A Polemic with Barth).

Kautskij, K., 'Ešče raz klassovaja bor'ba i etika' (Polemika s Fersterom), (Once Again the Class Struggle and Ethics – A Polemic with Foerster).

Kautskij, K., 'Kannibal'skaja etika (Polemika s Kvesselem), (Cannibal Ethics – A Polemic with Quessel).

[The preceding five articles all appear in this anthology].

Kautskij, K., *Marksova teorija gosudarstva v osveščenii Kunova* (The Marxist Theory of the State as Interpreted by Cunow), translated from German by P. Vinogradskaja, with a preface by L. Rudaš, Moscow, Izd. Socialističeskoj Akademii, 1924. See Chapter III: 'Marks, kak etik: (Marx as an Ethical Theorist), pp. 19–22.

Kautskij, K., *Etika i materialističeskoe ponimanie istorii* (Ethics and the Materialist Conception of History), translated by K. Kogan and B. Jakovenko, St. Petersburg, 1906.

Also, translated by F. Kapeljuš, St. Petersburg, Izd. 'Mysl'', 1906, 90 p.

Also, edited by Dan, Izd. 'Novyj Mir', 1906.

Also, Odessa, Izd. Kippera, 1906.

Also, edited by Lunarčarskij, Izd. 'Znanie'.

Also, with appended article 'Žizn', nauka, i etika' (Life, Science, and Ethics), 1906.

Also, included in *Pervyj sbornik* (First Anthology), St. Petersburg, Izd. V. Korčagina, 1906, pp. 153–88.

Also, translated by M. Gel'rot, Odessa, Izd. A. Tkača, 1906.

Also, translated by P. Ratner, edited by A. Lunarčarskij, Petrograd, Izd. Petrogradskogo Soveta, 1918.

Also, translated by I. Postman, with appended articles: (1) Kautskij, 'Žizn', nauka, i etika' (Life, Science and Ethics), (2) Aksel'rod (Ortodoks), 'Etika Kautskogo' (Kautsky's Ethics). Moscow, Giz., 1922.

Also, (same translation and same appendix as the preceding), Moscow, Izd. 'Novaja Moskva', 1922, 191 pp.

Excerpts from this work entitled 'The Ethics of Kant' and 'The Foundations of Morality' are included in this anthology.

Kautskij, K., *Žizn', nauka, i etika. Polemika s O. Bauerom* (Life, Science, and Ethics, A Polemic with O. Bauer), translated by V. Veličkina, St. Petersburg, 1906, 31 p.

Also, Moscow, Izd. 'Kommunist', 1918.

Also, included in the anthology *Etičeskaja problema v istoričeskom materializme*, Moscow, Izd. 'Pul's Žizni', 1907.

Also, in the form of an appendix to *Etika i materialističeskoe ponimanie istorii*, Moscow, Izd. Skirmunta, 1906; similarly in the edition by Giz., Moscow, 1922, pp. 131–50.

Also included in this anthology.

Kautskij, K., ' "Novoe učenie o nravstvennosti" Mengera' (The 'New Doctrine of Morality' of Menger), translated from German by M. M–n, *Vestnik Žizni*, 1906, 5, 43–53.

Kollontaj, A., 'Moral' kak orudie klassovogo gospodstva i klassovoj bor'by' (Morality as a Weapon of Class Rule and the Class Struggle), *Molodaja Gvardija*, 1922, nos. 6 and 7, pp. 128–36.

Kollontaj, A., *Novaja moral' i rabočij klass* (The New Morality and the Working Class), Moscow, Izd. VCIK, 1918, 61p.

Kollontaj, A., 'Problema nravstvennosti s postivnoj točke zrenija' (The Problem of Morality from a Positive Point of View), *Obrazovanie*, 1905, 10, 11.

Kratov, A., 'Kommunizm i nravstvennost' (Etika v marksistskom miroponimanii)', (Communism and Morality – Ethics in the Marxist World Conception), *Junyj Proletarij*, 1922, nos. 1, 2.

Krživickij, L., *Etika v ee istoričeskom razvitii* (Ethics in its Historical Development), St. Petersburg, Izd. 'Vestnik Znanija', 1907. Also, Moscow, Izd. 'Novaja Moskva', 1924.

Kutter, *Oni dolžny. V zaščitu socialno-demokratičeskoj etiki* (They are Obligated, In Defense of Social Democratic Ethics), translated by M. Pokrovskij, Moscow, Izd. Mjagkova, 1906.

Kvessel', L., 'Obez'jana v roli vospitatelja' (The Monkey in the Role of Educator); 'Otvet Kautskomy' (An Answer to Kautsky). Both articles included in the present anthology.

Labriola, Antonio, *Istoričeskij materializm. (Očerki materialističeskogo ponimanija istorii)* (Historical Materialism. Essays in the Materialist Conception of History), translated by A. N. Gorlin, Petrograd, GIZ, 1922, pp. 142–49. Also published under the title *K voprosu o materialističeskom ponimanii istorii* (Toward the Problem of the Materialist Conception of History), Moscow, Izd. N. I. Berezina i M. Semenova, pp. 64–69.

Landri, A., 'K. Marks', in the anthology *Etjudy po moral'noj filosofii XIX v.* Studies in the Moral Philosophy of the XIXth Century), Moscow, Izd. 'Tvorčeskaja Mysl'', 1908.

Lafarg, P., *Ekonomičeskij determinizm Karla Marksa* (The Economic Determinism of Karl Marx), Moscow, Izd. 'Moskovskij Rabočij', 1923. See the essays: 'Proisxoždenie idei dobra' (Origin of the Idea of the Good), pp. 141–65; 'Proisxoždenie idei spravedlivosti' (Origin of the Idea of Justice), pp. 109–40. The last two essays were also issued as a separate edition by M. Malyx, Moscow, 1906.

Lozinskij, E., 'Sovremennye filosofskie iskanija' (Contemporary Philosophical Quests), *Mir Bozij*, 1904, 10, 84–108.

Lozinskij, E., 'Sovremennye etičeskie iskanija' (Contemporary Ethical Quests), *Obrazovanie*, 1904, 8, pp. 80–103; 9, 31–46. (A Critique of Kantian Ethics).

Lunačarskij, A., 'K voprosu ob ocenke' (Toward the Problem of Evaluation); see his *Etjudy*, Moscow, GIZ, 1922, pp. 53–71. Printed also in his *Etjudy polemičeskie i kritičeskie* (Polemical and Critical Etudes), Moscow.

Lunačarskij, A., 'Moral' i svoboda' (Morality and Freedom), *Krasnaja Nov'*, 1923, Book 7 (December), pp. 130–36. Also in *Put' Kommunizma*, Krasnodar, 1922, 2, 91–97.

Lunačarskij, A., 'Proletarskaja etika' (Proletarian Ethics), *Vestnik Žizni*, 1906, 6.

Lunačarskij, A., *Moral' s marksistskoj točke zrenija* (Morality from the Marxist Point of View), Izd. 'Akademija', 1925.

Lunačarskij, A., ' "Problemy idealizma" s točki zrenija kritičeskogo realizma' ('The Problem Idealism' from the Viewpoint of Critical Realism), *Obrazovanie*, 1903, 2. See the Chapter 'O probleme morali' (On the Problem of Morality), pp. 130–50.

Lunačarskij, A., [under the pseudonym A. Barsov], 'Etika i marksizm' (Ethics and Marxism), *Vestnik Žizni*, 1906, 1, 1924. (In response to Kautsky's *Ethics and the Materialist Conception of History*).

Luppol, I., 'Social'naja etika Mabli i Morelli' (The Social Ethics of Mably and Morelly), *Trudy Instituta Krasnoj Professury*, GIZ, 1923, vol. 1, pp. 42–58.

Marks, K., 'Moralizujuščaja kritika i kritikujuščaja moral'' (Moralising Criticism and Criticising Morality), *Pod Znamenem Marksizma*, 1923, 4–5, 21–42. With notes by D. Rjazanov.

Marks, K., 'Declaration of Principles of the International Association of Workingmen' (1864). See the First Appendix to the book *Zamečanija na programmu germanskoj rabočej partii* (*Kritika Gotskoj programmy*) (Notes on the Program of the German Workers' Party – Critique of the Gotha Program), with an introductory article by K. Korsch, translated from German by N. Alekseeva, Petrograd, GIZ, 1923, pp. 76–77.

Marks, K., *Pervyj Manifest meždunarodnogo Tovariščestva Rabočix (1864)* (First Manifesto of the International Brotherhood of Workers, 1864), St. Petersburg, Izd. 'proletarij', 1906, p. 15. First printed in the Russian language in Geneva in 1903. Also, 2nd edition, 1906. Aĩso St. Petersburg, Izd. 'Mysl'', 1917.

Marks, K., 'Pis'mo k Engel'su (ot 4 nojabrja 1864)' (Letter to Engels, 4 November, 1864). See K. Marks in F. Engel's, *Pis'ma* (Letters), translated with notes by V. Adoratskij, Moscow, Izd., 'Moskovskij Rabočij', 1922, pp. 197–201.

Marks, K., (and Engel's, F.), *Svjatoj Maks* (*Kritika učenja Štirnera*), (Saint Max – A Critique of the Doctrine of Stirner), Moscow, Giz., 1920, p. 246. 'O vozrastajuščem licemerii buržuazii' (On the Growing Hypocrisy of the Bourgeoisie).

Marksizm i etika. Sbornik statej (Marxism and Ethics. An Anthology of Articles), 1st edition, Kiev, Gosudarstvennoe Izdatel'stvo Ukrainy, 1923, 318pp.

Martov, L., 'Marks s Kantom, Kant s Gindenburgom' (Marx with Kant, Kant with Hindenburg), *Letopis'*, 1916, 3, 164–70. Also Petrograd, Izd. 'Socialist', 1917.

Martov, L., 'Prostota xuže vorovstva' (A Simplicity Worse than Theft), Petrograd, Izd. 'Socialist', 1917, 31 p.

Mering, F., 'Suščestvuet li edinaja etika?' (Does There Exist a Single Ethics?), in the anthology *Marksizm i etika*.

Mering, F., 'Etika i klassovaja bor'ba' (Ethics and the Class Struggle), *ibid*.

Mering, F., 'Etika, etika . . . bez konca' (Ethics, Ethics . . . Without End), *ibid*.

N. N., *O proletarskoj etike* (On Proletarian Ethics), with a preface and edited by N. Rozkov, Moscow, Izd. Mjagkov, 1906. Also Moscow, Izd. VCIK, 1918. Also, Kar'kov, Izd. 'Proletarij', 1923.

Nezdanov, P., *Nravstvennost' pered sudom ekonomičeskogo materializma* (Morality Under the Judgment of Economic Materialism), Moscow, 1903, 337p. (The author 'reconciles' Marx with Kant).

Orlov, I., 'Materializm i razvitie nravstvennosti' (Materialism and the Development of Morality), in the anthology *Voinstvujuščij materialist* (The Militant Materialist), Izd. 'Materialist', vol. 1, 1924, pp. 53–80.

Pannekek, A., *Etika i socializm* (Ethics and Socialism), translated by P. Gurevič, St. Petersburg, Izd. 'Mir', 1907.

Plekhanov, G. V., *N. G. Černyševskij*, Izd. 'Šipovnik'. See the Chapter 'Učenie o nravstvennosti' (The Doctrine of Morality), pp. 109–20.

Plekhanov, G. V., 'O moral'nyx vozzrenija Gol'baxa i Gel'vecija' (On the Moral Views of

Holbach and Helvetius). See *Očerki istorii materializma* (Essays in the History of Materialism), *Sobrannie sočinenija* (Collected Works), vol. 1, pp. 39–46 and 82–90.

Plekhanov, G. V., 'Primečanija k russkomu perevodu knigi F. Engel'sa Ljudvig Fejerbax' (Notes to the Russian Translation of F. Engels' *Ludwig Feuerbach*), Moscow, Izd. 'Kransnaja Nov'', 1923, pp. 133–40.

Plekhanov, G. V., 'O vojne' (On the War), *Sovremennyj Mir*, 1915, 1, 192–96.

Plekhanov, G. V., 'Ešče o vojne' (Once Again on the War), *Sovremennyj Mir*, 1915, 8, 217–52.

Preobraženskij, *O morali i klassovyx normax* (On Morality and Class Norms), GIZ, 1923, 114p.

Rozkov, N., 'Istorija, moral', i politika' (History, Morality and Politics), *Pravda* (the journal), 1901, 1. It appeared also in the first part of his *Istoričeskie i sociologičeskie očerki* (Historical and Sociological Essays), Moscow, 1906, pp. 1–19.

Stolpner, B., and Juškevič, P., *Istorija filosofii v marksistskom osveščenii* (The History of Philosophy in a Marxist Interpretation), Part One, Moscow, Izd. 'Mir', 1924, 292p.; Part Two, 436p. (Consists of a collection of articles and excerpts from the writings of Marx, Engels, Plekhanov, Lenin, Kautsky, and others).

Struve, P., 'Filosofija ideal'nogo dobra ili apologija real'nogo zla' (Kritika st. V. Solov'eva: 'Ekonomičeskij vopros s nravstvennoj točki zrenija'), (The Philosophy of Ideal Good and an Apology for Real Evil), (A critique of V. Solov'ev's article: 'The Economic Question from a Moral Point of View), in the anthology *Na Raznye Temy* (On Various Themes), St. Petersburg, 1901, pp. 187–97.

Tarnovskij, E., 'Etičeskaja problema marksizma' (The Ethical Problem of Marxism), *Vestnik Evropy*, 1908, 10.

Troickij, A., 'Etičeskie vzgljady Gel'vecija' (The Ethical Views of Helvetius), *Trudy Instituta Krasnoj Professury*, vol. 1, Giz., 1923, pp. 35–41.

Vinogradskaja, N., 'Etika Kanta s točki zrenija istoričeskogo materializma' (Kantian Ethics from the Viewpoint of Historical Materialism), *Pod Znamenem Marksizma*, 1924, 4 and 5.

Vol'skij, S., *Filosofija bor'by, Opyt postroenija etiki marksizma* (The Philosophy of Struggle, An Attempt to Construct an Ethic for Marxism), Moscow, Izd. 'Slovo', 1909, 311p.

Vol'tman, L., *Sistema moral'nogo soznanija v svjazi s otnošeniem kritičeskoj filosofii k darvinizmu i socializmu* (The System of Moral Consciousness in Connection with the Relation of Critical Philosophy to Darwinism and Socialism), translated under the direction of M. Filippov, St. Petersburg, Izd. Zjabickogo i Pjatina, 1901.

Vol'tman, L., 'Etika i istoričeskij materializm' (Ethics and Historical Materialism). See his book *Istoričeskij materializm* (Historical Materialism), translated from the German by M. Filippov, St. Petersburg, 1901, pp. 294–305. (The author takes the Kantian viewpoint).

SELECTED BIBLIOGRAPHY

(A Bibliography of works from 1945 to 1962 has been published by R. T. DeGeorge in *Studies in Soviet Thought*, 1963, 82–103; a bibliography of works through 1971 has been published by P. Ehlen in his *Die philosophische Ethik in der Sowjetunion* (Munich, Anton Pustet, 1972), pp. 433–55).

Acton, H. B., *The Illusion of the Epoch*, London, Cohen and West, Ltd., 1955, 278p.

Adler, M., *Kausalität und Teleologie im Streite um die Wissenschaft*, in Adler, M., and Hilferding, R., *Marx-Studien, Blätter zur Theorie und Politik des wissenschaftlichen Sozialismus*, vol. 1, Vienna, Wiener Volksbuchhandlung, 1904, pp. 193–433.

Adler, M., *Marxistische Probleme, Beitrag zur Theorie der materialistischen Geschichts-auffassung und Dialektik*, Stuttgart, Verlag von I. H. W. Dietz Nachf. G.m.b.H., 1931, 316p.

Aksel'rod, L., *Filosofskie očerki: otvet filosofskim kritikam istoričeskogo materializma* (Philosophical Essays: an Answer to Philosophical Critics of Historical Materialism), St. Petersburg, Izd. M. M. Druzininoj, 1906, 233p.

Aksel'rod, L., 'Prostye zakony nravstvennosti i prava' (Simple Laws of Morality and Right), *Delo*, 1916, 1; reprinted in Rozanov, Ja. S., ed., *Marksizm i etika*, pp. 219–231.

Anisimov, S. F., *Nravstvennyj progress i religija* (Moral Progress and Religion), Moscow, "Mysl' ", 1965, 183p.

Anisimov, S. F., Švarcman, K. A., Rubinskij, L. I., Osadčij, A. Ja., 'Aktual'nye voprosy razvitija marksistsko-leninskoj etiki' (Current Problems in the Development of Marx-ist-Leninist Ethics), VF, 1975, 2, 153–58.

Arxangel'skij, L. M., *Kategorii marksistskoj etiki* (The Categories of Marxist Ethics), Moscow, Socekgiz, 1963, 271p.

Arxangel'skij, L. M., *Kurs leckij po marksistsko-leninskoj etiki* (A Course of Lectures in Marxist-Leninist Ethics), Moscow, Vysšaja škola, 1974, 318p.

Arxangel'skij, L. M., 'Nravstvennoe razvitie ličnosti v uslovijax socializma' (The Moral Development of the Individual under Socialist Conditions), FN, 1975, 4, 14–21.

Arxangel'skij, L. M., 'O filosofskom xaraktere marksistskoj etike i ee strukture' (On the Philosophical Character of Marxist Ethics and its Structure), FN, 1970, 1, 110–18.

Arxangel'skij, L. M., 'Rol' i mesto nravstvennogo vospitanija v sisteme formirovanija novogo čeloveka' (The Role and Place of Moral Education in the System for Forming the New Man), VF, 1977, 2, 13–23.

Arxangel'skij, L. M., 'Sověščanie po etike učenyx socialističeskix stran [Warsaw, June, 1973] (Conference on ethics of Scientists from the Socialist Countries, Warsaw, June, 1973), FN, 1974, 1, 159–61.

Arxangel'skij, L. M., 'Suščnost' etičeskix kategorij' (The Essence of Ethical Categories), FN, 1961, 3, 117–25.

Arxangel'skij, L. M., Višnevskij, Ju. R., 'Ob'ekt issledovanija – nravstvennoe soznanie'

(Object of Investigation – Moral Consciousness), *Struktura Morali*, 2nd issue, 1973, 52–70 [Sverdlovskij Ural'skij gosudarstvennyj universitet].

Asmus, V. F., *Immanuil Kant*, Moscow, 'Nauka', 1973, 535p.

Averin, N. M., 'O značenii moralizatorstva v etičeskom analize' (On the Significance of Moralizing in Ethical Analysis), FN, 1974, 3, 130.

Averin, N. M., 'Priroda obščečelovečeskogo v morali' (The Nature of the Universally-Human in Morality), FN, 1973, 2, 33–40.

Avineri, S., ed., *Karl Marx on Colonialism and Modernization*, Garden City, N.Y., Doubleday & Co., 1968, 464p.

Bakradze, K. S., *Sistema i method filosofii Gegelja* (The System and Method of the Philosophy of Hegel), Tbilisi, Izd. Tbilisskogo universiteta, 1958; reprinted as vol. 2 of his *Izbrannye filosofskie trudy* (Selected Philosophical Works), Tbilisi, Izd. Tbilisskogo universiteta, 1973, 463p.

Bakśtanovskij, V. I., 'Dialektika cel' i sredstv v moral'nom vybore' (The Dialectic of Ends and Means in Moral Choice), FN, 1977, 1, 34–42.

Bakuradze, O. M., 'Istina i cennost" (Truth and Value), VF, 1966, 7, 45–48.

Bakuradze, O. M., 'Svoboda i neobxodimost" [Avtoreferat] (Freedom and Necessity), Doctoral dissertation, author's summary, Tbilisi, 1964, 46p.

Balakina, I. F., 'Probleme cennostej – vnimanie issledovatelej' (The Problem of Values – Attention Researchers), VF, 1965, 152–57.

Bandzeladze, G. D., *Etika* (Ethics), 2nd edition of *Opyt izloženija sistema marksistskoj etiki*, Tbilisi, 'Sabčota Sakartvelo', 1970, 465p.

Bandzeladze, G. D., 'Opyt issledovanija osnov marksistskoj etiki' [avtoreferat] (An Essay in the Investigation of the Foundations of Marxist Ethics), Doctoral dissertation, author's summary, Tbilisi, 1963, 73p.

Bandzeladze, G. D., *Opyt izloženija sistema marksistskoj etiki* (An Essay in the Exposition of the System of Marxist Ethics), Tbilisi, 'Sabčota Sakartvelo', 1963, 474p.

Bandzeladze, G. D., ed., *Aktual'nye problemy marksistskoj etiki* [*sbornik statej*] (Current Problems of Marxist Ethics [an Anthology]), Tbilisi, Izd. Tbilisskogo gosudarstvennogo universiteta, 1967, 495p.

Berdiajew, N., 'Friedrich Albert Lange und die kritische Philosophie in ihren Beziehungen zum Sozialismus', *Neue Zeit*, 1899–1900, 28(2), 132–40, 164–74, 196–207.

Berdjaev, N., *Novoe srednevekov'e: Razmyšlenie o sud'be Rossii i Evropy* (The New Middle Ages: Thoughts on the Fate of Russia and Europe), Berlin, Obelisk, 1924, 142p.

Berdjaev, N., *Smysl istorii* (The Meaning of History), Berlin, Obelisk, 1923, 268p.

Berdjaev, N., *Sub'ektivizm i individualizm v obščestvennoj filosofii* (Subjectivism and Individualism in Social Philosophy), St. Petersburg, Električeskaja tipografija, 1901, 267p.

Berlin, I., *Karl Marx, his Life and Environment*, 2nd edition, London, Oxford University Press, 1948, 280p.

Bernstein, E., *Die Voraussetzungen des Sozialismus und die Aufgaben der Sozialdemokratie*, 1899; translated as *Evolutionary Socialism, A Critique and Affirmation*, by E. C. Harvey, New York, Schocken Books, 1961, 224p.

Blakeley, T. J., *Soviet Theory of Knowledge*, Dordrecht-Holland, D. Reidel Publishing Company, 1964, 203p.

Bljumkin, V. A., 'Ešče raz o predmete etike' (Once Again on the Object of Ethics), FN, 1972, 1, 29–35.

Bogomolov, A. S., 'Filosofija Gegelja i sovremennost" (The Philosophy of Hegel and the Present), *Kommunist*, 1970, 14, 99–110.

Bogomolov, A. S., 'Gegel' i naše vremja' (Hegel and Our Time), *Vestnik Moskovskogo universiteta, Filosofija*, 1970, 4, 3–14.

Borisov, A. G., 'Osobennosti otricatel'nyx javlenij v soznanii i povedenii otdel'nyx ljudej v uslovijax razvitogo socializma' (Particular Features of Negative Phenomena in the Consciousness and Behavior of Individual Persons under Conditions of Developed Socialism), FN, 1977, 3, 49–56.

Borovskij, M. I., *Determinizm i nravstvennoe povedenie ličnosti* (Determinism and the Moral Behavior of the Individual), Minsk, 'Nauka i texnika', 1974, 222p. [reviewed by Arxangel'skij and Ivančuk, VF, 1975, 8, 178].

Borovskij, M. I., *O kriterii nravstvennosti* (On the Criterion of Morality), Minsk, Izd. 'Nauka i Texnika', 1970, 168p.

Brandt, R. B., *Ethical Theory*, Englewood Cliffs, N. J., Prentice-Hall, Inc., 1959, 538p.

Celikova, O. P., *Kommunističeskij ideal' i nravstvennoe razvitie ličnosti* (The Communist Ideal and the Moral Development of the Individual), Moscow, Izd. 'Nauka', 1970, 207p.

[Celikova, O. P.], 'Osobennosti vyraženija v jazyke moral'no-etičeskogo soderžanija' (Peculiarities in the Linguistic Expression of Moral-Ethical Contents), in *Moral i etičeskaja teorija*, pp. 144–93.

Cohen, H., 'Einleitung mit kritischem Nachtrag' to the 5th German edition of F. A. Lange, *Geschichte des Materialismus*, Leipzig, J. Baedeker, 1896.

Cohen, H., *Ethik des reinen Willens*, 3rd edition, Berlin, B. Cassirer, 1921, 672p.

Cohen, H., *Kants Begründung der Ethik*, Berlin, F. Dümmler (Harrwitz und Gossman), 1877, 328p.

Crocker, L. G., *An Age of Crisis: Man and the World in Eighteenth Century Thought*, The Johns Hopkins Press, 1959, 469p.

Crocker, L. G., *Nature and Culture: Ethical Thought in the French Enlightenment*, Baltimore, The Johns Hopkins Press, 1964, 540p.

Čagin, B. A., Šaxnovič, M. I., and Meleščenko, Z. N., eds., *Očerk istorii etiki* (Essay in the History of Ethics), Moscow, Izd. 'Mysl'', 1969, 430p.

Čermenina, A. P., 'Problema otvetstvennosti v etike' [Avtoreferat] (The Problem of Responsibility in Ethics), Candidate's dissertation, author's summary, Leningrad, 1965, 21p.

Černokozova, V. N., and Černokozov, I. I., *Osnovy kommunističeskoj morali* (Fundamentals of Communist Morality), Moscow, 'Molodaja gvardija', 1971, 336p.

Davidovič, V. E., *Problema čelovečeskoj svobody* (The Problem of Human Freedom), L'vov, Izd. L'vovskogo universiteta, 1967, 248p.

Deborin, A. M., *Filosofija i politika* (Philosophy and Politics), Moscow, Izd. AN SSSR, 1961, 747p.

Deborin, A. M., 'Revizionizm pod maskoj ortodoksii' (Revisionism in the Guise of Orthodoxy), *Pod Znamenem Marksizma*, 1927, 9, 5–48; 1927, 12, 5–33; 1928, 1, 5–44.

Deborin, A. M., [review of Forlender, *Kant i Marks*], *Sovremennyj mir*, 1909, vol. 9, 115–17.

DeGeorge, R. T., 'The Foundations of Marxist-Leninist Ethics', *Studies in Soviet Thought*, 1963, 3, 121–33.

DeGeorge, R. T., *Patterns of Soviet Thought*, Ann Arbor, University of Michigan Press, 1966, 293 p.

DeGeorge, R. T., *Soviet Ethics and Morality*, Ann Arbor, University of Michigan Press, 1969, 184 p.

DeGeorge, R. T., 'Soviet Ethics and Soviet Society', *Studies in Soviet Thought*, 1964, 3, 206–17.

Drobnickij, O. G., 'Kant – etik i moralist' (Kant – Ethical Theorist and Moralist), VF, 1974, 4, 141–53 [published posthumously].

Drobnickij, O. G., *Mir oživšix predmetov, Problema cennosti i marksistskaja filosofija* (The World of Revivified Objects, The Problem of Value and Marxist Philosophy), Moscow, Izd. političeskoj literatury, 1967, 351 p.

Drobnickij, O. G., 'Moral'noe soznanie i ego struktura' (Moral Consciousness and its Structure), VF, 1972, 2, 31–42.

Drobnickij, O. G., 'Nekotorye aspekty problemy cennostej' (Some Aspects of the Problem of Values), in *Problema cennosti v filosofii*, pp. 25–40.

Drobnickij, O. G., *Ponjatie morali* The Concept of Morality), Moscow, 'Nauka', 1974, 388 p. [published posthumously].

Drobnickij, O. G., 'Priroda moral'nogo soznanija' (The Nature of Moral Consciousness), VF, 1968, 2, 26–37.

Drobnickij, O. G., 'Problema cennosti i marksistskaja filosofija' (The Problem of Value and Marxist Philosophy), VF, 1966, 7, 33–44.

Drobnickij, O. G., 'Struktura moral'nogo soznanija' (The Structure of Moral Consciousness), VF, 1972, 6, 51–62.

Drobnickij, O. G., 'Teoretičeskie osnovy etiki Kanta' (The Theoretical Foundations of Kant's Ethics), Ch. IV of Ojzerman, T. I., ed., *Filosofija Kanta i Sovremennost'*, Moscow, Izd. 'Mysl'', 1974, 469 p.

Drobnickij, O. G., and Kon, I. S., eds., *Slovar' po etike* (Dictionary of Ethics), 2nd edition, Moscow, Izd. političeskoj literatury, 1970, 398 p.

Drobnickij, O. G., and Kuz'mina, T. A., *Kritika sovremennyx buržuaznyx etičeskix koncepcij* (A Critique of Contemporary Bourgeois Ethical Conceptions), Moscow, 'Vysšaja škola', 1967, 383 p.

Dubko, E. L., 'Sud'ba morali v psixoanalize' (The Fate of Morality in Psychoanalysis), FN, 1976, 3, 90–96.

Džioev, O. I., *Materialističeskoe ponimanie istorii i buržuaznaja filosofija* (The Materialist Conception of History and Bourgeois Philosophy), Tbilisi, Izd. 'Mecniereba', 1974, 119 p.

Džioev, O. I., *Priroda istoričeskoj neobxodimosti* (The Nature of Historical Necessity), Tbilisi, Izd. 'Mecniereba', 1967, 136 p.

Egides, P. M., 'Marksistskaja etika o smysle žizni' (Marxist Ethics on the Meaning of Life), VF, 1963, 8, 25–36.

Egides, P. M., 'Osnovnoj vopros etiki kak filosofskoj nauki i problema nravstvennogo otčuždenija' (The Fundamental Problem of Ethics as a Philosophical Science and the Problem of Moral Alienation), in Bandzeladze, ed., *Aktual'nye problemy marksistskoj etiki*, pp. 59–108.

Ehlen, P., *Die philosophische Ethik in der Sowjetunion, Analyse und Diskussion*, Munich, Anton Pustet, 1972, 461 p.

Engels, F., *Ljudvig Fejerbax i konec klassičeskoj nemeckoj filosofii* (Ludwig Feuerbach and the End of Classical German Philosophy), 2nd edition, translated and edited by G. V. Plekhanov, Geneva, 1905; available in English in Plekhanov, G. V., *Selected Philosophical Works*, vol. 1, London, Lawrence & Wishart, 1961.

Engels, F., *Ludwig Feuerbach and the End of Classical German Philosophy*, in *Karl Marx and Frederick Engels, Basic Writings on Politics and Philosophy*, edited by L. S. Feuer, Garden City, N. Y., Doubleday & Company, Inc., Anchor Books, 1959, pp. 195–242.

Engels, F., *Herr Eugen Dühring's Revolution in Science (Anti-Dühring)*, New York, International Publishers, 1939, 1966, 365p.

Ermolaeva, V. E., 'Etika i logika' (Ethics and Logic), VF, 1968, 11, 78–83.

Eichhorn, W., *Wie ist Ethik als Wissenschaft möglich?*, Berlin, VEB Deutscher Verlag der Wissenschaften, 1965, 176p.

Feuerbach, L., *The Fiery Brook: Selected Writings of Ludwig Feuerbach*, translated by Z. Hanfi, Garden City, N. Y., Doubleday & Company, Anchor Books, 1972, 302p.

Filosofija Gegelja i sovremennost' (The Philosophy of Hegel and the Present), Moscow, Izd. 'Mysl'', 1973, 431p.

Filosofskaja enciklopedija, F. V. Konstantinov, Editor-in-chief, Moscow, 'Sovetiskaja enciklopedija', 1960–1970, 5 volumes.

Foerster, F. W., 'Klassenkampf und Ethik', *Neue Zeit*, 1900–01, 19(1), 438–41.

Foerster, F. W., 'Soziale Demokratie und Ethik – ein neues Kapitel aus dem englischen Munizipalsozialismus', *Soziale Praxis*, 1901, vol. 10, 4.

Frank, S., *Nravstvennyj vodorazdel v russkoj revoljucii* (The Moral Watershed in the Russian Revolution), Moscow, Izd. G. A. Lemana i S. I. Saxarova, 1917, 14p.

Frankena, W. K., *Ethics*, Englewood Cliffs, N. J., Prentice-Hall, 1963, 109p.

Fritzhand, M., *Główne zagadnienia i kierunki metaetyki: o metaetyce, intuicjonizme, i emotywizmie* (Main Problems and Directions of Metaethics: On Metaethics, Intuitivism and Emotivism), Warsaw, Książka i Wiedza, 1970, 428p.

Fritzhand, M., *Myśl Etyczna Młodego Marksa* (The Ethical Thought of the Young Marx), Warsaw, Książka i Wiedza, 1961, 349p.

Fritzhand, M., *W kręgu etyki marksistowskiej: szkice i polemiki etyczne* (In the Marxist Ethical Framework: Essays and Polemic in Ethics), Warsaw, Książka i Wiedza, 1966, 338p.

Furščik, M., 'O liberal'nom i marksistskom ponimanii etiki' (On the Liberal and the Marxist Understanding of Ethics), *Bolshevik*, 1930, 6.

Fussell, P., *The Great War and Modern Memory*, New York, Oxford University Press, 1975, 363p.

Gak, G. M., 'Obščestvennye i ličnye interesy i ix sočetanie pri socializme' (Social and Individual Interests and their Combination under Socialism), VF, 1955, 4, 17–28.

Ganžin, V. T., Sarov, V. D., Simpozium po etike učenyx GDR i SSSR v Moskovskom universiteta [May–June, 1974] (Symposium on Ethics of Scientists from the DDR and USSR in Moscow University), FN, 1975, 3, 128–32.

Gegel' i dialektičeskij materializm: Sbornik statej k 100-letuja so dnja smerti Gegelja (Hegel and Dialectical Materialism: An Anthology for the 100th Anniversary of the Death of Hegel), Institut Filosofii, Kommunističeskaja Akademija, Moscow, Partijnoe Izd., 1932.

Gegel' i filosofija v Rossii, 30-e gody XIX v. – 20-e gody XX v. (Hegel and Philosophy in Russia, 1830's to the 1920's), Moscow, 'Nauka', 1974, 264p.

Golovko, N. A., Konovalova, L. V., 'Konferencija etikov socialističeskix stran Evropy [Warsaw, June, 1973]' (Conference of Ethical Theorists from the Socialist Countries of Europe), VF, 1973, 12, 164–65.

Golovko, N. A. and Markov, V. S., 'Za naučnost' i konkretnost' v razrabotke problem etiki' (For Science and Concreteness in Solving the Problems of Ethics), VF, 1968, 8, 148–55.

Gontarev, G. A., and Xajkin, A. L., 'Razvitie marksistskoj etičeskoj mysli v SSSR' (The Development of Marxist Ethical Thought in the USSR), FN, 1967, 5, 79–87.

Gorskij, D. P., 'Istina i ee kriterij' (Truth and its Criterion), VF, 1962, 2, 121–33.

Gumnickij, G. N., 'K voprosu o kriterii nravstvennogo progressa' (On the Question of the Criterion of Moral Progress), Učenie zapiski Ivanovskogo pedogogičeskogo instituta, 1973, vol. 114, 140–54.

Gumnickij, G. N., 'Pis'mo k redakciju' (Letter to the Editor), FN, 1973, 5, 157–58.

Gumnickij, G. N., 'Smysl žizni, sčast'e, moral'' (The Meaning of Life, Happiness, Morality), VF, 1967, 5, 102–05.

Gurenko, M. M., 'Issledovanie klassovogo xaraktera morali' (Investigation of the Class Character of Morality), VF, 1974, 1, 133–38.

Gusejnov, A., Kvasov, G., 'Etičeskaja nauka v socialističeskom obščestve' (Ethical Science in Socialist Society), Kommunist, 1976, 3, 70–79.

Hegel, G. W. F., Hegel's Philosophy of Nature, translated by A. V. Miller (with a Foreword by J. N. Findlay), Oxford, Clarendon Press, 1970, 450p.

Hegel, G. W. F., Hegel's Philosophy of Right, translated by T. M. Knox, Oxford, Claredon Press, 1952, 1967, 382p.

Hegel, G. W. F., The Philosophy of History, translated by J. Sibree, New York, Dover Publications, 1956, 457p.

Hegel, G. W. F., The Science of Logic, translated by A. V. Miller (with a Foreword by J. N. Findlay), London, Allen & Unwin, 1969, 845p.

Hodges, D. C., Socialist Humanism, The Outcome of Classical European Morality, St. Louis, Warren H. Green, Inc., 1974, 362p.

Huxley, T. H., 'Evolution and Ethics' (Romanes Lecture, 1893), reprinted in Thomas H. Huxley and Julian Huxley, Touchstone for Ethics, 1893–1943, New York, Harper & Brothers, 1947, 257p.

Ivin, A. A., 'Deontičeskaja logika' (Deontic Logic), VF, 1966, 12, 160–71.

Ivin, A. A., 'Logičeskie teorii absoljutnyx i otnositel'nyx normativnyx ponjatij' (Logical Theories of Absolute and Relative Normative Concepts), Vestnik Moskovskogo universiteta, 1970, 6, 58–67.

Ivin, A. A., 'Nekotorye problemy teorii deontičeskix modal'nostij' (Some Problems of the Theory of Deontic Modalities), in Logičeskaja semantika i modal'naja logika (Logical Semantics and Modal Logic), Moscow, 'Nauka', 1967, 280p.

Ivin, A. A., 'O logike ocenok' (On the Logic of Values), VF, 1968, 8, 53–63.

Ivin, A. A., Osnovanija logiki ocenok (Foundations of the Logic of Values), Moscow, Izd. Moskovskogo universiteta, 1970, 231p.

Jakuba, E. A., Pravo i nravstvennost' kak regulatory obščestvennyx otnošenij pri socializme (Law and Morality as Regulators of Social Relations Under Socialism), Xar'kov, Izd. Xar'kovskogo universiteta, 1970, 208p.

Jakubson, Ja. G., 'Kategorija dobra i ee mesto v marksistsko-leninskoj etike' [Avtoreferat] (The Category of the Good and its Place in Marxist-Leninist Ethics), Candidate dissertation, author's summary, Leningrad, 1968.

Jaurès, J., *De Primis socialismi Germanici lineamentis apud Luterum, Kant, Fichte, et Hegel*, Tolosae, Chauvin, 1891; available in French as *Les origines du socialisme allemande; thèse latine de Jean Jaurès*, translated by A. Veber, Paris, Les Ecrivains réunis, 1927.

Joravsky, D., *Soviet Marxism and Natural Science, 1917–1932*, London, Routledge and Kegan Paul, 1961, 433p.

Jordan, Z. A., *The Evolution of Dialectical Materialism*, New York, St. Martin's Press, 1967, 490p.

Kamenka, E., *The Ethical Foundations of Marxism*, New York, Frederick A. Praeger, 1962, 208p.

Kamenka, E., *Marxism and Ethics*, London, Macmillan, 1969, 72p.

Kamyšan, M. A., 'Ob ob'ektivnom kriterii nravstvennogo progress' (On an Objective Criterion of Moral Progress), FN, 1962, 5, 90–97.

Kant, I., *Critique of Pure Reason*, translated by N. K. Smith, London, Macmillan & Co., Ltd., 1963, 681p.

Kant, I., *Groundwork of the Metaphysic of Morals*, translated by H. J. Paton, in *The Moral Law*, London, Hutchinson University Library, 1948, 142p.

Kautsky, K., *Ethik und materialistische Geschichtsauffassung*, Stuttgart, J. H. W. Dietz, 1906; available in English as *Ethics and the Materialist Conception of History*, translated by J. B. Askew, 4th edition, revised, Chicago, Charles H. Kerr & Co., 206p.

Kautsky, K., 'Klassenkampf und Ethik', *Neue Zeit*, 1900–01, 19(1), 233–42.

Kautsky, K., 'Leben, Wissenschaft, und Ethik', *Neue Zeit*, 1905–06, 24(2), 516–20.

Kautsky, K., 'Nochmals Klassenkampf und Ethik', *Neue Zeit*, 1900–01, 19(1), 468–72.

Kautsky, K., 'Die sozialen Triebe in der Menschenwelt', *Neue Zeit*, 1884, 2, 13–19, 49–59, 118–25.

Kautsky, K., 'Die sozialen Triebe in der Tierwelt', *Neue Zeit*, 1883, 1, 20–27, 67–73.

Kautsky, K., 'Der Ursprung der Moral', *Neue Zeit*, 1906–07, 25(1), 213–17, 252–58.

Kierkegaard, S., *Kierkegaard's Concluding Unscientific Postscript*, translated by D. F. Swenson and W. Lowrie, Princeton, Princeton University Press, 1941, 579p.

Kissel', M. A., and Emdin, M. V., *Etika Gegelja i krizis sovremmenoj buržuaznoj etiki* (The Ethics of Hegel and the Crisis of Contemporary Bourgeois Ethics), Leningrad, Izd. Leningradskogo universiteta, 1966, 123p.

Kline, G. L., 'Changing Attitudes Toward the Individual', in C. E. Black, ed., *The Transformation of Russian Society*, Cambridge, Harvard University Press, 1960, pp. 606–25.

Kline, G. L., 'Leszek Kołakowski and the Revision of Marxism', in G. L. Kline, ed., *European Philosophy Today*, Chicago, Quadrangle Books, 1965, pp. 113–63.

Kline, G. L., 'Theoretische Ethik im Russichen Frühmarxismus', *Forschungen zur Osteuropäischen Geschichte* (West Berlin), 1963, 269–79.

Kline, 'Was Marx an Ethical Humanist?', *Studies in Soviet Thought*, 1969, 9, 91–103.

Klušin, V. I., *Bor'ba za istoričeskij materializm v Leningradskom gosudarstvennom universitete (1918–1925)* (The Struggle for Historical Materialism in Leningrad State University, 1918–1925), Leningrad, Izd. Leningradskogo universiteta, 1970, 116p.

Kobljakov, V. P., *Moral' i ee social'nye funkcii v razvitom socialističeskom obščestve* (Morality and its Social Functions in Developed Socialist Society), Leningrad, Izd. 'Znanie', 1975, 40p.

Kobljakov, V. P., 'Ob istinnosti moral'nyx suždenij' (On the Truth of Moral Judgments), VF, 1968, 5, 61–71.

Kobljakov, V. P., 'Specifika moral'nogo otraženija i moral'noj istiny [Avtoreferat] (The Characteristics of Moral Reflection and Moral Truth), Candidate dissertation, author's summary, Leningrad, 1968, 10p.

Kobljakov, V. P., and Konovalova, L. V., *Predmet i sistema etiki* (The Object and the System of Ethics), Moscow and Sofija, 1973.

Kołakowski, L., *Toward a Marxist Humanism*, translated by J. Z. Peel, New York, Grove Press, 1968, 220p.

Kompaneec, T. A., Kurgan, G. U., Osadčij, A. Ja., et al., 'Etičeskie issledovanija v SSSR (1973–75) [Obzor]' (Research in Ethics in the USSR, 1973–75. A Survey), *Vestnik Moskovskogo universiteta, Series 8, Filosofija*, 1976, 4, 74–83; and 5, 73–81.

Kon, I. S., *Sociologija ličnosti* (The Sociology of the Individual), Moscow, Izd. polit
českoj literatury, 1967, 383p.

Korsch, K., *Marxism and Philosophy*, translated by F. Halliday, New York, Modern Reader, 1970, 175p.

Krutova, O. N., *Čelovek i moral'* (*Metodologičeskie problemy leninskogo analiza nravstvennosti*) (Man and Morality – Methodological Problems of the Leninist Analysis of Morality), Moscow, 'Molodaja gvardija', 1971, 336p.

Lange, F. A., *Geschichte des Materialismus und Kritik seiner Bedeutung in der Gegenwart*, 1st edition, Iserlohn, J. Baedeker, 1866, 563p.

Lenin, V. I., *Materialism and Empirio-Criticism*, Moscow, Cooperative Publishing Soviet of Foreign Workers in the U.S.S.R., 1937, 396p.

Lenin, V. I., *Philosophical Notebooks*, in vol. 38 of his *Collected Works*, 4th edition, Moscow, Foreign Languages Publishing House, 1963, 638p.

Lichtheim, G., *Marxism, An Historical and Critical Study*, 2nd revised edition, New York, Frederick A. Praeger, 1965, 412p.

Lobkowicz, N., 'Materialism and Matter in Marxism-Leninism', in *The Concept of Matter*, E. McMullin, ed., Notre Dame, University of Notre Dame, 1963, 624p.

Loeser, F., *Deontik, Planung und Leitung der moralischen Entwicklung*, Berlin, VEB Deutscher Verlag der Wissenschaften, 1966, 292p.

Löwith, K., *From Hegel to Nietzsche*, translated by D. E. Green, Garden City, N. Y., Doubleday & Company, Anchor Books, 1967, 468p.

Lozinskij, E., 'Neo-Kantianskoe tečenie v marksizme' (The Neo-Kantian Tendency in Marxism), *Žizn': literaturnyj, naučnyj, i političeskij žurnal'*, St. Petersburg, 1900, 12, 132–54.

Luppol, I., 'Social'naja etika Mabli i Morelli' (The Social Ethics of Mably and Morelly), *Trudy Instituta Krasnoj Professury*, vol. 1, pp. 42–58, Giz., 1923.

McLellan, D., *The Young Hegelians and Karl Marx*, New York, Frederick A. Praeger, 1969, 170p.

Maeckij, Z., 'Problema moral'nogo konflikta. Obzor sovremennoj Pol'skoj etičeskoj literatury [Stat'ja iz Pol'si]' (The Problem of Moral Conflict. A Survey of Contemporary Ethical Literature [An article from Poland]), FN, 1973, 6, 96–101.

Mandelbaum, M., 'Some Neglected Philosophic Problems Regarding History', *Journal of Philosophy*, 1952, 10, 317–23.

Marx, K., *Capital*, vol. 1, edited by F. Engels, New York, International Publishers, 1967, 807p.

Marx, K., *Grundrisse: Foundations of the Critique of Political Economy* (*Rough Draft*), translated by M. Nicolaus, Great Britain, Penguin Books, Ltd., 1973, 898p.

Marx, K., *Karl Marx, Early Writings*, translated and edited by T. B. Bottomore, New York, McGraw-Hill Book Company, 1964, 227p.

Marx, K., *Writings of the Young Marx on Philosophy and Society*, L. D. Easton and K. H. Guddat, editors and translators, Garden City, N. Y., Doubleday & Company, Anchor Books, 1967, 506p.

Marx, K., and Engels, F., *Collected Works*, London, Lawrence & Wishart, 1975ff. and New York, International Publishers, 1975ff.

Marx, K., and Engels, F., *The German Ideology*, edited by C. J. Arthur, London, Lawrence & Wishart, 1970, 158p.

Marx, K., and Engels, F., *Marx & Engels: Basic Writings on Politics and Philosophy*, edited by L. W. Feuer, Garden City, N. Y., Doubleday & Company, Anchor Books, 1959, 497p.

Matkovskaja, I. Ja., 'U istokov revoljucionnoj nravstvennosti' (At the Sources of Revolutionary Morality), VF, 1975, 1, 138–47.

Mehring, F., 'Allerlei Ethik', *Neue Zeit*, 1892–93, 11(1), 265–70.

Mehring, F., 'Ethik und Klassenkampf', *Neue Zeit*, 1892–93, 11(1), 700–02.

[Mehring, F.], 'Kant und der Sozialismus', *Neue Zeit*, 1899–1900, 18(2), 1–4.

Miller, R., 'Socialističeskaja ličnost' i etika' (The Socialist Personality and Ethics), VF, 1974, 3, 139–46.

Mil'ner-Irinin, Ja. A., *Etika, ili principy istinnoj čelovečnosti* (Ethics, or the Principles of True Humanity), Moscow, 1963, manuscript.

Mil'ner-Irinin, Ja. A., 'Etika, ili principy istinnoj čelovečnosti (princip sovesti)' (Ethics, or the Principles of True Humanity – The Principle of Conscience), in Bandzeladze, editor, *Aktual'nye problemy marksistskoj etiki*, pp. 253–302.

Mil'ner-Irinin, Ja. A., 'Etika – nauka o dolžnom' (Ethics – the Science of that which Ought to Be), in Bandzeladze, editor, *Aktual'nye problemy marksistskoj etiki*, pp. 15–58.

Moral' i etičeskaja teorija, Nekotorye aktual'nye problemy (Morality and Ethical Theory, Some Current Problems), Moscow, 'Nauka', 1974, 295p.

Novikov, S., 'O liberal'no-men'ševistskom i marksistsko-bol'ševistskom ponimanii etiki' (On the Liberal-Menshevik and the Marxist-Bolshevik Understanding of Ethics), *Pod Znamenem Marksizma*, 1930, 5, 150–86.

Oken, L., *Lehrbuch der Naturphilosophie*, 3rd edition, Zürich, F. Schulthess, 1843; translated by A. Tulk as *Elements of Physiophilosophy*, London, The Ray Society, 1847, Landmarks of Science Series Microprint.

Parygin, B. D., *Social'naja psixologija kak nauka* (Social Psychology as a Science), Leningrad, Izd. Leningradskogo universiteta, 1965, 208p.

Pavlova, L. I., *Nravstvennye cennosti našego sovremennika. Rekomendatel'nyj ukazatel' literatury* (The Moral Values of our Contemporary. An index of recommended literature), Moscow, 'Kniga', 1970, 96p.

Perry, R. B., *Philosophy of the Recent Past*, New York, Charles Scribner's Sons, 1926, 230p.

Petrosjan, M. I., *Gumanizm, Opyt filosofsko-etičeskogo i sociologičeskogo issledovanija problemy* (Humanism, A Philosophico-Ethical and Sociological Investigation of the Problem), Moscow, Izd. social'no-ekonomičeskoj literatury, 'Mysl'', 1964, 335p.;

available in English as *Humanism, Its Philosophical, Ethical and Sociological Aspects*, Moscow, Progress Publishers, 1972, 307p.

Petrov, E. F., *Egoizm: filosofsko-etičeskij očerk* (Egoism: a Philosophical-Ethical Essay), Moscow, 'Nauka', 1969, 207p.

Pico della Mirandola, *Oration on the Dignity of Man*, translated by E. L. Forbes, in *The Renaissance Philosophy of Man*, edited by E. Cassirer *et al.*, Chicago, University of Chicago Press, 1948, 404p.

Plekhanov, G. V., *Essays in the History of Materialism*, translated by R. Fox, New York, Howard Fertig, 1967, 287p.

Plekhanov, G. V., *In Defence of Materialism: the Development of the Monist View of History*, translated by A. Rothstein, London, Lawrence & Wishart, 1947, 303p.

Plekhanov, G. V., *Sočinenija* (Works), edited by D. Rjazanov, Moscow, Gos. Izd., 1922– 28, 24 volumes.

Popov, S. I., ' "Etičeskij socializm" – idejnaja osnova sovremennogo social-reformizma' ('Ethical Socialism' – The Ideological Basis of Contemporary Social Reformism), VF, 1974, 6, 27–38.

Problema cennosti v filosofii (The Problem of Value in Philosophy), Leningrad, Izd. 'Nauka', 1966, 261p.

Problemy kategorij marksistsko-leninskoj etike, Materialy simpoziuma, posvjaščennogo 100-letija so dnja roždenija V. I. Lenina (Problems of the Categories of Marxist-Leninist Ethics, Materials of the Symposium Dedicated to the 100th Anniversary of the Birth of V. I. Lenin), Novosibirsk, 1969, 343p.

Program of the Communist Party of the Soviet Union, 1961, reprinted in *The U.S.S.R. and the Future*, edited by L. Schapiro, New York, Frederick A. Praeger, 1963, 324p.

Radlov, E., *Etika* (Ethics), Petrograd, Nauka i škola, 1921, 80p.

Razumovskij, I., 'O marksistskom i eklektičeskom ponimanii etiki' (On the Marxist and the Eclectic Conception of Ethics), *Pod Znamenem Marksizma*, 1930, 5, 187–221.

Rubel, M., *Karl Marx, Pages Choisies. Pour une Ethique Socialiste*, Paris, Librairie Marcel Rivière et Cie, 1948, 440p.

Rybakova, N. V., and Xolostova, T. V., [review of Xarčev and Jakovlev, *Očerki istorii marksistsko-leninskoj etiki v SSSR*], VF, 1974, 1, 169f.

Samsonova, T. V., *Teoretičeskie problemy etiki* (Theoretical Problems of Ethics), Moscow, Izd. Moskovskogo universiteta, 1966, 111p.

Schmidt, A., *The Concept of Nature in Karl Marx*, translated by B. Fowkes, Atlantic Highlands, N. J., Humanities Press, 1973, 251p.

Schmidt, C., 'Sozialismus und Ethik', *Sozialistische Monatshefte*, 1900, 9, 522–31.

Selivanov, F. A., *Etika, Očerk* (Ethics, An Essay), Tomsk, Izd. Tomskogo universiteta, 1961, 187p.

Sidorenko, N. I., Vlijanie usvoenija moral'nyx norm na moral'nye čuvstva' (The Influence of Assimilation of Moral Norms of Moral Feelings), FN, 1976, 4, 136–38.

'Simpozium po probleme cennostej' (Symposium on the Problem of Values), FN, 1966, 2, 139–45.

'Simpozium po teorii cennostej: doklady i soobščenija' (Symposium on the Theory of Values: Reports and Communications), Tbilisi, October, 1965, unpublished.

Social'naja suščnost' i funkcii nravstvennosti (The Social Essence and Functions of Morality), Moscow, Izd. Moskovskogo universiteta, 1975, 128p.

Sogomonov, Ju. V., *Dobro i zlo* (Good and Evil), Moscow, Izd. političeskoj literatury,

1965, 96p.

Starikov, D., 'Real'naja nravstvennost'' (Real Morality), *Voprosy literatury*, 1964, 7, 26–31.

Stojanović, S., *Between Ideals and Reality, A Critique of Socialism and its Future*, translated by G. S. Sher, New York, Oxford University Press, 1973, 222p.

Struve, P., 'Die Marxsche Theorie der sozialen Entwicklung', *Archiv für Soziale Gesetzgebung und Statistik*, 1899, vol. 14, 658ff.

Šinkaruk, V. I., *Logika, dialektika, i teorija poznanija Gegelja: problema toždestva logiki, dialektiki, i teorii poznanija v filosofii Gegelja* (Hegel's Logic, Dialectic, and Theory of Knowledge: the problem of the identity of the logic, dialectic, and theory of knowledge in Hegel's philosophy), Kiev, Izd. Kievskogo universiteta, 1964, 294p.

Šiškin, A. F., 'Etologija i etika' (Ethology and Ethics), VF, 1974, 9, 111–22.

Šiškin, A. F., *Iz istorii etičeskix učenij* (From the History of Ethical Doctrines), Moscow, Izd. političeskoj literatury, 1959, 344p.

Šiškin, A. F., 'Marksistskaja koncepcija čeloveka i sovremennyj naturalizm v etike' (The Marxist Conception of Man and Contemporary Naturalism in Ethics), VF, 1977, 7, 94–108.

Šiškin, A. F., 'O nekotoryx voprosax issledovatel'skoj raboty v oblasti etiki' (Concerning Several Questions of Research Work in the Area of Ethics), VF, 1973, 1, 14–26.

Šiškin, A. F., 'O nravstvennyx cennostjax v sovremennom mire' (On Moral Values in the Contemporary World), VF, 1977, 11, 60–75.

Šiškin, A. F., *Osnovy marksistskoj etiki* (Fundamentals of Marxist Ethics), Moscow, Izd. instituta meždunarodnyx otnošenij, 1961, 528p.

Šiškin, A. F., ed., *Marksistskaja etika, Xrestomatija* (Marxist Ethics, A Reader), Moscow, Izd. instituta meždunarodnyx otnošenij, 1961, 511p.

Šiškin, A. F., and Švarcman, K. A., *XX vek i moral'nye cennosti čelovečestva* (The 20th Century and the Moral Values of Humanity), Moscow, Izd. 'Mysl'', 1968, 271p.

Šiškin, A. F., and Švarcman, K. A., 'Mirovozzrenie i moral', filosofija i etika' (Worldview and Morality, Philosophy and Ethics), VF, 1971, 8, 38–50.

Šiškin, V. F., *Tak skladyvalas' revoljucionnaja moral', Istoričeskij očerk* (Thus Revolutionary Morality Was Formed, An Historical Essay), Moscow, Izd. 'Mysl'', 1967, 360p.

Šixardina, T. N., 'Rol' morali v regulirovanii dejatel'nosti ličnosti' (The Role of Morality in Regulating the Activity of the Individual), FN, 1977, 2, 18–27.

Štein, V. S., 'Problema prostyx norm nravstvennosti i spravedlivosti v marksistsko-leninskoj etike' (The Problem of Simple Norms of Morality and Justice in Marxist-Leninist Ethics), in Bandzeladze, editor, *Aktual'nye problemy marksistskoj etiki*, pp. 124–82.

Švarcman, K. A., *Etika . . . bez morali, Kritika sovremennyx buržuaznyx etičeskix teorij* (Ethics . . . Without Morality, A Critique of Contemporary Bourgeois Ethical Theories), Moscow, 'Mysl'', 1964, 264p.

Švarcman, K. A., *Teoretičeskie problemy etiki* (Theoretical Problems of Ethics), Moscow, Vysšaja škola, 1969, 94p.

Švarcman, K. A., ' 'Texnologija povedenija' – B. Skinner i voprosy morali' ('The Technology of Behavior' – B. Skinner and Questions of Morality), VF, 1975, 11, 155–62.

Švarcman, K. A., and Borodixina, E. I., 'Soderžanie i metodika propagandy etičeskix znanij' (The Content and Method of Ethical Propaganda), VF, 1976, 7, 165–67.

Švarcman, K. A., and Gaevoj, V. S., 'Problema formirovanija socialističeskoj morali' (The Problem of Forming Socialist Morality) [review article], VF, 1974, 8, 162–64.

Taylor, C., *Hegel*, Cambridge, U.K., Cambridge University Press, 1975, 580p.

Titarenko, A. I., *Antiidei: Opyt social'no-etičeskaja analiza* (Anti-ideas: An Essay in Socio-Ethical Analysis), Moscow, Politizdat., 1976, 399p.

Titarenko, A. I., *Moral' i politika* (Morality and Politics), Moscow, Izd. političeskoj literatury, 1969, 264p.

Titarenko, A. I., 'Istoričeskie struktury nravstvennogo soznanija' (Historical Structures of Moral Consciousness), FN, 1973, 6, 12–25.

Titarenko, A. I., *Kriterij nravstvennogo progressa* (The Criterion of Moral Progress), Moscow, 'Mysl", 1967, 190p.

Titarenko, A. I., *Nravstvennyj progress* (Moral Progress), Moscow, Izd. Moskovskogo universiteta, 1969, 176p.

Titarenko, A. I., 'Problema kriterija nravstvennogo progressa i nekotorye anglo-amerikanskie idealističeskie filosofsko-etičeskie koncepcii [Avtoreferat]' (The Problem of the Criterion of Moral Progress and Some Anglo-American Idealist Philosophico-Ethical Conceptions), Doctoral dissertation, author's summary, Moscow, 1968, 24p.

Titarenko, A. I., 'Specifika i struktura morali' (Specific Features and Structure of Morality), in *Moral' i etičeskaja teorija*, pp. 7–49.

Titarenko, A. I., *Struktury nravstvennogo soznanija, Opyt etiko-filosofskogo issledovanija* (The Structures of Moral Consciousness, An Essay in Ethico-Philosophical Investigation), Moscow, Izd. 'Mysl", 1974, 278p.

Titarenko, A. I., ed., *Marksistskaja etika* (Marxist Ethics), Moscow, Politizdat., 1976, 335p.

Titarenko, A. I., Karvackaja, G. F., and Titov, V. A., 'Etika: problemy i perspektivy' (Ethics: Problems and Perspectives), FN, 1972, 4, 145–55.

Tugan-Baranovskij, M., *Sovremennyj socializm v svoem istoričeskom razvitii* (Contemporary Socialism in its Historical Development), St. Petersburg, 1906; translated by M. I. Redmount as *Modern Socialism in its Historical Development*, London, Swan Sonnenschein & Co., Ltd., 1910, 232p.

Tugarinov, V. P., *O cennostjax žizni i kul'tury* (On the Values of Life and Culture), Leningrad, Izd. Leningradskogo universiteta, 1960, 156p.

Tugarinov, V. P., *Teorija cennostej v marksizme* (The Theory of Values in Marxism), Leningrad, Izd. Leningradskogo universiteta, 1968, 124p.

Utkin, S., *Očerki po marksistsko-leninskoj etike* (Essays in Marxist-Leninist Ethics), Moscow, Izd. social'no-ekonomičeskoj literatury, 1962, 422p.

Utkin, S., *Osnovy marksistsko-leninskoj etiki* (Fundamentals of Marxist-Leninist Ethics), Rostov on Don, Izd. Rostovskogo universiteta, 1961, 240p.

Vasilenko, V. A., 'Cennosti i cennostnye otnošenija' (Values and Value Relations), in *Problema cennosti v filosofii*, pp. 41–49.

Vasilenko, V. A., Gudenko, V. I., 'Ob'ektivnoe i sub'ektivnoe v morali' (The Objective and the Subjective in Morality), *Vestnik Moskovskogo universiteta*, Series 7, Filosofija, 1977, 3, 41–51.

'Važnaja vexa v razvitii marksistsko-leninskoj etiki [Vsesojuznaja mežvuzavaja konferencija, Moscow, Sept., 1974]' (An Important Milestone in Marxist-Leninist Ethics [All-Union Inter-collegiate Conference]), *Vestnik Moskovskogo universiteta*, Series 8, Filosofija, 1975, 2, 90–95.

de la Vega, R., and Sandkühler, H. J., eds., *Marxismus und Ethik, Texte zum neu-kantianischen Socialismus*, Frankfurt, Suhrkamp Verlag, 1970, 373p.

Vinogradskaja, N., 'Etika Kanta s točki zrenija istoričeskogo materializma' (The Ethics of Kant from the Point of View of Historical Materialism), *Pod znamenem marksizma*, 1924, nos. 4 and 5.

Volkogonov, D. A., *Voinskaja etika* (Military Ethics), Moscow, Voenizdat, 1976.

Vol'skij, S., [Sokolov, A. V.], *Filosofija bor'by: opyt postroenija etiki marksizma* (The Philosophy of Struggle: an Essay in the Construction of a Marxist Ethics), Moscow, 1909, 311p.

Vorländer, K., *Kant und der Sozialismus*, Berlin, Verlag von Reuther & Reichard, 1900, 69p.

Vorländer, K., *Kant und Marx*, Tübingen, Verlag von J. C. B. Mohr (Paul Siebeck), 1911, 293p.

'Vsesojuznaja naučnaja konferencija po etike' (All-Union Conference on Ethics), FN, 1975, 4, 157–62.

Woltmann, L., *Die Darwinische Theorie und der Sozialismus, Ein Beitrag zur Naturges-chichte der menschlichen Gesellschaft*, Düsseldorf, Hermann Michels, 1899, 397p.

Woltmann, L., *Der historische Materialismus, Darstellung und Kritik der Marxistischen Weltanschauung*, Düsseldorf, Hermann Michels, 1900, 430p.

Woltmann, L., *System des moralischen Bewusstseins mit besonderer Darlegung des Verhältnisses der kritischen Philosophie zu Darwinismus und Sozialismus*, Düsseldorf, Hermann Michels, 1898, 392p.

Xajkin, A. L., ed., *Voprosy marksistsko-leninskoj etiki. Materialy k naučnoj konferencii posvjaščennoj 50-letija Velikoj Oktjabr'skoj socialističeskoj revoljucii* (Problems of Marxist-Leninist Ethics. Materials for a Scientific Conference Dedicated to the 50th Year of the Great October Socialist Revolution), Tambov, 1967, 263p.

Xarčev, A. G., 'K itogam diskussii o kategorijax etike' (On the Results of the Discussion of Ethical Categories), FN, 1965, 2, 124–31.

Xarčev, A. G., 'Sootnošenie internacional'nogo i nacional'nogo v moral'nyx cennostjax socializma' (The Inter-relation of International and National Values in Socialism), *Sociologičeskie issledovanija*, 1975, 1, 53–63.

Xarčev, A. G., 'Vospitanie i žiznedejatel'nost' ličnosti' (Upbringing and Life-Activity of the Individual), VF, 1975, 12, 62ff.

Xarčev, A. G., and Ivanov, V. G., 'Ob istorizme v etike' (On Historicism in Ethics), FN, 1969, 1, 44–52.

Xarčev, A. G., and Jakovlev, B. D., *Očerki istorii marksistsko-leninskoj etiki v SSSR* Essays on the History of Marxist-Leninist Ethics in the USSR), Leningrad, 'Nauka', 1972, 219p.

Zdravomyslov, A. G., *Problema interesa v sociologičeskoj teorii* (The Problem of Interest in Sociological Theory), Leningrad, Izd. Leningradskogo universiteta, 1964, 72p.

INDEX

SOVIETICA

Publications and Monographs of the Institute of East-European Studies
at the University of Fribourg/Switzerland
and the Center for East Europe, Russia and Asia
at Boston College and the Seminar for Politicial Theory and Philosophy
at the University of Munich

1. BOCHEŃSKI, J. M. and BLAKELEY, TH. J. (eds.): *Bibliographie der sowjetischen Philosophie.* I: *Die 'Voprosy filosofii' 1947–1956.* 1959, VIII + 75 pp.
2. BOCHEŃSKI, J. M. and BLAKELEY, TH. J. (eds.): *Bibliographie der sowjetischen Philosophie.* II: *Bücher 1947–1956; Bücher und Aufsätze 1957–1958; Namenverzeichnis 1947–1958.* 1959, VIII + 109 pp.
3. BOCHEŃSKI, J. M.: *Die dogmatischen Grundlagen der sowjetischen Philosophie (Stand 1958). Zusammenfassung der 'Osnovy Marksistskoj Filosofii' mit Register.* 1959, XII + 84 pp.
4. LOBKOWICZ, NICOLAS (ed.): *Das Widerspruchsprinzip in der neueren sowjetischen Philosophie.* 1960, VI + 89 pp.
5. MÜLLER-MARKUS, SIEGFRIED: *Einstein und die Sowjetphilosophie. Krisis einer Lehre.* I: *Die Grundlagen. Die spezielle Relativitätstheorie.* 1960. (Out of print.)
6. BLAKELEY, TH. J.: *Soviet Scholasticism.* 1961, XIII + 176 pp.
7. BOCHEŃSKI, J. M. and BLAKELEY, TH. J. (eds.): *Studies in Soviet Thought,* I. 1961, IX + 141 pp.
8. LOBKOWICZ, NICOLAS: *Marxismus-Leninismus in der ČSR. Die tschechoslowakische Philosophie seit 1945.* 1962, XVI + 268 pp.
9. BOCHEŃSKI, J. M. and BLAKELEY, TH. J. (eds.): *Bibliographie der sowjetischen Philosophie.* III: *Bücher und Aufsätze 1959–1960.* 1962, X + 73 pp.
10. BOCHEŃSKI, J. M. and BLAKELEY, TH. J. (eds.): *Bibliographie der sowjetischen Philosophie.* IV: *Ergänzungen 1947–1960.* 1963, XII + 158 pp.
11. FLEISCHER, HELMUT: *Kleines Textbuch der kommunistischen Ideologie. Auszüge aus dem Lehrbuch 'Osnovy marksizma-leninizma', mit Register.* 1963, XIII + 116 pp.
12. JORDAN, ZBIGNIEW, A.: *Philosophy and Ideology. The Development of Philosophy and Marxism-Leninism in Poland since the Second World War.* 1963, XII + 600 pp.
13. VRTAČIČ, LUDVIK: *Einführung in den jugoslawischen Marxismus-Leninismus Organisation. Bibliographie.* 1963, X + 208 pp.
14. BOCHEŃSKI, J. M.: *The Dogmatic Principles of Soviet Philosophy (as of 1958). Synopsis of the 'Osnovy Marksistkoj Filosofii' with complete index.* 1963, XII + 78 pp.
15. BIRKUJOV, B. V.: *Two Soviet Studies on Frege.* Translated from the Russian and edited by Ignacio Angelelli. 1964, XXII + 101 pp.

16. BLAKELEY, TH. J.: *Soviet Theory of Knowledge*. 1964, VII + 203 pp.
17. BOCHEŃSKI, J. M. and BLAKELEY, TH. J. (eds.): *Bibliographie der sowjetischen Philosophie*. V: *Register 1947–1960*. 1964, VI + 143 pp.
18. BLAKELEY, THOMAS J.: *Soviet Philosophy. A General Introduction to Contemporary Soviet Thought*. 1964, VI + 81 pp.
19. BALLESTREM, KAREL G.: *Russian Philosophical Terminology* (in Russian, English, German, and French). 1964, VIII + 116 pp.
20. FLEISCHER, HELMUT: *Short Handbook of Communist Ideology. Synopsis of the 'Osnovy marksizma-leninizma' with complete index*. 1965, XIII + 97 pp.
21. PLANTY-BONJOUR, G.: *Les catégories du matérialisme dialectique. L'ontologie soviétique contemporaine*. 1965, VI + 206 pp.
22. MÜLLER-MARKUS, SIEGFRIED: *Einstein und die Sowjetphilosophie. Krisis einer Lehre*. II: *Die allgemeine Relativitätstheorie*. 1966, X + 509 pp.
23. LASZLO, ERVIN: *The Communist Ideology in Hungary. Handbook for Basic Research*. 1966, VIII + 351 pp.
24. PLANTY-BONJOUR, G.: *The Categories of Dialectical Materialism. Contemporary Soviet Ontology*. 1967, VI + 182 pp.
25. LASZLO, ERVIN: *Philosophy in the Soviet Union. A Survey of the Mid-Sixties*. 1967, VIII + 208 pp.
26. RAPP, FRIEDRICH: *Gesetz und Determination in der Sowjetphilosophie. Zur Gesetzeskonzeption des dialektischen Materialismus unter besonderer Berücksichtigung der Diskussion über dynamische und statische Gesetzmässigkeit in der zeitgenössischen Sowjetphilosophie*. 1968, XI + 474 pp.
27. BALLESTREM, KARL G.: *Die sowjetische Erkenntnismetaphysik und ihr Verhältnis zu Hegel*. 1968, IX + 189 pp.
28. BOCHEŃSKI, J. M. and BLAKELEY, TH. J. (eds.): *Bibliographie der sowjetischen Philosophie*. VI: *Bücher und Aufsätze 1961–1963*. 1968, XI + 195 pp.
29. BOCHEŃSKI, J. M. and BLAKELEY, TH. J. (eds.): *Bibliographie der sowjetischen Philosophie*. VII: *Bücher und Aufsätze 1964–1966. Register*. 1968, X + 311 pp.
30. PAYNE, T. R.: *S. L. Rubinštejn and the Philosophical Foundations of Soviet Psychology*. 1968, X + 184 pp.
31. KIRSCHENMANN, PETER PAUL: *Information and Reflection. On Some Problems of Cybernetics and How Contemporary Dialectical Materialism Copes with Them*. 1970, XV + 225 pp.
32. O'ROURKE, JAMES J.: *The Problem of Freedom in Marxist Thought*. 1974, XII + 231 pp.
33. SARLEMIJN, ANDRIES: *Hegel's Dialectic*. 1975, XIII + 189 pp.
34. DAHM, HELMUT: *Vladimir Solovyev and Max Scheler: Attempt at a Comparative Interpretation A Contribution to the History of Phenomenology*. 1975, XI + 324 pp.
35. BOESELAGER, WOLFHARD F.: *The Soviet Critique of Neopositivism. The History and Structure of the Critique of Logical Positivism and Related Doctrines by Soviet Philosophers in the Years 1947–1967*. 1965, VII + 157 pp.
36. DEGEORGE, RICHARD T. and SCANLAN, JAMES P. (eds.): *Marxism and Religion in Eastern Europe. Papers Presented at the Banff International Slavic Conference, September 4–7, 1974*. 1976, XVI + 182 pp.
37. BLAKELEY, T. J. (ed.): *Themes in Soviet Marxist Philosophy. Selected Articles from the 'Filosofskaja Enciklopedija'*. 1975, XII + 224 pp.

38. GAVIN, W. J. and BLAKELEY, T. J.: *Russia and America: A Philosophical Comparison. Development and Change of Outlook from the 19th to the 20th Century.* 1976, X + 114 pp.
40. GRIER, P. T.: *Marxist Ethical Theory in the Soviet Union.* 1978, xviii + 271 pp.

In Press:

39. LIEBICH, A.: *Between Ideology and Utopia. The Politics and Philosophy of August Cieszkowski.* 1978.
41. JENSEN, K. M.: *Beyond Marx and Mach. Aleksandr Bogdanov's* Philosophy of Living Experience. 1978.